COMPLETE HANDBOOK OF

HORSES
and HORSE RIDING

COMPLETE HANDBOOK OF
HORSES
and HORSE RIDING

A COMPREHENSIVE ENCYCLOPEDIA AND IDENTIFIER FOR
OVER 90 MAJOR BREEDS AND TYPES; A DETAILED MANUAL
OF HORSE CARE COVERING HEALTH, DIET AND
GROOMING; AND A DEFINITIVE STEP-BY-STEP RIDING
COURSE FROM STARTING OUT TO ACHIEVING EXCELLENCE

Judith Draper | Debby Sly | Sarah Muir

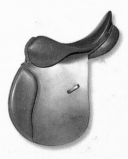

LORENZ BOOKS

This edition is published by Lorenz Books

Lorenz Books is an imprint of Anness Publishing Ltd
Hermes House, 88–89 Blackfriars Road, London SE1 8HA
tel. 020 7401 2077; fax 020 7633 9499
www.lorenzbooks.com; info@anness.com

© Anness Publishing Ltd 1999, 2004

UK agent: The Manning Partnership Ltd, 6 The Old Dairy, Melcombe Road, Bath BA2 3LR;
tel. 01225 478444; fax 01225 478440; sales@manning-partnership.co.uk

UK distributor: Grantham Book Services Ltd,
Isaac Newton Way, Alma Park Industrial Estate, Grantham, Lincs NG31 9SD;
tel. 01476 541080; fax 01476 541061; orders@gbs.tbs-ltd.co.uk

North American agent/distributor: National Book Network,
4501 Forbes Boulevard, Suite 200, Lanham, MD 20706;
tel. 301 459 3366; fax 301 429 5746; www.nbnbooks.com

Australian agent/distributor: Pan Macmillan Australia,
Level 18, St Martins Tower, 31 Market St, Sydney, NSW 2000;
tel. 1300 135 113; fax 1300 135 103; customer.service@macmillan.com.au

New Zealand agent/distributor: David Bateman Ltd,
30 Tarndale Grove, Off Bush Road, Albany, Auckland;
tel. (09) 415 7664; fax (09) 415 8892

Publisher Joanna Lorenz
Project Editor Felicity Forster
Designer Michael Morey
Illustrator Rodney Paull
Indexer Dawn Butcher
Editorial Reader Kate Henderson
Production Controllers Jessica Arendt and Ben Worley

Previously published as *The Ultimate Book of the Horse and Rider*

1 3 5 7 9 10 8 6 4 2

Contents

INTRODUCTION

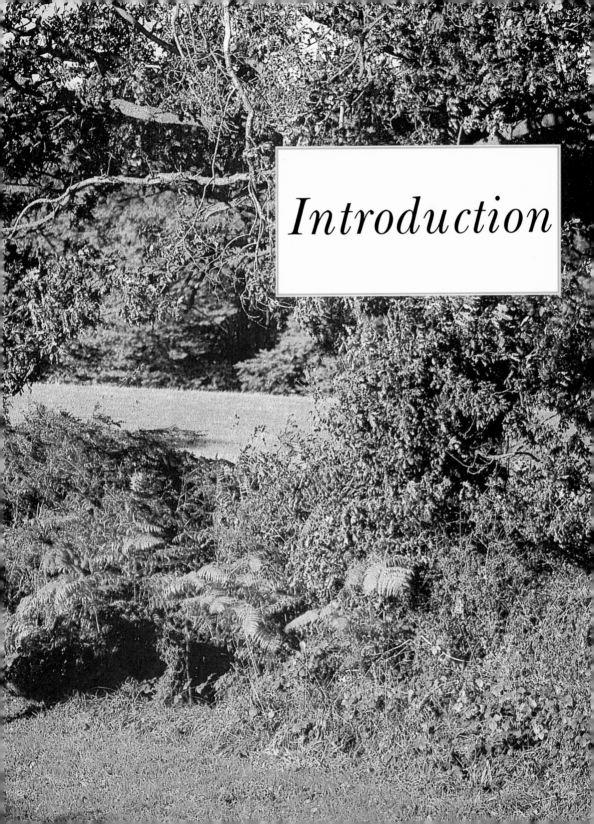

Introduction

The World of the Horse and Rider

The horse is one of the most beautiful and complex animals, and has fascinated mankind for many thousands of years. The purpose of this book is to capture some of the magic associated with horses – why so many have devoted their lives to them. It also aims, on a more practical level, to provide invaluable information for anyone with an equestrian interest, whether you ride for pleasure or competition, are planning on buying your first horse or pony, or just love horses.

Your Horse and You

This book starts by tracing the history of the horse, from its prehistoric ancestor – the Eohippus – to the modern *Equus caballus*, that we know as today's horse.

Breeds of the World is a comprehensive pictorial guide to the diverse variety of breeds and types of horse and pony around the world, from Appaloosas to Welsh Cobs, and from hacks to polo ponies. Each breed and type is described in detail, including its main characteristics, how the breed has developed and its uses.

Buying your own horse is a major step which most people who ride will want to do at some point. The section **Buying a Horse** provides a detailed guide to the subject, from how to choose the right horse or pony to suit you and your needs, to where to look for a horse, trying it and getting it vetted.

■ BELOW
The Shagya, a Syrian-bred Arab horse with a dished face, large wide-set eyes, a short back and high-set tail.

■ BOTTOM
Choosing the right horse is never easy – there are so many different breeds with different temperaments and characteristics. You need to find an animal that suits you.

■ RIGHT
Owning a horse brings with it a huge responsibility;
you should not consider it without making sure you
are fully aware of the commitment involved in
feeding, grooming, general stable management and
first aid.

■ BELOW
There are a number of different types of bedding
to consider for your stable. This horse is lying down
on shredded paper, which provides a dust-free bed,
especially good for horses with allergies to straw or
respiratory problems.

■ BELOW RIGHT
The amount of feed your horse needs depends on
many variables, such as how much exercise he has
and how much time he spends outside grazing.
When providing a haynet like this one, make sure
it is tied high enough to prevent the horse from
catching a foot in it.

Once you have bought your new horse or pony, this is where the fun – and hard work – begins. As the owner, you are responsible for your horse's health and welfare. With this in mind, **Keeping a Horse** provides useful information on the day-to-day management of horses and ponies, whether they live in a field or are stabled, including practical information about feeding, bedding and field management.

The **Daily Care** of the horse looks at how to keep your horse healthy and ensure that he has enough exercise to keep him fit, as well as how to recognize when he may be unwell. There is a useful guide to common ailments and how they should be treated. The horse's feet are also thoroughly discussed, including the anatomy of the hooves and the typical ailments which affect them.

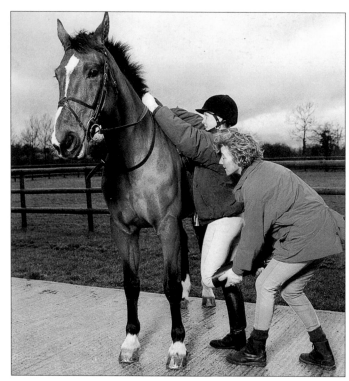

❚ LEFT
Once your horse is tacked up and ready, it's time to climb aboard. It's much easier to mount a horse with a helper to give you a leg-up to support you. This method is a good way to learn how to mount, and it is also far less stressful on the horse's back.

❚ BELOW LEFT
Position the stirrup iron so that your foot can go into it easily. For the near-side foot (left foot), turn the stirrup leather in an anticlockwise direction before placing your foot into the iron.

❚ BELOW RIGHT
Learning to ride requires patience and practice. Each pace – walk, trot, canter and gallop – gives you a different sense of speed and motion.

Riding horses is a demanding yet ultimately fulfilling pastime which has brought a great deal of pleasure and fun to many (although it is not without its many disappointments, as any rider will tell you!). It is important to remember that whatever your ambition, whether it be to compete at the highest level or to go on a gentle hack through beautiful countryside, riding should be enjoyable for you and your horse. The relationship between the rider and his or her mount should always be a partnership.

Learning the art of horsemanship requires dedication and patience on the part of the pupil – the rider never stops learning. Horses, like humans,

■ RIGHT
Cantering brings with it an exhilarating feeling of
speed and power, combined with a wonderful sense
of freedom. The horse and rider should appear to
be moving as one.

■ BELOW
The bridle is one of the first pieces of riding
equipment you will learn to use. When putting on
the bridle, you should hold the horse's nose with
your left hand, hold the bridle in your right hand,
bring it in front of the horse's face and then gently
lift it into his mouth.

are individuals, and we can learn as much from them
as they can from us.

The section **Learning to Ride** will prove invaluable
to anyone with an interest in riding, including first-
time riders, those returning to riding after a period of
time, or anyone who feels they need to do a little
"revision". We look at where to learn, the basic
clothing and equipment the rider needs, how to
prepare the horse for riding, and how the rider
communicates with his or her horse.

Although there is no substitute for actually being
on a horse, when you are learning to ride the time
spent in the saddle is often relatively little (it may be
only an hour a week), so it is useful for the budding
equestrian to be able to read and learn more about
horsemanship. Such knowledge will hopefully be able
to be put into practice the next time you ride.

In **Mastering the Paces** we look at how the horse
moves, showing the four paces – walk, trot, canter and
gallop – in detail, as well as the transitions between
these paces. As the rider gains confidence and
balance and learns how to coordinate himself, he

▌ RIGHT
Show jumping is an Olympic sport, combining
technical ability, athleticism and balance.
Competition riding can bring out the best in
horse and rider.

▌ BELOW
Most horses can be trained to jump. This horse
has jumped too high for these fences, but with
practice will be able to negotiate different distances
and heights.

can then develop his skills and learn more about
influencing his horse – for example, the half-halt,
lateral work, variations within paces and the counter
canter – creating and building upon the all-important
rider-horse partnership.

Preparing for Take-off is a useful section on
learning how to jump. Starting with simple exercises
over trot poles and low fences in the arena, we
progress to the exhilaration of riding around a cross-
country course, how to cope with difficult terrain and
preparing for the unexpected.

As your riding skills develop further you may want
to take part in competitions, so in **The Competition
World** we describe the wide variety of equestrian
sports which exist, and how to choose one that suits
you and your horse's temperament. From the
pleasure and excitement of jumping or mounted
games, the grace of dressage or vaulting, to the special
demands of endurance riding or the thrill of taking
part in a race, there's something for every rider in this
section – along with the idea that the main aim of
competing should be to have fun.

▌ ABOVE
Learning to jump requires practice. This horse is
jumping smoothly over a fence; the horse is
collected and the rider well-positioned.

▌ LEFT
Riders with good overall horsemanship skills can
put themselves to the test by competing in horse
trials or eventing.

▌ BELOW
Taking part in a dressage competition is the perfect
opportunity to show off your horse. Dressage is a
very popular sport and is as enjoyable to watch as it
is to partake in.

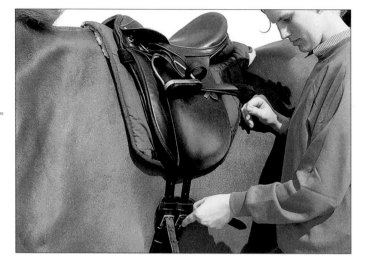

▌ LEFT
The saddle is one of the most important pieces of
equipment you will need to buy, and because of the
skill and craftsmanship involved in producing a
saddle, it is usually the most expensive. Take
good care of your saddle and you will enjoy it for
many years.

▌ BELOW
It is advisable to seek professional help when
choosing a new saddle, to ensure that it fits
the horse correctly and is suitable for your
riding needs.

Riding, like skiing, sailing and many other activities, requires specialist clothing and equipment. A visit to your local saddlery or tack shop will confirm the bewildering array of tack and equipment on sale – not all of it necessarily essential. With this in mind we have provided a detailed guide to **Saddlery and Equipment**, focusing on the everyday saddle and bridle, as well as explaining how and why many of the more unusual items of equipment are used.

The Saddle is an essential piece of riding equipment and one of the most expensive items the owner has to buy for his or her horse. There are saddles designed to suit every style of riding, so we explain which is the best for you and your chosen type

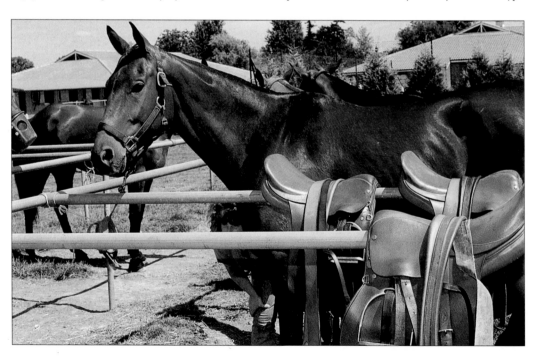

▌ BELOW
Choosing the right bridle and bit can be a daunting task – they come in a huge variety of shapes and sizes. The traditional bridle is made of leather.

▌ BOTTOM
Combined with the rider's legs, voice and body position, the bridle and bit provide the communication which allows the rider to control the horse.

of riding. There is also a section on essential saddle accessories including girths, stirrups, breastplates and saddle cloths, as well as a guide to saddle care.

The bridle is an equally important piece of equipment, and like the saddle should be chosen carefully, with the comfort of the horse and the safety of the rider firmly in mind. The subject of **Bridles and Bits** is a complex one and it is important to choose the right combination of tack to suit the horse and the rider – too mild a bit and you could be left with an unstoppable horse, too strong and you could unwittingly inflict pain on the horse. We explain the different types of bridle and noseband, and look in detail at bits and bitting, describing the various bit groups and the different actions they have on the horse.

▮ RIGHT
A dressage whip may be used when schooling a horse – this long whip can be used to give a gentle flick without the rider having to let go of the reins.

▮ BELOW
Not only is grooming essential for the health of your horse – removing dust, dead skin and hair, and providing massage for improving muscle tone – it also makes your horse look absolutely spectacular for competitions.

The novice rider will not need **Training Aids and Gadgets** (aids are used to develop a well-schooled, obedient horse and gadgets are used to prevent an aspect of the horse's behaviour), but nonetheless it is wise to be aware of what is available and how each item works. We explain how and when such aids are used, as well as the effect each one has on the horse.

Grooming is an essential part of the daily care of your horse, important for his health as well as his appearance. In **Grooming Equipment** we show the basic kit you will need and explain in detail how to groom your horse, from picking his feet out and daily brushing, to clipping the horse and the finishing touches required for a competition.

■ BELOW
This horse is dressed for travelling, with a poll guard for the head, rugs to keep him warm, hock and knee boots to protect his legs, and a bandage to protect his tail.

■ BOTTOM RIGHT
Stable bandages provide warmth and protection. They should always be used with padding underneath, otherwise pressure sores may form.

The horse in the wild has evolved to withstand the rigours of outdoor life, but many riding horses lead an "unnatural" life. As we place greater demands on the horse, expecting improvements in athletic performance and transporting horses to and from competitions, the need for special **Horse Clothing and Equipment** has increased. From boots and bandages to protect your horse's legs, to rugs and blankets which keep the horse warm and dry, the range of horse clothing is enormous. We guide you through the maze of clothing and equipment available, as well as providing an invaluable, step-by-step guide to putting on boots, bandages and rugs, so your horse will be protected from head to tail.

Finally, we come to **The Rider's Clothes**. Like the horse the rider needs special clothing and equipment for his or her chosen discipline. Much of today's riding clothing – especially competition attire – is influenced by tradition. For instance, the jacket worn by the show rider is based on the traditional coat worn by a huntsman.

This is not to say that fashion does not have an influence. As sports such as endurance riding become more popular, so new fabrics and colours are introduced to update the rider's wardrobe.

The most important considerations for any rider are comfort in the saddle and safety. Clothing for riding has developed to meet both these requirements. This section looks at the basic items that every rider needs: a protective hat, sensible footwear, and jodhpurs or breeches, and explains the correct dress for competitive riding. We also look at artificial aids (whips and spurs) explaining how and when they should be used by the rider.

We hope that you enjoy *The Ultimate Book of the Horse and Rider* and that it will prove to be an invaluable source of information for horse riders and horse lovers alike. Whatever your equestrian ambitions might be, never forget the great pleasure and satisfaction that being involved with horses can give, and that ultimately the most successful relationships between horses and people are based on mutual respect – a true partnership.

❚ LEFT
For most competitions you need to wear a riding coat, breeches and boots, a shirt with a collar and tie, or a collarless shirt with a hunting tie or stock. A rider dressed for top-level dressage wears a top hat, tail coat and waistcoat.

■ RIGHT
For more ordinary,
everyday riding,
choose clothes that are
neat and safe. Tall
leather boots will
provide protection
and keep your feet and
lower legs dry, gloves
will give you a good
grip on the reins, and
a hard hat provides
essential protection
for your head.

Breeds of
the World

Introduction

The lives of humans and horses have been bound together
for many thousands of years. Appreciated first as just another
source of food, the predecessors of the modern horse were
hunted like any other wild animal. In time there came a
steady process of domestication as nomadic peoples began to
herd horses in the same way as they did goats and other
animals. Ultimately, however, it was as a means of swift
transport that the horse really came into his own. Men learnt
to ride. Their whole lives were transformed. Horses became
their chief means of transportation, remaining so until well
into the twentieth century. Domestication, coupled with a
gradual increase in human population, signalled the end of
the truly wild horse. Today, even those horses which live in
herds on the few remaining extensive areas of suitable
grassland are not truly wild, for they are all "managed" by
humans to one degree or another. Nevertheless horses retain
much of the instinctive behaviour which enabled them to
exist without man's intervention and it is necessary to
understand what makes them "tick" if we are to enjoy our
continuing association with them.

The History of the Horse

The modern horse, *Equus caballus*, belongs to the family *Equidae*, which also includes asses and zebras. *Equidae* are placed in the order Perissodactyla, to which tapirs and rhinoceroses belong and which descended from the Condylarthra, a group of primitive, long extinct mammals which were the ancestors of all hoofed mammals.

Fossil remains have made it possible to trace at least some aspects of the evolution of the modern horse over a period of some sixty million years, indicating how it gradually adapted to changes in its environment. The known history of the modern horse starts with Eohippus, also called the Dawn Horse, which is known to have lived in North America during the Eocene epoch (fifty-four to thirty-eight million years ago). An animal no larger than a small dog, Eohippus was designed for life as a forest browser moving around on soft soil. It had four toes on its forefeet, three on its back feet and pads similar to a dog's. Its small, low-crowned teeth were

suited to eating leaves and other low, soft vegetation. It would probably have had a camouflage colouring to help it to escape predators. During the Oligocene epoch (thirty-seven to twenty-six million years

ago) first Mesohippus then Merychippus, showed distinct changes: the legs became longer, the back straighter (Eohippus had an arched back) and the whole animal larger. One toe disappeared on the forefoot, leaving three toes on both fore and hindfeet. The teeth also showed signs of change, the pre-molars becoming more like true molars.

In this slow process of evolution, the most significant change of all occurred during the Miocene epoch (twenty-five to seven million years ago) when forests gave

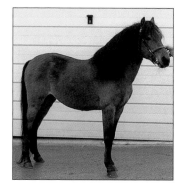

■ RIGHT
Horse Type 4 resembled this refined little Caspian
Pony. The Caspian was "re-discovered" in 1965.

■ BELOW RIGHT
Pony Type 1 lived in north-west Europe and looked
like the present-day Exmoor Pony.

way to grassland and the horse's ancestors
became plains dwellers. This significant
change in environment called for teeth
designed for grazing, as opposed to
browsing, a longer neck to make grazing
easier, longer legs to facilitate flight from
predators and feet suitable for harder
terrain. During this time the single toe, or
hoof, began to evolve: the outer toes no
longer touched the ground and the
central toe became larger and stronger.

Then the history of the horse family
becomes somewhat more complex, with
various sub-families developing.
Eventually, however, these became extinct
and it was Pliohippus which provided the
link in the chain from Eohippus to the
modern Equus. Pliohippus evolved some
ten to five million years ago and had long
legs with a single hoof on each. Its direct
successor, Equus, the genus of modern
horse, finally emerged a million years ago.

During the Ice Ages of the Pleistocene
epoch, Equus migrated via the land
bridges which then existed to Europe, Asia
and Africa. However, the disappearance of
these land bridges (e.g. across what are
now the Strait of Gibraltar and the Bering
Strait) when the ice receded about 10,000
years ago meant that if an animal had
become extinct in one continent, that

continent could not be repopulated – at
least not without the help of man. This is
exactly what happened in America: for
some unexplained reason the horse
disappeared. It was not seen again until
European colonists reintroduced it
thousands of years later.

All members of the modern *Equidae*
family are swift runners with only one
functional toe on each foot (the modern
horse's ergot – the horny growth at the
back of the fetlock – is believed to be the

vestiges of the pad of its ancestor,
Eohippus). All live in herds and all have
cheek teeth designed to grind plant-food.

Present-day horses and ponies are said
to trace back to three distinct types,
produced by variations in their natural
environment. Northern Europe provided
a slow-moving, heavy horse *(Equus
silvaticus)* from which the world's heavy
horse breeds are derived. Then there was
the primitive Asiatic Wild Horse, survivors
of which were found still living wild as late
as 1881 (and called the Przewalski Horse);
and finally the rather more refined
Tarpan, from eastern Europe.

Later on, by the time that man began
domesticating the horse, four sub-species
had evolved: two pony types and two horse
types. Pony Type 1 inhabited the north-
west of Europe and resembled the
modern Exmoor Pony. Pony Type 2,
which was bigger and more heavily built,
lived in northern Eurasia. The Highland
Pony is probably the nearest modern-day
equivalent. Horse Type 3 was a little bigger
still, but much more lightweight in build
and suited to hot climates. Its nearest
equivalent is thought to be the Akhal-Teke.
Horse Type 4, found in western Asia, was
the smallest but the most refined and was
the forerunner of the Caspian Pony.

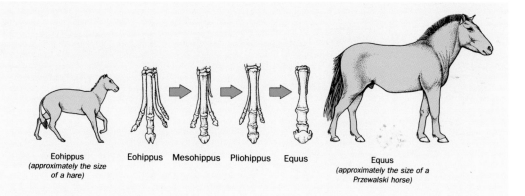

Eohippus
(approximately the size
of a hare)

Eohippus   Mesohippus   Pliohippus   Equus

Equus
(approximately the size of a
Przewalski horse)

Horses in the Wild

The horse is a herbivore, that is, an eater of plants. Like all herbivores horses are basically grass eaters. In the wild the horse is a nomadic grazer and spends up to twenty hours out of every twenty-four grazing. When food is plentiful a wild horse thrives and puts on weight; when it is scarce, and weather conditions harsh, he loses condition. Nature, as usual, has arranged for foals to be born in the spring when the weather is mild and the grass lush – thus ensuring that the mares have a plentiful supply of food, which in turn ensures ample milk for the foals. Mares come into season every twenty-one days during the spring and summer, until around September or October, and the gestation period is approximately eleven months.

Horses are by nature herd animals. In the wild they live in social groups within a larger group (the herd), each small group comprising a stallion, some mares, their

▌LEFT
This Dartmoor Pony is typical of a number of breeds which, although they have been domesticated for a very long time, have retained the ability to thrive in semi-wild conditions.

foals and yearlings and perhaps one or two two-year-olds. Depending on the power of the stallion, the total size of the group is usually in the region of a dozen. Young, timid stallions and old ones who no longer have any mares often live in bachelor groups – horses do not like to be alone. Just as family life is important to them, so is friendship. Horses indulge in mutual grooming with their teeth, they play together and relax and doze together. A stallion will groom a favourite mare even when she is not in season (grooming is also used to stimulate a mare sexually) and will play with the foals – though eventually he will drive out the more

mature colts who must then either join a bachelor group or begin to collect their own band of mares.

Horses communicate with each other by a number of means, both vocal and physical. Their "vocabulary" includes neighing, nickering, squealing and, more rarely, roaring. A loud neigh enables a horse to make contact with another from whom it has been separated; a quieter, lower nicker may be used by a stallion to a mare, a mare to her foal or between friends as a greeting; squeals are signs of excitement and are used when horses are in close contact, particularly sexual contact; horses may emit loud roars and

▌ LEFT
Horses are constantly on the alert. These semi-feral Camargue mares are aware of everything going on around them.

screams during a fight that has serious intentions, as opposed to the sort of play-fighting indulged in by young colts, and a mare may well scream her disapproval at a stallion who pesters her when she is not ready to be mated.

Body posture is another means of communication. A relaxed horse looks relaxed: a hind foot resting, head lowered, eyes partly closed, lower lip drooping. An

excited stallion prances around, head tucked in, tail raised, his whole outline saying "look at me". A startled horse looks tense and alert, signs which indicate to its companions that there is cause for alarm.

Smell is also important to horses. Mares and foals recognize each other by smell. When meeting, horses will put their noses close together, often blowing down their nostrils, before deciding whether or not to be friends. Smell also plays a part in sexual communication – a stallion smells the vulva and urine of an in-season mare and can tell the difference between the dung of another stallion and that of a mare (he will urinate over a mare's dung but add his own dung to that left by a stallion).

A horse's ears, too, being tremendously mobile, say a good deal about what he is thinking – where his attention is focused,

what mood he is in. Drooping ears indicate that the horse is in a dozy state, alert ones that something has caught his attention; ears that are turned back may show that the horse's attention is focused behind him or they may indicate submission or fear; ears laid flat denote anger or fear.

Having eyes set on the sides of his head, the horse can see almost all round him, the only blind spots being immediately behind and a little way in front of his head – he can keep an approaching object in focus merely by turning his head slightly. The horse's sense of touch is enhanced by the whiskers on his muzzle which enable him to judge how far an object is from the end of his nose and may also be useful for assessing texture, for example when he is grazing.

The horse's long legs enable him to travel at speed, essential for an animal whose natural form of defence is to run away. Since he is not equipped to fight predators such as wolves, lions and snakes, his chief means of survival is flight. This helps to explain why domesticated horses often prefer to shelter from bad weather by standing by a hedge or wall rather than making use of a specially provided man-made building: horses feel safer in the open air where they can easily gallop off if anything frightens them.

▌ LEFT
All horses and ponies are by nature herd animals, living in small social groups comprising a stallion, his mares and various offspring.

▌ RIGHT
Nature has equipped the Shetland Pony to withstand harsh winter weather. The thick coat ensures that the pony stays warm and the skin never gets wet.

Conformation

Conformation, or the horse's overall make and shape, varies a good deal from breed to breed. What constitutes "ideal" conformation varies according to the work which the horse is required to perform. In spite of these necessary variations, however, certain guidelines can be followed when looking for desirable conformation. They relate to proportion: if a horse is correctly proportioned he will be better balanced, less prone to unsoundness and more able to perform his allotted tasks than a horse with less harmonious proportions. Indeed, many a horse with conformational defects has been condemned as "difficult" when it is simply his shape which prevents him from carrying out what his master requires.

A horse is deemed to have "correct" proportions when certain measurements are equal. For example: the length of the head, the depth of the body at the girth,

the distance from the point of the hock to the ground, the distance from the chestnut on the foreleg to the ground, the distance from the croup to the fold of the stifle and from the fold of the stifle to the point of the hock should all be the same.

The domesticated horse is required to work, which means that certain features of his conformation are of particular importance. If a horse is deep through the girth, that is from the top of the wither to below the elbow, then his lungs will have plenty of room to expand – essential for any working horse. The length of his back is also important, particularly for the ridden horse. Too long, and it will be inclined to weakness; too short, and it may restrict the action.

Starting at the front, it is important that the horse's head is in proportion to his overall size. An over-large, heavy head will upset the overall balance, putting

extra weight on the forehand, which already carries 60 per cent of the horse's total weight. Too small a head will also affect the balance. The upper and lower jaws should meet evenly at the front – if they do not this will inhibit the horse's ability to bite food such as grass. The nostrils should be large and wide, and large eyes are preferable to small ones, which experience has shown often denote a less than generous temperament. The set of the head is also important. If there is not sufficient clearance between the mandible (the lower jaw) and the atlas (the top bone in the neck), the horse will have difficulty in flexing at the poll, a requirement in the more collected gaits. There should be room for two fingers' width when the horse's head is raised.

In the riding horse the neck should be fairly long and curved. There should be no tendency to fleshiness around the

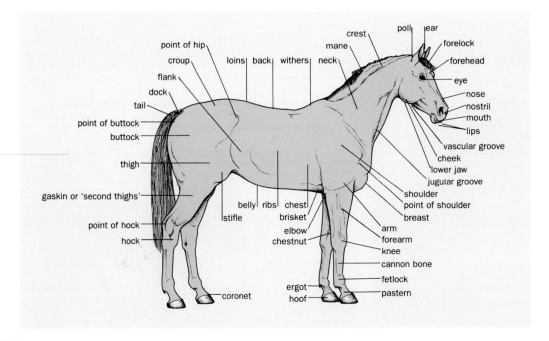

▌ LEFT
The long neck and sloping shoulder of the
Thoroughbred are associated with speed. Depth
through the girth ensures plenty of room for the
lungs to expand.

rounded and look like a matching pair.
"Boxy" upright feet are prone to jarring.
Large, flat feet may be more prone to
bruising of the sole and to corns. The
hindfeet, which bear less of the horse's
overall weight when he is stationary,
should be more oval in shape than the
forefeet. Viewed from the side the slope of
both fore and hindfeet should be a
continuation of the slope of the pastern.
The feet should point directly forwards.

throat, which again would restrict the
flexion of the head. This is particularly
important in the riding horse. A long neck
is associated with speed, a shorter one with
strength. Hence the heavy draught breeds
lack the length of neck seen, for instance,
in the Thoroughbred. The shoulder
should be well sloped (the angle of the
scapula gives the slope). Such
conformation enables the horse to take
longer strides than a straight shoulder,
which results in short, restricted action. A
straight shoulder may produce jarring,
which can be detrimental to the forelimb.
Horses with straight shoulders tend to give
an uncomfortable ride, too. The shoulder
should be muscular but not "loaded", i.e.
too heavy. The withers should be of a
good height and well defined. If they are
too high, it may be difficult to fit a saddle.
If they are poorly defined, it may be
difficult to keep a saddle in place. With
the draught horse, which must wear a
collar and for whom pulling power is
more important than extended paces, a
slightly straighter shoulder is acceptable.

The chest and body should be
reasonably broad, but not excessively so,
otherwise the horse's movement will be
affected. Narrowness in the chest, giving
the forelegs the appearance of "coming
out of one hole" is a serious fault, causing
the foreleg joints to brush against each
other. The back should rise slightly to the
croup, and be well muscled. Short, well-
muscled loins are essential: the lumbar
vertebrae have no support from the ribs,
yet it is the loins which transfer the thrust
from the engine (the hindquarters) to the
body. The croup of the fully grown horse
should be the same height as the withers
and should not be too sloping, a feature
which, combined with a low-set tail, is
usually a sign of weakness. Croup-high
horses throw extra weight on to the
forehand, thus putting more strain on
the forelimbs.

The horse's engine is in the back, that
is in the hindquarters. They should
therefore be strong and muscular. When
standing still the hindlegs should not be
stretched out behind him or tucked under
him – a line dropped vertically from the
point of the buttock to the ground should
touch the hock and run down the rear of
the cannon bone.

The forelegs should be straight and
strong, with long, muscular forearms and
large, flat knees. Short cannons indicate
strength and there should be a good
measurement of bone (the measurement
being taken around the cannon below the
knee). The amount of bone determines
the weight-carrying ability of the horse.
The amount of bone varies with the type
of horse but as a rough guide a
lightweight riding horse standing 16.2hh
should have a minimum of 8 inches
(20cm) of bone, a heavyweight horse of
the same height at least 9 inches (23cm).

The pasterns should be of medium
length and slope. The forefeet should be

COMMON CONFORMATIONAL DEFECTS

Back at the knee – where the knees,
when viewed from the side, tend to
extend backwards.

Calf knees – knees which are shallow
from front to back.

Cow hocks – hocks which, when viewed
from behind, turn inwards, as in a cow.

Ewe neck – where the top line of the neck
is concave and the lower line convex.

Herring-gutted – where the horse has an
upward slope from front to back on the
underside of the belly.

Over at the knee – where the knees
protrude forwards.

Pigeon toes – toes which turn inwards.

Roach back – where the spine has an
exaggerated upward curve.

Sickle hocks – hocks which when viewed
from the side have a concave line in front of
the hocks and a slanting cannon bone.

Slab-sided – where the ribs are flat as
opposed to "well-sprung".

Splay-footed – where the toes
turn outwards.

Sway back – where the back has an
exaggerated hollow.

Tied in below the knee – where the
measurement of bone just below the knee is
less than that farther down the cannon bone.

Colours and Markings

Equine coat colouring is controlled by numerous genes acting in combination to produce a multitude of variations in pigmentation. These genes, which are inherited, are located on paired structures known as chromosomes: the modern horse has 64 chromosomes, half of which are inherited from the sire and the other half from the dam. Some genes are dominant, others are recessive. For example, in horses chestnut is recessive to all other colours, bay is dominant to black, and grey is dominant to bay and black. The dominant greying gene can result in horses which are born with a dark coat turning progressively more grey as they

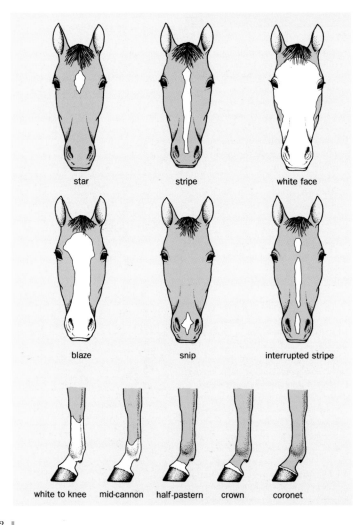

star

stripe

white face

blaze

snip

interrupted stripe

white to knee   mid-cannon   half-pastern   crown   coronet

FACIAL MARKINGS

These include: Star, stripe and interrupted stripe, snip, blaze, white face, white muzzle

LEG MARKINGS

For registration purposes leg markings are described in detail, using points of the anatomy: e.g. white to fetlock, white to knee, white to hock, etc.

Two less specific terms are also in popular use: sock (white colouring from the coronet up to the knee), stocking (white colouring from the coronet up to and over the knee or hock).

HOOF COLOURS

The horn of the hoofs can vary from blue or black to white and may be marked with dark stripes.

grow older. This is especially noticeable in the Lipizzaner, whose foals are born dark and, with rare exceptions, turn grey as they mature. Albinos occur where there is a congenital deficiency of colouring pigment. The hair is white, the skin pink and eyes often blue.

A horse is always described by its coat colouring, followed by other distinguishing features, where applicable, such as white markings and the colour of the mane and tail.

Some horses have more than one clearly defined coat colour. Broken or part-coloured horses such as piebalds and skewbalds (known as Pintos or Paint Horses in America) have irregular patches of two different colours while Spotted Horses show a variety of spotted markings. Black legs go with bay body colouring.

Horses' eyes are normally dark, although blue eyes also occur.

EQUINE COLOURS

Grey A mixture of black and white hairs throughout. The coat varies from light to iron (very dark). The skin is black.

Fleabitten Grey Grey coat flecked with brown specks.

Dappled Grey Light grey base coat with dark grey rings.

Bay Reddish coat with black mane, tail and "points" (i.e. limbs). The coat colour may vary from red to brown or yellowish.

Black All black except for occasional white marks on the legs and/or head.

Chestnut Varies from a pale golden colour to a rich, red gold. The mane and tail may be lighter or darker than the coat colour.

Liver Chestnut The darkest of the chestnut shades.

Sorrel A light-red chesnut.

Brown A mixture of black and brown hairs, with black limbs, mane and tail. A very dark brown horse may appear almost black.

Roan A body colour with white hairs interspersed, which lightens the overall effect.

Strawberry Roan Chestnut body colour with white hair giving a pinkish-red tinge.

Blue Roan Black or brown body colour with white hair giving a blue tinge.

Dun Light sandy-coloured coat with black mane and tail, often accompanied by a dark, dorsal eel-stripe extending from the line of the neck to the tail, and sometimes by "zebra markings" (stripes) on the withers and legs – the vestiges of a primitive form of camouflage. Dun can vary from yellow to "mouse", depending on the diffusion of pigment. The skin is black.

Palomino Gold coat with white mane and tail.

Spotted Small, more or less circular patches of hair of a different colour from the main body colour and distributed over various areas of the body.

Piebald Large, irregular patches of black and white.

Skewbald Large, irregular patches of white and any other colour except black.

Cream Cream-coloured coat with unpigmented skin (also known as cremello).

White Markings White markings on the face and legs and, occasionally, on the body, are a valuable means of distinguishing one horse from another and are therefore noted in detail on veterinary certificates and registration papers.

Brindle Brown or grey streaked or patched with a darker colour.

▌ OPPOSITE
ABOVE
The predominant coat colour of the Lipizzaner is grey, but foals are born dark and it takes several years for the coat to change to the typical "white" colouring associated with the breed.

▌ RIGHT
Spotted coat patterns have existed – and often been highly prized – throughout man's long relationship with the horse. Spotted horses are particularly associated with the Nez Percé Indians of North America.

Horses

There are more than 150 different breeds and types of horses in the world. The development of each of them has been influenced by man. Domestication resulted in selective breeding and, in many instances, more nutritious feeding, both of which led to an increase in the size or the quality (or both) of the horse. However, the biggest influencing factor was the work which humans required their particular horses to perform. Those who needed to move heavy loads bred for strength, while others in need of fast transportation bred for speed. The terms coldblood and warmblood (which have nothing to do with temperature) are used to describe horses. Coldblood refers to the heavy draught breeds which are believed to be descended from the prehistoric horse of northern Europe. Warmblood refers to the lighter, riding type of horse. Nowadays the term "warmblood" is used in connection with the horses being bred for competition riding. The breeds in this book are organized by continent, then sub-divided into countries within each continent.

"Wild" Horses

PRZEWALSKI HORSE

The horse no longer exists as a truly wild animal, although the Asiatic Wild Horse, believed to be one of the precursors of the domesticated horse, can still be seen in zoos in various parts of the world. The Asiatic Wild Horse *(Equus przewalskii przewalskii Poliakoff)* was "discovered" – or rather a small herd was – as recently as 1881 in the Tachin Schara Nuru Mountains on the edge of the Gobi desert by the Russian explorer Colonel N.M. Przewalski. Before that it was believed to have been extinct, over-hunted for its meat by Mongolian tribesmen. The Przewalski Horse, as it is widely known, differs genetically from the domesticated

horse, having 66 chromosomes instead of 64. In appearance it has several "primitive" features: a large head, with the eyes set high up rather than to the side of the head as in the case of the modern horse;

long ears; thick neck; heavy body with a dark dorsal strip and zebra markings on the legs. The Przewalski stands about 12–13hh and is always yellowish dun with a light-coloured nose and dark mane and

▮ ABOVE
These Kaimanawa horses live in feral herds in New Zealand's North Island. Like the Brumbies of Australia they are unpopular with stockmen because they compete for food with domestic animals

▮ PREVIOUS PAGE OPPOSITE

A Mustang.

▮ PREVIOUS PAGE
A Trakehner.

▮ LEFT
The Asiatic Wild Horse or Przewalski Horse is the only surviving race of the species from which domestic horses are descended. Its chromosome count differs from that of the domesticated horse.

tail. The mane, which grows upright, is shed each spring and there is no forelock. Intractable by nature – it cannot be trained for riding – the Przewalski can survive on a minimum of food and endure extremes of heat and cold.

TARPAN

Eastern Europe and European Russia were the home of the Tarpan, another horse widely believed to have been an ancestor of the modern horse. It survived in the wild until the nineteenth century. One authority claims that the last true Tarpan in captivity died in 1919, in which case the Tarpan which exists today, running semi-wild in reserves in Poland, must be a "reconstruction", almost certainly bred from the Konik, which it strongly resembled. Experiments with crossing Przewalski stallions and Konik mares have also produced an animal which looks very like the original Tarpan. The Tarpan was (and is) more lightly built than the Przewalski, standing about 13hh and with

a brown or mouse dun coat, dark mane and tail and, frequently, primitive dorsal stripe and zebra markings.

BRUMBY

Australia's "wild" horse, the Brumby, is not a true wild horse, equine animals having been unknown in Australasia until the arrival of European settlers a few hundred years ago (the assumption being that because there were no land bridges linking the Americas with Australia, Eohippus and its descendants had no means of migrating there). The Brumbies which live in feral herds in the Northern Territory and, to a lesser extent, in central Australia, are descended from settlers' horses who wandered off into the bush, producing offspring that grew up under wild conditions. When rounded up and broken in some Brumbies have, over the years, been useful to man but today they are generally regarded as a pest and are culled because they compete for food with domestic animals.

See also Camargue, Mustang, Sorraia.

■ ABOVE LEFT
The primitive looking Konik pony is found in Poland and is a descendant of the Tarpan. Crossed with Przewalski stallions, Konik mares produce Tarpan "look-alikes".

■ LEFT
The Sorraia pony, which can be found living in semi-feral conditions in Portugal, is believed to be of ancient origin.

Arab

The oldest and purest of all horse breeds, the Arab is considered by many people to be the most beautiful equine animal in the world. With its refined head and dished profile, expressive eyes, high spirits and unique, floating action, it is undoubtedly one of the most exquisite of creatures. Although it has certainly been bred with great care for many centuries, its exact origins are unclear. Depictions of horses

BREED DESCRIPTION

Height 14.2 – 15hh.

Colour Predominantly chestnut, grey, bay and black.

Conformation Small head with broad forehead, fine muzzle, concave profile, wide nostrils and small ears; deep, clearly defined jowl with the throat set into it in a distinctly arched curve; graceful, curving neck; long, sloping shoulders with well-defined withers; deep, roomy body with broad, deep chest and short, level back; high-set tail; hard, clean limbs with well-defined tendons and dense, fine bone; hard, well-shaped feet; fine, silky mane and tail.

INTERESTING FACTS

The unique outline of the Arab is determined by the formation of its skeleton, which differs from other equine breeds in several respects. The Arab has 17 ribs (other horses have 18); five lumbar vertebrae (other horses have six), and 16 tail vertebrae (other horses have 18).

in ancient art suggest that horses of Arab type lived in the Arabian peninsula as long ago as 2,000 – 3,000BC. Like the desert tribes with whom they have lived for so long, Arab horses became superbly well adapted to life in a harsh environment, having extreme powers of endurance, tremendous soundness and the ability to thrive on the most meagre of rations.

More than any other horse, it is the Arab which has influenced the development of equine

▌ TOP
Large eyes and nostrils are typical of the Arab. The short, refined head, with its dished profile, is one of the breed's most distinctive features.

▌ LEFT
The Arab's comparatively small size belies its weight-carrying ability. Standing no more than 15hh it will nevertheless carry a fully grown man with ease.

breeds throughout the world. This Arabian influence was initiated in the seventh and early eighth centuries AD when the followers of Islam spread across North Africa and into Spain. The horses they took with them were greatly superior to the native stock of other lands and so began a process of upgrading, through the introduction of

Arab blood, that was to go on for many centuries and, indeed, still goes on today.

Pure-bred Arabian horses are now bred throughout the world. As well as appearing in the show ring, they are particularly suited to the sport of endurance riding. In recent times, too, there has been a resurgence of interest in Arab racing.

❚ ABOVE LEFT
The Arab horse often appears to float over the ground. This remarkable action, coupled with a gentle temperament, makes it a popular riding horse throughout the world.

❚ ABOVE RIGHT
The breed's legendary stamina makes it the perfect choice for endurance riding which at the top level involves covering a distance of 100 miles (161km) in a day.

❚ LEFT
With its elegance, spirit and exceptional looks, it is easy to see why the Arab is often considered to be the world's most beautiful horse.

Barb

The Barb comes from Morocco, Algeria and Tunisia – the coastal regions of these North African countries were formerly known as the Barbary Coast, "Barbary" meaning foreign or, more specifically, non-Christian lands. Opinions differ as to the Barb's origins, lack of documentary evidence making it impossible to do more than hazard an educated guess. According to one school of thought, the Barb may trace back to an isolated group of wild horses which survived the Ice Age. If that were true, it would make the Barb an even older breed than the Arab. Another theory links the Barb to the Akhal-Teke, the horse of the Turkmens.

Although it is unlikely that the breed's true origins will ever be revealed, what is certain is that the Barb has had more influence on the development of equine breeds throughout the world than any other horse except the Arab. As with the Arab, it was the spread of Islam which led to the forerunners of today's Barbs reaching Europe from the early eighth century onwards (the first Muslim army, seven thousand strong, landed in Spain in the spring of 711). Once established on the Iberian peninsula the Barb horse played a major role in the development of the Andalusian, which subsequently became one of the major influences in horse breeding all over the world. Among the many historical references to

BELOW
The Barb lacks the refinement and elegance of the Arab but is equally tough and enduring.

BREED DESCRIPTION

Height Around 14.2 – 15.2hh.

Colour Predominantly grey, bay, brown and black.

Conformation Narrow head with convex profile; arched neck; flat shoulders with well-defined withers; short, strong body; sloping hindquarters with fairly low-set tail; rather slender, but strong, limbs; narrow, but hard, feet.

"Barbary" horses perhaps the most famous is Roan Barbary, belonging to the English king, Richard II (1367–1400). During the sixteenth century Henry VIII imported a number of Barbary horses into England and a century later the Barb played an important part in the evolution of the Thoroughbred. Elsewhere the influence of the Barb is still evident in the Argentinian Criollo and the American Mustang.

Despite its importance as a progenitor of other breeds, the Barb has achieved less widespread renown than the Arab, no doubt because it lacks the Arab's unique visual appeal, being much less refined and generally less impressive in appearance. Nevertheless it has the same boundless stamina and endurance, the same ability to thrive on meagre rations, the same sure-footedness – and an impressive turn of speed over short distances.

■ BELOW
Dressed in ceremonial attire, Barb horses and their
Moroccan riders are a colourful sight at a modern
"Fantasia".

INTERESTING FACTS

The most well-known Barb horses of modern
times were those ridden by the Spahis, men
of the Algerian and Tunisian cavalry
regiments in the French army. The Spahis
originally came from Turkey but were
incorporated into their army by the French
when the latter occupied Algiers and Tunis.
Barb horses still feature in the exciting
present-day North African festivals recalling
these countries' military pasts.

■ BELOW
In the dramatic rifle-firing charge seen at North
African festivals, Barb horses demonstrate their
impressive speed over a short distance.

41

Andalusian

As its name suggests, the Andalusian comes from the sun-baked region of southern Spain which is close to North Africa. While it is without doubt an ancient breed, its origins are uncertain. Whatever native horses existed in Spain when the Muslim invaders arrived in 711 – they may well have resembled the primitive Sorraian Pony still found today in Portugal – must surely have been crossed subsequently with

the invaders' Barb horses, which were imported in such great numbers.

After the last Muslim state, Granada, had fallen to the Christians in 1492, Spain began to assume a new importance in the western world and so, too, did her horses. Taken to the Americas by the sixteenth-century

Conquistadores, Spanish horses provided the foundation stock for the majority of new breeds developed by the settlers. In Europe, meanwhile, the Spanish horse became the preferred mount of monarchs and of the great riding masters, including the Englishman, William Cavendish, Duke of Newcastle, who in the seventeenth century wrote that: "If well chosen it is the noblest horse in the world; the most beautiful that can be. He is of great spirit and of great courage and docile; has the proudest walk, the proudest trot…the loftiest gallop and is the lovingest and gentlest horse and fittest of all for a king in Day of Triumph." The Lipizzaner is a direct descendant of the Andalusian, while other famous European breeds influenced by Spanish blood include the Frederiksborg, the Friesian (which in turn

BREED DESCRIPTION

Height 15 – 15.2hh.

Colour Predominantly grey (including "mulberry" – a dappled, purplish grey) and bay.

Conformation Handsome head with broad forehead and large, kind eyes; fairly long, thick but elegant neck; long, well-sloped shoulders with well-defined withers; short, strong body with broad chest and well-sprung ribs; very broad, strong, rounded hindquarters with rather low-set tail; medium length limbs, clean cut and elegant but strong; long and very luxuriant mane and tail.

Grey is one of the predominant Andalusian colours, along with bay. Spotted strains were once popular and were responsible for the founding of the Appaloosa breed in America.

■ LEFT
On point duty in present-day Barcelona. Thanks to its excellent temperament and willing nature, the Andalusian is an ideal all-purpose riding horse.

INTERESTING FACTS

The Andalusian horse's survival down the centuries, which included some pretty turbulent times, was aided by the monastic orders, particularly the Carthusians, who became especially skilful at horse breeding. In times of danger, horses were moved from the great studs to remote monasteries for safe keeping. The Carthusians were instrumental in maintaining purity of line and produced animals of consistently high quality.

influenced the Oldenburg), the Holstein and the Connemara.

The Andalusian is one of the most elegant of horses. Possessing tremendous presence, lofty paces, agility and a gentle, willing nature, it makes an excellent all-round riding horse and is particularly well suited to the movements of the *haute école* (high school). It can also be seen to great effect taking part in the colourful annual *ferias*, or fairs, of its native Andalusia.

■ RIGHT
The breed's proud bearing and lofty action lend themselves perfectly to the movements of the *haute école*, or high school.

Thoroughbred

The life of man has been inextricably interwoven with that of the horse for more than 4,000 years but in all that time no achievement has excelled the "invention" of the Thoroughbred. Quite apart from being the world's supreme racehorse, the Thoroughbred has played a vital part in the upgrading of numerous old horse and pony breeds and in establishing as many new ones.

Henry VIII set the process in motion during the sixteenth century when he

founded the famous Royal Paddocks at Hampton Court. His daughter, Elizabeth I, founded another stud at Tutbury, in Staffordshire. Both monarchs imported horses from Spain and Italy to cross with native stock. Under subsequent monarchs – James I, Charles I and Charles II – horse breeding and racing gained impetus. By the beginning of the seventeenth century regular race meetings were being staged at Newmarket, Chester, Doncaster and Lincoln. Many noblemen took up the

---

BREED DESCRIPTION

Height Variable. May be as small as 14.2hh or over 17hh. Average 16 – 16.2hh.

Colour All solid colours, the most common being bay, chestnut and brown. Also grey, black and roan. White markings are permissible.

Conformation Variable, but the best specimens have excellent conformation characterized by a refined, intelligent head; elegant neck; well-sloped shoulders; short, strong body with great depth through the girth; strong, muscular hindquarters with well -set tail; clean, hard legs with well let-down hocks and a minimum of 8 inches (20cm) of bone below the knee.

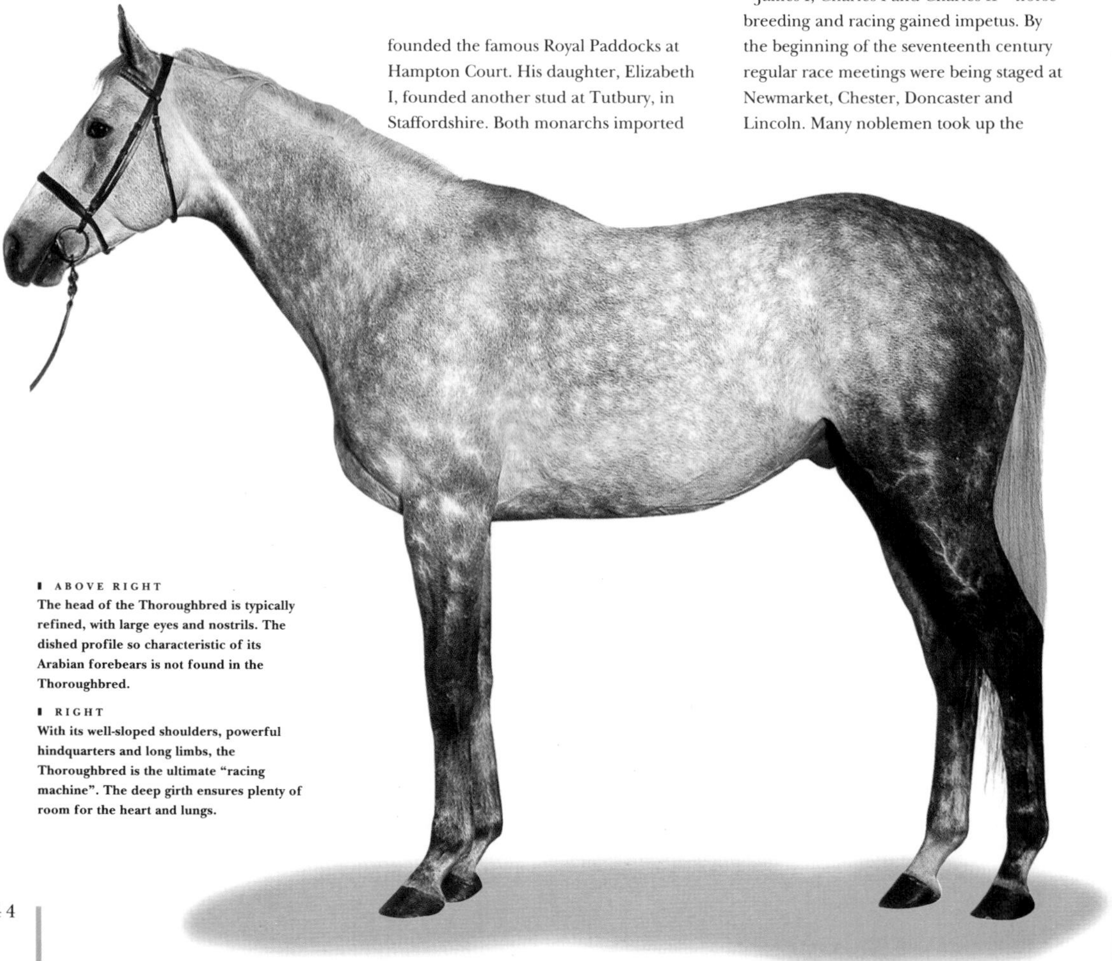

▌ ABOVE RIGHT
The head of the Thoroughbred is typically refined, with large eyes and nostrils. The dished profile so characteristic of its Arabian forebears is not found in the Thoroughbred.

▌ RIGHT
With its well-sloped shoulders, powerful hindquarters and long limbs, the Thoroughbred is the ultimate "racing machine". The deep girth ensures plenty of room for the heart and lungs.

■ RIGHT
The bigger, slower developing stamp of Thoroughbred often makes a first-rate steeplechaser. Chasing calls for courage, stamina and speed, qualities for which the Thoroughbred is renowned.

■ BELOW RIGHT
Thanks to carefully kept records (in the *General Stud Book*) dating back some two centuries, it is possible to trace the pedigree of this foal to one of the breed's handful of foundation sires.

■ BOTTOM
Thoroughbreds hurdling at speed at Cheltenham, spiritual home of the sport of jump racing. The Thoroughbred's athletic prowess makes it equally suitable for sports such as hunting and three-day eventing.

breeding of horses for racing, sending agents overseas to seek out good stallions. Records of the time repeatedly refer to Barb, Barbary, Arabian, Hobby and Galloway horses (the Irish Hobby and Scottish Galloway were famous "running"' horses of the day) – and it is on this blood that the modern Thoroughbred was founded.

The exact breeding of the Thoroughbred's forebears will never be known since horses often changed names when they

changed hands and the terms "Arabian", "Barb" and "Turk", were frequently used inaccurately. However, what is certain is that during the last quarter of the seventeenth century and the first quarter of the eighteenth, Englishmen or their agents bought a number of eastern stallions, crossed them with English mares of mixed pedigree and started a dynasty of great racehorses. The most famous of these stallions were the Byerley Turk, the Darley Arabian and the Godolphin Arabian, who are recognized as the founding fathers of the Thoroughbred. In 1791 *An Introduction to a General Stud Book* appeared and following the publication of several more preliminary editions, there came, in 1808, Volume I of the *General Stud Book*. A horse is classed as Thoroughbred if both its parents are entered in the *General Stud Book* (or in the equivalent official Thoroughbred stud books in other countries).

The Thoroughbred is a handsome horse, alert, spirited and full of presence. It has an easy, ground-covering stride at the gallop and possesses boundless courage and immense stamina, qualities which stand it in good stead on the racecourse, in the hunting field and in three-day eventing.

INTERESTING FACTS

The Byerley Turk was captured by Captain Byerley at Buda in the 1680s, ridden by him at the Battle of the Boyne and sent to England to stand at stud. His great-grandson Tartar sired Herod, one of the most important sires in Thoroughbred history. The Darley Arabian, foaled in 1700, was acquired by Thomas Darley and sent to England from the Syrian port of Aleppo. He was responsible for founding the Eclipse line – Eclipse was one of the greatest racehorses of all time. The Godolphin Arabian was foaled in the Yemen in 1724, exported to Tunis via Syria and later given by the Bey of Tunis to the King of France, who subsequently sold him to Edward Coke, from Derbyshire. He was eventually acquired by Lord Godolphin and was responsible for founding the Matchem line. The Herod, Eclipse and Matchem lines, plus the Highflyer (Highflyer was a son of Herod) are the four principal tail-male lines of the modern Thoroughbred.

Anglo-Arab

A more substantial horse than the pure-bred Arab, the Anglo-Arab is produced by mixing Arab and Thoroughbred blood. The Anglo-Arab can result from a first cross between a Thoroughbred stallion and an Arab mare or vice versa. It can also be produced by breeding Thoroughbred to Anglo-Arab or Arab to Anglo-Arab, or Anglo-Arab to Anglo-Arab. As a result of these different permutations, the amount of Arab blood varies a good deal. So, too, does the size and appearance of the horse. The biggest horses are often produced by using an Arab stallion on a Thoroughbred mare and the best examples of the Anglo-Arab will inherit the endurance and stamina of the Arab and the speed and scope of the Thoroughbred, but not the latter's rather high-strung temperament.

France has been a notable producer of Anglo-Arabs since the first half of the nineteenth century. The French Anglo-Arab traces back to two eastern stallions, Massoud (an Arab) and Aslam (which is said to be of Turkish origin). They were imported from Syria and crossed with three imported English Thoroughbred

BREED DESCRIPTION

Height Around 15.3 – 16.3hh.

Colour Usually chestnut, bay or brown.

Conformation Variable, but the best specimens tend towards good Thoroughbred conformation: intelligent head with straight profile, expressive eyes and alert ears; long neck with more prominent withers than the Arab; sloping shoulders; short, strong body – rather more sturdy than the Thoroughbred – with deep chest; somewhat long hindquarters; good, sound limbs; strong, well-shaped feet.

▮ **TOP LEFT**
The head of the Anglo-Arab is closer in appearance to that of the Thoroughbred than the Arab. The Anglo lacks the dished profile of the pure-bred.

▮ **LEFT**
The overall conformation is noticeably more Thoroughbred than Arab, although many Anglo-Arabs are more sturdily built than the average Thoroughbred.

▌ LEFT
The crossing of
Thoroughbred with
Arab blood has
produced some
outstanding
competition horses in
the Olympic
disciplines, including
dressage.

mares, Daer, Comus Mare and Selim Mare. Their three daughters, Delphine, Clovis and Danaë became the foundation stock of France's first breed of sports horse. At one time the Anglo-Arab was much used in France by the military and as a general riding and competition horse. More recently it has been an influential factor in the development of the modern sports horse, the Selle Français.

▌ BELOW
In recent years French Anglo-Arabs such as this one have achieved great success in top-level three-day eventing, holding their own against the best of the Thoroughbreds and Warmbloods.

INTERESTING FACTS

Before the development of the Selle Français, the French Anglo-Arab was highly successful in the competitive disciplines, particularly show jumping. Many of the horses ridden by the dual Olympic champion Pierre Jonquères d'Oriola were Anglo-Arabs, the most famous being the little gelding Marquis III (a very successful Grand Prix and Nations' Cup horse) and Ali-Baba, on whom d'Oriola won his first Olympic title at Helsinki in 1952. More recently French Anglo-Arabs have been successful performers with the French three-day event team. They include Twist la Beige (winner of the European Championship in 1993) and Newport and Newlot (both European team silver medallists).

Noriker

Bred and developed over several thousand years in the mountain regions of Austria, the Noriker is an attractive looking light draught horse. Strong and hardy, this horse is noted particularly for its calm temperament, sound limbs and sure-footedness. These characteristics make it an ideal all-round work horse over difficult mountainous terrain.

As with most horses, despite its ancient origins there was no formal breeding programme until fairly recent times. The Prince-Archbishop of Salzburg is credited with forming a stud book some 400 years ago. It was then that standards were drawn up, for both mares and stallions, and stud farms established.

Because of its toughness and capacity for hard work the Noriker became popular throughout Europe. Different strains evolved, including the Bavarian, now known as the South German Coldblood and found in Upper and Lower Bavaria. Various colour lines, tracing back to Andalusian and Neapolitan horses, also had an influence on today's breed and were responsible for the dappled and brindle colourings.

BREED DESCRIPTION

Height Stallions 16 – 17hh.
Mares 15.3 – 17hh.

Colour Brown, chestnut, black, grey and brindle. White body markings are not acceptable. Too many or too large white markings on the head and limbs are not desirable.

Conformation Straight profile, wide nostrils, medium-sized eyes; medium-length neck with thick, curly mane; good sloping shoulders; broad, deep chest; medium-length, well-muscled back; long limbs with powerful forearms, large clean joints, well-muscled second thigh and good, sound feet.

INTERESTING FACTS

The breed takes its name from the ancient state of Noricum (during the Roman Empire Noricum was roughly approximate to present-day Austria). However, the Noriker can be traced back to pre-Roman times, when a heavy war horse was developed in Thessalonica. Horses of this type were taken to Noricum by the Romans. In due course they were crossed with other coldblooded horses of the region and became admirably adapted to the harsh conditions of their new environment.

❚ ABOVE
Most Norikers are brown but the breed embraces a wide range of coat colours, including this attractive dark chestnut with flaxen mane.

❚ LEFT
The Noriker's sturdy build and good limbs and feet make it an ideal work horse in mountainous regions. Like most mountain breeds, it is a good mover, with a particularly active trot.

Belgian Draught

One of the world's finest and historically most important heavy horses, the Belgian Draught is an ancient breed, closely connected to the Ardennais. The Flanders Horse, as the breed was known during the Middle Ages, had an influence on the development of several other renowned "heavies", including the Shire, the Suffolk Punch and particularly the Clydesdale. Nowadays the Belgian Draught is also known as the Brabant, after its main breeding area in central Belgium.

Despite widespread mechanization, this gentle giant of a horse, known for its kind nature and willingness to work, can still be found in modest numbers in many areas of Belgium and is also much appreciated in North America.

Over the years breeders have managed to maintain the excellence of these horses by a policy of strict selection and some inbreeding. The result is a handsome individual – its short neck, strong shoulders, short limbs, deep-girthed body and huge hindquarters, coupled with the most amenable of temperaments, make it the ideal draught horse for work on the land and there is no finer sight in the equestrian world than a team of these magnificent animals hitched to a smart brewers' dray.

▌ ABOVE
The Belgian Draught is an impressive horse, combining great strength with a gentle temperament and willingness to work. Despite its size, it is economical to keep.

BREED DESCRIPTION

Height 16.2 – 17hh.

Colour Predominantly red-roan with black points, chestnut and sorrel. Bay, dun and grey also occur.

Conformation Small, rather plain head but with intelligent expression; short, muscular neck; massive shoulders; short, deep, compact body; rounded, powerful hindquarters; short, strong limbs with plenty of feather and well-shaped, medium-sized feet.

INTERESTING FACTS

Towards the end of the last century there were three recognized types of Brabant horse, each based on a different bloodline. Those from the celebrated stallion Orange I, known as the Gros de la Dendre line, were mainly bay in colour. A stallion called Bayard founded the Gris du Hainaut line, with its greys, red-roans and sorrels. A third line, the Colosses de la Méhaigne, descended from the bay stallion Jean I. Today the descendants of these bloodlines all come under the general title of Belgian Draught or Brabant.

▌ ABOVE LEFT
The head is rather plain but the eyes have the kindly expression associated with so many of the heavy breeds.

▌ LEFT
Massive hindquarters are typical of the breed. These horses have docked tails.

Frederiksborg

The stud after which the Frederiksborg is named was founded by King Frederick II during the 1560s and was famous as a provider of quality horses to the courts of Europe. The stud's foundation stock came from Spain and was subsequently crossed with the Spanish horse's close relative, the Neapolitan. The horses thus produced were both elegant and spirited and well suited to the dual requirements of the day: as a mount for work in the manège and as a charger for the cavalry.

▮ RIGHT
The Frederiksborg's somewhat plain head has a kind, intelligent look about it. Most examples of the breed, like this horse, are chestnut.

BREED DESCRIPTION

Height 15.3 – 16hh.

Colour Chestnut.

Conformation Intelligent, if somewhat plain, head; short, upright neck; strong but rather upright shoulders; strong back that tends to be long; high-set tail; good, strong feet.

The breed continued to develop through the introduction of eastern and British half-bred stallions and for several centuries the Frederiksborg was one of the most sought-after horses in Europe. Eventually, so numerous were the exports of the Frederiksborg from Denmark that stock became seriously depleted, with the result that during the first half of the nineteenth century the stud turned instead to Thoroughbred breeding. This venture was not a success and in 1871 the stud was dispersed. Fortunately, however, Frederiksborgs did not disappear altogether: private breeders went on producing them, mainly for use as light harness horses.

Frederiksborgs are still bred in Denmark, although recent demands for an outstanding sports horse have led to the development of a new horse, the Danish Warmblood, based mainly on Swedish, German and Polish stallions. Frederiksborg blood does occasionally appear in today's Danish Warmblood pedigrees, chiefly through the female line.

INTERESTING FACTS

The Frederiksborg played a significant part in the development of a much more well-known breed, the Lipizzaner, famous for its association with the Spanish Riding School in Vienna. The white stallion Pluto, from the Royal Danish Court Stud, was one of the six stallions on which the Lipizzaner breed is based. Pluto was foaled in 1765, the earliest of the six. More than two centuries later his descendants are still performing at the Spanish Riding School where they can be identified by the "Pluto" prefix to their names.

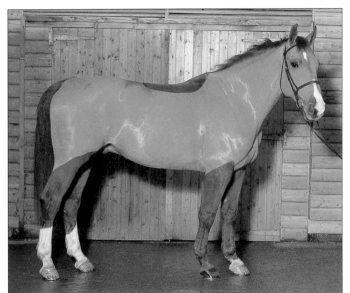

▮ LEFT
The rather long back, short neck and upright shoulders are more typical of the light harness horse than the riding horse.

Jutland

Except for the feathering of its lower legs, Denmark's heavy horse bears an uncanny resemblance to the British breed, the Suffolk Punch. This resemblance is perhaps not so surprising, because the present-day Jutland was greatly influenced by the Suffolk blood introduced via the English stallion Oppenheim LXII, who stood at stud in Denmark during the 1860s.

The breed goes back much further than that, however. Heavy horses have been bred on the Jutland Peninsula for many centuries, certainly as far back as the twelfth century, when they were in great demand as war horses. Combining enormous strength with the most willing

BREED DESCRIPTION

Height 15 – 16hh.

Colour Predominantly dark chestnut with light mane and tail.

Conformation Heavy, rather plain head, but with kind expression; short, thick neck; strong, muscular shoulders; exceptionally deep body with broad chest; round, muscular hindquarters; short limbs with plenty of bone.

INTERESTING FACTS

The Jutland was an influential factor in the development of the Schleswig, a draught horse which takes its name from the northernmost region of Germany and which towards the end of the nineteenth century was in demand for pulling trams and buses. Infusions of Jutland blood from neighbouring Denmark were being used by German breeders well into this century. The Schleswig closely resembles the Jutland and the Suffolk, both in build and colour. However, the use of carefully selected Boulonnais and Breton stallions from France has led to the appearance of some greys and bays.

of natures, the Jutland horse made the ideal mount for the heavily armoured knights of the Middle Ages. Cleveland Bay and Yorkshire Coach Horse blood is said to have been used in the development of the Jutland, but it is unquestionably the Suffolk which has been the dominant factor, even to its chestnut colouring.

Mechanization has reduced the numbers of these attractive horses but some can still be seen, either at shows or pulling drays in the cities or, occasionally, working the land.

▌ ABOVE
In common with all heavy breeds, the handsome Jutland has been the victim of mechanization but a few are still working.

▌ LEFT
The Jutland is usually chestnut, a colour inherited through the Suffolk Punch element in its ancestry.

Danish Warmblood

The Danish Warmblood is one of a number of horses specifically developed for use in modern equestrian pursuits, particularly the competitive disciplines of dressage, show jumping and three-day eventing.

The Danes have a long tradition as horse breeders: their first organized studs date from the fourteenth century. However, the market for horses has changed enormously this century, and especially during the last few decades. In many countries the relentless march of mechanization has transformed the horse from an essential means of transport to a "leisure" animal. In the wake of this transformation the Danes found that their native breeds – the Frederiksborg and its cousin, the spotted Knabstrup (a popular circus horse) – were not going to measure up as competitive sports horses.

To remedy this deficiency, a breeding programme was set up in 1962 to produce a new type of Danish riding horse.

BREED DESCRIPTION

Height 15.3 – 16.3hh.

Colour All colours occur.

Conformation Quality head; long, well set-on neck; good shoulders with prominent withers; muscular back and loins; long croup; strong limbs with long forearms, well-defined joints and good bone.

▌ RIGHT
The Danish Warmblood shows the typical conformation of the modern sports horse: well-sloped shoulders, strong back and quarters, and good, sound limbs and feet.

▌ ABOVE RIGHT
Like many other warmblood horses, the Danish Warmblood bears a distinctive brand mark on its hindquarters for identification purposes.

ABOVE
Warmblood horses
have been specifically
developed for use in
competitive sports
such as show jumping.

ABOVE RIGHT
A good deal of
German blood has
been used in the
development of the
Danish Warmblood.
This is reflected in its
quality head.

RIGHT
Perhaps the most
famous of all Danish
Warmbloods is the
dressage stallion
Matador, winner of the
silver medal at the
1990 World Equestrian
Games.

Carefully selected stallions, chiefly
Swedish, Trakehner, Hanoverian,
Holstein and Polish, were crossed with
the various local-bred mares to improve
the basic stamp of horse. Stringent
grading was introduced for both stallions
and mares to ensure that only the best
were granted entry to the stud books.
The breeding programme has been a
tremendous success. The resultant Danish
Warmblood is a handsome individual, well
proportioned and possessed of excellent
paces. It combines courage with a good
temperament and makes an outstanding
dressage horse.

Ariègeois

The Ariègeois, which lives in the Pyrenean mountains in the south-west of France, is a breed of great antiquity. It closely resembles the horses of southern Gaul described in Caesar's commentaries on

BREED DESCRIPTION

Height 13.1 – 14.3hh (the latter is rarely attained in its native habitat, although it may be on richer, lowland grazing).

Colour Solid black. Normally no white stockings or markings on the head, although the flank may be lightly flecked with white.

Conformation Light-boned, expressive head with flat forehead, straight profile, fairly short, hairy ears and bright, alert eyes with a gentle expression; fairly short, straight neck; rather straight shoulders; long but strong back and broad chest; round hindquarters with sloping croup; short, fairly slender limbs with a tendency to cow hocks; good, strong feet..

the Gallic Wars. Its home is the high valley of the Ariège river, from which it takes its name. Well adapted to the worst excesses of its mountain environment, it is impervious to cold and outstandingly sure-footed – ice-covered mountain trails hold no terrors for the little Ariègeois.

A versatile, hardy creature, the Ariègeois has for centuries been used as a packhorse, though it can just as easily function as a small riding horse or work the land on the steepest of hill farms, where modern machinery cannot venture.

▮ TOP
Like all mountain breeds, the Ariègeois has very active paces. It has exceptionally strong hooves and is noted for its sure-footedness.

▮ LEFT
The Ariègeois has a fairly long, but nevertheless strong, back, a powerfully built neck and deep girth. The sloping croup and low-set tail are characteristic.

Norman Cob

The Norman Cob is a light draught horse, still in use on small farms in the La Manche region of Normandy. Normandy has long been famed for its horse breeding, notably at the historic studs of Le Pin (founded as a royal stud in the mid-seventeenth century) and Saint-Lô, where the ancestors of the modern Cob were bred.

Stocky and compact, like the English Cob after which it was named, the Norman Cob was developed as a distinct breed at the beginning of this century. It was at that time that the breeders of half-bred horses first began to distinguish between those animals suitable for use as riding horses, particularly for the army, and those of less quality and sturdier build, more suited to light draught work.

The Norman Cob, as the heavier type was subsequently named, became a popular workhorse, especially in the La Manche region – even the powerful Percheron failed to supplant it there.

Over the years there has been a tendency for the Norman Cob to become heavier, to cope with the work required of it, but although it is undoubtedly sturdy and muscular, it lacks the massive stature of the true heavy horse and has never lost the energetic action, particularly at trot, characteristic of the half-bred horse.

❚ RIGHT
The Norman Cob has always been noted for its energetic action. The lively, free-moving trot is characteristic of the breed.

❚ BELOW
The Norman Cob has the same kindly expression as the English Cob after which it is named.

INTERESTING FACTS

The tail of the Norman Cob is still traditionally docked. Down the centuries this mutilation of horses' tails has been carried out for a variety of reasons: fashion, to prevent the tail becoming entangled with harness and equipment and, in ancient times, probably to serve some ritual purpose. It used to be the fashion to dock the tail of the English Cob, but the practice became illegal in Great Britain under the Docking and Nicking Act, 1948. Quite apart from the trauma of the operation, docking deprives the horse of a vital means of protection against flies.

BREED DESCRIPTION

Height 15.3 – 16.3hh.

Colour Chestnut, bay or bay-brown; occasionally red-roan or grey.

Conformation Overall strong, stocky build with short, well-proportioned limbs.

❚ LEFT
Strong and stockily built, the Norman Cob is a well-proportioned light draught horse. It lacks the massive proportions of the true heavy horse.

Camargue

BELOW LEFT
Small, strong and always grey, the Camargue has been an inspiration for artists and poets down the centuries.

BELOW
The breed's ancient origins can be detected in the somewhat heavy, square head, which is reminiscent of that of the primitive horse.

The tough little Camargue, the native horse of the inhospitable wastes of the Rhône delta in southern France, was not recognized as a breed until January 1968 yet it is almost certainly of ancient origin. It bears a strong resemblance to the horses depicted in the cave paintings of Lascaux, dating from 15,000 BC. Moreover, the even older horse skeletons unearthed at Solutré in south-east France in the nineteenth century could well be those of the breed's forebears.

During its long occupation of the marshlands, the indigenous horse must

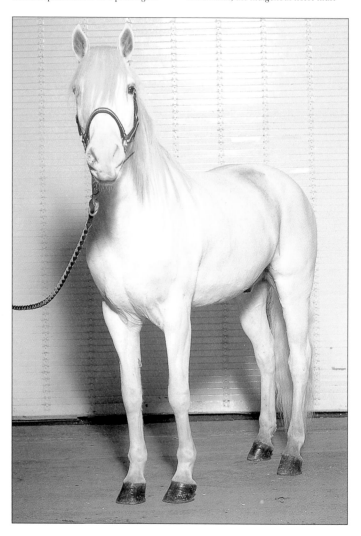

have been influenced by influxes of North African blood, but it has retained certain characteristics of the primitive horse, particularly in its rather heavy, square head.

The horses have always played an integral part in the everyday life of the Camargue, providing the guardians, or herdsmen, with strong, sure-footed mounts for their work with the herds of fighting bulls traditionally raised in the area. Despite its relatively small size, the Camargue horse has the strength and courage to carry a grown man safely over the most treacherous wetland terrain.

The herds, or *manades*, of Camargue horses, each with its own stallion, enjoy a semi-wild existence, being rounded up annually for inspection, branding of young stock, selection of suitable breeding stock and gelding of non-breeding males. Although the practice of fencing off pastureland and draining large areas for the cultivation of crops has, over the years, reduced the need for herdsmen, the horses are still very much a feature of the area. They have taken on a new role as mounts for the increasing number of tourists to the Camargue, which is famed for its wealth of wildlife.

BREED DESCRIPTION

Height 13.1 – 14.1hh.

Colour Grey.

Conformation Rather large, square head with short, wide-set ears; short neck; short, upright shoulders; fairly short back and deep chest; muscular hindquarters with short, sloping croup and long, bushy tail; strong, well-formed limbs with big knees and very hard, sound feet.

INTERESTING FACTS

The half-wild Camargue horses have long held a romantic fascination for artists and writers. In his poem "Horses on the Camargue", Roy Campbell penned these typically evocative lines:

*...in a shroud of silence like the dead,
I heard a sudden harmony of hooves,
And, turning, saw afar
A hundred snowy horses unconfined,
The silver runaways of Neptune's car
Racing, spray-curled, like waves before
the wind.
Sons of the Mistral, fleet
As him with whose strong gusts they love
to flee,
Who shod the flying thunders of their feet
And plumed them with the snortings of
the sea.*

BELOW LEFT
Despite their semi-wild existence Camargue horses are perfectly amenable to training, as this French trick-riding expert demonstrates.

BELOW
The inhospitable wastes of the Rhône delta have produced a breed renowned for its toughness, strength and sure-footedness.

BOTTOM
Herding the fighting bulls reared in the region is the breed's traditional role. Despite its small size, the Camargue horse will carry a herdsman with great ease.

Ardennais

One of the world's premier heavy horses, the powerful but exceptionally docile Ardennais is of ancient origin and is named after its mountainous homeland region on the French–Belgian border.

The Ardennais used to be less massive – as late as the nineteenth century it was used not only for draught work but also for riding. Arab blood was introduced around 1810 and infusions of

BREED DESCRIPTION

Height 15 – 16hh.

Colour Roan, red-roan, iron grey, dark or liver chestnut and bay are the preferred colours. Bay-brown, light chestnut and palomino are admissible. Black, dappled grey and all other colours are inadmissible.

Conformation Straight profile with slightly prominent eye sockets, low, flat forehead, large expressive eyes, pricked ears and wide, open nostrils; medium-length neck, well set-on and generally arched; very strong shoulders; medium-heavy body with deep chest, rather short back and muscular loins; wide, rounded hindquarters; fairly short, strong and muscular limbs.

▌ BELOW
Massively built, but extremely docile, the bigger type of Ardennais makes the perfect partner for heavy agricultural work.

Thoroughbred, Percheron and Boulonnais were added later. These attempts to improve the breed were not a great success and were abandoned, but the Ardennais nevertheless continued to be a most useful animal. Its energy and stamina made it invaluable to the military during the Revolution, at the time of Empire and particularly during the ill-fated Russian campaign. During World

War I the Ardennais was in great demand as an artillery horse.

It was the requirements of agriculture and other heavy draught work which led to the development of a heavier stamp of horse and today, in addition to the original small Ardennais, two other types are recognized: a larger version of the Ardennais, known as the Auxois and the heavier, larger framed Ardennais du Nord (formerly known as the Trait du Nord), the result of using outcrosses to the Belgian Draught.

INTERESTING FACTS

In their writings some 2,000 years ago both the Greek historian Herodotus and the Roman emperor Julius Caesar made particular mention of the horses of north-eastern France, then known as northern Gaul, extolling their stamina and toughness. Skeletons unearthed in the region suggest that these horses stood 15hh – the height of the smaller type of Ardennais still seen today. These were the ancestors of the modern Ardennais.

▌ ABOVE
The Ardennais can still be found working on the land. Its ability to thrive on a minimum of feed makes it an economical proposition for the farmers of small holdings.

▌ BELOW
Roan is a very typical coat colouring of the breed. The eyes are invariably large, with an intelligent, gentle expression.

Selle Français

France has been well to the fore in the development of a modern sports horse, the Cheval de Selle Français (French Saddle Horse) being one of the great warmblood breeding success stories of the twentieth century. The term Selle Français came into use in December 1958 and the first stud book was published in 1965.

The French, with their great tradition of horse breeding, laid the foundations for their modern, quality riding horse as far back as the early nineteenth century, when many regions of the country began to import English Thoroughbred and half-

BREED DESCRIPTION

Height: Medium weight small, 15.3hh and under; medium, 15.3 – 16.1hh; large, over 16.1hh.

Height: Heavyweight small, under 16hh; large, 16hh and over. (The classification "medium" or "heavy" is based on the horse's weight-carrying ability, judged on conformation.)

Colour Predominantly chestnut, though all colours are permissible.

Conformation Refined head; long, elegant neck; sloping shoulders; strong body with well-sprung ribs; broad, powerful hindquarters; strong limbs with particularly powerful forearms, pronounced joints and good bone.

▌ ABOVE
A quality head, set on a long, elegant neck, is typical of the Selle Français. The breed is one of the world's most successful competition horses.

▌ RIGHT
English Thoroughbred and French Trotter blood provided the base for the Selle Français. Its harmonious proportions and overall appearance are very reminiscent of the Thoroughbred.

■ BELOW
Some Selle Français horses such as The Fellow (in the red colours) have the speed to take on, and beat, full Thoroughbreds on the racecourse.

■ BELOW
Some Selle Français horses such as The Fellow (in the red colours) have the speed to take on, and beat, full Thoroughbreds on the racecourse.

■ BOTTOM LEFT
The breed excels at show jumping. This attractive bay mare, Miss, won team and individual silver medals at the 1994 World Equestrian Games.

INTERESTING FACTS

Although the most important influence on the Selle Français has undoubtedly been the Thoroughbred, the French Trotter has also been a factor, not least in the pedigrees of the famous show jumpers Galoubet and Jappeloup. Galoubet has trotter blood on his dam's side, albeit a couple of generations back. But the spring-heeled little Jappeloup, whose brilliant show-jumping career culminated with success in the individual championship at the 1988 Olympic Games in Seoul and a team gold medal in the 1990 World Equestrian Games, was actually by a trotter, Tyrol II, out of a Thoroughbred mare, Vénérable.

Interestingly, Jappeloup lacked the harmonious paces usually associated with the Selle Français. He was notoriously clumsy (many a human had their feet trodden on in his company) and a far from comfortable ride. This was almost certainly the result of his powerful hindquarters – he stood higher behind the saddle than in front, typical trotter conformation.

■ BELOW
Thanks to the Thoroughbred blood in their veins, Selle Français horses have the speed and stamina to succeed in three-day eventing.

bred stallions to cross with their local, less refined, mares (the chief exceptions were the Limousin and south-west regions which specialized in breeding Anglo-Arabs). In Normandy, always a stronghold of horse breeding, two important horses evolved: a fast trotter, later to become the French Trotter (many of the half-breds imported from England came from Norfolk Roadster stock) and the Anglo-Norman. The vast majority of today's Selle Français horses trace back to the Anglo-Norman.

French Warmblood breeding differs from that in neighbouring countries, where the grading system is all-important. Success in competition by stallions, mares and their progeny or relatives forms the basis for selection in France. It is a system which, in a comparatively short space of time, has produced a highly successful competition horse, in appearance reminiscent of the Thoroughbred (which provided its most famous foundation sires) and possessing the necessary spirit to survive the cut and thrust of modern competitive sports. The Selle Français shines, above all, at show jumping where its claims to fame include Jappeloup (1987 European and 1988 Olympic Champion), Quito de Baussy (1990 World Champion), I Love You (1983 World Cup winner) and Galoubet (1982 world team gold medallist).

French Trotter

France – the country with the greatest tradition of trotting racing outside the United States – developed its own strain of trotter by crossing English Thoroughbreds, half-breds and Norfolk Roadsters with robust Norman mares. The process began in the early nineteenth century. The first French trotting races, which were ridden, not driven, took place in 1806 on the Champ de Mars in Paris. As the sport began to increase in popularity, purpose-built race tracks were opened, the first being at Cherbourg in the 1830s, and the breed developed and improved. In 1861 an Imperial decree gave official encouragement to the sport, leading to the formation of its first governing body.

The Anglo-Norman developed into a fine trotter and five important bloodlines became established: Conquérant, Normand, Lavater, Phaeton and Fuchsia.

BREED DESCRIPTION

Height Average about 16.2hh. The larger horses tend to make the best ridden trotters.

Colour All colours admissible. Chestnut, bay and brown are predominant with some roan. Grey is rare.

Conformation Well-sloped shoulders, giving good ground-covering action; short, strong body; immensely powerful, often sloping, hindquarters.

▌ TOP RIGHT
The French Trotter has much of the Thoroughbred about its general appearance, although it is more sturdily built and rather less refined.

▌ RIGHT
Racing under saddle, as well as in harness, has ensured the continued quality of this old-established breed, which has played an important part in the development of the Selle Français.

▌ LEFT
French Trotters are
sometimes used in
the sport of skijoring,
in which the horse
pulls its human
partner on skis.

Conquérant and Normand were both by
the English half-bred Young Rattler. This
son of the Thoroughbred Rattler is
sometimes called "the French Messenger"
(Messenger being the foundation sire of
the Standardbred) because of the
enormous influence he has had on trotter
breeding in France. Lavater was another
example of the English connection, being
by a Norfolk Roadster. The most
prepotent of all the early stallions was
Fuchsia. Foaled in 1883 he sired nearly
400 trotters and more than 100 of his sons

produced winners. Some Standardbred
blood was introduced over the years to
give the breed more speed but the
Trotteur Français Stud Book was closed to
non-French-bred horses in 1937 and has
only been opened a fraction in recent
years to allow a very limited number of
carefully selected French/Standardbred
crosses to be admitted.

The French have never totally given
up ridden racing. Some ten per cent of
today's trotting races staged in France are
under saddle and they have an important
effect on breeding. Because ridden
trotters race under comparatively heavy
weights they must accordingly be well built
horses with good balance and level action.
These quality horses have played a large
part in maintaining the overall standard of
the French Trotter.

▌ ABOVE RIGHT
Powerful hindquarters
are typical of the
breed, the best
examples of which can
trot at speeds not
much less than those
of the galloping
Thoroughbred.

▌ RIGHT
Specially designed
vehicles are used to
replace the bike-wheel
sulky for racing on
snow. Unlike pacers,
trotters always race
without hobbles on
their legs.

Percheron

The elegant, free-moving Percheron originated in La Perche, in the south of Normandy. Its ancestors were Arabian horses brought to Europe by the Moors. The oriental influence is believed to have begun following the defeat of the Moors by Charles Martel near Poitiers in AD 732, and was continued after the First Crusade in 1099, when Robert, Comte de Rotrou, imported more Arab horses into France. Much later, during the eighteenth century, Arab stallions at the Royal Stud at Le Pin were made available to breeders of Percherons to upgrade their stock. The

eastern influence continued until relatively recent times, one of the most important early Percheron stallions, Jean le Blanc (foaled in about 1830), being the son of the Arab stallion Gallipoly. The Percheron's great strength and courage, coupled with its sound limbs and

LEFT
The Percheron has a fine head with prominent, alert eyes and wide, open nostrils.

ABOVE RIGHT
The breed is noted for its broad, deep chest, powerful forearms and excellent feet.

RIGHT
Well-proportioned and clean-limbed (that is, without feather on the lower legs), the Percheron is an elegant horse possessed of surprisingly free-moving paces considering its great size.

INTERESTING FACTS

One of the tallest horses on record was a Percheron named Dr Le Gear. Foaled in 1902, he stood 21hh or 7 feet (213.4m) at the withers and weighed just under 27cwt (1,370kg).

FAR LEFT
The quality and excellent movement of the modern Percheron reflect the Arab influence on the breed.

LEFT
Pause for a snack for a working horse. Percherons are so docile that they can be trained to work in a very short time.

BELOW
Thanks to its good action and amenable temperament, the Percheron goes equally well under saddle and in harness.

longevity, made it tremendously popular in various fields: as a war horse, as a carriage horse and on the land. For some four decades during the late nineteenth and early twentieth centuries it was in great demand world wide, both for work purposes and as an improver of other heavy breeds. French breeders exported a great number of Percherons, which proved to be the most adaptable of horses whatever the climate. Many went to England, some to Australia (the Percheron is said to be the first heavy horse to be taken there) and South America, and the breed became particularly popular in North America, where the black coat colouring was preferred to the grey. American buyers also favoured a heavyweight horse which, together with the need elsewhere for big horses to work on the railways, encouraged the breeding of more massive animals. Despite its great size, however, the modern Percheron is very much a quality animal, retaining the long, low action of its ancestors.

BREED DESCRIPTION

Height 15.2 – 17hh. Average 16.1hh.

Colour Grey or black.

Conformation Fine head, with broad, square forehead, fine, long ears, prominent, alert eyes, straight profile and flat nose with wide, open nostrils; long, arched neck with fairly thick mane; sloping shoulders with prominent withers; broad, deep chest with fairly prominent sternum, short, straight back and loins with great depth through the girth and well-sprung ribs; long, sloping hindquarters; clean, sound limbs with prominent, powerful forearms and long, muscular thighs, large knees and hocks, small, strong fetlock joints and good, strong feet.

Breton

Short-legged and heavily built, the Breton is a surprisingly active heavy horse, with an especially lively trot: characteristics that testify to its Norfolk Roadster and, even further back, Arab ancestry. Like so many southern European horse breeders, those in Brittany used horses brought back from the Middle East by the Crusaders to cross with their more plebeian native stock adding, in more recent times, infusions of blood from England and a number of continental countries – the latter not always with successful results.

Down the centuries there has always been more than one type of Breton horse. Two were identified in the Middle Ages, the Sommier and the Roussin. The Sommier was descended from stock bred mainly in the north of Brittany and was used for pack and agricultural work. The Roussin, a much lighter stamp of animal, was found in the south and some central parts of the region and was a popular

▌BELOW
Chestnut is the most usual colour for the Breton. The beautiful, kind eyes are set in a wide, somewhat square head.

saddle horse, noted for its comfortable, ambling gait.

Although the Breton is no longer thought of as a saddle horse, it does still come in different types – a large and small draught, and a coach-horse type known as the Postier, which is built on less massive lines than the draught horse. The Postier owes its lighter conformation and brilliant paces to infusions of Norfolk Roadster blood from England during the nineteenth century.

An early-maturing animal, the Breton is highly regarded in the French meat trade for the high yield and quality of meat it produces. However, it is still also valued as a draught animal and some Bretons can still be seen working on the land, particularly in the vineyards.

INTERESTING FACTS

The Breton is a hardy, adaptable animal and a most willing worker. Because of its ability to work in hot climates, it has been used for upgrading purposes by breeders in Italy, Spain and even as far afield as Japan.

BREED DESCRIPTION

Height 15 – 16.1hh.

Colour Mainly chestnut; some red roan, bay and grey; black rarely occurs.

Conformation Squarish head with straight profile, open nostrils, bright eyes and small, fairly low-set ears; short, strong and slightly arched neck; rather short but sloping shoulders; short, broad and strong body with well-sprung ribs; very powerful hindquarters; short, strong limbs with very muscular thighs and forearms.

▌RIGHT
Stocky and short-legged, the Breton is nevertheless a very active mover and has been used over the years as a warhorse, draught horse, pack-horse, coach horse – and even a riding horse.

Boulonnais

The gentle Boulonnais, the most elegant of all the heavy horse breeds, traces back to Roman times. It is a native of north-west France and, like the Percheron, was greatly influenced by oriental blood. The Arab influence occurred more than once. First there was the arrival of the Roman armies, with their horses of eastern origin, who massed on the French coast before invading Britain. Then there were the Crusaders, who brought more eastern horses back with them. Two great noblemen in particular, Robert, Comte d'Artois and Eustache, Comte de Boulogne, are credited with importing Arab horses for use in their stables at this time. There was a slight change of direction during the fourteenth century, when Mecklenburg blood from Germany was introduced in order to breed a sturdier animal capable of carrying knights with their new, plated armour.

The term Boulonnais dates from the seventeenth century and reflects the main breeding region of that name on the north French coast. Sadly, the number of Boulonnais horses was seriously depleted during World War I because their chief breeding grounds were right at the heart of the battle zone. World War II had a second serious impact on the breed just as it was recovering. These two setbacks, plus the rapid spread of mechanization following World War II all but signalled the death blow of this fine horse. Fortunately it did survive, thanks to the efforts of a few dedicated enthusiasts, and although the meat trade features as one of the prime outlets for breeders, some Boulonnais horses may still be seen working small farms, where they can prove more effective and economical than tractors. Despite its size and substantial build, it is still possible to detect traces of the breed's Arab ancestry both in the small, refined head, with its large, expressive eyes, and in its outgoing nature.

INTERESTING FACTS

Two types of Boulonnais evolved: a large, heavy version for use in agriculture and industry, and a smaller, lighter horse suitable for less strenuous work on small-holdings and in light draught work. At one time the small type was known as the *maréeur* or *mareyeur* (fish merchant) because it was used for the transportation of fish from Boulogne to Paris. Nowadays the small type is used in agriculture, the meat trade favouring the larger animal.

BREED DESCRIPTION

Height 15.3 – 16.3hh.

Colour All shades of grey.

Conformation Elegant head, short and broad overall, with straight profile, wide forehead, slightly prominent eye sockets, strong, rounded, widely spaced jowls, large, bright eyes, small, erect ears, open nostrils and small mouth (in mares the head is slightly longer and less heavy); thick, often arched, neck with thick mane; muscular shoulders with fairly prominent withers; broad, straight back, broad chest and well-sprung ribs; round, muscular hindquarters with fairly high-set, thick tail; strong limbs with very prominent muscular projections in the forearms and thighs, short, thick cannons, large, flat joints and no feather.

Trakehner

Of all the warmbloods, the Trakehner is the closest in appearance to the Thoroughbred. Organized breeding of this attractive riding horse began in 1732, when Friedrich Wilhelm I of Prussia established the Royal Trakehner Stud Administration in East Prussia (now part of Poland). A great deal of Thoroughbred and Arab blood was used to upgrade the local horses. These were descendants of the tough little Schweiken breed known to the Teutonic knights who colonized the region during the early thirteenth century. The Schweiken was a descendant of the

Konik pony, which traces back to the primitive Tarpan.

Towards the end of the eighteenth century a determined effort was made to improve the Trakehner, or East Prussian, as it was also known. Inferior breeding stock at the Royal Stud was drastically weeded out, a process which led to the swift development of the Trakehner. It was soon much in demand, first as a carriage horse and subsequently as an army remount.

Renowned for its twin qualities of elegance and toughness, the Trakehner flourished for nearly two centuries – until the disastrous upheaval of World War II. During the autumn and winter of 1944 the breed suffered catastrophic losses as desperate efforts were made to evacuate the horses before the arrival of the advancing Russian troops. Of the

thousands of Trakehners, many of them mares with foals at foot, who set off on the 900 mile (1,450km) journey west across Europe, few survived. Before their flight there were more than 25,000 horses registered in the East Prussian stud book. A mere 1,200 or so made it to the West

▌ ABOVE RIGHT
The Trakehner is noted for its refined head. Large eyes and a small, tapered muzzle enhance the overall impression of quality.

▌ RIGHT
The Trakehner's elegant outline owes much to the Thoroughbred influence. The Trakehner, in its turn, has been used in the development of the Dutch, Danish and Swedish Warmbloods.

BREED DESCRIPTION

Height Average 16 – 16.2hh.

Colour Any solid colour.

Conformation Refined head with large eyes and small muzzle; elegant, tapering neck; well-sloped shoulders; strong, medium-length body, well ribbed-up; well-rounded hindquarters; hard limbs with short cannons and excellent, sound feet.

INTERESTING FACTS

One of the most famous examples of the Trakehner is the show jumper Abdullah, a handsome grey stallion who competed for the United States. Ridden by Conrad Homfeld, he won a team gold medal and the individual silver at the 1984 Olympic Games and was victorious in the World Cup the following year. Abdullah was originally exported *in utero* to Canada and was foaled in 1970. After his retirement from competition he was used for breeding in many countries, thanks to the use of frozen semen.

■ LEFT
Like the Thorough-bred, the Trakehner is possessed of courage and stamina, qualities which make it suitable for tough sports such as carriage driving.

■ BELOW LEFT
The powers of endurance which helped the breed survive the harsh times of World War II stand the breed in good stead in the modern sport of eventing.

■ BELOW
The show-jumping stallion Abdullah demonstrated the breed's fine qualities to great advantage when winning a team gold medal at the 1984 Olympic Games.

and many of these failed to survive in the very harsh economic conditions of post-war Germany.

Incredibly, thanks to the dedicated efforts of the keepers of the original stud book, the Trakehner did not die out. The surviving equine evacuees were tracked down and re-registered in West Germany and, as breeding resumed and numbers increased, the Trakehner began to take its place in the modern equestrian world. Valued for its good conformation and action, its spirited temperament and its endurance, it has found favour both as a competition horse and as an improver of other warmbloods.

Hanoverian

George II, Elector of Hanover and King of England, was instrumental in the establishment of this famous German warmblood, thanks to the foundation of the state stud at Celle in 1735. The aim was to provide local people with the services of good quality stallions at nominal fees, the original horses being Holsteins of predominantly Andalusian and Neapolitan blood. Thanks to the later

▌ LEFT
Previously bred as an all-purpose work horse, the modern Hanoverian has been refined for use in equestrian sports.

BREED DESCRIPTION

Height 15.3 – 16.2hh.

Colour All solid colours.

Conformation Medium-sized head, clean cut and expressive, with large, lively eyes and good free cheek bones; long, fine neck; large, sloping shoulders with pronounced withers; strong, deep body; muscular hindquarters with well set-on tail; well-muscled limbs with large, pronounced joints and well-formed, hard hooves.

▌ ABOVE RIGHT
Thoroughbreds and Trakehners were used in the development of the present-day Hanoverian. Their influence can be seen in the breed's clean-cut head.

▌ RIGHT
The Hanoverian is noted more for its strength than its speed, hence the many successes of its representatives in dressage and show jumping.

▌ LEFT
Hanoverians have
found favour
throughout the world
as show jumpers.
Amadeus Z, bred in
Belgium, is seen
competing for Holland
at the 1994 World
Equestrian Games.

importation of English horses, including
Thoroughbreds, the Hanoverian gradually
began to show more quality, the aim being
to produce a good all-purpose animal that
was capable of working on the land but
also suitable for ridden work and for use
as a light carriage horse.

In common with so many other horse-
breeding enterprises, the development of
the Hanoverian at Celle was adversely
affected by war. By the end of the
eighteenth century the stud had over 100
stallions, but by 1816, after the
Napoleonic wars, a mere thirty remained.
To help make up for these losses, more
outside blood was brought in, especially
Thoroughbred. But the time came when
the breed was tending to become too light
for the work required of it and this
influence was accordingly reduced.

After World War II, however, the
Hanoverian had to be adapted to a new
way of life if the breed was to survive and
Thoroughbred blood was again
introduced, along with Trakehner, to
produce a warmblood suited to the
demands of the leisure-horse market.

The modern Hanoverian is lighter
and less coarse than of old and is noted
for its good, honest temperament. In
common with other German warmbloods,
stallions are only licensed if they pass the
required veterinary inspection and, after
licensing, must pass ridden performance
tests. Hanoverians are among the world's
most sought-after sports horses, their
strength and athleticism making them
especially suitable for dressage and
show jumping.

▌ LEFT
Dressage is the other
sport at which the
Hanoverian excels.
With its great strength
and true, energetic
action, it is well suited
to this demanding
discipline.

Holstein

The Holstein is probably the oldest of the German warmbloods, dating back several centuries. As early as the seventeenth century horses bred in the region were much in demand in France, Denmark and Italy. The old Holstein horses contained mixed blood, including German, Neapolitan, Spanish and oriental. During the nineteenth century they were crossed with Yorkshire Coach Horses, a policy which helped give the breed a distinctive high knee action, great presence and an exceptionally tractable nature. Holsteins became renowned for being tough but handsome carriage horses and subsequently as army remounts.

The Traventhall Stud, founded by the Prussians in 1867 in Schleswig-Holstein, is considered the modern Holstein's birthplace. However, this stud is no longer

▌ ABOVE
This handsome head, with its alert, intelligent
expression, is typical of the Holstein.

in operation and the breeds main base is now at Elmshorn.

To produce a stamp of horse suitable for today's requirements, some Thoroughbred blood was used in the period after World War II, which resulted in a lighter type of horse with less high, "carriage-horse" action and a better shoulder. Although the infusions of Thoroughbred blood may have made the Holstein rather more excitable than it was

▌ LEFT
Formerly bred for use as a carriage horse
and army remount, the Holstein was
upgraded into a better-quality animal
through the introduction of a certain
amount of Thoroughbred blood.

One of the most celebrated Holstein horses of all time was the big bay gelding Meteor, the only show jumper to have won a medal at three Olympic Games. Foaled in 1943, he won the individual bronze medal at the 1952 Games and four years later helped Germany win the team gold in Stockholm, where he finished fourth individually. In Rome in 1960, at the age of 17, he won a second team gold medal and finished sixth in the individual contest. Ridden by Fritz Thiedemann, an exceptionally talented all-round horseman, Meteor was an outstanding ambassador for the Holstein breed. He died in 1966 and is buried at Elmshorn, the breed's headquarters.

▌ FAR LEFT
Show jumping is a sport at which the Holstein, with its intelligent and bold character, has excelled for many years.

▌ BELOW
The breed is noted for its powerful action, which is used to good effect in Grand Prix dressage.

of old, it has, generally speaking, retained its good temperament. Its intelligence and boldness make it a first-rate mount for top-level dressage and show jumping.

Holstein horses are not bred in such quantity as some other warmbloods nor is their breeding area particularly large. Possibly as a result, there is less variation in overall type.

▌ BELOW
Originally prized as tough, active carriage horses, Holsteins can still be seen in harness in the competitive discipline of four-in-hand driving.

BREED DESCRIPTION

Height Approximately 16 – 17hh.

Colour All colours permissible. Bay with black points and brown predominate. Grey is quite common, chestnut less so.

Conformation Expressive head, well set-on and in proportion to the size of the horse, with big, bright eyes; long, muscular and slightly arched neck; long, sloping shoulders; strong back, deep, wide chest and muscular loins; strong, muscular hindquarters with well-muscled thighs, stifles and gaskins; short, strong cannon bones, flat knees, big, clean hocks, medium-length pasterns and good, hard feet.

Oldenburg

The Oldenburg, Germany's heaviest type of warmblood, was originally developed as a coach horse and was based on the old Friesian horses bred in the region between the River Weser and the Netherlands. The breed takes its name from Count Anton Gunther von Oldenburg (1603–67), who played a leading part in its development, crossing stallions from Italy and Spain with the native stock. Later breeders introduced Thoroughbred, Cleveland Bay, Hanoverian and Norman blood. The result was a big upstanding horse, measuring a good 17hh, and fairly heavily built. Unlike most large animals, however, it matured early which undoubtedly popularized it as a work horse.

■ LEFT
The Oldenburg was originally bred as a coach horse. It is the heaviest of the German Warmbloods.

BREED DESCRIPTION

Height Approximately 16 – 17hh.

Colour Predominantly brown, black and bay.

Conformation Rather plain head, occasionally with a Roman nose; fairly long, very strong neck; sloping, muscular shoulders; powerfully built body with deep chest; strong hindquarters with high-set tail; fairly short limbs with large joints and plenty of bone.

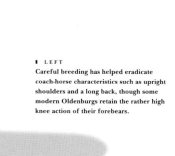

■ LEFT
Careful breeding has helped eradicate coach-horse characteristics such as upright shoulders and a long back, though some modern Oldenburgs retain the rather high knee action of their forebears.

▌ LEFT
The German rider
Franke Sloothaak on
his way to becoming
World Show Jumping
Champion in 1994.
His mount is the
Oldenburg mare,
Weihaiwej.

As coach horses gave way to motorized transport in the early twentieth century, breeders had of necessity to change the type of the Oldenburg and look more to the production of a general-purpose farm horse. More recently, further infusions of Thoroughbred blood, and some Selle Français, have produced a horse which is considerably finer than its coaching ancestors and well able to hold its own in the competitive sports, working equally well under saddle or in harness. The Oldenburg still tends to be a big individual compared with other warmbloods but many of the coach-horse characteristics, such as an upright shoulder and long back, have been eliminated. The knee action still tends to be a little on the high side.

Oldenburg horses are exported to many countries and have proved particularly popular in the United States.

▌ BELOW
From coach horse to dressage horse: refinement of the breed has been brought about through the introduction of Thoroughbred and Selle Français blood, making the present-day Oldenburg an outstanding sports horse.

INTERESTING FACTS

Olympic Bonfire, an Oldenburg gelding foaled in 1983, won the World Dressage Freestyle to Music Championship in 1994 when ridden by the leading Dutch rider, Anky van Grunsven.

Westphalian

Closely related to the Hanoverian, the Westphalian is bred in the region of Nordrhein-Westfalen, in the north-west of Germany. Its main breeding centre, Warendorf, is famous for being the home of German equestrianism (the National Federation is based there). The area has a long tradition of horse breeding. It is known that in the early nineteenth century East Prussian stallions were made available to local mare owners to enable them to upgrade their stock. Over the years various outcrosses were made, involving Oldenburg, Hanoverian, Friesian, Anglo-Norman and trotter blood and it was not until this century that breeders finally settled for just one influence: the Hanoverian. Today's Westphalian shares the bloodlines of the present-day Hanoverian, although there are also several important ones which have developed specifically in the Westphalia region.

BREED DESCRIPTION

Height 15.3 – 16.2hh.

Colour All solid colours.

Conformation Intelligent head with good width between the eyes; well-shaped neck; deep, broad body; powerful hindquarters, although they can be a little flat.

▌ ABOVE
The Westphalian has the same clean-cut good looks as the Hanoverian, with whom it shares a common ancestry.

▌ RIGHT
The conformation is typical of that of the modern sports horse: a good length of neck, deep body and powerful hindquarters. It tends to be a little longer in the leg than the Hanoverian.

INTERESTING FACTS

Famous Westphalian horses include Rembrandt (Olympic dressage champion in 1988 and 1992, ridden by Nicole Uphoff-Becker); Ahlerich (Olympic dressage champion in 1984, ridden by Reiner Klimke); Fire (winner of the World Show Jumping Championship in 1982, ridden by Norbert Koof) and Roman (winner of the World Show Jumping Championship in 1978, ridden by Gerd Wiltfang). Rembrandt, one of the most handsome representatives of the breed, was the first horse in the history of the Olympic Games to win two individual gold medals for dressage. He was European champion in 1989 and also took the individual title at the first World Equestrian Games, held in Stockholm in 1990.

❚ ABOVE RIGHT
Two Step is a Westphalian who has found fame as a show jumper. Originally named Polydektes, he is by Polydor, one of the breed's most successful sires of competition horses.

❚ RIGHT
Ahlerich was one of the breed's most outstanding performers in the world of dressage. He crowned a gloriously successful Grand Prix career with victory at the 1984 Olympic Games in Los Angeles.

Schleswig

A sturdy, compact heavy horse, the Schleswig comes from the northernmost region of Germany, Schleswig-Holstein, which borders on to Denmark and which was, indeed, at various times actually part of that country. It is not surprising, therefore, that the Schleswig bears a marked resemblance to the Jutland, the Danish heavy breed to which it is closely related. The Schleswig was developed during the second half of the nineteenth century as a medium-sized draught horse. Infusions of lighter blood, including Yorkshire Coach Horse and Thoroughbred, were made towards the end of the century but these had no lasting effect on the breed. Popular as a tram and bus horse, and for use on the land and in forestry, the breed survived World War I (during which its homeland was under Danish rule) although it was seriously depleted in both numbers and quality. The subsequent introduction of Breton and Boulonnais blood from

▌ BELOW
The head is rather plain but the expression is kindly.

▌ BOTTOM
The Schleswig is generally chestnut in colour.

BREED DESCRIPTION

Height 15.2 – 16hh.

Colour Predominantly chestnut, occasionally bay or grey.

Conformation Large, rather plain head, but with a kind eye; short, crested neck; very powerful shoulders; rather long body, though with good depth through the girth; well-muscled hindquarters; short, strong limbs with some feather.

France proved highly successful. The Schleswig recovered and flourished in large numbers until the years immediately following World War II. In time, however, mechanization took its usual toll, and numbers dwindled drastically. In recent years some of the surviving Schleswigs have been bred back to Jutlands, in order to increase the breed's size.

INTERESTING FACTS

The attractive Schleswig horse, which often has a flaxen mane and tail, is extremely powerfully built and weighs in the region of 1,766lb (800kg).

South German

This strong and agile heavy horse is descended from the Austrian Noriker, which was introduced into Bavaria, in southern Germany, towards the end of the nineteenth century. With a view to improving and developing their own stamp of horse, breeders in Upper Bavaria added some Holstein and Oldenburg blood, while those in Lower Bavaria experimented with an extraordinary variety of outcrosses, from Oldenburg and Cleveland Bay to Clydesdale and Belgian Draught. In time, however, German breeders reverted to using the original Noriker blood for upgrading purposes. Originally called the Pinzgauer Noriker, after the region in Salzburg province from which that particular strain of the Austrian heavy horse came, the German version of the breed became known as the South German Heavy Horse. Today it is bred mainly in Bavaria and Baden Wurtemburg. It still resembles the Noriker, although it is inclined to stand a little less tall. It is a well-proportioned horse, with a calm, docile temperament, and can be seen in parades and at shows as well as, occasionally, at work in agriculture.

▌ BELOW
The South German Coldblood has a large head and, typically, a docile expression.

▌ BOTTOM
The South German resembles the Noriker but is a little smaller.

The South German heavy horse is a popular attraction at shows. As well as being used by trick riders, it takes part in races – which it clearly enjoys!

BREED DESCRIPTION

Height Around 15.3hh.

Colour Brown, bay and chestnut.

Conformation Rather large head, with kind eye; short, strong neck; powerful shoulders; strong back with deep girth; good limbs with a little feather.

Cleveland Bay

A race of bay-coloured horses was being bred, primarily for pack work, in the north east of England as far back as mediaeval times. It was the preferred means of transport of the chapmen, or travelling salesmen of the day, and was accordingly known as the Chapman Horse. Taking the Chapman Horse as their base, seventeenth-century breeders used some of the Andalusian and Barb stallions that were being brought into the country at that time to produce a fine coach horse, renowned for its active paces and great stamina. This became known as the Cleveland Bay after the area where it

was chiefly bred. As roads improved, and a faster type of coach horse became necessary, some Thoroughbred blood was introduced, usually by means of putting half-bred stallions to Cleveland mares. This lighter, faster version of the

Cleveland Bay was called the Yorkshire Coach Horse. It had its own breed society, founded in 1886, and stud book. But the coming of motorized transport signalled the demise of coach horses everywhere and the Yorkshire breed was no exception.

■ ABOVE
The Cleveland Bay is the descendant of a race of bay-coloured horses bred in north-eastern England since medieval times.

■ LEFT
A handsome, upstanding stamp of horse, the Cleveland Bay produces excellent hunters when crossed with the Thoroughbred.

■ LEFT AND
FAR LEFT
Cleveland Bay horses
at the Royal Mews in
London testify to the
interest taken in the
preservation of this
historic breed by
Queen Elizabeth II.

Its stud book was finally closed in 1936, by
which time the breed had virtually died
out. Fortunately the Cleveland Bay
survived, albeit in small numbers. Crossed
with the Thoroughbred, the breed
produces fine upstanding heavyweight
hunters and excellent carriage horses. The
Cleveland Bay has a true, straight and free
action (high action is not characteristic of
the breed), moves freely from the
shoulder and covers the ground well. As
well as making an excellent hunter and
carriage horse, the Cleveland Bay, when
crossed with the Thoroughbred, has also
produced some first-rate show jumpers.

BREED DESCRIPTION

Height 16 – 16.2hh, though height does
not disqualify an otherwise good animal.

Colour Bay with black points.

Conformation Bold head, not too small,
with large, well-set, kind eyes and large, fine
ears; long, lean neck; deep, sloping,
muscular shoulders; deep, wide body, with
muscular loins, powerful hindquarters and
well set-on tail; clean limbs (without
feather), with muscular forearms, thighs and
second thighs, large knees and hocks, and
strong, sloping pasterns; good, sound feet.

INTERESTING FACTS

The survival of the Cleveland Bay was aided in
no small measure by Queen Elizabeth II. A colt
named Mulgrave Supreme, due to be sent to
the United States, was bought by the Queen,
subsequently broken to saddle and to harness
and then made available to breeders of
Cleveland Bays, both pure- and part-bred,
throughout Britain. This tremendously
successful promotional exercise sparked off
renewed enthusiasm among breeders. Prince
Philip further enhanced the breed's profile by
driving, for many years, teams of pure- and
part-bred Cleveland Bays at international level.

■ RIGHT
For many years HRH
The Duke of
Edinburgh drove a
team of Cleveland
Bays in international
four-in-hand events.
They have excellent
ground-covering
action, well suited to
work both in harness
and under saddle.

Hackney

The Hackney, with its high-stepping action, is a native of England though it is prized the world over as a carriage horse, especially in the show ring. The Hackney horse originated in the late seventeenth and early eighteenth centuries and is a descendant of the famous English trotting horses of the time, the Yorkshire Trotter and the Norfolk Roadster. These horses had a common ancestor, a horse known as the Original Shales, who was foaled in 1755 and was by the Thoroughbred Blaze out of a mare described as a "hackney". Blaze was by Flying Childers, generally recognized as being the first great racehorse. Blaze and his progeny, notably his two sons, Driver and Scot Shales, had a considerable influence on the development of the trotters of eastern England. Despite their shared ancestry,

BREED DESCRIPTION

Height Hackney pony not exceeding 14hh. Hackney horse 15 – 15.3hh.

Colour Usually dark brown, black, bay or chestnut.

Conformation Small, convex head with small muzzle, large eyes and small ears; fairly long, well-formed neck; powerful shoulders and low withers; compact body, with great depth of chest; short legs with strong, well let-down hocks and well-shaped feet.

the horses bred in Yorkshire and Norfolk developed somewhat different characteristics – those of Yorkshire origin tended to have more quality than those from Norfolk, which were more cob-like in appearance – but these regional

INTERESTING FACTS

The derivation of the word hackney is doubtful but it is thought to come from the Old French *haquenée*, "an ambling horse or mare, especially for ladies to ride on", and may be related to the Old Spanish and Portuguese *facanea* and Spanish *hacanea*. In the fourteenth century the word was latinized in England as *hakeneius*.

▌ LEFT
Hackneys are popular
in show rings
throughout the world.
Here they are being
driven in an unusual
three-horse
combination known as
a unicorn, comprising
two wheelers and a
leader.

distinctions later disappeared.

The Hackney pony was developed
during the second half of the eighteenth
century – earlier use of the term "Hackney
ponies" almost certainly referred to small
part-bred Hackney horses. It was the very
enterprising Westmorland breeder,
Christopher Wyndham Wilson, a
remarkable man whose achievements
included inventing the silo to store winter
feed for farm animals, who was largely

responsible for the development of the
true Hackney pony. Wilson used a variety
of pony breeds, especially the Fell, as his
foundation mares, crossing them with a
good-looking Hackney horse named Sir
George, who was sired in 1866 and stood
less than 14hh. His policy of inbreeding to
the prepotent Sir George enabled Wilson
to achieve his aim of developing a
Hackney with real pony characteristics and
in due course other breeders followed his

lead. The original height limit for ponies,
as recommended by the Hackney Horse
Society, was 14.2hh but this was
subsequently reduced to 14hh. The high-
stepping action for which the Hackney is
renowned was not developed until the
second half of the nineteenth century,
when it became the fashion to drive
elegant, showy carriage horses. It is partly
inherited, partly taught and can be
enhanced by training.

▌ RIGHT
In classes for single
turnouts the Hackney
is harnessed to a
lightweight vehicle
with pneumatic tyres.

▌ OPPOSITE
The Hackney has a
compact body,
powerful shoulders
and a deep chest. The
limbs are strong and
the feet invariably well
formed.

Shire

England's most magnificent looking heavy horse is descended from the mediaeval warhorse known as the Great Horse, which was later given the name of the English Black. It was developed by crossing imported Flanders and Friesian horses with native stock to produce first a military mount and subsequently a farm and general draught horse. The introduction of the term "blacks" for these heavy horses is attributed to Oliver Cromwell, and was probably used originally to describe the imported Friesians, which are always black in colour. The main breeding areas of the

BREED DESCRIPTION

Height Stallions 16.2 – 17.2hh. Mares 16 – 17hh.

Colour Black, brown, bay or grey.

Conformation Lean head (neither too large nor too small), wide between the eyes, slightly Roman nose, large, prominent eyes with docile expression, and long, lean, sharp, sensitive ears; fairly long, slightly arched neck; deep, oblique shoulders, wide enough to support a collar; short, strong, muscular back, broad chest and wide, sweeping, muscular hindquarters with well let-down thighs; clean, hard limbs with 11–12 inches (28–30cm) of bone and broad, deep, flat hocks, set at the correct angle for leverage; fine, straight, silky feather; deep, solid feet with thick walls and open coronets.

▌ ABOVE RIGHT
The Roman nose, long, sharp ears, large eyes and docile expression are typical of the Shire, the archetypal "gentle giant".

▌ RIGHT
The magnificent Shire is descended from the medieval warhorse known as the Great Horse. It weighs in excess of 20cwt (1,016kg).

I RIGHT
A team of twenty Shires makes a magnificent sight at
an English horse show, admirably displaying the
breed's tractable nature.

I BELOW
A foal dozes in the summer sun. While Shires will
never be seen in the same numbers as in olden times,
the breed has enough enthusiasts to ensure its future.

INTERESTING FACTS

One of the earliest records of a Shire stallion
standing at stud is of the horse known as
the Packington Blind Horse. He was named
after the village of Packington, near Ashby-
de-la-Zouche, where he lived between 1755
and 1770. This horse, and horses said to be
his progeny, had a significant influence on
the breed during its formative years.

English Black were the Fen country and
the Midland shires of Leicestershire,
Lincolnshire, Derbyshire and
Staffordshire, from which the breed
eventually took its name. In the early days
the breed displayed regional variations,
horses bred in the Fens tending to be
bigger, heavier and somewhat coarser
than those from the "Shires". Those from
Derbyshire and Leicestershire were
predominantly black, while Staffordshire
horses were more often brown.

It was not until the late nineteenth
century that the breeding of these horses
became formalized, as a result of the
publication of the first stud book. In 1878
a breed society was set up under the title
of the Old English Cart Horse Society.
The name was changed in 1884 to the
Shire Horse Society and the breed has
been known as the Shire ever since.

Following the formation of the breed
society, the Shire went from strength to
strength, competing with great success in
the leading agricultural shows of the time
and attracting the interest of foreign
buyers. Shire horses were soon being
exported as far afield as North and
South America, Russia and Australia. They
also became an indispensable part of daily
life in Britain. With their qualities of
strength, stamina, soundness and good
temperament, these gentle giants could be
seen ploughing the land, hauling timber
and pulling farm wagons, railway vans,
brewers' drays and coal carts. Although
mechanization took its customary toll, a
Shire "revival" began in the 1960s and
today these wonderful horses can again be
seen at shows, ploughing the land and,
not least, pulling brewers' drays on short-
haul routes in cities.

I LEFT AND ABOVE
Shires hitched to brewers' drays are a popular
sight at many British horse and agricultural shows.
Some are still used for short-haul work in inner
cities, where they are more economical than
motorized transport.

Suffolk

Britain's oldest heavy breed, the Suffolk or Suffolk Punch, is named after the East Anglian county where it has been bred since the sixteenth century. Little is known of its origins, but as far back as 1506 there is an historical reference to a distinctive type of Suffolk horse. The Suffolk was developed as a farm horse and with its tremendously strong shoulders and clean legs (i.e. free of feather) it is ideally suited to working on the very heavy clay soils of East Anglia.

The breed is unique in that all Suffolks trace back to a single stallion, known as Crisp's Horse of Ufford, foaled in 1760.

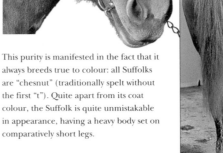

▌ LEFT
This mare shows the typical broad forehead and full, bright eyes of the Suffolk. All Suffolks are chesnut in colour – traditionally spelt without the middle "t".

▌ BELOW
Although there is plenty of width between the forelegs, the hindfeet are set close together. Such conformation prevents the horse damaging crops when working in the fields.

This purity is manifested in the fact that it always breeds true to colour: all Suffolks are "chesnut" (traditionally spelt without the first "t"). Quite apart from its coat colour, the Suffolk is quite unmistakable in appearance, having a heavy body set on comparatively short legs.

▌ RIGHT
With its heavy body and short legs the Suffolk admirably fits its popular name, "Punch". Its legs are always free of feather – an essential prerequisite for a horse bred to work on heavy clay soils.

BREED DESCRIPTION

Height 16 – 16.3hh.

Colour Always "chesnut", of which seven shades are recognized, ranging from a pale mealy tone to a very dark, almost brown, shade. The most common is a bright reddish shade. A little white may occur on the face and the mane and tail are sometimes pale in colour.

Conformation Quite large head, with broad forehead; deep, tapering neck; long, muscular shoulders; deep, well-rounded body with strong quarters and well-set tail; fairly short, straight limbs with plenty of bone, sloping pasterns and no coarse hair; hard, sound, medium-sized feet.

INTERESTING FACTS

The ability of the Suffolk to thrive on less rations than other working heavy horses is well illustrated by the experiences of one farmer who, during the early part of this century, compared the feed requirements of two dozen cross-bred farm horses which he used for several years on one farm, and those of twenty-five Suffolks which he used for a similar period on another. While all the horses ate the same quantities of bulk food – hay, mangolds and chaff – the cross-breds each required 75lb (34kg) of corn per week, increasing by some 14–21lbs (6.4-9.5kg) per week as they grew older, while the Suffolks, even the older ones, kept their condition on a regular 50lb (22.7kg) per week.

Despite its size the Suffolk is a remarkably economical horse to keep, thriving and working on comparatively small rations. It matures early – Suffolks can be put to light work at two years of age and go into full work at three. It has an exceptionally amenable temperament and it is noted for its great soundness and longevity – it is common for horses to be in use and mares to be producing foals into their late teens and Suffolks often live until they are nearly thirty. The Suffolk's remarkable qualities combined to make it one of the most popular agricultural and draught horses of all time and, not surprisingly, its popularity spread abroad. There have been Suffolks in the United States for many years and representatives of the breed have also been exported to Australia, Africa, Russia and Pakistan (where they were used to produce army horses). Like the Shire, the Suffolk survived the coming of mechanization and can still be seen occasionally working the land, pulling drays and at shows, principally in eastern England.

❚ ABOVE RIGHT
A pair of present-day Suffolks drawing a vehicle of yesteryear.

❚ RIGHT
Suffolks can still be seen at their traditional work, ploughing. Early maturing, sound, long-lived and economical to feed, the breed possesses all the attributes so vital in a draught horse in the days before mechanization.

Clydesdale

Scotland's breed of heavy horse, as its name suggests, originated in that area of Lanarkshire through which the Clyde river runs. Today's Clydesdale, which developed more recently than the other British heavy breeds, began to evolve during the second half of the eighteenth century when imported Flemish stallions were used to improve the stock, descended from pack animals, of local farmers. Before that, during the early part of the century, a breeder named Paterson of Lochlyoch had begun to produce horses which, by all accounts, bore a distinct resemblance to the modern Clydesdale, certainly as far as colour was concerned. The stallion Glancer, to whom many Clydesdales can be traced back, was out of a mare known as Lampit's Mare, who was believed to be a

BREED DESCRIPTION

Height Stallions 17.1 – 18hh. Mares 16.3 – 17.2hh

Colour Bay, brown or black. Chestnut is rare. Often with a good deal of white on the face and legs, which may run up on to the body, particularly as flashes on the stomach.

Conformation Strong, intelligent head, with broad forehead, wide muzzle, large nostrils, bright, clear eyes and big ears; long, well-arched neck; sloping shoulders with high withers; short back with well-sprung ribs and muscular hindquarters; straight limbs with forelegs set well under the shoulders, long pasterns and a fair amount of fine feather; round, open feet.

▌ OPPOSITE PAGE
The brisk, ground-covering paces of the Clydesdale make it eminently suitable for both agricultural and heavy haulage work.

▌ ABOVE
Large, kind eyes and big ears give these Clydesdales the gentle, sensible expression typical of the breed. Unlike the Shire, the Clydesdale never has a Roman nose.

▌ LEFT
Although the Clydesdale is closely related to the Shire, it has a number of distinguishing features, the most readily discernible of which is the large amount of white often seen on the limbs and extending up to the lower parts of the body.

❚ BELOW
Wearing traditional Scottish harness decorations,
the Clydesdale makes a fine sight in the show ring.

INTERESTING FACTS

One of the most famous and
influential stallions in the development
of the Clydesdale was a dark brown
horse named Prince of Wales, foaled in
Ayrshire in 1866. He was a mixture of
English and Scottish blood and had
outstanding action. His stud fee of £40,
by no means a small sum for those days,
was well worth paying – young horses
sired by him fetched anywhere from
£2,000 to £3,000.

descendant of the Lochlyoch horses.

Shire blood was used in the breed's
development – indeed the two leading
Clydesdale breeders during the second
half of the nineteenth century, Lawrence
Drew and David Riddell, believed the
Clydesdale and the Shire to be of the same
origin, and regularly interbred the two.

The Clydesdale Horse Society was
formed in 1877 and the first stud book was
published the following year. By this time
interest in the breed had spread to other
countries and Clydesdales were soon

being exported, often in large numbers, to
work the vast wheatlands of North America;
others went to Australia, South America
and Russia. It was, without doubt, the
Clydesdale's docile nature combined with
elegance and great activity that endeared
it to heavy horse enthusiasts all over the
world. Describing his action, the breed
society says that the inside of every shoe
should be made visible to anyone walking
behind. The Clydesdale is an exceptionally
sound horse, great emphasis having always
been placed on good limbs and feet.

❚ RIGHT
Many Clydesdales
were exported to
North America to work
in agriculture. Their
descendants can still
be seen, though in
rather different roles.
This team is being
used to haul the
starting stalls at Santa
Anita Racetrack.

Furioso

Hungary has long enjoyed a world-wide reputation as a horse-breeding country and as a producer of fine horsemen. The famous stud farm at Mezőhegyes, founded in 1784 by the Emperor Josef II, quickly became established as one of the great breeding centres of Europe. One of the most important breeds developed there was the Furioso, which was produced by crossing Thoroughbreds with mainly Hungarian mares. The chief influences were the English Thoroughbred stallion, Furioso, after whom the breed was named and who was acquired by Mezőhegyes in 1841, and another English horse, North Star, who was imported during the 1850s. Using these two bloodlines Mezőhegyes began producing quality carriage horses and good, heavyweight riding horses. For a time these two bloodlines were kept separate, with North Star proving a particularly successful sire of harness racehorses. He was descended from the

BREED DESCRIPTION

Height About 16hh.

Colour Any solid colour.

Conformation Fine head (denoting its Thoroughbred ancestry); well-sloped shoulders; strong back; good strong limbs and feet.

1793 Derby winner, Waxy (a grandson of the great Eclipse), and is said to trace back to Norfolk Roadster blood, which could account for his progeny's success in harness. Towards the end of the nineteenth century the North Star and Furioso strains were merged, after which the Furioso became the dominant force.

INTERESTING FACTS

The Csikos horse herders of Hungary are renowned for their trick-riding skills. Their breathtaking displays, often performed with Furioso horses, are famous all over the world.

▌ TOP
The present-day Furioso is a quality all-purpose riding horse, built on somewhat heavier lines than its Thoroughbred ancestors.

▌ LEFT
Large herds of horses, including the Furioso, have traditionally been raised on the grasslands of Hungary.

Nonius

Like the Furioso, the more heavily built Nonius evolved at the Mezöhegyes stud farm founded by the Emperor Josef II. The breed's foundation sire was an Anglo-Norman horse by the name of Nonius Senior. He was foaled in 1810, captured in

BREED DESCRIPTION

Height Large type 15.3 – 16.2hh. Small type 14.3 – 15.3hh.

Colour Predominantly bay, with some black, brown and chestnut.

Conformation Attractive, honest head; sloping shoulders; broad, strong back; strong hindquarters; sound limbs.

France by the Austrians in 1814 and installed at Mezöhegyes in 1816. Nonius was said to be by a half-bred English stallion out of a Norman mare and almost certainly had Norfolk Roadster blood in him. He was by all accounts not the most prepossessing individual and would have won no prizes for conformation, but during his sixteen years at stud he became a tremendously successful sire. Mated with mares of various breeds, including Arab, Lipizzaner, Spanish and Turkish, as well as Hungarian, he produced good quality horses, the best of which were mated back to him. In this way a distinctive type emerged – to be known as the Nonius.

During the 1860s, infusions of Thoroughbred blood were made, a policy which led to the development of two different types of Nonius: one, a large horse suited to light agricultural work and as a carriage horse, the other, a smaller, finer animal suitable for riding. In more recent times, as the need for farm horses diminished, the larger type of Nonius was used mainly for driving, a skill at which Hungarian horsemen have long excelled. Both types of Nonius combine active paces with a calm, willing temperament.

▌ BELOW
The head, though lacking refinement, reflects the breed's kind, tractable nature.

▌ BELOW
Thoroughbred, Norman and Norfolk Roadster blood all played a part in the development of the Nonius. Today's sturdily built individuals make good all-round riding and driving horses.

INTERESTING FACTS

There are two distinct types of harness used for driving purposes. These Nonius horses are wearing breast harness. For pulling heavy loads horses wear collars to enable them to use the full strength of their shoulders.

Hungarian Half-bred

The Hungarians began producing leisure and sports horses during the 1960s, continuing their tradition of breeding fine horses. They imported Hanoverians and Holsteins to cross with the Furioso and the Gidran in order to develop an animal suited to modern requirements. The Gidran, which to all intents and purposes is the Hungarian Anglo-Arab, can be traced back to an Arabian stallion known as Gidran Senior, imported into Hungary in 1816. Gidran's son, Gidran II, bred from a Spanish mare, became the foundation sire of the type which bears his name.

Initially a variety of mares were used, but later Thoroughbred blood was introduced and, subsequently, more Arab blood. This breeding policy

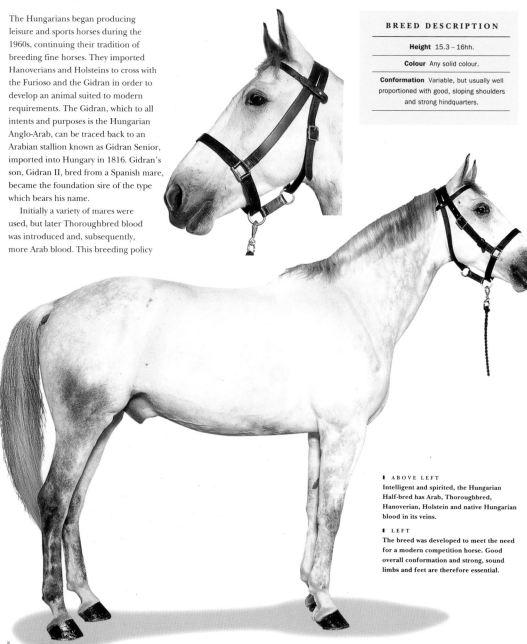

BREED DESCRIPTION

Height 15.3 – 16hh.

Colour Any solid colour.

Conformation Variable, but usually well proportioned with good, sloping shoulders and strong hindquarters.

▌ ABOVE LEFT
Intelligent and spirited, the Hungarian Half-bred has Arab, Thoroughbred, Hanoverian, Holstein and native Hungarian blood in its veins.

▌ LEFT
The breed was developed to meet the need for a modern competition horse. Good overall conformation and strong, sound limbs and feet are therefore essential.

The Hungarian Half-bred has a good
temperament which lends itself to training for
a wide variety of activities – as this daring trick
riding display proves.

■ LEFT
Speed, stamina and a
ground-covering stride
make the half-bred a
suitable partner for
the tough sport of
three-day eventing.

■ BELOW
Hungarian Half-breds
have achieved their
greatest competition
successes in the
gruelling sport of four-
in-hand driving. They
have been exported to
many countries for this
purpose.

resulted in a quality horse with a
good, ground-covering gallop. The
breed was developed at Hungary's
chief studs – the old-established one
at Mezőhegyes; the Kisber, named after
the Hungarian-bred horse who won the
British Derby in 1876, and the Kecskemet,
which is famous for its cross-bred
driving horses, based on Lipizzaner and
trotter blood.

Hungarian Half-breds have achieved
outstanding success in the sport of international four-in-hand driving, where they
have competed not just in the hands of
the traditionally dashing and skilful
Hungarian drivers but also for a number
of other European nations, notably
Switzerland and Britain.

Shagya

The Shagya is a strain of Arabian horse bred in Hungary and descended from a stallion of the same name. Shagya was a Syrian-bred horse, foaled in 1830 and imported to the Hungarian stud at Babolna some six years later. Shagya was used to cover quality mares which, although they were of mixed blood (including Hungarian, Thoroughbred and Spanish, as well as Arabian) were distinctly "eastern" in overall appearance. By employing the practice of inbreeding, the Babolna Stud produced the distinctive type of Arab horse seen today. The Shagya is rather taller and has a noticeably bigger frame than other Arabs (Shagya himself

▌ ABOVE LEFT
The wide-set eyes and tapered muzzle, with its large nostrils, are typical of the Shagya.

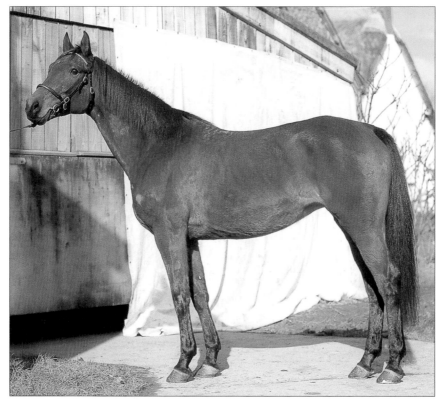

▌ LEFT
The Shagya tends to have a rather more substantial frame than the pure-bred Arab, though its overall outline is very similar.

INTERESTING FACTS

The Babolna Stud, home of the Shagya Arab, was founded in 1789 by the Emperor Joseph II. Hungary has one of the oldest traditions of organized horse breeding in the world, its first recorded stud (founded by Prince Arpad, who died in 907) dating back more than 1,000 years. During the mid-eighteenth century horse breeding began to slip into a gradual decline and it was Joseph II who was largely responsible for revitalizing it. He founded the Veterinary College in Budapest, decreed the building of the famous Mezőhegyes stud farm in 1785 and subsequently Babolna, thus paving the way for the golden age that Hungarian horses enjoyed during the nineteenth century.

BREED DESCRIPTION

Height 14 – 15hh.

Colour Predominantly grey but all other Arab colours occur.

Conformation Refined head, with dished profile, small, tapered muzzle and large eyes; elegant, curved neck; sloping shoulders; short, slightly concave back with strong loins, level croup and high-set tail; good, strong limbs with especially good, well-formed feet.

was a little taller than normal for an Arab, standing over 15.2hh). But the overall appearance, with its beautiful, dished face, large eyes, short back and high-set tail, are all characteristic of the pure-bred Arab. Combining toughness with elegance, the Shagya was bred as a riding horse and found favour as a cavalry mount in the days before mechanization. Nowadays it is bred for leisure riding and is exported to a number of countries.

▮ ABOVE
Mares and foals at the Babolna Stud in Hungary, home of the Shagya Arab. Babolna was founded by Royal decree more than 200 years ago.

▮ BELOW
Grey is the breed's predominant colour, although all other Arab colours also occur. Shagya Arabs often stand a little taller than their pure-bred relatives.

Icelandic

The little Icelandic horse is probably
the purest horse breed in the world. Its
ancestors were taken to Iceland by ninth-
century settlers, travelling from western
Norway and the north of Britain. They
were small, sturdy horses who adapted well
to the rigorous Icelandic climate. Later
some imports were made of eastern
horses, but these had such a detrimental
effect upon the original stock that in
AD 930 the Althing (parliament) passed a
law forbidding the import of further
horses. Although this law seems to have
been flouted occasionally, for the last 800
years there have been no infusions of
outside blood. As a result the Icelandic
horse has changed little since the age of
the Vikings.

It is an outstandingly tough, weather-
resistant little horse (although it stands no
more than 13.2hh it is always referred to
by the Icelanders as a horse, not a pony).
A strong swimmer – there were no bridges
over Iceland's numerous turbulent rivers
until the beginning of this century – it is
also remarkably sure-footed. It can be seen
carrying a full-grown man at speed, with
ease and safety, over mountainous terrain
during the traditional autumn sheep
round-ups.

Some Icelandic horses are noted for
their keen sense of direction and

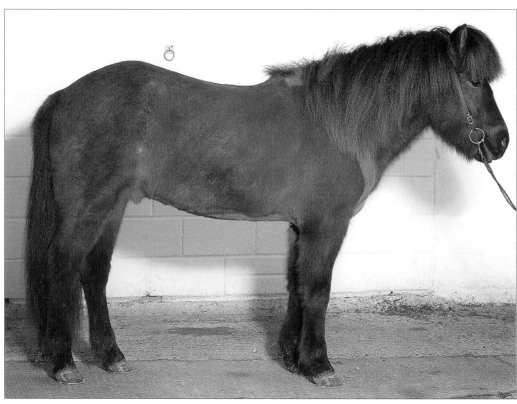

▌ LEFT
Icelandic Horses, which have changed little since Viking times, come in a wide range of attractive coat colours, including dun, palomino, piebald and skewbald.

BREED DESCRIPTION

Height 12.3 – 13.2hh.

Colour Any.

Conformation Fairly heavy head; short, well-carried neck; compact body with short back and deep girth; sloping, wedge-shaped, very strong, muscular hindquarters; strong limbs with short cannons and strong hocks; strong, well-shaped feet.

extraordinary homing instinct. After the annual round-up, while sheep are penned and sorted into each farmer's flock, horses are often turned loose and will set off alone down the valleys to their homes. There are also many recorded instances of horses that have been sold to another part of the country travelling for weeks to return to their original homes.

While some local selection of breeding stock probably took place from time to time, it was not until 1879 that Iceland undertook a practical selective breeding programme. It was begun in Skagafjördur, the country's most famous horse-breeding area. Conformation is naturally taken into account, but it is the quality of the horse's gaits which is of prime importance. These are: the fetgangur (walk), the brökk (trot – used when crossing rough country), the stökk (gallop), the skeid (lateral pace – used to cover short distances at high

speed) and the tölt (a running walk used to cover broken ground). The tölt is a gait of four equal beats – the sequence being near hind, near fore, off hind, off fore – with which the horse achieves great speed.

▌ BELOW
Notwithstanding its diminutive size, the breed is immensely strong and fast. It is a popular all-round riding horse in many countries outside its native Iceland.

INTERESTING FACTS

In days gone by horse fights were a popular form of entertainment in Iceland. Playing on the natural instinct of stallions to fight each other for possession of a mare, Icelanders would set two specially trained stallions against one another, using goads to urge them on. This pastime was so dangerous that it was a common occurrence for handlers to be injured or even killed.

Irish Draught

Irish horses are renowned for being the best hunters in the world and none more so than those produced by crossing the Thoroughbred with the versatile Irish Draught. Although there are no early formal records or stud books, Ireland's light draught horse is known to trace back many centuries, to the time when Norman horses were introduced to Ireland and crossed with the native animals, which at

■ LEFT
A typically handsome, intelligent Irish Draught head. The breed is renowned for its innate good sense, coupled with boldness and athleticism.

that time were small of stature. Later infusions of Andalusian – and, probably, eastern – blood helped improve the overall quality (and height) of the Irish horses. The result was

very much an all-round horse, totally suited to the Irish country way of life: capable of working on the small Irish farms but active enough to be harnessed to a trap or to carry a rider safely across country. The modern Irish Draught is generally accepted to have evolved from the crossing of imported Thoroughbred stallions with the best of these country-bred mares. The numbers of these splendid horses declined in Ireland following the famine of 1847 and some heavy horses were introduced from Britain, but this tended to lead to a coarsening of the Irish Draught. To save the best of the remaining stock, in the early years of this century a scheme of subsidies was introduced by the government, for approved stallions of Irish Draught and hunter type. As a result the active, clean-legged general-purpose

■ RIGHT
Substance and plenty of bone are the hallmarks of the modern Irish Draught. The conformation should incorporate all the features of the correctly built riding horse.

BREED DESCRIPTION

Height Stallions 16hh and over. Mares 15.2hh and over.

Colour All solid colours.

Conformation Small, intelligent head; sloping shoulders; strong body with deep chest and oval rib cage; powerful hindquarters; strong limbs with plenty of flat bone and no feather.

Irish Draught horse survived and in 1917 the Department of Agriculture introduced "a scheme to establish a Book for Horses of the Irish Draught type", in which 375 mares and 44 stallions were entered as being suitable and sound. The Irish Draught Horse Society was formed in 1976.

The excellence of Irish-bred horses owes much to the limestone pastures on which they are raised. The mineral-rich land contributes to the growth of strong bone and the production of good, upstanding animals. Today's Irish Draught has plenty of substance but is also an attractive looking, well-balanced, quality horse, with straight, athletic action. It is noted for its intelligence and kind temperament. It has an inherent ability to cross the most testing of hunting country with total assurance and because of its jumping prowess is a successful producer of top-level show jumpers.

INTERESTING FACTS

Since World War II many of the world's leading show-jumping horses have been Irish bred, with a fair percentage being by registered Irish Draught stallions. One of the most famous names in show-jumping breeding is King of Diamonds, an Irish Draught who sired many famous horses, including Special Envoy – who has jumped with great success for Brazil, ridden first by Nelson Pessoa then by his son Rodrigo – and Mill Pearl, ridden by the United States Olympic champion Joe Fargis.

Maremmano

Maremmano horses are bred in Tuscany and are the traditional mounts of the *butteri*, or cattlemen. Maremma, a coastal tract on the Tyrrhenian Sea extending from Piombino to Orbetello, is a former marshland which was drained in ancient times but later reverted to being an unhealthy wasteland. Drainage was reintroduced earlier this century and the area is now used as pastureland.

The origins of the Maremmano horses are obscure but it is likely that they are descended from the Neapolitan horses (founded on Arab, Barb and Spanish

■ RIGHT
The Maremmano is a strong horse possessed of a quiet temperament, and although not particularly speedy it makes a useful all-round riding horse.

blood) made famous in the sixteenth century by Federico Grisone. Grisone was the founder of the Neapolitan riding academy and regarded as the first of the great classical riding masters after the

Greek, Xenophon (c. 430–350 BC). A good deal of outcrossing took place later – some involving imported English horses, including the Norfolk Roadster – so that the horses which became known as the

■ LEFT
Maremmano horses vary a good deal in type and conformation. This horse is much more refined than many examples of the breed, with an especially elegant head.

■ BELOW
A Maremmano wearing the traditional tack of the
buttero, or Italian cowboy. Its toughness and
reliability make the breed an ideal mount for
working with cattle.

BREED DESCRIPTION

Height Variable, usually around 15.3hh.

Colour Any solid colour.

Conformation Variable. Overall appearance
somewhat coarse, with rather upright
shoulders, flat withers and low-set tail,
though conformational improvements are
being made through the introduction of
Thoroughbred blood.

Maremmano were something of a mixture
and of no fixed type. By no means the
most beautiful looking of horses, nor the
speediest, they are nevertheless good,
honest workers, combining strength and
toughness with a calm temperament.
Amenable by nature and economical to
feed, they have proved useful as army and
police horses, as well as in agriculture –
they are strong enough to perform light
draught work – and cattle herding.

INTERESTING FACTS

During the seventeenth century Italy became
one of the world leaders for horse breeding.
Most famous of all was the Neapolitan, of
which the Maremmano is possibly a descendant.

Murgese

Originating from the Orfano plain and the hill districts near Gravina, the original Murgese horse can be traced back at least 500 years. During the late fifteenth and early sixteenth centuries the governor of the port of Monopoli, which for some years belonged to the Venetian Republic, kept a stock of Murgese stallions and several hundred brood mares in order to provide remounts for the cavalry. However, somewhere down the years the breed died out and the modern version dates only from the 1920s.

The Murgese is basically a light draught horse, though inferior in quality to the Irish Draught and showing no great uniformity of type. It can be ridden, but a better stamp of riding horse is produced by putting a Murgese mare to a Thoroughbred or warmblood stallion, the latter giving the progeny more quality, and paces better suited to a saddle horse.

BREED DESCRIPTION

Height 15 – 16hh.

Colour Usually chestnut, though other solid colours occur.

Conformation Variable. Overall appearance suggests a light draught horse. The head tends to be plain, though with an honest expression, and the hindquarters rather poor, with a low-set tail.

■ ABOVE
Although basically best suited to light draught work, the Murgese can make a useful riding horse. This example of the breed has been fully trained as a police horse.

■ TOP LEFT
Although the predominant coat colouring is chestnut, some dark colours do occur.

■ LEFT
The Murgese is Italy's breed of light draught horse. However, it lacks definitive type and the overall quality of the light draught horse of Ireland.

Italian Heavy Draught

Italy's premier heavy horse, the Italian
Heavy Draught – also known as the
Agricultural Heavy Horse – bears a distinct
resemblance to the handsome Breton,
which has had an important influence
upon its development. The Italian Heavy
Draught originated at Ferrara in the north
of the country during the second half of
the nineteenth century, when Neapolitan
blood was crossed with Arab and Hackney

BREED DESCRIPTION

Height Stallions 15 – 16hh.
Mares 14 – 15hh.

Colour Predominantly chestnut with flaxen
mane and tail. Occasionally dark bay.

Conformation Square head with broad
forehead, large eyes and nostrils and small,
mobile ears; muscular, slightly arched neck;
well-sloped shoulders; deep chest, short,
strong back with broad, slightly sloping
croup; short strong limbs with muscular
forearms and large joints, short pasterns and
large, well-shaped feet.

to produce an active, lightweight
workhorse. In due course the need arose
both for a heavier agricultural animal and
a heavy artillery horse, and breeders
accordingly began introducing new blood,
notably Boulonnais. Then, in the 1920s,
pure-bred Breton stallions were used to
establish the stamp of horse now known as
the Italian Heavy Draught.

An attractive looking horse, stocky and
muscular in build, the Italian Heavy
Draught is noted for its conformation and
active paces. It is capable of maintaining a
good speed even when pulling heavy
loads. The limbs are short and very strong
with well-developed muscles and large
joints. Although the need for draught
horses has decreased in Italy, as elsewhere,
the Italian Heavy Draught can still be seen
at work on some of the smaller farms, and
is also used for meat production.

INTERESTING FACTS

A stud book for Italian Draught Horses was
opened in 1961. Horses accepted for
registration are branded on the nearside of
the hindquarters with the breed mark, a
five-runged ladder within a shield.

Friesian

The Friesian is one of Europe's oldest horses and down the centuries it has had an influence on a number of other breeds, notably the Oldenburg in Germany and Britain's Fell and Dales ponies. The breed's homeland is Friesland, in the

■ LEFT
The Friesian's friendly disposition is evident in its kind but alert expression. The rather long head is set on a well-arched neck.

north of the Netherlands. The remains of an ancient coldblood type of heavy horse have been unearthed there, from which the modern Friesian is believed to be descended. Eastern blood, introduced into the Netherlands during the time of

BREED DESCRIPTION

Height 15 – 16hh.

Colour Always black.

Conformation Rather long head, with short ears and alert expression; elegant, arched neck with long, flowing mane; powerful shoulders; strong, compact body with strong, sloping hindquarters and rather low-set, very full, tail; short, strong limbs with good bone and a fair amount of feather.

■ RIGHT
Excellent overall conformation is the hallmark of the breed. The body is compact, the limbs strong and the feet hard and sound.

■ LEFT
An attractive turnout
much appreciated
throughout its native
land: a Friesian driven
to a traditional high-
wheeled gig.

■ BELOW
Appreciation of
Friesians is not
restricted to Holland.
This handsome team
was pictured in a busy
London street.

INTERESTING FACTS

The Friesians' noble bearing makes them
ideal for ceremonial occasions. These
horses were part of a six-strong team pulling
the Dutch Royal Carriage at the opening
ceremony of the 1994 World Equestrian
Games in The Hague.

the Crusades, had an influence on the
development of the Friesian, as did the
Andalusian during the Eighty Years' War,
when the Netherlands were occupied by
the Spanish. The Friesian horse which
thus developed was an active all-rounder,
suitable for work on the land but, because
of its ability to trot at speed, also useful as
a harness horse and for riding.

During the nineteenth century, when
trotting became extremely popular,
breeders sought to improve the Friesian's
already active, high-stepping trot, by
outcrossing to trotters. This led to the
Friesian becoming lighter in build and less
useful as a farm horse. By the beginning of
World War I its numbers were seriously
depleted and the decline continued
between the wars. However, lack of fuel
during World War II led to a revival in the
breed's fortunes as farmers once again
turned to it for draught work.

During the second half of this century
there has been a resurgence of interest in
the breed and it is now very popular as a
carriage horse. A well-balanced horse with
proud bearing, the Friesian looks
exceptionally attractive when pulling a
traditional high-wheeled Friesian gig. The
breed is noted for its kind temperament.

Gelderland

A number of different breeds went into the making of the Gelderland, which comes from the region of the same name in the central Netherlands and was developed during the nineteenth century. Native mares were crossed with, among others, English, French, German, Hungarian and Polish stallions to produce a good stamp of dual-purpose horse, one that was big and strong enough to do farm work or pull a carriage but not so heavy that it could not be used for riding. Hackney blood was also used in a

INTERESTING FACTS

The Gelderland is one of two types of all-purpose horse developed in the Netherlands, the other being its northern neighbour, the Gröningen. The Gröningen is somewhat heavier than the Gelderland. It has Friesian and Oldenburg blood in its ancestry, as well as some Suffolk Punch. Like the Gelderland, it has played an important part in the development of the Dutch Warmblood.

breeding programme that was noted for its well-founded principles of selection, only horses that had proved themselves to be good, sound workers being used at stud. As mechanization spread, and horses were needed less for use on the land, breeders introduced Thoroughbred blood to lighten the Gelderland.

A typical carriage type of horse, the modern Gelderland, with its excellent shoulders and good, free action, has been used successfully in the sport of four-in-hand driving and has also provided one of the main bases for the production of the Netherlands' sports horse, the Dutch Warmblood.

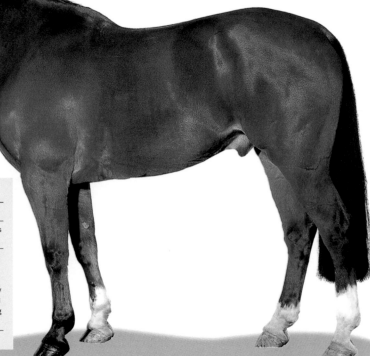

■ RIGHT
Good shoulders are a characteristic of Gelderland conformation, ensuring free movement at all paces.

BREED DESCRIPTION

Height About 16hh.

Colour Predominantly chestnut, sometimes bay or grey.

Conformation Rather plain, sensible looking head, with a tendency to a convex profile; strong neck; good shoulders, with fairly low withers; fairly long but strong body with good depth through the girth; powerful hindquarters with high-set tail; short, strong limbs with good, sound feet.

Dutch Warmblood

The production of the Netherlands' highly successful leisure and competition horse began with the selection of the best Gelderland and Gröningen mares, who were then mated with Thoroughbred stallions. The latter, also carefully selected, were imported from all over the world, including Britain, Ireland, France and the United States. Many of these came from the best racing lines, a fact which was to prove highly beneficial: as time went on Dutch breeders found that the stallions

LEFT
Milton is a grandson of the Trakehner Marco Polo, one of the most influential Dutch Warmblood stallions.

INTERESTING FACTS

One of the most important stallions in the breeding of Dutch Warmbloods was the Trakehner Marco Polo (1965–1976). By the Thoroughbred Poet, he was only small but he produced some top-class show jumpers. They included Marius, who was ridden with great international success by Britain's Caroline Bradley. In Britain Marius combined his competitive career with stud duties and had the distinction of siring Milton, the world's most successful show jumper.

BREED DESCRIPTION

Height 16 – 17hh.

Colour Any solid colour, with bay and brown the most usual.

Conformation Quality head, with alert, intelligent expression; good, sloping shoulders with pronounced withers; strong back and hindquarters; good, sound limbs, with plenty of bone and short cannons; good, sound feet.

Dutch breeders use a highly efficient, performance-based selection system to produce their horses and, despite its relative newness, the Dutch Warmblood has already demonstrated the correctness of their approach by achieving success at top international level in dressage, show jumping and carriage driving. Dutch

Warmbloods have been used in the establishment of other warmblood strains, too, notably in Britain, the United States, Australia and New Zealand.

who produced the best warmbloods had themselves enjoyed successful racing careers. In addition to Thoroughbreds, some Trakehner stallions were used in the early years, and a number of Holstein mares were imported and put to Gelderland or Gröningen stallions. Later on warmbloods of the type which the Dutch breeders were seeking to develop, such as the Holstein and Selle Français, were introduced into the breeding programme, and a dash of Hanoverian and Westphalian blood was added. At the same time there was a gradual decrease in the amount of Gelderland and Gröningen blood used. The result is a riding horse of harmonious proportions, with straight, true action, an easy, ground-covering stride at all paces and a good temperament.

LEFT
The Dutch Warmblood is a quality horse possessed of a good temperament. The correct proportions of its conformation result in excellent action, thus ensuring its suitability for modern competitive sports.

Lusitano

As its appearance suggests, the Portuguese Lusitano is a close relative of the Andalusian in neighbouring Spain. Indeed, until quite recent times the horses bred on the Iberian peninsula were regarded as being one and the same. It was not until the early years of the twentieth century that the two countries decided to establish independent stud books.

Since opening their own stud book the Portuguese have made great strides in monitoring and improving their breeding programme. They have been diligent in preserving the Lusitano's greatly admired qualities of strength and courage. These attributes led to the breed being very highly esteemed as a warhorse (the best Iberian horses have always been bred along the long frontier between

Portugal and Spain where endless battles were fought).

These same qualities also make the Lusitano an ideal mount for the demanding sport of mounted bullfighting. In Portugal, where it is considered a disgrace for a horse to be injured during a bullfight, the horses are extremely well

trained, using their inherent powers of acceleration and manoeuvrability to evade the bull.

As they have proved down the centuries, Lusitano horses are most amenable to training. Intelligent, gentle and affectionate, they work hard and enthusiastically. Possessed of good natural

BREED DESCRIPTION

Height Generally 15.1 – 15.3hh. Some horses reach over 16hh.

Colour Often grey or bay, but any true colour is found, including dun and chestnut.

Conformation Long, noble head, typically with a convex profile, finely curved nose and large, generous eyes; powerful, arched neck, deep at the base and set at a slightly wide angle to the shoulders, giving the impression of being fairly upright; powerful shoulders; short-coupled body with deep rib cage, broad, powerful loins, gently sloping croup and rather low-set tail; fine, clean legs with excellent dense bone; abundant silky mane and tail.

▌ ABOVE LEFT
This noble head and powerful, arched neck are characteristic of the Lusitano. The breed is also noted for its silky mane and tail.

▌ LEFT
The overall outline of the Lusitano is virtually the same as that of its close relative, the Andalusian.

I BELOW
The bay colouring of this mare at the Alter Stud is
typical of the Alter Real Lusitanos.

I BOTTOM
Portugal's horses are renowned for their muscular
strength, great impulsion and elevated paces.

INTERESTING FACTS

The Lusitano horse gives an exceptionally
smooth, comfortable ride. Agile and
intelligent, it makes the ideal mount for the
mounted bullfighter.

balance and with agile, elevated paces,
they give a smooth comfortable ride.
With their proud bearing and tremendous
joie de vivre they have, not surprisingly,
always excelled at high school work.
However, it is not only in the manège that
the breed excels. More and more
Lusitanos are proving themselves well
suited to modern sports such as show
jumping and carriage driving. People who
work with them testify to the great
understanding which quickly develops
between horse and human.

ALTER REAL

The Alter Real is not a distinct breed but
an offshoot of the Lusitano. It takes its
name from the town of Alter do Chão, in
the Portuguese province of Alentejo, the
world "real" meaning royal in Portuguese.
The royal stud founded at Alter supplied
the royal manège in Lisbon with high-
school and carriage horses. The stud
flourished for many years, producing a
fine line of horses which were valued not

only in Portugal but all over the
Peninsula. However, the stud's progress
suffered serious interruption on a
number of occasions, notably during
the Peninsular War, and the Alter Real
horses went into decline. Attempts to
resurrect the strain towards the end of
the nineteenth century by importing
English, Norman and German blood
were not successful, nor was a subsequent
attempt, using Arab horses. Through
the introduction of Andalusian blood at
the end of the century, the Alter Real
Lusitanos were finally re-established
but after the fall of the monarchy in
the early twentieth century, many horses
were sold or destroyed. The Alter Real
line would have died out but for the
efforts of the d'Andrade family, who
during the early 1940s saved two
stallions and a handful of mares and
instigated a breeding programme.
Today the Alter Stud is state run and
again produces horses for high school
work. The Alter Real is essentially a
Lusitano, although it is always bay, brown
or black in colour.

Bashkir

The small Bashkir horse comes from the southern foothills of the Ural mountains, taking its name from the region of Bashkirsky where it is kept in herds. It goes equally well in harness and under saddle and for centuries has been used as a pack and general work horse as well as a supplier of meat and milk. Stockily built,

BREED DESCRIPTION

Height 13.3 – 14hh.

Colour Predominantly bay, chestnut and brown.

Conformation Massive head; short, fleshy neck; low withers; wide, deep body with broad, straight back; comparatively short legs with substantial bone; good, hard feet.

with a thick coat, mane and tail, it can survive in the open in temperatures as low as -22° to -40° Fahrenheit (-30° to -40° C). It is able to withstand ferocious blizzard conditions and will dig through snow a metre deep to find food. Furthermore, its tremendously hard feet enable it to work without being shod. The Bashkir is undoubtedly one of the hardiest breeds of

INTERESTING FACTS

Bashkir mares are renowned for their milk yields. During the lactation period of some seven to eight months, a mare will produce upwards of 330 gallons (1,500 litres). In a number of areas of the former USSR horses are still run in herds and their milk is used to produce the fermented liquor known as kumis, which is both drunk by the local herdsmen and bottled on a large scale for consumption elsewhere.

horse or pony in the world.

A type of Bashkir also exists in the north-west of the United States, prompting the theory that these horses' ancestors travelled over the former land-bridge between Asia and North America (now the Bering Strait). The horse, however, is generally believed to have become extinct on the North American continent as long ago as the Ice Age and was not reintroduced until Spanish explorers of the modern era "discovered" the land. It is therefore much more likely that the Bashkir was introduced from Russia in fairly recent times.

■ ABOVE LEFT
The Bashkir's head is heavily built and set on a short, fleshy neck. The chest is broad.

■ LEFT
With its stocky build, short strong limbs and exceptionally hard feet, the Bashkir is well equipped for life in a harsh environment – though, as this picture shows, it also thrives in less rigorous surroundings.

Don

Don horses were made famous by the Don Cossacks, who between 1812 and 1814 helped drive Napoleon's invading troops from Russia. The Cossacks' horses were descended from those of the nomadic steppe people and were of mixed blood. Early influences would have included the Nagai from Mongolia, the Karabakh (a type of light riding horse), the Turkmen and the Persian Arab. During the nineteenth century infusions of Orlov and Thoroughbred blood were made and outcrosses were also made to the part-bred Arab horses produced at the Strelets Stud in the Ukraine. All these crosses, used to upgrade the old Cossack strain, ceased at the beginning of this century, since when no more outside blood has been used in the breeding of Don horses.

Like most Russian breeds, the Don was traditionally reared in herds on the vast expanses of the steppes, and accordingly developed into a tough individual, capable of thriving with minimal help from humans. It was ideally suited to its original role as an army remount while nowadays it is used for general riding purposes.

Various inherent conformational defects tend to limit the quality of its paces but its strong constitution makes it a suitable mount for endurance riding.

■ TOP
Don horses are predominantly chestnut. Calm and willing workers, they go equally well in harness and under saddle and have great endurance.

■ ABOVE
The Don tends to lack good riding horse conformation: straight shoulders and rather upright pasterns are common faults.

BREED DESCRIPTION

Height 15.3 – 16.2hh.

Colour Predominantly chestnut and brown, often with a golden sheen.

Conformation Medium-sized head with wide forehead; average length neck; strong body with broad, straight back and loins and rounded croup; rather sloping hindquarters; straight limbs with well-muscled forearms and second thighs, but a tendency to calf knees (an inward curve below the knee), sickle hocks and upright pasterns; short, thin mane and tail.

Budenny

A breed of relatively recent origin, the Budenny was created by crossing Don and Chernomor mares with Thoroughbred stallions (the Chernomor was the horse used by Cossacks who settled in the Kuban during the eighteenth century and was similar to the Don, though somewhat smaller and lighter in build). The chief purpose was to produce a good army remount, possessed of great endurance. Breeding was centred in the Rostov region, using a process of careful selection. The best mares were bred to the

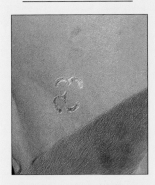

Russian horses are often hot branded as an aid to identification. The chestnut horse on the facing page has also been freeze-branded on the saddle patch. This is a valuable form of individual identity marking which helps to deter horse thieves because the owner can easily be traced.

▌ ABOVE RIGHT
The Thoroughbred influence on the present-day Budenny is particularly noticeable in the refinement of head, with its lean good looks, bright, intelligent eyes and alert ears.

▌ RIGHT
The overall conformation, while showing good depth through the girth and a reasonably well-sloped shoulder, lacks the harmonious proportions of the Thoroughbred, notably in the hind limbs, which are inclined to be a bit weak.

best Anglo-Don stallions. The brood mares were both well fed and, unusually in Russian horse breeding at the time, stabled during the worst of the winter weather, thus ensuring that they produced better, healthier foals than they might otherwise have done if forced to burn up their resources merely on keeping themselves warm. The young stock were tested on the racecourse between two and four years of age.

The robust constitution of the Don horse and the excellent action of the Thoroughbred proved to be a good combination and as a result the Rostov military stud farm was soon turning out an

BREED DESCRIPTION

Height 16hh.

Colour Predominantly chestnut, some bay and brown. The coats of some Budenny horses have a golden sheen (a throwback to the Chernomor and Don horses).

Conformation Well-proportioned head with straight or slightly concave profile; long, straight neck; reasonably well-sloped shoulders with high withers; comparatively heavy body with short, straight back and long croup; fine, straight limbs, though with a tendency to small joints and rather weak hindlegs; usually well-shaped feet.

upstanding horse, with a tractable nature, which proved suitable for both riding and light draught work. Named the Budenny, it was officially recognized as a breed in 1949.

As the need for army remounts ceased and interest turned to pleasure riding and sport, more Thoroughbred was added to improve the Budenny. Although the Thoroughbred influence is quite evident in the overall light build, the Budenny has a noticeably heavier body while the legs tend to be a bit light on bone. Today the breed is used as a general purpose riding horse, especially in the sports of show jumping, dressage and steeplechasing.

❚ RIGHT
The predominant Budenny coat colouring is chestnut. Some horses have a striking golden sheen.

Kabardin

Sure-footedness and a well-developed sense of self-preservation are the hallmarks of the Kabardin and little wonder, for its home is the northern Caucasus, where it has for centuries been accustomed to carrying men over the toughest mountain terrain. It traces back

■ ABOVE
The Kabardin's head is long and Roman noses are not uncommon. The ears are very mobile and the horse has a kind, calm expression.

■ RIGHT
Having evolved in the mountains, Kabardin horses are very athletic and well balanced. They make good jumpers.

to the sixteenth century and is derived from the horses of the steppe tribes who were crossed with Turkmen, Persian and Karabakh horses. Originally the Kabardin was itself fairly small. Raised in herds, which were (and still are) grazed on the high pastures during the summer and in the foothills during the winter, it developed into a typical mountain breed: tough, sturdy and possessing great endurance.

The numbers of Kabardin horses were seriously depleted as a result of the Revolution and it was during the 1920s, when efforts were made to re-establish the breed, that a bigger stamp of horse began to be produced, one suitable as an army remount and for agricultural work. The Malokarachaev and Malkin Studs became the producers of the best modern Kabardin horses, which are used to improve stock in neighbouring areas as well as for general riding and driving purposes.

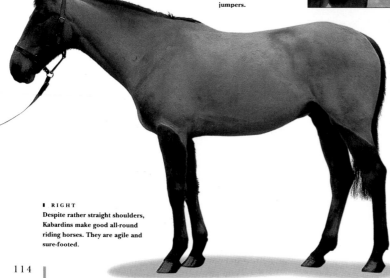

■ RIGHT
Despite rather straight shoulders, Kabardins make good all-round riding horses. They are agile and sure-footed.

Tersk

Like the Kabardin, the Tersk comes from the northern Caucasus, though it is a breed of more recent origin, having been developed from 1921 onwards at the Tersk and Stavropol Studs.

The Tersk is based on Strelets horses, the part-bred Arabs which were formerly bred at the Strelets Stud in the Ukraine. The Strelets was produced by crossing

BREED DESCRIPTION

Height Stallions 15hh. Mares 14.3hh.

Colour Predominantly light grey or "white" with a silvery sheen.

Conformation Fine head with large, expressive eyes and medium-length, mobile ears; medium-length neck set high on well-sloped shoulders; strong body with deep chest, wide back and muscular loins; fine legs with well-defined tendons; fine mane and tail.

INTERESTING FACTS

Nowadays most of the world's Tersk horses are produced at the Stavropol Stud. Stavropol is in the northern Caucasus between the Black Sea and the Caspian Sea.

■ BELOW
Tersk horses are invariably refined and elegant. Their predominantly light grey colouring adds to their attraction.

■ BOTTOM
The breed shows unmistakable signs of its Arab ancestry though it is usually a little taller than the pure-bred Arab.

pure-bred Arabs with, among others, high quality Orlovs and Anglo-Arabs (some Thoroughbred blood was also used, though this was not a dominant factor).

The result was a horse with a distinctly Arabian look about it but one which was bigger built than the pure-breds.

By the 1920s there were very few Strelets in existence. The few that did remain, including two stallions, were taken to the Tersk Stud in an attempt to increase their numbers. The mares were put to pure-bred Arab stallions; and various cross-bred mares, including Strelets x Kabardin and Arab x Don, were covered by the Strelets stallions. After some thirty years the new type, known as the Tersk, became fixed. It has inherited the general appearance of the Arab, though it stands a little taller, and also its elegant paces. A handsome horse, usually grey in colour, it combines a kind temperament with tremendous energy, attributes which have made it a favourite in circuses and also as a sports horse.

Orlov Trotter

The Orlov shares with the Standardbred and the French Trotter the distinction of being one of the world's foremost breeds of trotting horse. Indeed, before the development of the Standardbred it was probably the most famous of all trotters. Although the Orlov is less well known now outside its native land than the other two members of the triumvirate, it nevertheless plays an important role both in Russian harness racing and in the upgrading of other Russian breeds.

The Orlov takes its name from Count Alexis Orlov (1737–1809), founder of the Orlov Stud near Moscow. The Count imported from Greece a grey Arab stallion called Smetanka. Despite Smetanka's short stud career, he was to prove highly influential in the development of this popular breed. Smetanka's grey son

Polkan, bred out of a Danish mare and foaled in 1784, produced Bars I, who became the foundation sire of the Orlov Trotter.

The breed was developed by Count Orlov and his stud manager V.I. Shishkin at the then newly founded Khrenov Stud in the province of Voronezh

BREED DESCRIPTION

Height Stallions 16hh. Mares 15.3hh.

Colour Predominantly grey. Bay and black are commonly found. Chestnut is rare.

Conformation Small, often somewhat coarse head; long, often swan-shaped, neck set high on the withers; long, straight back with muscular loins and broad, powerful croup; fine, squarely set legs with a minimum of 8 inches (20cm) of bone below the knee.

▌LEFT
Most fast-trotting horses are fairly long in the back and the Orlov is no exception. The good measurement of bone below the knee denotes its strength.

INTERESTING FACTS

Count Alexis Orlov, the breed's founder, was a soldier famous for his courage and audacity. In 1762 he played a part in the assassination of Peter III. The Count's older brother, Grigorei, who distinguished himself during the Seven Years' War, had attracted the attention of Peter's wife, soon to become Catherine II. However, having helped place her on the throne, Grigorei found himself ousted from the Empress's favour by his fellow conspirator, the handsome Prince Potemkin. Alexis is reputed to have knocked out Potemkin's eye – and turned to horse breeding as a diversion from affairs at court!

I RIGHT
The Russian Trotter is part Orlov, part
Standardbred. It is faster on the racetrack than
the Orlov.

to which the stock from the Moscow stud
was transferred in 1788. Bars I was used to
breed from Arab, Dutch and Danish
mares as well as half-breds imported from
England. Inbreeding back to Bars I was
practised extensively. During the early
part of the nineteenth century the breed
continued to improve thanks to the
systematic training and racing of trotters
in Russia.

Later, as the Standardbred began
to demonstrate its supremacy on
the racetrack, the Russians started
importing horses from America to
cross with the Orlov. The resultant
half-breed, subsequently known as
the Russian Trotter, proved faster than
the Orlov. Imports of Standardbreds
ceased at the outbreak of World War I
but in recent times the traffic has
resumed to maintain the speed of the
Russian Trotter.

I BELOW
As well as being raced
in their native country,
Orlovs are well suited
to the modern sport of
four-in-hand driving.
They are exported for
this purpose.

I BELOW
This horse, hitched to
a training vehicle,
demonstrates the
Orlov's tremendously
powerful action.

Vladimir Heavy Draught

The Clydesdale played a significant part in the development of the Vladimir, a heavy draught horse created in the provinces of Vladimir and Ivanovo, to the north-east of Moscow. During the early years of this century stallions of various heavy breeds were imported from Britain and France to cross with the local mares of the region in order to produce a good-quality heavy work horse. Among the most influential of the foundation stallions were the Clydesdales Lord James, Border Brand, both imported in 1910, and Glen Albin (1923). Shire stallions were also used, though to a lesser extent, and some Cleveland Bay, Suffolk, Ardennais and

Percheron blood is also said to have been introduced. The experiment met with success, the result being a powerfully built heavy horse, well suited to all types of heavy agricultural and draught work. Named the Vladimir Heavy Draught, it was recognized as a breed in 1946.

Its docile nature makes it easy to handle, while its active paces – no doubt inherited from its Clydesdale forebears – mean that despite its massive build it can be used to pull the famous Russian troikas. Another bonus is its early maturity: the Vladimir is so well developed by the age of three that it can start work and also be used at stud, where the stallions are noted

■ OPPOSITE ABOVE
The Vladimir Heavy Draught combines great
strength with the most docile of natures – note this
horse's kindly expression.

■ OPPOSITE BELOW
Clydesdale blood was used with great success in the
development of this breed, which is renowned for
its powerful build and active paces.

BREED DESCRIPTION

Height Stallions 16.1hh. Mares 15.3hh.

Colour Predominantly bay, also black
and chestnut with white markings on head
and legs.

Conformation Large, long head with convex
profile; long, muscular neck; pronounced
withers; wide chest, rather long, broad back
and long, broad, sloping croup; long limbs;
some horses carry feather.

for their good fertility rate. Minus points
include, in some horses, a rather long
back, which is not conducive to strength,
and a flat-sided rib cage (the reverse of
"well sprung" or rounded ribs, which
enable the lungs to work to maximum
efficiency). The Vladimir is the largest of
the Russian heavy breeds. Stallions have a
girth of some 6 feet 9 inches (207cm) and
weigh in the region of 1,688lb (758kg).
Mares are only a little smaller, with a girth
of 6 feet 5 inches (196cm) and a weight of
1,507lb (685kg).

INTERESTING FACTS

Other heavy horses in the former USSR
include the Russian Heavy Draught, founded
a century or so ago, and based largely on
the Ardennais, and the Soviet Heavy
Draught, which was founded by crossing
Belgian Heavy Draught stallions with local
harness-type mares. Both were registered as
breeds in 1952. The Russian Heavy Draught
is quick to mature and remarkably long lived.
It was formerly known as the
"Russian Ardennes".

LATVIAN
The Latvian is a powerfully built harness
horse renowned for its weight-pulling
ability. It is of recent origin, dating only
from the early 1920s when local mares
were crossed with German, English and
French horses to produce an all-round
worker possessed of strength, stamina
and good, active paces. There are two
distinct types of Latvian horse: a heavy
harness type which is based largely on
Oldenburg, Norfolk Roadster and
Anglo-Norman outcrosses and a lighter
version which has a preponderance of
Hanoverian blood.

Latvian horses have good overall
conformation and great freedom of
movement. Stallions stand up to 16.2hh,
mares up to 16hh. Black is the
predominant colour of the heavier type,
while most of the lighter weight horses
are chestnut.

The Latvian harness horse was
recognized as a breed in 1952 and
although some outcrosses to Oldenburg
and Hanoverian horses have been made
since, these have been on a fairly limited
scale. The breed is especially noted for
its placid temperament which, together
with its strength and energy, make it a
popular working animal.

North Swedish

Forestry is the chief area of employment for the North Swedish horse, a small, compact, agile draught horse ideally suited to moving timber in confined spaces, over difficult terrain and often in inclement weather conditions.

The breed is descended from the ancient native work horse of Sweden which was influenced by the Døle horses from neighbouring Norway. At some time during the nineteenth century, outcrosses were made to horses of lighter build from outside Scandinavia but towards the end of the century there was a move to produce a heavier stamp of horse, more suited to pulling the heavier types of machinery which were then becoming available. Consequently stallions from larger breeds, such as the Clydesdale, were imported.

BREED DESCRIPTION

Height Stallions around 15.2hh. Mares around 15hh.

Colour Any solid colour.

Conformation Fairly large head with longish ears; short, crested neck; strong, sloping shoulders; rather long, but deep, strong back; rounded hindquarters with sloping croup; short, strong limbs with good bone; the mane and tail are usually very abundant.

The possibility of the old Swedish horse dying out altogether as a result of these crosses prompted interested parties to form an association to save it, the aim being to breed from the old-type stock still found in the remoter parts of the north of the country, using Døle stallions. Government support during the early years of the twentieth century aided this aim and during the 1920s performance testing was introduced as a means of selection, something which is still used today. Horses are tested for their draught aptitude as well as draught efficiency. The former test involves pulling a sled laden with logs, the judges awarding points according to the horse's performance and its condition after the work. For the efficiency test the horse is hitched to a wagon and its actual pulling power is measured by a dynamometer.

Lumbering is an area where heavy horses can prove more efficient and more cost effective than mechanized transport, and the North Swedish Horse continues to thrive in its traditional environment.

▌ LEFT
Small and compact, the North Swedish horse is particularly strong through the neck and shoulders. Its short limbs have plenty of bone.

North Swedish horses make good all-round draught animals. They are, however, most often associated with agricultural work and, more especially, forestry. They begin work as three-year-olds and within a couple of years are sufficiently mature to be capable of working an eight-hour day. Stallions weigh anything from 1,440 to 1,655lb (650–750kg) and mares 1,200 to 1,545lb (550–700kg).

Swedish Warmblood

Sweden has been renowned for its fine riding and carriage horses for many centuries, so it is not surprising that the Swedish Warmblood should have had such an impact on present-day competitive sports, particularly top-level dressage.

The Skåne province of what is now southern Sweden (the area had previously been under Danish rule) was noted for its horse breeding as long ago as the twelfth century, when Archbishop Absalon raised remounts there for his cavalry. Then in the mid-seventeenth century, Charles X of Sweden founded the Royal Stud at Flyinge, to the north-east of Malmo, to supply horses for the royal stables and the

■ LEFT
This handsome head is typical of the Swedish Warmblood, which is noted for its intelligence and pleasant disposition.

■ BOTTOM
Although overall conformation varies, most examples of the breed have a long, elegant neck and well-proportioned limbs and hindquarters.

army. Down the years horses from a wide variety of breeds were used at the stud to produce a quality cavalry horse. They included Holsteins, Hanoverians, East Prussians, Frederiksborgs, Arabs,

Thoroughbreds and Oldenburgs, with the East Prussian and Hanoverian blood being particularly influential.

Officers of the Swedish cavalry mounted on Swedish horses enjoyed tremendous success in all three equestrian disciplines (dressage, show jumping and three-day eventing) at Olympic level both before and after World War I. The Swiss army bought many Swedish horses after World War II, a number of whom found fame in the dressage world. When mechanization signalled the demise of the cavalry horse it was a natural progression for the Swedes to channel their horse-breeding efforts towards leisure and

RIGHT
Warmblood mares with
their foals put on a
fine show to an
appreciative crowd
during the 1990 World
Equestrian Games in
Stockholm.

BOTTOM LEFT
Thanks to infusions
of outside blood,
including
Thoroughbred, the
breed has become a
good all-round sports
horse.

BOTTOM RIGHT
Swedish Warmbloods
have traditionally
excelled at the
demanding
discipline of Grand
Prix dressage.

BREED DESCRIPTION

Height 15 – 17hh.

Colour Any solid colour.

Conformation Variable, but usually a
handsome head, with wide forehead and
kind, intelligent eyes; long neck; shoulders
sometimes tend to be rather straight,
depending on the bloodline; well-
proportioned body, hindquarters and limbs.

INTERESTING FACTS

Swedish-bred dressage horses which have
found fame at the Olympic Games include
Piaff, winner of the individual gold medal in
Munich in 1972, when ridden by the West
German, Liselott Linsenhoff. Piaff's sire was
Gaspari, who competed for Sweden in the
1960 Games in Rome, where another
Swedish horse, Wald, won the individual
silver medal in the hands of the Swiss rider,
Gustav Fischer. In Tokyo in 1964 Fischer's
compatriot, Henri Chammartin, was the
individual gold medallist on yet another
Swedish horse, Woermann. Also Swedish
bred was Gauguin de Lully, winner of the
individual bronze medal at the Seoul Games
in 1988, again competing for Switzerland.

competition. There was no doubting the
Swedish Warmblood's prowess as a
dressage horse and in recent times top
jumping blood has been introduced from
France, Germany and Holland. Carefully
selected Thoroughbred stallions have also
been used on warmblood mares.

To maintain the excellence of the

breed, in terms of both conformation and
temperament, Swedish Warmblood
stallions are graded and must pass a
performance test, veterinary examination
and assessment of type, conformation and
action. There is also a system of progeny
testing, the results of which are available
to mare owners seeking a suitable stallion.

Akhal-Teke

One of the most striking looking horses anywhere in the world, the Akhal-Teke, or Turkmen, has been bred for some 3,000 years in the desert oases of Turkmenistan, a region to the north of Iran and to the east of the Caspian Sea. Although the Turkmen people probably introduced a certain amount of Arabian and Persian blood at some stage, its isolated homeland has kept the Akhal-Teke freer from outside influences than many riding

■ LEFT
The Akhal-Teke's head is always very fine, with large expressive eyes and beautifully shaped ears.

■ BELOW
The luminous sheen on the coat of this horse is typical of the breed, as is the lean overall appearance.

■ RIGHT
Akhal-Tekes make good all-round riding horses, their legendary stamina making them excellent mounts for competitive endurance riding.

■ BOTTOM RIGHT
Despite being raised for centuries in desert conditions, the breed adapts perfectly well to life in the much less rigorous climate of western Europe.

BREED DESCRIPTION

Height 15.1 – 15.2hh.

Colour Bay and chestnut, often with a remarkable golden sheen; also grey and black.

Conformation Very fine head with wide nostrils, large, expressive eyes and long, beautifully shaped ears; long, straight and often thin neck set high on the shoulders; sloping shoulder with high withers; long, often weak back, shallow rib cage and a tendency to poor loins, lacking in muscle; narrow hindquarters but with muscular croup and long, muscular thighs; strong, straight forelegs with long forearm, and long hindlegs which tend to be sickle shaped with cow hocks; small but hard feet; sparse mane and tail; thin skin.

horses. Raised to withstand the extreme conditions of the desert – fiercely hot days alternating with cold nights – the Akhal-Teke developed into a tough, lean horse, whose undoubted conformational defects are offset by its fast paces, stamina and tremendous hardiness. This hardiness owes much to the rigorous lifestyle imposed upon it over many centuries. The traditional Turkmen method of horse management did not included stabling. The animals were wrapped in felt, with only their heads uncovered, and kept on tethers. Their diet included meagre amounts of dry lucerne, barley and some mutton fat. Foals were weaned very young and the horses raced as yearlings. Nowadays Akhal-Tekes are kept along more modern lines, out at grass by day and stabled by night. They are still raced, though not until they are two- or three-year-olds, as is the custom in the Thoroughbred racing world.

Spirited and athletic, they are used for general riding purposes, including show jumping and dressage, and at stud in the development of other riding horse breeds. Their phenomenal stamina also makes them the ideal mount for endurance rides, since they are capable of covering great distances, in extremes of temperature, on the most modest of rations. One of the most celebrated of all endurance rides took place in 1935, when Akhal-Teke horses travelled from Ashkabad to Moscow (their journey included crossing the Karakum desert), completing a distance of 2,580 miles (4,152km) in 84 days.

INTERESTING FACTS

The Akhal-Teke used to be renowned for its devotion to its rider – which is not surprising if one tale told about the Turkmen training techniques is true. According to this story, a young horse would be kept alone in a pit or enclosure. Stones would be thrown at it by everyone but the owner. Only he would treat it kindly and offer it food. Thus the horse learnt to trust only one man and to fear all others. This could account for the breed's sometimes difficult temperament.

Morgan

The American Morgan horse is highly unusual in that it can be traced back to just one stallion, the extraordinary little Justin Morgan, who stood a mere 14hh but who excelled in weight-pulling contests and races, both under saddle and in harness.

Justin Morgan was probably foaled in 1789 and was originally named Figure, later taking the name of his first recorded owner, Thomas Justin Morgan, who came from farming stock in Vermont but who was also a music teacher and church composer. How Justin Morgan was bred has never been satisfactorily resolved because of the lack of recorded evidence. Plausible claims have been made for Thoroughbred, Arab, Welsh Cob and Dutch ancestry. What is beyond dispute is that despite his small stature – he weighed no more than 850lb (386kg) – Justin Morgan proved himself a remarkably strong work horse, and he undoubtedly

The head of the Morgan is expressive, with large, prominent eyes and shapely ears set rather wide apart. Mares may have slightly longer ears than stallions.

worked extremely hard for a succession of owners. He was used for ploughing, as a harness horse and in woodland clearance and was never beaten in log-hauling matches against rivals weighing nearly half as much again.

He was, moreover, a wonderfully prepotent sire, passing on to his progeny all his own remarkable attributes of strength, endurance, speed and, not least, his gentle temperament. Three of his sons were to have a particular influence on

the development of the breed of which he was the founder: Sherman Morgan, foaled around 1808, Woodbury Morgan (1816) and Bulrush Morgan (1812). The Sherman Morgan line was noted for its excellent harness horses and had an important influence on the foundation of other breeds in the US: the Quarter Horse, Saddlebred, Standardbred and Tennessee Walker. The Woodbury Morgans were much in demand as saddle and parade

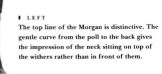

The top line of the Morgan is distinctive. The gentle curve from the poll to the back gives the impression of the neck sitting on top of the withers rather than in front of them.

BREED DESCRIPTION

Height 14.1 – 15.2hh with some individuals over or under.

Colour Bay, chestnut, brown or black. No white markings permitted above the knee or hock, except on the face.

Conformation Expressive head, with straight or slightly dished profile, broad forehead, large eyes and short, alert ears; slightly arched neck; sloping shoulders and well-defined withers; compact, deep body, with short back, well-sprung ribs, broad loins and deep flank; well-muscled hindquarters with high-set tail; straight, sound legs, with short cannons, flat bone and sufficiently long, sloping pasterns to provide light, springy step; good, sound feet with dense horn; full, soft mane and tail.

horses, while the Bulrush Morgans were noted for their trotting speed.

Like so many other breeds, the Morgan horse went into decline with the coming of motorized transport, but thanks to the efforts of enthusiastic members of the Morgan Horse Club, founded in 1909, the breed survived. Today there is a thriving population of Morgan horses in the United States plus recognized breed clubs in Canada, Britain, Australia, Spain, New Zealand, Germany, Italy and Sweden. The Morgan is kept as a show horse and is also to be seen competing in a variety of spheres, such as cutting horse, stock horse and reining horse classes, hunter-jumper division, dressage and roadster and carriage driving competitions.

INTERESTING FACTS

A Morgan horse named Comanche, the mount of Captain Myles Keogh, was the only non-Indian survivor of the Battle of the Little Big Horn in 1876. He recovered from his many wounds and lived to the ripe old age of 29.

I ABOVE
The versatile Morgan horse is equally at home in harness and under saddle.

I LEFT
Morgan horses are well up to carrying the weight of adult riders. The action is straight and springy.

Quarter Horse

The Quarter Horse, as its name implies, excels at racing over a short distance – a quarter of a mile to be precise. It traces back to the horses taken to America by the Spanish Conquistadores. During the seventeenth and eighteenth centuries the waves of English settlers in the eastern states used the local Spanish-based stock to cross with their own, imported horses to produce a good, all-round work horse, suitable for every type of ridden work, for tilling the land and for work in harness. Tough and stocky, these horses became the settlers' "right-hand men". Spreading westward, they became indispensable during the great days of cattle herding

when the chief requirement was for a totally dependable mount, one which was athletic and fearless working among cattle. In time these horses developed an innate "cow sense" and could anticipate the movements of a steer, stopping and turning at breakneck speed.

It was the Englishman's growing enthusiasm for racing which led to these all-purpose horses being raced in impromptu contests: on the road, in a clearing, anywhere where a couple of

▌ ABOVE LEFT
The head of the Quarter Horse is short and wide with large, intelligent eyes, alert ears and a small muzzle.

▌ ABOVE RIGHT
The chest is broad and deep, and the forelegs wide set. The muscling on the insides of the forearms gives the appearance of a well-defined inverted V.

▌ RIGHT
The breed is noted for its strong, close-coupled back and deep girth. Well-muscled hindquarters and strong, low-set hocks give the horse its tremendous acceleration.

BREED DESCRIPTION

Height 14.3 – 16hh for mature stallions and mares.

Colour Any solid colour.

Conformation Short, wide head, with small muzzle, large, wide-set, intelligent eyes and medium-length, alert ears; fairly long, flexible neck; sloping shoulders and well-defined withers; compact body with broad chest, deep girth, short back, well-sprung ribs and powerful loins; broad, deep, heavy and well-muscled hindquarters with long, gently sloped croup; good limbs, with short cannons, broad, flat, low-set hocks, muscular thighs and gaskins and medium-length pasterns; oblong feet with deep, open heels.

horses could be galloped upsides for a few hundred yards. The Quarter Horse, as it was dubbed, developed immensely powerful hindquarters, which could propel it into a flat-out gallop virtually from a standing start, and the speed to sprint over short distances. Eventually, however, as Thoroughbred racing became established, interest in Quarter Horse racing dwindled. Still later, when mechanization brought about a lessening of the horse's importance in ranching, the Quarter Horse, in common with riding horses all over the world, became a leisure riding horse.

Today the Quarter Horse enjoys great popularity in Western-style competitions such as barrel racing, in rodeos and, once again, in racing over short distances. Thanks to a revival of interest in the latter sport, Quarter Horses now compete on proper tracks for big purses.

INTERESTING FACTS

The American Quarter Horse Association was formed in 1940. Its registry is now the largest of any breed in the world, with more than two million horses listed.

❚ ABOVE
Quarter Horses have an innate "cow sense" and are able to anticipate the movements of a steer.

❚ BELOW LEFT
The Quarter Horse makes an ideal mount for traditional Western sports.

❚ BELOW RIGHT
The breed is well known for its pleasant disposition and gentleness and as a result is used in a wide variety of activities.

Saddlebred

Formerly known as the Kentucky Saddler, the elegant Saddlebred was developed by the early nineteenth-century settlers in the southern states of North America. To meet their requirements for a quality utility horse, the plantation owners interbred horses of various kinds, including the Narragansett Pacer (a speedy strain of pacing horse from Rhode Island) and the Thoroughbred. The end result was a good-looking animal who gave an exceptionally comfortable ride – essential for long hours spent in the saddle on crop-inspection tours – but was equally well suited to pulling a carriage. In 1891 a group of leading breeders established the American Saddle Horse Breeders' Association and a Saddle Horse Registry was set up.

Blessed with the most amiable disposition, intelligence, speed and natural balance, the Saddlebred could (and still can) be used for all manner of different purposes, including working with cattle. Not surprisingly it has made the transition from work horse to pleasure

BREED DESCRIPTION

Height 15 – 17hh; average about 15.3hh.

Colour Usually chestnut, bay, brown, black or grey; also palomino, spotted and occasionally roan.

Conformation Well-shaped head with large eyes set well apart, small, alert ears and wide nostrils; long, arched neck; sloping shoulders with sharp withers; short, strong back; well-muscled hindquarters with level croup and high-set tail; straight, strong limbs with long, sloping pasterns; good, sound hooves, open at the heels.

TOP
Everything about the Saddlebred's head suggests quality, refinement and intelligence. The neck is always long and elegantly arched.

LEFT
The Saddlebred's top line is distinctive: the croup is long and level, the back short and the well-defined withers higher than in most other light breeds.

■ LEFT
Long, well-sloped
pasterns contribute to
the comfortable paces
for which the breed is
famous.

■ BELOW
As well as being
popular riding horses,
Saddlebreds go equally
well in harness. The
peculiar tail carriage is
not natural, being
achieved through an
operation and
maintained by keeping
the tail in a device
known as a tail set
when the horse is
stabled.

horse with no difficulty whatsoever and
can be seen today competing in show
classes under saddle and in harness.

In the show ring, ridden Saddlebreds
are classified either as three-gaited or five-
gaited. The three-gaited horses are shown
at walk, trot and canter. The walk is
springy, the trot has high action and the
canter is slow, smooth and rhythmic. The
five-gaited horses show these three paces
plus two others: the slow gait and the rack.
The slow gait is a high-stepping, four-beat
gait executed in a slow, restrained manner.
The rack is a fast, flashy, four-beat gait in
which each foot strikes the ground at equal
intervals and which is free from any lateral
movement or pacing. The practice of
growing the feet unnaturally long (to
enhance the action), and operating on the
tail to make it unnaturally high set,
developed for the show ring.

Outside the artificial confines of the
show ring, in its handsome natural state,
the Saddlebred makes an excellent all-
round riding horse – easy to train, fast,
possessing great stamina and having a
good jump, too.

INTERESTING FACTS

In their natural state the Saddlebred's
strong hooves are well formed. For showing
purposes they are grown to an unnatural
length and shod with heavy shoes.

Standardbred

The American Standardbred is to harness racing what the English Thoroughbred is to flat racing and steeplechasing. During the past century or more, every country where harness racing flourishes has imported Standardbred horses to upgrade its own trotters and pacers.

BREED DESCRIPTION

Height 14 – 16hh.

Colour All solid colours, predominantly bay, brown, black and chestnut.

Conformation The Standardbred is a powerfully built horse, of rather less quality and refinement than the Thoroughbred and somewhat longer in the body and shorter in the leg. The shoulders are long and sloping and the croup invariably high.

▌ OPPOSITE PAGE
The gaits are so inherent that Standardbreds often show a marked preference for the trot (shown here) or the pace over the gallop, even when they are at liberty.

Strangely enough the foundation sire of the Standardbred was a horse who only ever raced at the gallop: the English Thoroughbred, Messenger. A grey tracing back to the Darley Arabian, Messenger was foaled in 1780 and raced on the flat for three seasons, winning eight of his fourteen starts. Exported to Philadelphia in May 1788, he stood at stud in America for twenty years, covering mainly Thoroughbred mares to start with then, after racing was suppressed in New York, all types of non-Thoroughbreds. Some of his descendants became fine flat

▌ ABOVE
The head of the Standardbred is not exactly refined but the overall aspect is workmanlike and the expression sensible.

▌ LEFT
In comparison with that other great racehorse, the Thoroughbred, the breed is rather long in the back and short in the leg. The shoulders are invariably long and well sloped, giving the horse the necessary freedom of movement.

racehorses but it was his ability to throw good trotting stock (not so much his immediate progeny as their descendants) that earned him lasting fame. His great grandson, Hambletonian, became a prolific sire of trotters and Hambletonian's four sons, George Wilkes, Dictator, Happy Medium and Electioneer, founded the sire lines responsible for virtually all harness racehorses in the USA today. Hambletonian was out of the Charles Kent Mare, who was inbred to Messenger, and descended, through her sire, Bellfounder, from the famous Norfolk Trotter, Old Shales.

In addition to the dominant Messenger line, two other important influences on the early development of the Standardbred were the Clays (descendants of a Barb stallion imported from Tripoli in 1820) and the Morgan horse. Neither produced important families within the breed but both are believed to have helped establish its characteristic gait.

The first register of trotters was published in 1871 and the term "Standardbred" was introduced eight years later when a set of qualifications was drawn up for the admission of horses into the register. The original "standard", from which the breed takes its name, was judged to be the ability of a horse to cover a mile (1.6km) in 2 minutes 30 seconds (as trotters and pacers improved, this time had to be reduced). Standardbreds race either at the pace (a lateral gait) or the trot (a diagonal pace). Up until the last couple of decades of the nineteenth century, trotters were more popular than the marginally faster pacers, but this is not so today.

▪ ABOVE
Although the pace is one of the breed's natural gaits it is usual for pacing racehorses to wear hobbles to encourage them to maintain the lateral movement.

▪ LEFT
Racing harness includes many items not generally seen in other horse sports. The shadow rolls on this horse's bridle are designed to prevent him from seeing and taking fright at shadows or "foreign objects" on the ground.

Missouri Fox Trotter

Although a stud book for the Missouri Fox Trotting Horse was not opened until 1948, the breed began to evolve in the early part of the nineteenth century. Settlers travelling westwards across the Mississippi river from Kentucky, Tennessee and Virginia took with them a variety of horses, including Thoroughbreds, eastern-bred stock and Morgans, and then interbred them to produce a horse suited to the conditions of their new home in the Ozark Hills region of Missouri.

The chief requirement, especially of doctors, sheriffs, stock raisers and the like, was for a horse that could be ridden for long periods, often over rough terrain, with a minimum of fatigue either to horse or rider. The answer was found in the gait known as the fox trot, in which the horse walks with its forelegs but trots behind. The Fox Trotter does not put its hindfeet down with the jarring action characteristic of the

BREED DESCRIPTION

Height 14 – 16hh.

Colour Any. Most commonly sorrel and chestnut sorrel with white markings.

Conformation Neat, clean, intelligent head with pointed, well-shaped ears, large, bright eyes and a tapered muzzle; graceful neck, in proportion to length of body; well-sloped, muscular shoulders; deep, strong body with deep, full chest and short, strong back; strong, muscular limbs; strong, well-made feet.

▌ ABOVE
This neat, intelligent looking head, with its bright eyes and well-shaped ears, is typical of the Missouri Fox Trotter.

▌ RIGHT
The body is deep, the back short and the overall impression one of compactness. Well-sloped shoulders ensure good riding action.

LEFT
The legendary comfort experienced when riding a Fox Trotter comes from the unusual action of the hindfeet, which slide forward under the horse as he puts them down, rather than hitting the ground with a jarring action.

INTERESTING FACTS

In the fox trot the horse's hindfeet disfigure the tracks of the forefeet, that is the hindfeet touch the front tracks and slide forward. The horse should travel in a collected manner, with animation, rhythm and style. The horse's tail is slightly elevated and moves in a bobbing rhythm with the gait. The flat-foot walk should also be performed with style and animation. It is an animated four-beat gait in which the horse overstrides its front track with the hindfeet. The typical canter of the Fox Trotter is collected, with the head and tail slightly elevated.

normal trot, but slides them along under him. The result is a smooth, comfortable gait at which the horse can travel for extended periods without tiring. The ability to walk in front and trot behind is inherited but it can also be enhanced with training. The overall quality of the Fox

show classes in which it is judged 40 per cent for the fox trot, 20 per cent for the flat foot walk, 20 per cent for the canter and 20 per cent for conformation, the only exceptions being two-year-olds, who are judged 50 per cent for fox trot, 25 per cent for walk and 25 per cent for conformation.

BELOW LEFT
Originally bred as a means of transport, the present-day Fox Trotter is well suited to modern leisure riding. It is renowned for its sure-footedness.

BELOW
Unlike the Saddlebred and the Tennessee Walking Horse, the Missouri Fox Trotter is shown with normal-length feet. Artificial appliances such as weights and tail sets are forbidden.

Trotter was improved over the years through infusions of Saddlebred and Tennessee Walker blood and today the breed is noted for its compact, muscular build and its sure-footedness.

Having become obsolete as a means of transport, the Fox Trotter is now used as a pleasure horse, being ideally suited to trail (long-distance) riding. It is also ridden in

Tennessee Walking Horse

LEFT
The Tennessee Walking Horse is customarily ridden in a plain bit with long shanks and on a single rein which is held with a light hand and flexed wrist.

BELOW
The Walking Horse has the substance of the Standardbred and the style of the Saddlebred which are two of the breeds on which it is based.

The Tennessee Walking Horse traces back to the Narragansett Pacer and, like the Saddlebred and the Missouri Fox Trotter, it was developed as an exceptionally comfortable riding horse with gaits not found in other breeds. Originally known as the Southern Plantation Walking Horse or Tennessee Pacer, it was an invaluable mode of transport for planters carrying out crop inspections, being fast, robust, comfortable under saddle and having a most tractable temperament.

The foundation sire was a horse named Black Allan, who arrived in Tennessee in

1903. Black Allan's sire came from a line of Standardbred trotters, while his dam was a Morgan. Black Allan was crossed with the Tennessee Pacers of the time to produce the forerunners of the modern Walking Horse. Saddlebred blood was also introduced, the most important influence being that of Giovanni, who in 1914 was brought from Kentucky to stand at stud in Tennessee. By adding Saddlebred blood, breeders succeeded in producing a better quality, more refined, animal. Today's Walking Horse, which might be decribed as a somewhat more powerful version of

BREED DESCRIPTION

Height Average 15 .2hh.

Colour Any. Black and solid colours are most popular.

Conformation Intelligent but rather plain head; strong, arched neck; well-sloped shoulders; powerful body with broad chest; strong hindquarters; clean, hard limbs.

the Saddlebred, is therefore an amalgam of Thoroughbred, Standardbred, Morgan and Saddlebred blood. The Tennessee Walking Horse Breeders' Association was formed in Lewisburg, Tennessee, in 1935 and the Walking Horse was finally recognized as a breed in 1947.

Walking horses are fine all-round riding horses, their inherently kind nature making them especially suitable for novice riders. They are also popular horses in the show ring.

INTERESTING FACTS

The Tennessee Walking Horse's distinctive gaits – the flat-foot walk, the running walk and the canter – are inherited. Small foals can be seen performing the running walk beside their dams. Both walks are a loose, four-beat gait, with high action in front. As it moves, the horse nods its head in rhythm with the rise and fall of the hoofs, and the hindfeet overstride the tracks left by the front feet. The flat-foot walk should be loose, bold and square with plenty of shoulder motion. There should be a noticeable difference in the tempo between the two walks. The canter has a distinctive "rocking chair" motion.

LEFT
The breed's unique gaits are inherited – young foals are seen to "walk" alongside their mothers with the ease of older horses – but are encouraged with artificial aids applied to the forefeet.

FAR LEFT
An impressive collection of Walking Horse trophies won in America, where the breed is a popular show-ring attraction.

BELOW
The exaggerated outline of the show horse is produced in part by the extra-long forefeet. The rider sits way behind the normal saddle position (on what is generally held to be the weakest part of the horse's back).

Mustang

Mustangs, the "wild" horses of North America, are descended from the horses taken to the New World by the sixteenth-century Conquistadores. As Spanish colonizers began moving north from Mexico into what is now Texas, so the Indian tribes with whom they came into contact began to have their first experience of horses. Initially, the Indians were inclined to kill and eat any horses they captured from the settlers. In time, however, as they began to realize the value of the horse as a means of transport, they learnt how to handle and ride them.

By the second half of the seventeenth century, some tribes were taking horses from the Spaniards and using them in mounted raids against the newcomers – during which they would acquire more horses. So began the gradual spread of the horse to other tribes (either by trading or by theft) and the movement of the horse

■ LEFT
This Mustang shows unmistakable signs of its Spanish ancestry in its attractive head and luxurious growth of silky mane.

BREED DESCRIPTION

Height 13.2 – 15hh.

Colour Any.

Conformation Because of its mixed ancestry (the original Spanish stock was progressively diluted as a wide variety of settlers' horses, who either became lost or were abandoned, joined and interbred with the wild herds) there is a good deal of variation. The best are sturdily built with strong, clean limbs and feet.

northwards. Many of the horses who subsequently ran "wild" would have done so after getting loose during skirmishes between Indians and Spaniards. Others, perhaps those who were lame or needed resting, were probably turned loose, their owners intending to round them up later. Some domestic horses put out to graze on the range simply wandered off. Gradually these horses joined together to form feral

herds, which flourished in the wide open spaces of the Great Plains. By the late eighteenth and early nineteenth centuries there were huge numbers of "wild" horses grazing the plains – one authority estimates the number to have been as high as two million.

The turning point for the Mustang, as these feral horses became known, was the westward spread of civilization. Many were

■ RIGHT
Because of its chequered history, Mustang conformation is very variable. Not all horses are as sturdily built as this one.

█ LEFT
Centuries of living in a feral state led to the
development of a tough, enduring type of animal.

killed, others were rounded up for use as
draught animals, some were used for
cross-breeding. Large numbers were used
as army remounts in the Boer War. During
the twentieth century still more have been
killed for the meat and pet food trades.

Public pressure led to the introduction,
in 1971, of an act giving protection to wild
horses in the United States and there are
several ranges where they still live, albeit
in much reduced numbers. Domesticated
Mustangs often make good riding horses.
Because of their inherent toughness, they
are well suited to endurance rides.

█ LEFT
A fine stamp of Mustang which looks well under
saddle. The majority of domesticated Mustangs
make good all-round riding horses.

█ RIGHT
Decorated in
traditional style, these
horses reflect their
links with the Indian
tribes who came to rely
on the horses first
introduced into
America by the
Conquistadores.

Criollo

▌ BELOW
Originally the mount of the gauchos, or cowboys, of South America, the Criollo has achieved world-wide fame in the world of polo.

▌ BOTTOM
The sturdy, compact Criollo is one of the world's toughest horses, with strong short limbs, plenty of bone below the knee and exceptionally sound feet.

A descendant of the horses taken to South America by the sixteenth-century Spanish Conquistadores, the Criollo comes from Argentina and is one of the toughest breeds of horse in the world. Its hardiness is the result of many years of natural selection. Some of the Spanish horses and their descendants formed feral herds on the pampas, where the extremes of climate – intensely dry, hot summers and severe winters – would have proved intolerable to all but the sturdiest individuals. Those that survived adapted to their harsh environment remarkably well, no doubt helped by the fact that they were descended from Andalusian and Barb horses, both breeds noted for their endurance. The Criollo, as it became known, even developed a coat colour – Criollos are predominantly dun – which helped render it inconspicuous against

the dry pastureland of its habitat.

The Criollo became the favoured mount of the gauchos, the cowboys of the pampas, and an indispensable riding and packhorse for settlers in the huge and frequently inhospitable countries of South America. It can be found throughout the continent and although there are some variations, the result of adaptation to differences in habitat and climate, wherever it is bred it retains its basic qualities of stamina and soundness. Crossed with the Thoroughbred, the Criollo produces a fine polo pony, the Thoroughbred blood providing the extra speed required in the modern game.

BREED DESCRIPTION

Height Around 14 – 15hh.

Colour Usually dun with dark points and often with a dorsal stripe.

Conformation Medium-sized head, with wide-set eyes and alert ears; muscular neck; short, deep body with well-sprung ribs; short, strong limbs with plenty of bone and good, sound feet.

INTERESTING FACTS

The most famous example of the Criollo's extraordinary powers of endurance was "Tschiffely's Ride", a journey undertaken by the Swiss-born traveller and writer Aimé Felix Tschiffely (1895–1954). In 1925, together with two Criollos – the 16-year-old Mancha, and the 15-year-old Gata – Tschiffely set off from Buenos Aires to ride to Washington D.C. in the United States. Alternately riding one horse and leading the other as a packhorse, he completed the journey, over some of the most arduous terrain in the world, in two and a half years. The horses were then shipped back to South America, where they spent their retirement, Gata living to the age of 36 and Mancha to 40.

Peruvian Paso

The Paso (meaning "step") is another breed which owes its origins to the Barb and Andalusian horses introduced to South America by the Spaniards. The first horses to arrive in Peru were taken there in 1532 by Francisco Pizarro (c.1478–1541).

The Paso's characteristic lateral gait is thought to have been inherited from the Spanish "jennet", which was a riding horse akin to the old English ambler. The lateral movement has been preserved down the centuries; the Paso usually demonstrates a preference for it over the canter. The paso is unlike any other lateral gait in that the horse's forelegs arc out to the side as he moves. With his hindlegs he takes long, straight strides, carrying his hindquarters

BREED DESCRIPTION

Height 14 – 15.2hh.

Colour Any, but predominantly bay and chestnut.

Conformation Intelligent looking head; fairly short, muscular neck; strong shoulders; strong body with broad, deep chest; strong, rounded hindquarters; short, strong limbs and excellent feet.

low, with his hocks well under him. This combination of flowing foreleg movement and powerfully driving hindlegs gives a particularly smooth ride. The Paso is said to be able to reach speeds of up to 15mph (24kph) and to maintain the lateral gait over rough terrain for extended periods without tiring.

Fairly small and stockily built, the Paso is noted for its sure-footedness, its ability to thrive on meagre rations and its kind nature. It makes an ideal ranch and long-distance riding horse.

▌ RIGHT
Horse and rider make an attractive, workmanlike picture in their traditional Peruvian tack and costume. The Paso is up to carrying a good deal of weight.

▌ ABOVE
Compact and well-muscled, with powerful hindquarters and short, strong limbs, the Peruvian Paso is a tremendously strong individual.

▌ LEFT
The Paso's long silky mane (and tail) is reminiscent of that of its Spanish ancestors, introduced into South America during the sixteenth century.

INTERESTING FACTS

The Peruvian Paso is not the only horse to show a natural preference for a lateral gait but the curious outward arcing of the forelegs, which move rather like the arms of a swimmer, is unique to the breed.

Ponies

Broadly speaking a pony is a small horse, "small" usually meaning no higher at the withers than about 14.2hh (a hand is 4 inches). However, not all small horses can be classified as ponies. Arab horses, for example, often stand below 15hh but they are very much horses, with the proportions and characteristics of the horse. An unusually small Thoroughbred is certainly not a pony and the remarkable little Caspian, although it is classified as a pony, actually resembles a miniature horse.

True ponies have very distinct pony characteristics, which include a proportionately short length of leg in relationship to the depth of the body. True ponies are perhaps best exemplified by the Mountain and Moorland breeds of Britain and Ireland, remarkable animals which have existed in the comparative isolation of their island home for thousands of years. These ponies, which are now divided into nine distinct breeds, are possessed of extraordinary strength in relation to their size. Fashioned by a harsh environment, they are tough, sure-footed, able to exist on minimum rations and have an inherent sagacity often lacking in their larger cousins.

Haflinger

Austria's attractive Haflinger pony is named after the village of Hafling in the southern Tirol, the region where it was first bred hundreds of years ago. Its ancestors were indigenous mountain

BREED DESCRIPTION

Height Around 14hh.

Colour Chestnut with flaxen mane and tail.

Conformation Intelligent looking head, with large eyes, small ears and slightly dished profile; sloping shoulders; strong, deep body with fairly long back and muscular loins; powerful hindquarters; strong limbs and excellent feet.

▮ PREVIOUS PAGE
OPPOSITE
Exmoor ponies.

▮ PREVIOUS PAGE
A Norwegian Fjord
pony.

▮ LEFT
The "Hungarian Post" – Haflinger style! The breed combines strength with very active paces and can be trained to perform in a wide range of equestrian activities.

▮ BELOW LEFT
Haflingers are true all-rounders, equally adept at work in harness and under saddle. This handsome team was photographed in Switzerland.

▮ BELOW
The Haflinger's good temperament is easily discerned in this attractive head, with its large, kind eyes and alert expression.

horses and ponies which were upgraded with Arabian blood. All modern Haflingers trace back to a half-bred horse named El Bedavi XXII – who was bred in Austria and was a great grandson of the Arabian stallion, El Bedavi – and to El Bedavi XXII's son, Folie.

Over the years inbreeding has resulted in a pony of very definite type: small, but powerfully built, always chestnut in colour, hardy and sure-footed as befits a mountain

pony, and with the active paces of its Arab forebears.

With its amenable nature, the Haflinger makes an excellent all-round riding and driving pony. Before mechanization it was in great demand for agricultural work and as a pack-pony. Nowadays many Haflingers are used for leisure riding. The breed has been exported to a number of countries, and is especially popular in Germany and Switzerland. It is noted for its longevity.

INTERESTING FACTS

Haflingers which are entered in the breed's stud book are traditionally branded. The brand mark is the alpine flower, the edelweiss, at the centre of which is placed the letter "H".

Sorraia

LEFT
Dun is the predominant colour of the Sorraia, Portugal's small, semi-feral pony. The breed is of ancient origin and is exceptionally hardy.

BELOW
In build and overall outline the Sorraia is not unlike the primitive Tarpan. Some selective breeding is carried out in order to preserve the original form.

Formerly used for farm work and general riding purposes, the primitive looking Sorraia survives today mainly in small feral groups. Its homeland is in Portugal in the region between the rivers Sor and Raia, tributaries of the Sorraia, which flows into the Tagus estuary from the south.

The Sorraia pony is believed to be descended from the Asian Wild Horse and the Tarpan. It bears a remarkable likeness to the latter, with its small stature and large head. The Sorraia's colouring, predominantly dun, often with an eel-stripe and zebra markings on the legs, is also typical of the primitive equine type.

The Sorraia does not have the best conformation in the world. It is, however, an extremely tough individual, able to exist on poor forage and to withstand extremes of climate. The shoulders tend to be upright, the hindquarters weak and the limbs rather long and lacking in bone, though the feet are hard and sound.

BREED DESCRIPTION

Height 12 – 13hh.

Colour Predominantly dun, with black eel-stripe down the centre of the back and frequently with zebra markings on the legs and occasionally on the body; also grey.

Conformation Large, primitive looking head with convex profile; straight shoulders; poor hindquarters with low-set tail; long limbs, lacking in bone.

INTERESTING FACTS

The Sorraia is believed to be related to the Garrano, the pony of northern Portugal. The Garrano shows more quality than the Sorraia, the result of infusions of Arab blood. Although small, the Garrano is inherently hardy, and has been used for all types of farm work, as a pack-pony and for hauling timber.

Exmoor

The Exmoor is the oldest of Britain's Mountain and Moorland breeds and one of the oldest equine breeds in the world. This attractive pony has inhabited the wild moorland area of west Somerset and north Devon in the south-west of England for many centuries. Ponies of Exmoor type were certainly known during Roman times and may well have existed as far back as the Bronze Age, when they would have been used for pulling chariots. Mention is made of Exmoor ponies and their owners in the Domesday Book of 1085.

The remoteness of its habitat has meant that the Exmoor pony has been subjected to very little in the way of

"improvement" through the introduction of outside blood. The rigours of life on the moor have produced a tremendously hardy pony, strong enough to carry an adult rider in spite of the fact that the ponies stand no higher than 12.3hh.

The Exmoor Pony Society was founded in 1921 to improve and encourage the breeding of Exmoor ponies of the traditional moorland type. By carrying out rigorous inspections, it ensures that no pony lacking true Exmoor type is registered as a pure-bred. When ponies are passed for registration, they are branded on the shoulder with the

BREED DESCRIPTION

Height Stallions and geldings not exceeding 12.3hh. Mares not exceeding 12.2hh.

Colour Bay, brown or dun with black points. No white markings anywhere.

Conformation Clean-cut face with wide forehead, large, prominent eyes, wide nostrils and clean throat; good length of rein; well laid-back shoulders; strong body with deep, wide chest, well-sprung ribs and broad, level back; clean, short limbs and neat, hard feet.

▌ TOP
The Exmoor's attractive head, notable for its large eyes, small, mobile ears and intelligent expression, is full of true pony character.

▌ RIGHT
The Exmoor is a fine stamp of pony: hard and strong, vigorous, alert and symmetrical in appearance. Its general poise indicates its good natural balance.

I LEFT
An Exmoor foal in his native habitat. Ponies have inhabited the moor for many centuries and are totally adapted to life in a tough environment.

Society's star brand. Beneath this the pony's herd number appears, while on the nearside hindquarter there is the pony's own number within that herd.

Herds of ponies still run "wild" on the moor, although they are rounded up annually for inspection. The Exmoor's robust build and constitution make it an excellent riding pony and they are also used in the sport of driving.

INTERESTING FACTS

The most instantly recognizable features of the Exmoor are its mealy coloured muzzle and its large, prominent eyes. The latter are termed "toad" eyes because of their heavy top lids. The eyebrows are surrounded by light, buff-coloured hair.

I ABOVE
Correctly handled and schooled, the Exmoor, for all its great strength, makes a good riding pony for a small child.

I LEFT
The breed's inherent athleticism makes it a good all-round performance pony for an older child.

149

Dartmoor

Unlike its neighbour, the Exmoor, the Dartmoor Pony has been influenced by a number of breeds over the many centuries during which ponies have run free on the high moorland of Devon, in south-west England. Ponies are thought to have lived on the moor during Saxon times. Later the important trade route which existed between Exeter and Plymouth would have been travelled by horses of many different types, some of which would almost certainly have had an influence on the native stock. Arabs and Barbs, brought back by Crusaders, are also believed to have found their way onto the moor.

Climate and the hardships of existing in such a wild region would have ensured

that the animals roaming the moors achieved a certain degree of uniformity, particularly with regard to size. During the Industrial Revolution the requirements of the mining industry prompted a new development: the crossing of Dartmoor Ponies with the much smaller Shetland, in order to produce animals suited to working underground. This proved to be a

highly retrograde step as far as the Dartmoor Pony was concerned. The type of riding-quality pony that had evolved began to deteriorate. In order to set matters right, new blood had to be introduced, including Welsh Mountain Pony, Polo Pony and Hackney.

The first stud book for Dartmoors was opened in 1899 and the height limits for

■ LEFT
Strength and active paces make the Dartmoor a
good harness pony.

INTERESTING FACTS

There was a steady decline in the numbers of
ponies of true Dartmoor type after World War II
and many of those found on the moor were
only poor quality cross-breds. However, in
1988 the Dartmoor Pony Society Moor
Scheme was set up in order to encourage
farmers with unregistered pure-bred type
ponies to offer them for registration and to
provide them with the services of pedigree
stallions. The aim is to establish a pool of
pure-bred ponies – hardy enough to thrive on
the moor – to which breeders can then go for
true native pony characteristics. Suitable
mares from the moor are put in large enclosed
areas known as newtakes together with a
pedigree stallion. Their female progeny are
inspected and those which pass muster are
entered in a supplementary register of the
stud book. In due course these ponies will also
be mated to a fully registered stallion, and so
on until their descendants, on inspection, can
be admitted to the full stud book.

■ RIGHT
Dartmoors have a
calm temperament
and make good mounts
for children.

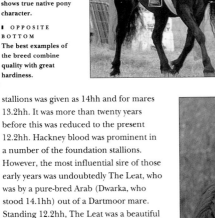

■ OPPOSITE TOP
The Dartmoor's neat,
well set-on head with
its small, alert ears,
shows true native pony
character.

■ OPPOSITE
BOTTOM
The best examples of
the breed combine
quality with great
hardiness.

■ BELOW
Although Dartmoor ponies declined in number and
quality after World War II, in recent times measures
have been introduced to ensure the preservation of
a pool of hardy pure-breds.

stallions was given as 14hh and for mares
13.2hh. It was more than twenty years
before this was reduced to the present
12.2hh. Hackney blood was prominent in
a number of the foundation stallions.
However, the most influential sire of those
early years was undoubtedly The Leat, who
was by a pure-bred Arab (Dwarka, who
stood 14.1hh) out of a Dartmoor mare.
Standing 12.2hh, The Leat was a beautiful
looking pony with excellent conformation.
During his short stud career only a
handful of his progeny were registered,
but many of the best present-day ponies
trace back to him.

At its best the Dartmoor is a hardy,
quality riding pony with smooth, low, free
action. Its sound constitution, intelligence
and excellent, calm temperament, make it
an ideal pony for a child.

Welsh Mountain

The rugged landscape of Wales is home to four distinct equine breeds: two ponies, designated Section A and Section B in the Welsh Pony and Cob Society Stud Book, and two cobs, designated Section C and Section D.

At the base of all Welsh breeding is the beautiful Welsh Mountain Pony, Section A, which has thrived for many centuries in the tough environment of its native land

▮ ABOVE
The eastern influence is clearly visible in the beautiful head, with its big eyes, wide nostrils and dished profile.

▮ LEFT
The Section B is larger than the Welsh Mountain Pony but the best examples have the same true pony character. The action is straight, quick and free.

▮ BELOW
Section A ponies like this one were used in the development of the Australian Pony, which is based on Welsh and Arab blood.

BREED DESCRIPTION

Height Not exceeding 12hh.

Colour Predominantly grey, though bay, chestnut and palomino occur and any solid colour is permitted.

Conformation Small, clean-cut head, tapering to the muzzle, with bold eyes, small, pointed ears and prominent, open nostrils; lengthy, well-carried neck; long, sloping shoulders; strong, muscular back with deep girth, well-sprung ribs and strong loins; lengthy, fine hindquarters with tail well set on and carried gaily; good, strong limbs, with long, strong forearm, well-developed knee, large, flat hocks and well-shaped feet, of dense, hard horn.

and is considered by many people to be the most beautiful of all ponies. The development of the breed is obscure, but it goes back at least to the times of the Romans, who crossed horses of eastern origin with the native Welsh stock. In more recent times, particularly during the eighteenth century, some Thoroughbred, Arab and Barb blood was introduced.

The modern Welsh Mountain Pony is courageous and spirited, yet kindly, and makes a superb child's riding pony. It is also an outstanding performer in the increasingly popular sport of carriage driving. It has evolved as a supremely hardy individual, able to endure harsh weather conditions and to thrive on sparse rations. It has been used to improve other breeds, including the New Forest, and also in the development of the British Riding Pony. The Welsh Mountain Pony is popular in many countries outside its native Wales. It has been exported to Europe, the United States, New Zealand and Australia.

INTERESTING FACTS

The Welsh Pony (Section B) is larger than the Mountain Pony, though it retains the true pony characteristics. Arab, small Thoroughbred and small Welsh Cob stallions were crossed with Mountain Pony mares to develop this quality riding pony, which stands up to 13.2hh. Formerly used for shepherding and hunting, Welsh Ponies are now much in demand as children's riding ponies.

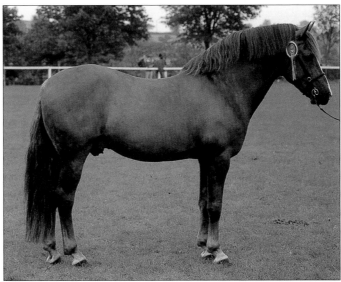

New Forest

Wild horses are known to have existed in the New Forest, in southern England, as far back as the time of Canute (c. 995–1035). The exact origins of today's New Forest Pony are, however, unknown although it has certainly been influenced down the years by a variety of other breeds. During the eighteenth century the Thoroughbred stallion Marske, the sire of the great racehorse Eclipse, was used for a time to

BREED DESCRIPTION

Height 13.3 – 14.2hh.

Colour Any colour except skewbald, piebald, or blue-eyed cream.

Conformation Rather large head; fairly short neck; well-sloped shoulders; deep body; strong hindquarters; straight limbs with plenty of bone and good hard, round feet.

serve New Forest mares and in the mid-nineteenth century an Arab stallion belonging to Queen Victoria was allowed to run with the herds. Hackney blood was also introduced. While these infusions of outside blood added to the pony's size, they were detrimental when it came to the preservation of true pony substance and to rectify the situation, outcrosses were made to stallions of other native breeds, including Dales, Dartmoor, Exmoor, Fell, Highland and, later, Welsh Mountain.

Today's New Forest Ponies, like many Exmoor and Welsh Mountain Ponies, still roam freely in their native habitat. Life in the Forest can be hard, the food supply often meagre and low in quality. This tough environment has produced a hardy, sure-footed animal. The pony's action is free, active and straight and its good temperament makes it easy to train. As a result they make excellent all-round riding and driving ponies. They are popular not only in their native country but also in mainland Europe, North America, Australia and New Zealand.

▐ TOP
The best type of New Forest Pony is strongly built and possesses good, well-sloped riding shoulders, powerful hindquarters and strong, sound limbs

▐ ABOVE LEFT
The New Forest's head indicates the breed's typically calm, tractable temperament.

INTERESTING FACTS

The ponies are owned by the New Forest Commoners, who carry out an annual "drift" or round-up in order to select those which are to be sold. The remaining breeding stock is then returned to the Forest.

Welsh Cob

The Welsh Cob (designated Section D in the Welsh Pony and Cob Society Stud Book) is derived from the Welsh Mountain Pony, of which it is, in essence, a larger version. It traces back at least to the twelfth century when eastern-type horses were brought back by the Crusaders and crossed with the local ponies. Subsequently infusions of Yorkshire Coach Horse, Norfolk Roadster and Arab blood were made.

Tough, sound, spirited and courageous, yet with an amenable temperament, the

❙ ABOVE
The action is straight, free and forceful. The whole foreleg is extended from the shoulders and as far forward as possible in all paces, with the hocks well flexed, producing powerful leverage.

❙ RIGHT
The Welsh Cob
Section D is described
by the breed society as
the embodiment of
strength and
hardiness.

BREED DESCRIPTION

Height Above 13.2hh – usually
14.2 – 15.2hh.

Colour Any, except piebald and skewbald.

Conformation Quality, pony head with bold,
widely set eyes and neat, well-set ears; long,
well-carried neck; strong, well laid-back
shoulders; strong, deep, muscular body;
muscular hindquarters; short, powerful limbs
with long, strong forearms, strong, muscular
second thighs, large, flat joints and well-
shaped feet.

INTERESTING FACTS

By crossing Welsh Mountain Pony mares with
small Welsh Cobs breeders produced the
Welsh Pony of Cob Type (Section C in the
Stud Book), a smaller version of the Cob and
a marvellous all-round riding and driving pony.
It shares all the characteristics of its larger
cousin, but does not stand over 13.2hh. Like
the Cob, it was formerly much used by hill
farmers and also to transport slate from the
mines of North Wales. After World War II it
was in danger of becoming extinct, but its
numbers have since recovered and nowadays
it enjoys popularity as a trekking pony, a small
hunter and as a driving pony.

▌ RIGHT
A popular attraction in the show ring, the Welsh
Cob is also a good hunter and a marvellous all-
round performer in competitive sports.

Welsh Cob was traditionally used for all
manner of heavy work on the hill farms,
being equally at home in harness and
under saddle. It was also formerly much in
demand by the army, particularly for
pulling guns and other heavy equipment.
Possessed of active paces and great
stamina, the Welsh Cob is renowned above
all for its spectacular trotting action,
inherited no doubt from the Norfolk
Roadster. Indeed, up until 1918, when
stallion licensing was introduced,
breeding stock was selected by means of
trotting matches. Nowadays, not
surprisingly, the breed enjoys notable
success in the sport of carriage driving.

Unique among the British Mountain
and Moorland breeds, the Cob has no
upper height limit, but whatever its size it
should retain true pony characteristics –
its quality head testifying to its Welsh
Mountain Pony ancestry. When crossed
with the Thoroughbred (particularly the
second cross) the Welsh Cob produces
excellent competition horses.

▌ RIGHT
A quality head, depth
through the girth and
strong limbs, with an
abundance of flat
bone, are prerequisites
of this sturdy breed.

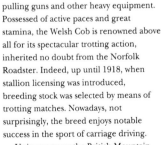

Highland

One of the strongest and heaviest of Britain's Mountain and Moorland breeds, the Highland Pony comes from the Highlands of Scotland and the islands off the west coast. Ponies are believed to have inhabited the region many thousands of years ago. The modern Highland Pony, sure-footed, hardy and long-lived, evolved as a result of various outcrosses, particularly Arab and Clydesdale. The Dukes of Atholl, influential breeders of Highland Ponies for several centuries, almost certainly introduced eastern blood as early as the sixteenth century.

Until fairly recently the breed was divided into two types: a more substantial mainland type, which stood up to 14.2hh,

and the lighter, somewhat smaller Western Isles type. Although the Highland Pony Society, founded in 1923, no longer recognizes these distinctions, differences in type can still be discerned to some extent.

The Highland is a strong, sturdily built pony, a real all-round worker which in its time has carried men to war, been the mount of shepherds, worked in harness, hauled timber, taken deer-stalkers into the hills and carried the shot stags – weighing

BREED DESCRIPTION

Height 13 – 14.2hh.

Colour Various shades of dun, also grey, brown, black and occasionally bay and liver chestnut with silver mane and tail.

Conformation Well-carried head with broad forehead, alert, kindly eyes and wide nostrils; strong, arched neck with clean throat; well laid-back shoulders; compact body with deep chest and well-sprung ribs; powerful hindquarters with strong, well-developed thigh and second thigh; strong limbs with short cannons, flat, hard bone and well-shaped, hard, dark hooves; silky feather, not over-heavy and ending in a prominent tuft at the fetlock; long, silky, flowing mane and tail.

■ LEFT
The Highland Pony is a willing worker. It is still used on Scottish estates to carry game panniers and to cart shot stags.

upwards of 16 stone (224lb/101kg) – back down. It is much used for pony trekking and makes a fine general-purpose riding pony, well able to carry an adult. Pure-breds can be seen taking part successfully in a number of competitive sports, including driving and dressage. Crossed with the Thoroughbred the Highland makes an excellent hunter and more than one successful three-day event horse has had Highland blood in its veins.

INTERESTING FACTS

One of the most striking features of the Highland is its colouring, particularly the various shades of dun: yellow, golden, mouse, cream and fox (yellow dun is believed to have been the breed's original colour). Most ponies show at least one of the characteristics of the primitive horse, i.e. a dorsal eel-stripe and zebra markings on the legs. These markings testify to the antiquity of the breed.

■ ABOVE
Highland Ponies are noted for the beauty of their coat colouring – including the whole range of duns – and for the silky texture of their abundant manes and tails.

■ BELOW
Versatility is one of the most valuable characteristics of the breed, which will haul timber as easily as it will carry a rider to hounds or go in harness.

■ OPPOSITE TOP
The Highland Pony's head is broad between the eyes, short from eyes to muzzle and well-carried on a strong, arched neck. The eyes have a kind expression.

■ OPPOSITE
Moulded by its harsh natural environment, the breed is strong, hardy, long lived and economical to feed. It is eminently sure-footed over the most treacherous terrain.

Shetland

Named after the remote group of islands situated to the far north-east of mainland Scotland and in the same northern latitude as south Greenland, the Shetland Pony is the smallest of the British native breeds. Its origins are uncertain but there have certainly been ponies in the Shetlands for many centuries and it may

▌ LEFT
The Shetland's profuse growth of mane and tail afford valuable protection from the severe weather of its northern homeland.

BREED DESCRIPTION

Height Not exceeding 40 inches (102cm) at three years or under. Not exceeding 42 inches (107cm) at four years or over.

Colour Any colour except spotted.

Conformation Small, well-carried head with broad forehead, bold, dark, intelligent eyes, small, erect ears and broad muzzle with wide open nostrils; strong, deep body with short back and muscular loins; broad, strong hindquarters; strong limbs, with good, flat bone and short cannons; tough, round, well-shaped feet.

well trace back to far more distant times.

Small of stature, it is nevertheless immensely strong – one of the strongest equine animals, in relation to size, in the world. Wonderfully well adapted to the vagaries of the islands' northern climate and the poor quality grazing, the Shetland is inherently hardy. Its action is free and straight, with a characteristic lift to its joints – the result of centuries of traversing rough, rocky or heather-covered terrain. An integral part of the lives of the

islanders, the ponies have traditionally been used both under saddle and as pack animals, carrying everything from grain to peat for fuel. They were formerly much in demand for coal mining, their small size and great strength making them perfect for work underground. Breeding flourished, though there was little attempt at selective breeding before the middle of the nineteenth century.

The Shetland has also found favour far from its native islands as a children's riding pony. It can be strong-willed but it is intelligent and responds to correct handling. With its active paces and manoeuvrability, it makes a particularly good driving pony and can be seen competing right up to international level.

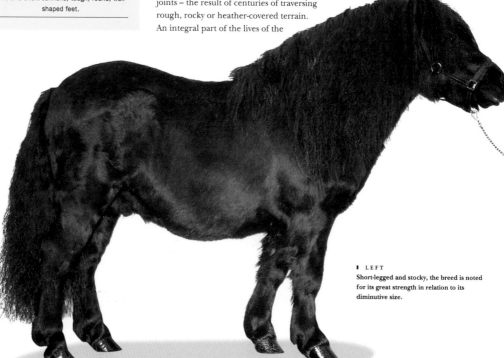

▌ LEFT
Short-legged and stocky, the breed is noted for its great strength in relation to its diminutive size.

I LEFT
Shetlands are very
active little ponies and
take part with great
enthusiasm in Shetland
"Grand Nationals",
which raise money for
charity.

I BELOW
In spring the Shetland
begins to shed its thick
winter coat, designed
to keep out extremes
of wet and cold.

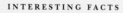

I ABOVE
Shetland Ponies can be wilful, but in the hands of a
competent child they make good riding ponies.

I RIGHT
Centuries of living on rough, rock-strewn terrain
have made the ponies both active and sure-footed.
Their feet are well-shaped and extremely hard.

INTERESTING FACTS

In winter the Shetland Pony grows a double
coat as protection against the inclement
climate of its native home. The coat has
"guard hairs", which shed rain and keep the
pony's skin completely dry, however severe
the weather. The mane and tail are profuse.

Dales

The Dales Pony comes from the Upper Dales (river valleys) of the eastern side of the Pennine Hills in northern England. It shares the same ancestors as its slightly larger neighbour, the Fell Pony, whose traditional home is on the western side of the Pennines. These ponies are believed to be descended from horses of the Roman period, when Friesians were introduced into northern England – this could have been the source of the Dales' predominantly black colouring. In more recent times various outcrosses are said to have been made, Norfolk Roadster among them. Some Welsh Cob blood was used during the nineteenth century and also Clydesdale. Despite the introduction of the latter, the Dales has retained its pony character, as can be seen in its neat head with its small, mobile ears.

The Dales is noted for its tremendously active paces and its great strength in relation to its size. At one time it played a vital part in lead mining, working both under- and overground, carrying loads of lead ore to the sea ports. It was also much

---

BREED DESCRIPTION

Height Not exceeding 14.2hh.

Colour Predominantly black, also bay, brown and, occasionally, grey.

Conformation Small, neat head, with wide forehead, bright eyes and small, erect ears; well-sloped shoulders; strong, deep body with short back, well-sprung ribs and strong loins; well-developed hindquarters; strong limbs with short straight cannons, good, clean joints and broad, very hard, well-shaped feet; fine, silky feather at the heel.

INTERESTING FACTS

Dales Ponies are inherently sure-footed. Their forebears are said to have been used by the Romans when constructing Hadrian's Wall in the inhospitable tract of country between the mouth of the River Tyne and the marshes of the Solway Firth in northern England.

---

used by the army. Stamina, courage and a docile temperament, coupled with its great strength and energy make the Dales a first-rate all-round riding and driving pony. It jumps, is intelligent, has a sensible, calm temperament and can carry an adult with ease.

▌ TOP
There have been native ponies on either side of the Pennines and in the Scottish borders for many centuries. They trace back in part to the Scottish Galloway although the Dales' black colouring probably comes from the influence of Friesian blood.

▌ LEFT
The breed is particularly renowned for its strong limbs, good bone and excellent feet.

Fell

Like its relative, the Dales, the Fell Pony is believed to be descended from the Friesian which was brought to northern England during Roman times. Down the centuries it, too, was almost certainly influenced by the now extinct Galloway, the mount of border reivers (raiders, particularly cattle thieves) who needed a strong, fast, sure-footed horse for their nefarious purposes.

BREED DESCRIPTION

Height Not exceeding 14hh.

Colour Black, brown, bay and grey, preferably with no white markings, though a star or a little white on the foot is allowed.

Conformation Small, well set-on head with broad forehead, bright, prominent eye, small, neat ears, large nostrils and fine throat and jaws; strong neck but not too heavy, giving a good length of rein; good, sloping shoulders; strong, deep body with muscular loins; strong hindquarters with well set-on tail; strong limbs with plenty of good flat bone below the knee and well-formed feet with characteristic blue horn.

The Fell has evolved as a somewhat smaller, lighter pony than the Dales (official recognition of a distinction between the two did not come until 1916, when the Dales Pony Improvement Society and the Fell Pony Society were formed). The Fell is, nevertheless, enormously strong and, like the Dales, was used as a pack-pony. During the eighteenth century it transported lead, coal and iron ore to the coast, carrying up to 16 stone (224lb/101kg) at a time in panniers. Some were used in pack-trains to carry produce such as wool as far as London.

The Fell is noted for its good paces, having a fast, active walk and a swift trot. Now that it is no longer in demand for pack work, shepherding and general farm work, it has become a popular all-round pleasure pony. It makes an excellent mount for trekking, goes superbly across country, both under saddle and in harness, and has the paces to do well in pure dressage.

❙ A B O V E
Fell ponies are native to the western side of the Pennines. They are slightly smaller than their near neighbours, the Dales, but have the same inherent toughness and active paces.

❙ B E L O W
The Fell makes a first-class riding pony. These ponies, pictured at a breed performance show, were competing in show jumping and mounted games as well as in show classes.

INTERESTING FACTS

HRH The Duke of Edinburgh competes in trials with a team of HM The Queen's Fell Ponies. With their lively trot and great stamina they are well suited to the marathon phase, run over a distance of 16 miles.

Connemara

Elegant, hardy, intelligent, possessed of tremendous agility and jumping prowess, the Connemara is arguably the best performance pony in the world. It is Ireland's only indigenous breed; it takes its name from the wild, rocky region on the western seaboard of Ireland where ponies have existed, in one form or another, since ancient times.

How this paragon among ponies developed is unclear. One theory is that it is descended from Barb and Spanish horses introduced into the west of Ireland as early as the sixth century BC, when the Celts overran the whole of Europe. These

LEFT
The Connemara's beautiful head possesses great refinement. Grey is the breed's predominant colour.

horses would then have been crossed with the indigenous stock. Also, during subsequent centuries of trade between the west coast of Ireland and the Iberian peninsula it is highly likely that quantities of horses would have been imported. The breed undoubtedly does show signs of Spanish and eastern blood to this day. The suggestion that the Connemara is descended from horses of the Spanish Armada that swam ashore after being shipwrecked in 1588 is nowadays dismissed by most experts as mere fancy!

Arab stallions are known to have been imported by landowners during the middle of the nineteenth century, but it is impossible to say what influence, if any, they had on the Connemara. During the latter part of the century, however, Welsh

BREED DESCRIPTION

Height Not exceeding 14.2hh.

Colour Predominantly grey but also brown, dun, black and occasionally chestnut and roan.

Conformation Short head, often with slightly dished profile, with broad forehead, dark, full eyes, small ears; long, arched neck giving good length of rein; well-sloped shoulders; deep, compact body; strong hindquarters with high-set tail; good strong limbs with short cannons and plenty of bone below the knee; strong, sound feet.

RIGHT
Excellent conformation - notably the well-sloped shoulders - make the Connemara a superb riding pony, possessed of strength, free-going movement and superb balance.

blood was certainly introduced and did play a part: one of the Welsh stallions, Prince Llewellyn, sired Dynamite out of a native mare. Dynamite in turn sired Cannon Ball (foaled in 1904), who is the first stallion listed in the Connemara Stud Book. Other attempts to "improve" the breed included the use of Thoroughbred, Hackney and Clydesdale blood.

Finally, in 1923, the Connemara Pony Breeders' Society was founded in Galway. It had the backing of the Department of Agriculture and the intention was to improve the breed from within, by seeking out the best type of mare and an appropriate number of similar quality

▌ ABOVE
Connemaras in their natural habitat of western Ireland.

▌ BELOW
Traditional pony power: carting seaweed in Galway.

stallions to use as foundation stock. The result of these efforts is an outstanding, quality pony of fixed type, courageous but sensible, able to excel in virtually all sports, from show jumping and three-day eventing to dressage and driving. When crossed with the Thoroughbred it produces a top-class performance horse.

▌ ABOVE
As a ridden pony the Connemara cannot be bettered. Spirited but sensible, courageous but kind, it is an ideal mount for children and adults alike.

Fjord

Norway's unusual looking Fjord Pony is believed to have inhabited Norway and probably other parts of Scandinavia since prehistoric times. At a quick glance it is not unlike the Przewalski's Horse (the Asiatic Wild Horse) in appearance, though the head is much less heavy and "primitive", being more pony-like in size and shape. Ponies resembling the Fjord are depicted in Viking art. They can be seen fighting, a pastime which was also popular in Iceland and which may have been engaged in for sport, as a form of performance testing or, probably, a combination of both.

Hundreds if not thousands of years spent in a mountainous habitat have

produced a pony that is perfectly adapted to its environment. Sturdy and muscular, the Fjord has short, strong legs with good joints and hard, sound feet. Down the centuries its inherent sure-footedness, strength, soundness and tremendous stamina have made it an invaluable

helpmate to farmers. Used to coping with severe weather conditions and undaunted by the most rugged terrain, it also proved the perfect pack-pony for use on mountain trails.

Nowadays the Fjord Pony can be found in a number of countries outside Scandinavia, including Germany, Denmark and England. It makes a good general-purpose riding pony and also goes well in harness.

BREED DESCRIPTION

Height 13 – 14hh.

Colour Most shades of dun with a black dorsal eel-stripe and, often, zebra markings on the legs.

Conformation Pony-type head with broad forehead and small ears; muscular neck; strong, deep body; fairly low-set tail; short, strong limbs with good joints, short cannons and plenty of bone; hard, sound feet.

Although its natural
environment is the
mountains, the
adaptable Fjord can be
found in many other
types of country,
where it is valued both
for its attractive
appearance and its
performance ability.

■ OPPOSITE TOP
The Fjord has a true pony head, with small ears,
large, wide-set eyes and a small muzzle which is
lighter in colour than the rest of the coat.

■ OPPOSITE
The pony's stocky build testifies to its great
strength. Deep through the girth and with a
particularly muscular neck and strong legs,
it is a great little worker in areas not accessible
to machines.

■ LEFT
The striking colouring
of the mane and tail,
with their black and
silver hair, is unique to
the Fjord Pony.

■ RIGHT
Fjords make excellent driving ponies. They have a
kind, willing temperament but are active movers
and, like all mountain breeds, exceptionally sure-
footed.

INTERESTING FACTS

One of the most distinctive features of the
Fjord Pony is its unusual mane and tail
colouring. Both mane and tail have black
hairs in the centre, with silver on the
outside. The stiff mane is traditionally cut in
a curve with the dark inner hair standing
higher than the outer silver hair.

Caspian

In 1965 an exciting discovery was made in northern Iran, in a remote, mountainous region not far from the Caspian Sea. Some three dozen miniature horses, no taller than a small pony but with the outward characteristics of a diminutive horse, were found. Detailed scientific examination revealed that these little horses had certain physical characteristics that did not match those of other horses: an extra full-sized molar on each side of the upper jaw; a scapula that was a different shape from that usually found in equine animals, and a slightly different formation of the three parietal bones in the head.

The Caspian Pony, as it has become known, is believed to be the direct descendant of the earliest equine animals that roamed the region around 3,000 BC. Bones have been excavated in Iran that point to the existence in the area of a very similar small horse at that period, a seal in the British Museum shows King Darius riding in a chariot drawn by horses of

Caspian type, and other artefacts of the period exist depicting similar small horses. It is thought possible that the Caspian is a far-off ancestor of the Arabian.

For many centuries the Caspian was mysteriously "lost". After its re-discovery a careful breeding programme was set up at studs in order to safeguard its future. Caspian Ponies can now be found in a number of European countries as well as Australia, New Zealand and the United States.

The Caspian is extremely hardy, and possesses great speed and endurance as well as a kind temperament. It has dense bone and exceptionally hard, tough feet, which do not require shoeing. It makes a good riding pony and despite its small size has remarkable jumping ability.

TOP
The skin on the Caspian's short, refined head is particularly fine. The ears should be no more than 4½ inches (11.5cm) long.

ABOVE
On account of its small size the breed is described as a pony, although it has all the attributes of a miniature horse.

INTERESTING FACTS

Despite its lack of height, the Caspian has wonderful natural action; it can keep up with a horse at walk, trot and canter. Even at this early age the foal shows tremendous length of stride.

Riding Pony

I BELOW
The Riding Pony looks like a miniature
Thoroughbred but should have the characteristics
of a pony, not a horse. A good length of neck and
well-sloped shoulders ensure the required freedom
of movement.

Any pony which can be ridden is,
technically, a "riding pony" but the Riding
Pony which has been developed in Britain
for showing purposes has evolved into a
very definite type. It is essentially a child's
hack, the equivalent of the adult rider's
Thoroughbred show hack. It is not,
therefore, surprising that small
Thoroughbreds have been used in its
development. Together with the Arab, the
Thoroughbred was crossed with native
ponies, particularly the Welsh and the
Dartmoor, to produce ponies of great
quality and excellent conformation. The
best examples, while resembling the
Thoroughbred in miniature, will not have
lost the bone and substance of the native
ponies and should certainly look like
ponies, not small horses.

Since it is by definition a child's mount,
the Riding Pony must have a sensible
nature and be safe for children to ride;
but since it is also a show pony, it must
have presence and the long, low, graceful
action of the Thoroughbred. The perfect
combination of these elements, together
with the retention of true pony character,
is the challenge faced by all breeders of
Riding Ponies. Riding Ponies may be
entered in the National Pony Society Stud
Book.

BREED DESCRIPTION

Height Show class divisions – up to
12.2hh, 12.2 – 13.2hh and 13.2 – 14.2hh.

Colour Any whole colour; white markings
are permissible.

Conformation Fine, quality head, with large,
well-spaced eyes and small ears; fairly long
neck; good sloping shoulders with clearly
defined withers; medium length back, deep
through the girth; well-muscled hindquarters
with well set-on tail; clean, hard limbs with flat
joints, short cannons and well let-down hocks;
good, sound feet of equal size; no feather.

INTERESTING FACTS

In the show ring, as well as the height divisions there are classes for ponies ridden
side-saddle, for pairs of ponies and for novice ponies. Ponies are judged on their
paces, conformation and manners but are not required to jump.

Pony of the Americas

This breed of spotted pony originated in the 1950s, the foundation sire, Black Hand, being the result of a mating between a Shetland pony stallion and an Appaloosa mare. Black Hand was the equivalent of a miniature Appaloosa. Interest in this concept of a spotted pony soon spread and the Pony of the Americas, as it became known, is now a popular all-round riding pony throughout the United States and also in Canada. It has its own breed society and stud book.

The Pony of the Americas stands no more than 13.2hh and must have one of the recognized Appaloosa colourings. It should be well proportioned, with substance, style and refinement – something like a miniature cross between a Quarter Horse and an Arabian. The pony's paces should be smooth and the action straight and free. The Pony of the Americas is a versatile performer. It is shown in Western pleasure and performance classes, as well as under English saddles and in harness. It has a kind nature and makes an ideal all-round riding pony for children.

▌ ABOVE
The head is clean cut and the pony has a kind eye, which reflects its docile, friendly nature.

▌ BELOW
In overall appearance the Pony of the Americas is not unlike the Quarter Horse, but with more refinement.

INTERESTING FACTS

Leslie Boomhower, of Mason City, Iowa, was responsible for the mating of Shetland to Appaloosa which produced the breed's foundation sire.

BREED DESCRIPTION

Height 11.2–13.2hh.

Colour Normal Appaloosa markings – leopard, snowflake, blanket, frost, marble.

Conformation Clean-cut head, sometimes with slightly dished profile, with large, kind, prominent eyes and medium-sized, alert ears; slightly arched neck; deep, sloping shoulders with prominent withers; round, full-ribbed, heavily muscled body with well-sprung ribs and short back and loins; muscular hindquarters with long, level croup; strong limbs, with good clean joints; wide, well-shaped feet.

American Shetland

Shetland Ponies were first imported into America during the 1880s and quickly became popular. In 1890, when the American Shetland Pony Club was formed, there were over two hundred listed American breeders – Buffalo Bill Cody featuring prominently among them. Today there are large numbers of American Shetlands but, although they retain the name "Shetland", they do not bear a great deal of resemblance to the native "Sheltie" of Britain's Shetland Isles.

The American Shetland is the result of crossing pure-bred Shetlands with Hackney Ponies, with the addition of a little Arab and Thoroughbred blood. In appearance it is more like a Hackney than a British native pony. It is more refined than the true Shetland, being somewhat narrower and longer in the body and with longer, more slender limbs. The head, too, has lost the true pony character. Its high, extravagant action, which testifies to the infusion of Hackney blood, makes the American Shetland a popular harness pony.

BREED DESCRIPTION

Height Up to around 42 inches (103cm).

Colour Any.

Conformation Fairly long head with straight or slightly dished profile; long, graceful neck with pronounced withers; sloping shoulders; short, strong body and hindquarters; fairly long limbs.

❚ LEFT
The American Shetland usually stands a couple of inches (5cm) taller than the true Shetland. The same range of colours occurs as in the original Scottish breed.

INTERESTING FACTS

The high-stepping action produced through the infusions of Hackney blood, has resulted in a pony well suited to harness classes. As with the American gaited horses, the action is enhanced by means of growing the feet longer than normal. Shetlands compete in classes for singles, pairs and tandems as well as in draught harness and under saddle.

❚ ABOVE
Due to the addition of Hackney, Arab and Thoroughbred blood, the American Shetland has lost, in varying degrees, the true native pony character of its British ancestors.

Types

Horses and ponies with unusual or exotic coat colours and patterns have occurred throughout history and have usually been highly prized by man, regardless of their breeding. In recent times registers or stud books have been opened in some countries for the most popular of these colour types – in fact some now qualify for the title "breeds". The term "breed" is used to describe horses who have been bred selectively over a period of time and who have, as a result, developed fixed characteristics. Horses belonging to a particular breed have their pedigrees recorded in a stud book. The term "type" describes a horse bred for a particular purpose, such as hunting. Any number of permutations can be (and are) used to produce a horse suitable for riding to hounds and hunters cannot therefore be described as a breed. Horse and pony types, although few in number compared with the established breeds, nevertheless have an important role to play in the world of leisure riding.

Appaloosa

The spotted coat colouring of the American Appaloosa traces back to stock imported by the Spanish Conquistadores. Spotted horses became particularly prized by the Nez Percé Indian tribe who lived in the region that is now northern Idaho, north-east Oregon and south-east Washington. The word Appaloosa is derived from Palouse country, an area named after the Palouse river.

The Nez Percé are said to be the first Indian tribe to have practised systematic breeding of horses. Following the defeat of the Indians by the US army during the latter half of the nineteenth century, the horses which escaped slaughter became

■ LEFT
The eye-catching markings of the American Appaloosa are derived from Spanish stock imported by the Conquistadores.

■ BELOW LEFT
The Appaloosa is a compact, muscular stamp of horse. The sparse mane and tail hair are characteristic of the breed.

scattered. It was not until the 1920s that efforts were made to re-establish the Appaloosa horse, using the descendants of those which survived as a basis. In 1938 the Appaloosa Horse Club was founded in Oregon. Its objectives were to collect records and historical data relating to the origin of the Appaloosa, to preserve, improve and standardize the breed and to set up a register for approved animals.

The re-establishment of the Appaloosa has been a great success and today the breed is widely used in all types of Western riding, for endurance riding and in the show ring in both hunter and jumper classes. Appaloosas are mainly associated

Registry the foal m[...]
"natural" Paint mar[...]
minimum of 2 inch[...]
If a horse does not[...]
colour requiremer[...]
registration requi[...]
solid-coloured foa[...]
mating between t[...]
Paint Horses), it r[...]
Breeding Stock R[...]

The spectrum[...]
Paint Horse enco[...]
known in the ho[...]
range from almo[...]
minimal amoun[...]
white with mini[...]
are distinguishe[...]
on the horse, th[...]
overo and tobia[...]

Overo horse[...]
characteristics:[...]
cross the back[...]
withers and th[...]
and often all f[...]
generally the [...]
scattered or s[...]
to as calico; h[...]

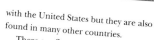

▮ LEFT
This horse and rider, decked out in traditional style, recall the time when spotted horses were the preferred mounts of the Nez Percé Indians.

▮ FAR LEFT
Spotted horses are popular in many countries outside the United States. There is a thriving Appaloosa society in Britain – this horse was photographed at the Royal Windsor Horse Show.

with the United States but they are also found in many other countries.

There are five main Appaloosa coat patterns: leopard – white colouring over the loins and hips with dark, round or egg-shaped spots; snowflake – dark spots all over a white body but usually dominant over the hips; blanket – white area over the hips without dark spots in the white; marble – mottled all over the body; frost – white specks with a dark background. Other distinguishing features include white sclera round the eyes and, often, vertical black and white stripes on the hooves. The mane and tail tend to be quite sparse.

▮ LEFT
Noted for its strong limbs and the excellence of its feet, the Appaloosa makes a good endurance riding horse.

175

Pai

Horses with
known as pic
found all ov
particularly
American I

In Amer
colouring r
Paint Hors
the horse r
American
founded i
horses wit
of contras
and distin
To qualif

Knabstrup

Spotted horses have been known – and have often been highly prized – since ancient times. They can be seen in early Chinese art and there were spotted strains of the Noriker (Austria's old-established light draught breed) and the Spanish horses which were so influential in the development of many of the world's modern breeds. Denmark's once-famous Knabstrup is of Spanish ancestry and dates back to the time of the Napoleonic Wars. At that time a spotted mare named Flaebehoppen was acquired by a butcher called Flaebe (hence her name). Flaebehoppen, an exceptionally fast mare possessed of great endurance, was bred by her next owner, Judge Lunn, to Frederiksborg horses and founded a line of spotted horses. Named the Knabstrup, after Lunn's estate, this strain was rather less substantial than the Frederiksborg but

INTERESTING FACTS

The breed's remarkable talents as a circus horse were demonstrated in America not so long ago when a centre-ring attraction consisted of a large Bengal tiger riding a Knabstrup horse. The horse wore protective harness – in case the big cat slipped and decided to hang on with his claws!

BREED DESCRIPTION

Height Around 15.2 – 16hh.

Colour Mainly white, with brown or black spots of varying size over the body, head and legs.

Conformation Variable, but the best examples have reasonably good overall conformation, with a kind, intelligent head. The mane and tail are usually sparse, as in the majority of spotted horses.

was tough and sound and, because of its attractive markings, became popular as a circus horse. Subsequent crossings back to the Frederiksborg reduced the number of pure-bred Knabstrup horses but examples of the breed are still to be found, though not in anywhere near the numbers of the American Appaloosa.

❚ TOP LEFT
The mottled skin colouring of the lips and muzzle, so typical of all spotted horses, can be clearly seen on this Knabstrup.

❚ LEFT
The characteristic white body hair with all-over dark spots, together with its intelligent, kind nature, made the Knabstrup a popular circus horse.

Spotted Pony

Spotted Ponies are known to have existed in Britain, and especially in Wales and the West Country, for many centuries. The Romans are said to have brought spotted horses into the country and some of the ancestors of today's Spotted Ponies would have been imported Spanish horses. The creation of a breed society for these striking looking animals is, however, of very recent origin. A British register for spotted horses and ponies was created in 1947 and then in 1976 the organizing society was split, with ponies up to 14.2hh coming under the aegis of the British Spotted Pony Society and larger animals being entered in the British Appaloosa registers.

To qualify for registration ponies must display some of the following features: white sclera round the eye; mottled skin – this part-dark, part-pink skin is usually most evident around the genitals, lips, muzzle, eyes and inside the ears; and striped hooves. If ponies are of solid colour but have proven spotted breeding,

BREED DESCRIPTION

Height Not exceeding 14.2hh.

Colour Leopard (spots of any colour on white or light background); few spot leopard (white base coat with few spots); snowflake (white spots on dark base coat); blanket (area of white over hips and hindquarters, with or without spots, any base colour).

Conformation Quality pony head with big, bold eyes set well apart, small, neat, well-placed ears, prominent, open nostrils and clean, well-defined throat; good length of neck, moderately lean in mares, inclined to be more cresty in stallions (slightly heavier neck allowed in cob type); good, strong, sloping shoulders, well laid back, with well-defined withers; strong, muscular body with deep girth and well-sprung ribs; lengthy, strong, well-muscled hindquarters with well set-on tail (slightly finer hindquarters in riding type); good limbs, with long, strong forearms, well-developed knee, well let-down hocks, short cannons; well-shaped, dense hooves.

INTERESTING FACTS

As with all colour types, breeding for spots is a question of genetics. Some ponies which have spotted coats when young may lose their spots as they grow older. They are known as "faders". Fading is caused by the dominant grey gene. Raised spots, that is ones that stand out above the rest of the pony's coat, rarely fade. The colour of the foal's coat cannot be used as a guide to the adult pony's colouring, since the colour often changes with the first change of coat.

they are eligible for entry in a separate register but they should preferably show some breed characteristics. Piebald and skewbald ponies are not eligible, nor are their progeny.

Spotted Ponies may be of small, riding or cob type, but all should show true pony character and must have bone, substance and active paces. They make good all-round performance ponies, both under saddle and in harness, and there is growing interest in ridden and in-hand show classes. British Spotted Ponies have been exported to Australia, North America and several European countries, including France, Germany and Holland. Indeed, the demand from overseas has led to so many good mares and stallions being exported that the breed society has now introduced performance and sire-rating awards in order to encourage breeders to keep more of the best stock at home.

▌ TOP LEFT
The British Spotted Pony has the large, expressive eyes, neat, mobile ears and open nostrils that are characteristic of all good types of pony.

▌ LEFT
Versatile and strong, the British Spotted Pony makes a good all-round riding pony and has also been used with great success in four-in-hand driving.

Hunter

As its name implies, a hunter is a horse used for riding to hounds. It is a type, not a breed, and there is no fixed "recipe" for producing a hunter. It is, however, generally accepted that the finest hunters are bred in Ireland, Britain and, to some extent, the United States.

The type of horse required for hunting varies according to the nature of the country hunted – a big, quality Thoroughbred type may be perfect for galloping and jumping over the grassland of the English "shires", but will be less than ideal for areas of heavy plough or trappy hill country, where boldness and speed are less important than steadiness and sure-footedness. Whatever the exact type of horse required, however, a hunter must have correct conformation, without which he is unlikely to stand up to the

hard work required of him. He must be well balanced and give a comfortable ride. He needs to be agile and fearless but also well mannered and controllable. He must have the necessary speed to keep up with hounds and the stamina to see him through a long day of physical exertion, often twice a week during the hunting season. He must also have jumping ability,

the exact degree depending on the type of country hunted.

The Irish hunter is often produced by crossing the Thoroughbred with the Irish Draught, while many of the best British hunters have an element of native pony blood, again laced with Thoroughbred. There is no fixed height and in hunter showing classes in Britain and Ireland the horses are divided according to their weight-carrying ability.

▌ ABOVE LEFT
In the show hunter, the judge is looking for as near perfect conformation as possible. The horse must also give a good ride and be well mannered.

▌ LEFT
Depth through the girth is essential to allow for expansion of the lungs. Well-sloped shoulders ensure free-going action. The horse's weight-carrying ability is determined by its overall build and the amount of bone (measured round the cannon, below the knee).

BREED DESCRIPTION

Height From 14.2hh upwards.

Colour Any.

Conformation Well set-on head and neck, giving good length of rein; well-sloped shoulders; strong, shortish back with well-sprung ribs and great depth through the girth; strong loins; powerful hindquarters; strong limbs with large joints and plenty of bone; strong, well-shaped feet.

Cob

The cob is a short-legged "stuffy" type of small horse, stocky in appearance and capable of carrying a heavyweight rider. Its kind, unflappable, willing nature and impeccable manners, coupled with its weight-carrying ability, make it an ideal mount for a heavyweight elderly rider – or indeed for anyone who is not particularly athletic.

As with the hunter, there is no set formula for breeding a cob. Many of the best are produced by chance, although Irish Draught blood is often used with great success, particularly when mixed with Thoroughbred. The cob's sturdy, muscular proportions are not designed for great speed, but it should none the less have active paces and be able to gallop and to jump well.

At one time the cob was used as an all-purpose horse, performing equally well in harness and under saddle. Nowadays it is most often seen as a riding horse – the best make excellent hunters.
Under British Show Hack and Cob Association

INTERESTING FACTS

In the show ring cobs are judged like hunters and are expected to show that they can gallop. The judge rides each exhibit in turn to assess the quality of ride they give.

rules, cobs are exhibited in two weight classes: as lightweights, capable of carrying up to 14 stone (196lb/89kg) and as heavyweights, capable of carrying over 14 stone. There are also working cob classes, in which the horses must jump a working hunter-type course of fences.

The cob's mane is traditionally hogged (cut short). It used to be the custom to dock the tail of cobs but this cruel practice was made illegal in Britain under the Docking and Nicking Act, 1948.

ABOVE RIGHT
Good conformation ensures that the cob possesses tremendous freedom of movement despite its chunky proportions.

RIGHT
The overall impression of this most workmanlike of horses should be one of intelligence, calmness and reliability.

TYPE DESCRIPTION

Height Up to about 15.3hh (in show classes not over 15.1hh).

Colour Any.

Conformation Intelligent-looking head, with no suggestion of coarseness; fairly short, arched neck; strong, sloping shoulders; broad, deep body with short back and powerful loins; strong, well-muscled hindquarters; short, strong limbs with plenty of bone; broad, open feet.

Hack

In Britain the hack is a supremely elegant, refined type of show horse – although the word "hack" is also used to describe any horse suitable for general riding purposes (as opposed to competitive sports, such as eventing or hunting).

The term hack goes back to the days before the motorization of transport, when "park hacks" were used by the most fashionable people of the day for leisure riding, notably in London's Rotten Row, in Hyde Park. In appearance and manners the park hack was impeccable, thus complementing its elegant, well turned-out rider. In the hunting world riders formerly made use of the "covert hack", a quality horse with less substance than a hunter, to take them to the meet – their grooms having ridden the hunters on beforehand at a leisurely pace to conserve their energy for the day ahead.

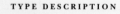

ABOVE
Gaiety and lightness of movement are essential attributes of the show hack.

Today's show hack is nearer to the park hack and is usually Thoroughbred, or near Thoroughbred. It is judged on conformation, presence, action, training, ride and manners – it should give a comfortable ride and its manners should be faultless. During judging, horses are usually required to give a solo show, designed to demonstrate the horse's correct training and obedience. It should include walk, trot and canter on both reins and a good halt, with the horse standing still on a loose rein.

TYPE DESCRIPTION

Height 14.2 – 15.3hh.

Colour Any solid colour.

Conformation Small, quality head; elegant neck; well-sloped shoulders with prominent withers; strong body with deep girth and well-sprung ribs; well-rounded hindquarters; good, sound limbs with at least 8 inches (20cm) of bone; good, sound feet.

INTERESTING FACTS

Hacks are shown in two height classes: small hack, for horses exceeding 14.2hh but not exceeding 15hh, and large hack, for horses exceeding 15hh but not exceeding 15.3hh. There are also classes for ladies' hacks (14.2 – 15.3hh) in which horses are shown under side-saddle.

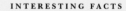
LEFT
The hack has the overall refinement of the Thoroughbred. It must give a smooth, comfortable ride and have perfect manners.

Polo Pony

▌ FOLLOWING PAGE
Mares and foals at grass in Kentucky.

▌ LEFT
A typically intelligent looking Argentinian polo pony. It is customary to hog the mane to prevent the hair obstructing the player's stick.

The ancient game of polo is believed to have originated in Persia some 2,500 years ago. It was subsequently played in India, the Far East and Tibet, reaching the western world – England and then North and South America – during the nineteenth century. Any pony used in the game is technically a polo pony but the modern polo pony has evolved as a definite type. Many of the best animals are bred in Argentina or at least are descended from Argentinian stock.

By the beginning of the twentieth century the sport was well established in Argentina, where breeders produced suitable mounts by crossing their Criollo horses with imported Welsh ponies. After the 14.2hh height limit for polo ponies was abolished in 1919 the Argentinians began introducing English Thoroughbred blood, which produced animals of greater quality and with more speed.

The polo pony must be capable of short bursts of speed but does not require the long stride of a racehorse. Far more important is a smooth action, which makes the rider's job of hitting the ball easier, the ability to accelerate and decelerate quickly, and to make fast turns. The essential qualities of the polo pony are courage, stamina and natural balance.

▌ RIGHT
Whatever their height, polo ponies are always referred to as "ponies", not horses.

TYPE DESCRIPTION

Height Around 15.1hh.

Colour Any.

Conformation Variable, the chief requirements being: fairly long, well-muscled neck; sloping shoulders with well-defined withers; strong, deep body with fairly short back and well-sprung ribs; well-rounded, muscular hindquarters; strong limbs with short cannons, good joints and plenty of bone; well-shaped, round feet.

INTERESTING FACTS

Between the two World Wars some of the best polo players were to be found in India, where the game was popular both with members of the native aristocracy and in the Indian army. The game there was immortalized by Rudyard Kipling (1865–1936) in *The Maltese Cat*, the story of an inter-regimental match seen through the eyes of the equine participants. A flea-bitten grey, brilliantly quick on his feet, "The Cat" knows more about "playing the game" than most humans!

Horse and
Pony Care

Buying a Horse

Everyone who takes part in sport on a regular basis reaches
the stage when they want their own equipment. Whether it is
a tennis racquet, a fencing foil, a pair of skis or a yacht,
owning rather than hiring makes life easier on two counts: the
equipment will be available whenever it is required and, most
importantly, the owner's performance will almost certainly
improve because that equipment will have been selected with
their skills and limitations in mind. Riders, however, are faced
with a problem not encountered by other sportsmen: their
most important piece of equipment is not a man-made object
which, to varying degrees, can be tailored to fit individual
needs. The horse is a living creature, with a mind, will and
personality of his own. He is an expensive animal both to buy
and to keep. Choosing the right one is not always easy;
choosing the wrong one can be disastrous, both for an
owner's bank balance and for his or her confidence. The
prospective horse owner should proceed with caution and the
rewards will be great.

Choosing the Right Horse

Before you buy a horse make an honest assessment of your riding ability, bearing in mind that most people tend to over-estimate their skill. Talented, experienced riders get the best from all sorts of horses, even those with difficult temperaments. They can school and bring on the young horse, improve the poorly educated older one and ensure that the well-trained performer is used to the best effect. A novice rider, who has only just mastered the basics of horsemanship, can do none of these things and should choose a mount accordingly. The novice needs a correctly schooled, well-mannered mount with a kind disposition, one who will look after his rider. The term "schoolmaster" is aptly used to describe these equine paragons.

For the majority of people cost is one of the most important factors and the purchase price will be determined by a number of things: the type, size and conformation of the horse or pony; its age; its temperament and manners; its performance capabilities (either proven or potential) and its level of schooling.

▮ PREVIOUS PAGE OPPOSITE
A Dartmoor pony: a suitable ride for a child.
▮ PREVIOUS PAGE
A Karbardin horse: ideal for endurance riding.
▮ LEFT
With the right horse, the experience of ownership will be enjoyable and rewarding for both horse and rider.

Generally speaking, an unbroken two- or three-year-old will be cheaper than a four- or five-year-old which has already received some schooling; after that the horse gradually increases in value until it reaches the age of about ten. Once into its teens, it will tend to decrease in value.

Apart from price, your choice of horse or pony will be determined by your size and weight; your riding ability; your stabling/grazing facilities; the amount of

▮ RIGHT
The majority of warmbloods, specifically developed as sports horses, make fine show jumpers. This horse is a Holstein.

▮ BELOW
The larger British native ponies, like this Highland, are suitable for adult riders as well as children. They are economical to keep.

time you have to look after it, and the use to which you intend to put it. For example, there is no point in spending a lot of money on a flighty Thoroughbred if you are a nervous rider who wants to do no more than go for quiet hacks; similarly, a pure-bred Arab is not going to take you to the top in the show-jumping world. As to size, much depends on your own build – someone with long legs will certainly be more comfortable on a big horse than someone with short legs and vice versa, and it is usually easier to ride well if you are neither under- nor over-horsed. Temperament and manners are a vital consideration, too. Nervous riders need placid (though not lazy) mounts if they are not to be frightened and put off riding altogether, while a bolder rider will be able to cope with, and enjoy, a more spirited ride.

❙ BELOW
If quiet hacks out are your aim, make sure you don't choose the horse who is too spirited.

❙ RIGHT
For endurance riding, choose a horse with proven stamina. Arabs and part-bred Arabs are particularly suited to the higher levels of this sport.

Then there is the question of how much time you can devote to looking after your horse. If you have a full-time job, and limited time for weekday exercising, life will be easier for you and your horse if he can live out or at least be turned out during the day.

If you are not planning to do a lot of strenuous competition work, then age need not be too much of a factor, though of course the older the animal the more work he is likely to have done and the more wear and tear there will have been on his legs and body by the time you buy him. However, for general riding purposes horses and ponies often go on well into their late teens and even early twenties. A young horse will, of course, have many more useful years ahead of him and will be easier to sell on for a good price. However, young horses are not suitable for the novice rider, who will be unable to give them the necessary schooling.

❙ BOTTOM
Experienced riders will be able to school young horses, but novice riders should learn on a more experienced horse.

Unless you are planning to become involved in an activity which requires a specific breed – such as a particular category of showing – you will have a wide variety of breeds and types to choose from. Always bear in mind, however, your intended use for the horse: for endurance riding he will need great stamina; for eventing, stamina plus speed; for dressage, excellent movement. While stallions often excel in the last named discipline and are increasingly seen in other types of equine competition as well, they do require more expert handling than geldings and mares, and are not suitable for the novice horse owner. Mares can be more moody and take rather more understanding than geldings (very often, though, a good competition mare is very good indeed). They do, of course, come into season regularly during the summer months and this can be a problem.

If you have good stabling and grazing facilities, you can keep any type or breed without a problem. Lack of stabling will tend to determine what you can or cannot buy, particularly if you live in a region where the winters are cold and wet and/or the summers excessively hot. A British native pony will do perfectly well living out all year round, provided supplementary feed is given in winter, as necessary. A thin-skinned Thoroughbred, on the other hand, may not thrive unless he has the shelter of a stable, at least at night. If you wish to keep your horse at peak fitness for competition work or hunting, you will certainly need the use of a stable.

Where to Buy

There are various ways to buy a horse. These include at a public sale, through a dealer, from a private vendor advertising in the equestrian or local press, or perhaps from the riding school where you have been taking lessons.

The novice rider is generally advised not to buy at a public sale. The problem is not that all sales are conducted by less than reputable people – that is certainly not the case – but that everything takes place so quickly and there may not be sufficient opportunity for the purchaser to ride the horse. Buying in this way calls for an expert, practised eye and it is incumbent upon the purchaser to be observant. For instance, if a horse offered for sale has an obvious physical defect, the onus is on the purchaser to see it – a subsequent plea of ignorance will not be accepted. On the other hand the horse must correspond to its description – a horse described as a show jumper must be able to jump – and the buyer is entitled to return it if this proves not to be the case (or, if necessary, to sue for damages).

Dealers are businessmen with a reputation to maintain and are unlikely to try to sell you a bad lot. Your local riding school may be able to put you in touch with one or, failing that, you may see them

advertising in the equestrian press. The advantages of buying through a dealer are that you will almost certainly have the choice of several horses and there should be plenty of opportunity to see them being handled and to ride them yourself. Some dealers may also allow you to try the horse at home and, if you have a horse to sell, may offer part-exchange terms.

Buying from a private vendor – and there are always a great many advertising in the equestrian and farming press as well as in local newspapers – may seem the simplest way of acquiring a horse but it is not necessarily the safest. Here the rule is *caveat emptor* (let the buyer beware), a common law maxim warning you that you cannot claim that your purchase is defective if you have not obtained express guarantees from the vendor. Many of the horses and ponies described in the "For Sale" columns are up for sale for perfectly genuine reasons but others may not be. It

is easy to compose an advertisement praising their good points but omitting their shortcomings. Just because a horse is good to box and shoe does not mean that he is quiet to clip or sensible in traffic. The brilliant jumper may refuse to go into a horsebox or trailer. The otherwise perfect equine specimen may, when you get him home, persist in jumping out of his paddock, refuse to be caught, or chew his stable, his rugs, his bandages – or all three. Often it is not so much what the advertisement does say but what it omits to say, so you must be prepared to ask the right questions.

If you have been attending a good riding school, the proprietor should be able to advise on the purchase of a horse or pony and may well have one on the premises which would suit you. The advantage here is that the instructor will have a good knowledge of your skills and limitations as a rider.

Trying a Horse

■ BELOW
When trying a horse, ride him at different paces
and have a jump if you wish.

When you learn of a horse which you think may suit your purpose, the first step is to make an appointment to see it and try it. Always take a more knowledgeable person along with you both to offer expert advice and to act as a witness to any sale. If you have no one who will do this as a friend, it is worth paying for an expert opinion.

Explain to the vendor exactly what you want to use the horse for and ask specific questions: is the horse good to box, clip, shoe, catch, in traffic, etc. Ask to see the horse led up outside and pay close attention to how he behaves while he is having his rugs removed and his bridle put on. Note the bit which is being used. Cast an eye around the inside of the stable and the door for signs of kick marks or chewing. It may be that this is not the horse's usual box but if it is, such signs could indicate a behavioural problem. Ask to see the horse stood up outside and view him from both sides to assess his conformation before having him walked and trotted up. Make sure that he is trotted up on a loose rein both away from you and towards you (leading a horse on a short rein can help to cover up defective action).

Before you ride him, watch the vendor put him through his paces to see how he goes with a familiar rider. Then ask your expert adviser to try him. If the vendor failed to ask the horse to do certain things, such as strike off on a particular leg at canter, it may be that there is a problem, and your adviser (who should have noticed even if you have not) can look into the matter. Finally, ride the horse yourself. Does he feel right for you: not too big, not too wide, not too narrow? Is there a good length of rein? Put him through his paces, have a jump if you wish, take him out on the road to make sure he is safe in traffic and generally try to get the feel of him.

It is not easy in a relatively short time to assess whether this is the horse you really

want to have on a long-term basis, so if possible arrange to have him at home on trial, say for a week. This will enable you to get to know his character, to ride him in more relaxed circumstances and also to get to know more about his general behaviour: is he well mannered in the stable, is he good in the company of other horses, will he willingly go away from other horses, is he safe in the company of dogs and in all traffic (not just cars) and so on. However well he suits you from the riding point of view, it is important that you should actually like him, too.

If you do decide to have a horse on trial, make sure that the arrangements are agreed and set down in writing – you will be responsible for feed, vet's bills and so on and will be liable for negligence.

Horses sold at public sales usually come with a warranty or warranties. A warranty is a statement of fact made before or during

a transaction – for example a horse may be "warranted sound". Privately sold horses do not always come with a warranty and if you ask the vendor for one and he or she declines, then you may have grounds for suspicion (on the other hand, in these days of increasing litigation, the vendor may simply be being extra cautious). When in doubt, consult your expert equestrian adviser and, if necessary, a solicitor. The law does give some protection to buyers of horses, as in the case of other merchandise, the big difference being that the horse is a living creature and therefore far less predictable than, say, a television or a refrigerator or a motor car.

When you do find the horse of your dreams and decide to purchase, buy him "subject to a veterinary certificate" and ask your own veterinary surgeon (not the vendor's) to carry out the inspection.

Vetting

If possible, you should be present when your veterinary surgeon carries out his examination of your proposed purchase so that he can discuss the horse with you.

The examination will begin with a preliminary visual inspection. The vet can deduce a good deal from the general attitude of the horse when approached: his stance might show signs of lameness; the condition of his stable could indicate behavioural problems such as box-walking (constant pacing round and round the stable), assuming that the vendor has not switched the horse to another box to hide the evidence; his head carriage can indicate problems of balance or vision; how he reacts to being handled will be indicative of his temperament.

The vet will take in the horse's general state of health, noting any discharges from the nose or eyes, the condition of the skin; and the presence of lesions, or heat in a

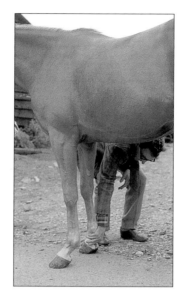

tendon or joint. He will also examine the eyes and heart.

Once outside his stable, the horse will be stood up squarely on flat ground while the vet makes a detailed appraisal of his conformation. This is followed by a manual examination of the entire horse:

OPTIONAL EXTRAS

For an additional charge various optional extra tests can be carried out. Blood tests may be used to detect anti-inflammatory drugs, designed to mask lameness. X-rays may be used where there is a suspicion of unsoundness (such as navicular disease) in the foot. Mares may be given a rectal examination if this is specifically requested.

the head, including the mouth and teeth, the neck, ribs, sternum, back, abdomen and the limbs. Once the horse has been examined at rest he will be walked and then trotted in hand both away from the vet and towards him to enable him to detect any signs of lameness. Turning the horse to either side on a tight circle, backing him for a few strides and lungeing him at trot on a hard, flat surface are other tests which may reveal problems of unsoundness.

Flexion tests may be carried out on the limbs, particularly if there is a suspicion of lameness. However, opinion differs on these flexion tests, as they can actually induce lameness if they are used with sufficient force.

▌ ABOVE LEFT
Vetting includes a
manual examination of
the entire horse.

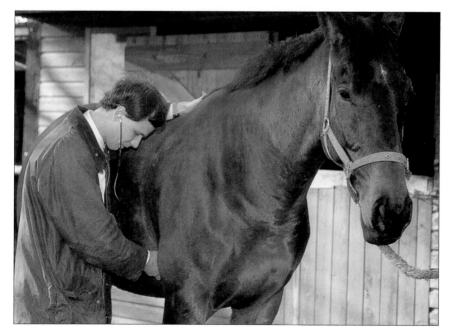

▌ LEFT
The vet will check the
horse's heart and
respiratory rates both
at rest and after
exercise.

LEFT
The horse is stood up outside the stable while a detailed appraisal is made of his conformation.

BELOW
During the vetting procedure the horse will be warmed up under saddle, then given a gallop. Fast work sometimes produces signs of an old lameness problem.

To test the horse's wind and heart he is tacked up, warmed up gently at walk, trot and canter and then given a gallop. The vet will note whether the horse dips its back when the saddle is put on and the rider mounts. Some horses habitually do this, in others it may be a sign of back problems. After exercise the vet will listen to the lungs for any signs of abnormal respiration and to the heart for any irregularity. After the horse has been cooled off he will be rested for half an hour, after which he will be trotted out again in hand. If the horse is suffering from muscular or arthritic problems, which might disappear while the horse is warm, they may well reappear after this period of rest. Signs of old lameness might also appear after fast exercise. A further examination of the heart and respiration may also be made. The vet will then complete the certificate.

The certificate includes a detailed identification of the horse, the vet's report and his opinion as to its suitability for purchase, bearing in mind the use for which it is required. It is important to remember that the certificate is not a guarantee, but an opinion expressed by a qualified person. The certificate means that the horse has been found to be free of certain disorders at the time of examination. It does not and cannot mean that the horse is and will remain completely free from disease – vets are certainly not clairvoyant. Nor does the certificate guarantee that the horse is free from so-called stable "vices" such as crib-biting or weaving. If you would like a written warranty to this effect, you must obtain it from the vendor.

Keeping a Horse

Horse ownership is a big responsibility and should not be entered into lightly. Certainly no one should consider it unless they have the necessary facilities and have first mastered the rudiments of horse care. These include a knowledge of feeding, grooming, general stable management and basic first aid. All horses and ponies need safe accommodation and daily attention – they cannot be set aside on a Sunday afternoon and forgotten about until the following weekend. Unlike small domesticated animals, who share their owners' home, they need large facilities of their own, maintenance of which takes time and money. Depending on the work required of them and their breed or type, horses can either be kept at grass or stabled, or a combination of the two (known as the combined system). The owner will therefore need access to grazing, a stable, a weatherproof storage area for feed, bedding and tools and somewhere secure to keep tack and other equipment.

THE HORSE AT GRASS

The horse is by nature a nomadic, grazing animal, so it is far more natural – and less stressful – to keep him in a paddock than in a stable. However, a fenced paddock, no matter how large, is still an unnatural environment for a horse and certain precautions must be taken if the horse is to be safe and secure.

▮ PREVIOUS PAGE OPPOSITE Stabled horses need constant care and attention.
▮ PREVIOUS PAGE Most small ponies are quite hardy and can live outside all year round.
▮ OPPOSITE Fit horses who spend part of the day at grass should wear bandages and boots to guard against injury.
▮ ABOVE Brood mares grazing in a well-fenced paddock.

Fencing

All fields used for grazing horses must be securely and safely fenced. Since it is the horse's nature to roam, if he sees a gap he will certainly go for it. Similarly, if there is anything on which the horse can injure himself, he will find it – the domesticated horse is notoriously accident prone.

Undoubtedly the most effective (but unfortunately also the most expensive) fencing is good **wooden post and rail**. It is sturdy, long lasting and looks attractive. The wooden support posts, which should be 4 inches (10cm) square, must be driven well into the ground since horses like to rub against fencing, particularly when they are changing their coats. For a 4 foot (1.2m) fence the posts should be no less than 6 feet 6 inches (2m) in length. The fence should be constructed of good-quality wood and treated with non-toxic preservative to give protection against the weather and to discourage horses from chewing it. The top rail should be level with the top of the posts, which should be cut on a slope to allow rain to run off. Where possible the rails should be attached to the inner side of the posts. This prevents the horse banging into the

▪ LEFT
Provided they are sufficiently high to deter the horse from jumping out, well-maintained stone walls are effective barriers.

▪ BELOW LEFT
Fixing the rails to the insides of the support posts prevents horses pushing them off when rubbing against them.

SAFETY CHECKLIST

☛ Make regular checks of all field boundaries.

☛ Repair any broken sections of boundary immediately.

☛ Keep wire fencing taut at all times.

☛ Set the lowest strand of a wire fence 18 inches (46cm) above the ground.

☛ Block off gaps in hedges with stout fencing – never use loose strands of wire.

☛ Never use pig or sheep netting – horses tend to put their feet through the squares of wire and can become caught up.

☛ Never use sheep posts, with sharp, upward pointing ends.

☛ Fence off potential danger areas, such as treacherous ground or ditches.

☛ When using electric fencing, ensure that it is visible – to humans as well as horses – by tying strips of strong plastic (for example, from feed or fertilizer bags) at intervals along the wire.

☛ Avoid metal or concrete fence posts – they will do far more damage than wooden ones should a horse collide with them.

■ OPPOSITE TOP
Good-quality wooden post and rail fencing makes the perfect horse-proof boundary and looks attractive.

■ BELOW RIGHT
Rusty metal, barbed wire and concrete posts are potentially lethal to horses. Sections of poor fencing like this should be replaced.

■ LEFT
Electric fencing can be very useful, especially for dividing paddocks into smaller sections. Horses quickly learn to respect it.

■ BOTTOM
Curved fencing with no right-angled corners is safest for horses.

Electric fencing has its uses, especially for temporarily dividing one area of a field from another, for example when resting one section of grazing.

Stone walls will also contain horses very well, provided they are sturdy and high enough – all boundaries should be a minimum of 4 feet (1.2m) high, otherwise horses might try to jump out. Like a hedge, a wall will afford some protection against the weather.

Modern **plastic fencing**, which comes in a variety of colours, may not look as "natural" as wood but it does have certain advantages: horses do not chew it, it does not rot and it will absorb impact without causing injury. Like wire, it should be correctly strained on strong, wooden posts.

Whatever the fencing used, right-angled or sharp corners should be avoided in paddocks where horses are kept. Rounding the corners of the field makes it less likely for a horse to injure himself when galloping about, either by coming to an abrupt halt (with the possibility of jarring the legs) or actually crashing into the boundary. Acute corners can also be traps for a timid horse who might find himself literally "cornered" by a more aggressive companion.

posts when galloping about and also prevents him from pushing a rail off if he leans or rubs against it.

A tall, thick **hedge,** provided it is without poisonous trees or shrubs, can also make a good boundary. Beech and hazel are particularly suitable since horses will not eat them. Unlike a fence, a hedge provides horses with shelter in bad weather. It will, however, require regular trimming to keep it in good order – if gaps begin to appear they must be fenced off.

Probably the best boundary of all is a combination of the two: a good dense hedge with a post and rail fence running immediately in front of it.

Cheaper, less attractive but equally effective fencing can be constructed with **wire mesh**. The mesh must have small, V-shaped openings so that there is no possibility of a horse catching his foot in the holes. Mesh fencing needs to be erected professionally to prevent sagging. It is also likely to stretch when leant on.

Plain wire fencing will provide a good horseproof barrier so long as it is well constructed. It should consist of four or five strands of wire attached to stout wooden posts, with strainers at the corners to keep them taut. An alternative, and one which makes the fence more easily visible to the horse, is to use a wooden rail in place of the top strand of wire. The strands of wire should be some 12 inches (30cm) apart and the placing of the lowest strand is particularly important. It should be about 18 inches (46cm) above the ground. Any lower and the horse may put

a leg through the strands and become caught up; any higher and he may be tempted to put his head underneath. Plain wire is more suitable than barbed wire. If the latter cannot be avoided, it must be kept absolutely taut – loose barbed wire can cause dreadful injuries if any part of the horse becomes caught up in it. Horses can also cut themselves if they rub against the barbs.

Gates

Good access to fields is most important. Gateways must be wide enough to allow not only horses to pass through safely but also large machinery (such as a tractor and harrow) which will be required from time to time to keep the pasture in good condition. For safety's sake it is better for gates to be situated away from busy roads. Wooden and metal gates are both suitable for horse paddocks. All gates should have cross bars for added strength.

It is best to have a gate hung by an expert to ensure that it does not sag, drag on the ground or swing. Gates must open easily otherwise a horse could try to push his way out while you are still struggling to open it. The safest way to hang a gate is so that it opens inwards into the field. This

SAFETY CHECKLIST

☛ Make regular checks of all gates.

☛ Replace/repair worn or damaged catches/hinges immediately.

☛ Keep gates securely fastened, using chains and padlocks at BOTH ends.

☛ Never fasten gates with bits of rope or string – horses can bite through them and they are easily removed by thieves.

☛ Avoid gates less than 6 feet (1.8m) wide – horses can easily bang themselves, especially their hips, as they go through.

☛ Avoid gates that open directly on to a main road – it is dangerous leading a horse straight out into traffic and will also make theft easier.

☛ Never use flimsy metal gates – they are too easily bent and broken.

☛ Avoid rusty metal gates – horses can easily injure themselves.

☛ Avoid straining gates by climbing over them.

☛ Avoid feeding horses close to the gateway – the ground will quickly become poached in winter.

▌ BELOW
Gate posts must be strong. Gates should be securely fastened at both ends with sturdy chains and padlocks.

will prevent a horse pushing it open as soon as you unfasten the catch. A wooden gate should be heavy and solidly built and, like fencing, should be treated with preservative. Galvanized metal gates will

▌ BOTTOM
This broken gate is totally unsuitable for a paddock. Rusty metal may cause serious injuries and flimsy barriers encourage horses to escape.

require regular painting. Gateposts need to be very strong and should be set about 3 feet (90cm) into the ground with concrete to keep them firm. They will require strong hinges and a horse-proof catch, that is one that the horse cannot unfasten with his teeth. All catches should be easy for a person to open with one hand. There should be no protruding hooks or other fastenings on which the horse could injure himself.

Horse stealing is not uncommon and so it is vital to secure all gates. Use heavy-duty chain with a strong padlock and fit one to BOTH ends of the gate so that would-be thieves cannot simply lift the gate off its hinges. Avoid climbing over gates as it tends to weaken them. If you must, always climb over the hinge end and do it quickly.

During wet weather the ground in gateways quickly becomes poached by horses being taken in and out on a daily basis or simply pacing up and down waiting to be fed. If possible, gates should be situated on well-drained ground, and not in a muddy hollow.

Shelters

In the wild, horses make use of natural shelter such as trees, banks or rocks for protection from extremes of wind, wet or heat or to escape from flies. For horses kept in the confines of a paddock it is essential to provide an equivalent form of protection. Most domesticated horses retain their natural instinct to shelter beside a good, thick hedge or under a tree rather than going inside a confining man-made structure. But not all paddocks have hedges and trees and so a wooden shelter may be the only alternative.

Since horses are happiest when kept in company with others of their kind, a field shelter needs to be large enough to accommodate the number of horses that graze together, without risk of squabbling and overcrowding. It should be positioned on well-drained ground. If this is not possible, the floor and the area around the shelter may need a hard surface, such as concrete. The shelter should be built with its back to the prevailing wind. It must be strongly constructed and treated with preservative. The roof must be sufficiently high to give horses plenty of

head room (thus avoiding possible injury) and should slope towards the back so that rainwater runs away from the entrance. Open-fronted shelters are the safest, because it is easy for a horse to escape should he be bullied by a companion. Any fixtures and fittings, such as mangers, hay racks, etc., must be strongly made and fitted at a good height from the ground, again to prevent injury. They should be checked regularly and repaired as necessary, as should the whole shelter.

Some types of smaller field shelter are designed with a bottom door which, when closed, converts the shelter into a stable.

This can be very useful if you have no other stabling but sometimes need to keep your horse or pony inside. It can also be used as an isolation box in the event of the horse contracting a contagious illness.

A less costly type of shelter may be provided by means of a wooden screen, erected in conjunction with the fencing. Windbreak screens need to be about 6 feet 6 inches (2m) high and can either be straight or double-sided, using a corner of the field. Multi-angled screens, affording protection from different directions, can be built free-standing in the open away from the fencing.

I TOP
A well-designed wooden field shelter with high, sloping roof, wide front opening and strong kicking boards.

I LEFT
This small shelter, with its narrow opening, is suitable for a single horse. With the addition of a door it could convert into a stable for emergency use if necessary.

201

Poisonous Plants, Shrubs and Trees

▮ BELOW LEFT
Horses appreciate the shelter afforded by mature trees such as this oak. But acorns, if eaten in large quantities, can be poisonous so they should be removed.

There are a good many plants, shrubs and trees which are poisonous to horses and ponies. Some, such as the **buttercup**, which are poisonous if eaten in large quantities when fresh, are not particularly palatable. On the other hand horses will readily eat yew, all parts of which are lethal. A quantity as small as 1lb (0.5kg) can kill a horse. All paddocks should be rigorously checked for dangerous plants before horses are put out to graze and regularly checked thereafter – remember that however well you tend your own grazing it can still be contaminated by seeds blowing from neighbouring land.

One of the most dangerous plants of all is **ragwort**, which is tall and easily recognized by its bright yellow flowers. Ragwort

SAFETY CHECKLIST

☞ Learn to recognize poisonous plants and trees.

☞ Before putting a horse in a new paddock, make a thorough check of grassland and hedges for signs of poisonous vegetation.

☞ Dig up and burn poisonous plants.

☞ Fence off any poisonous trees which cannot be removed – make sure they are well out of reach of horses or ponies.

☞ Make regular checks of all paddocks and hedges – remember that poisonous plants can spread from neighbouring land.

☞ Never leave poisonous plants which have been dug up lying about in the paddock – many plants, notably ragwort, are far more palatable to horses when wilted or dead.

☞ Practise good pasture management: a good, dense sward of grass helps prevent poisonous plants from seeding.

☞ If there are poisonous trees in the vicinity, keep an eye open for fallen twigs or branches – particularly during windy weather.

☞ If paddocks adjoin gardens, make regular checks for cuttings dumped over the fence by their owners – they may contain poisonous plants.

☞ After using chemical weedkillers keep horses off the grass for several weeks and at least until there has been a good downpour of rain.

contains alkaloids which poison the liver and the effects are cumulative: small doses eaten over a long period of time are just as lethal as a large amount eaten in a short time. There is no specific treatment for ragwort poisoning and the effects are usually fatal.

Ragwort can be eliminated by spraying – the best time is between late April and late May, before the flower shoots develop and while young plants are just becoming established. Or it can be dug up, though this can be hard work. All the roots must

■ CLOCKWISE FROM RIGHT
Ragwort, yew, laurel, rhododendron and privet: all
are highly dangerous to horses. Ragwort must be
eradicated from horse pasture; the trees and shrubs
must either be removed or fenced off out of reach.

be removed from the ground and the
flower heads should be burnt. Attempting
to control ragwort by cutting it when it is
in flower to prevent the production of
seeds is unlikely to solve the problem since
the plants will often grow more vigorously
the following year. If a paddock is really
badly infested with the plant, the best
solution is to plough the land and reseed
it. The better the grassland management
the less opportunity there will be for
ragwort to become established. The
denser the sward of grass the less likely
ragwort is to seed.

Foxgloves, which like ragwort become
more palatable when they are dried in hay
than when fresh, are also lethal to horses.
As little as ¼lb (100g) may prove fatal.
Symptoms of foxglove poisoning include
convulsions and difficulty in breathing. A
horse will die in a matter of hours.

Hemlock has a similarly disastrous
effect though it takes larger quantities
(around 5–10lb or 2.5–5kg) to cause
death. All members of the **nightshade**
family are poisonous, as is **monkshood**.
Horsetails, commonly found growing in
boggy conditions, are very dangerous if
eaten in large quantities in hay. Horses do
not usually eat the growing stems.

Shrubs and trees to be avoided at all
cost include **rhododendron** (small
quantities cause death through failure of
the respiratory system), **oleander**,
laburnum (especially the seeds), **box,
privet** and **laurel**. All parts of **yew**, living or
dead, are lethal in small quantities – again
there is no known antidote. **Meadow
saffron** contains a poison which may take
time to build up in the system, by which
time the horse is beyond help, and the
poisons present in **bracken** also have a

cumulative effect which causes poor
growth, lack of co-ordination and general
loss of condition. Care should be taken if
there are oak trees in or around a horse's
paddock. The crop of **acorns** varies from
year to year. If they are eaten in large
quantities, they can be harmful. They
should be raked up and removed.

Plants, shrubs and trees which are poisonous to horses include:
Bracken, buttercup, flax, foxglove, hemlock, horsetail, lupin, meadow saffron, nightshade, purple milk vetch, ragwort, St John's wort, yellow star thistle
Box, laurel, oleander, privet, rhododendron
Buckthorn, laburnum, magnolia, yew
Acorns

Water

■ LEFT
A natural supply of running water is ideal provided it is pollution free.

■ BELOW
A galvanized trough makes a suitable alternative.

■ BOTTOM LEFT
All water containers must be well filled and cleaned regularly.

Horses and ponies kept at grass must have constant access to a clean supply of water. A natural supply of running water, such as a stream or river, is ideal but nowadays it is all too likely that it may be polluted. If it is not, then horses and ponies may be allowed free access provided the bottom is gravel (if it is sandy the horse may ingest sand with the water).

The approach to the drinking area must be clean, fairly flat and safe. Steep banks are not suitable since the horses will slip and slide down and the bank will eventually collapse. If the stream is narrow, this could arrest the flow of water. Any fencing that crosses the stream or river must be checked regularly to ensure that horses cannot escape from their paddock by wandering off along the waterway. Streams which are not free flowing in summer are not suitable, since the water will tend to become stagnant. Horses should never be allowed access to polluted rivers, stagnant ponds or boggy areas: these should be securely fenced off.

The alternative to running water is a man-made container. A galvanized water trough, purpose-built, fed by mains water and controlled by a ballcock provides an efficient water supply, although there is

always the problem of pipes freezing in winter. The feed pipe needs to be buried to a suitable depth and the length of pipe which is above ground will need to be well lagged. It is essential that the ballcock is enclosed so that horses cannot damage it.

If mains water is not available, troughs can be filled by hosepipe or, if convenient, by bucket. Troughs such as this with static water will require baling out every week and refilling. Smaller containers, such as old stone sinks, plastic tubs and buckets can also be used but they will need more frequent filling. The advantage of small, lightweight containers is that they are easy to clean and they can be moved about to different areas of the field to prevent wear and tear on the ground. The disadvantage is that they are easily knocked over.

Standing a bucket or tub in an old car tyre is one solution to this problem.

Water troughs are best positioned parallel to a fence. Horses drink a lot so the approach to a trough will be in constant use. It should be hard – it may be necessary to lay concrete or hard core.

SAFETY CHECKLIST

- Check your horse's water supply every day.
- Bale out and clean all water containers regularly.
- During severe weather be prepared to break ice on water two or three times a day.
- Fence off all sources of stagnant water.
- Never place a water trough in the corner of a field where a horse may be trapped by one of its companions.
- Never place a water trough under deciduous trees or near a hedge where leaves, twigs and seeds can foul it.
- Avoid placing troughs in the middle of fields where they can become a source of injury.
- Recess water troughs into the line of the fence to minimize projections and the risk of injury.
- Never place a water trough slightly in front of a fence so that a horse could trap his leg between it and the fence.
- Avoid using containers such as old baths that have rough edges or dangerous projections.

Grass Management

BELOW
Grazing cattle with horses, or in rotation, helps control worms and weeds.

BELOW LEFT
Droppings must not be allowed to accumulate in the paddock. If they cannot be picked up regularly, they should be harrowed.

Careful management is required if a paddock is to withstand the horse's close-biting method of grazing and the constant wear and tear inflicted by his feet. Poor quality grazing quickly becomes "horse sick" – barren areas alternate with patches of intrusive, unpalatable weeds such as nettles, docks and thistles – and without a good grass sward it will also become badly poached in wet weather. Even good quality grazing will deteriorate if it is not given the right attention.

The ideal pasture is one that has been sown with seed selected and mixed specifically with horses in mind. A good basic mixture would contain 50 per cent of perennial rye grass, 25 per cent of creeping red fescue and 25 per cent of a mixture including crested dog's tail, meadow grass and a little wild white clover. Timothy should also be included if you intend to take hay from the paddock.

Rye grass grows well in most conditions although on poor, light soils it will decline after a few years if it is not fertilized. Two different types should be included in the mix. Creeping red fescue is particularly useful in difficult conditions (it is often used on sports grounds) and again two different types should be included. Smooth-stalked meadow grass will grow in dry, sandy soils while the rough-stalked variety, which horses find very palatable, thrives in moist, rich soils. Its dense, low growth helps prevent the intrusion of weeds and poisonous plants. Clover is useful because its root nodules contain nitrogen-producing bacteria. Its inclusion in the mix will help reduce the need for fertilizing. It is important to choose wild clover rather than one of the farm varieties, which grow very aggressively and can take over an entire paddock.

Even with the right basic mixture of grasses, the amount and quality of grazing produced will vary according to a number of natural factors. These include soil type, rainfall, wind and altitude. Soil should be

tested for its suitability to sustain grass. For example, if it is acidic it will need to be treated with lime (horses must be kept off the grazing until the lime has been washed in by rain).

The best grazing is produced on well-drained land. The installation of underground drainage is expensive but it may be essential where ground is so badly drained that it is both unproductive and easily poached by a horse's feet. Where drainage exists it is important to maintain it. Check ditches regularly, and remove any blockages which prevent water from running away freely (remember that blocked ditches on neighbouring land can prevent the free run of water from your paddock). Check all pipes leading into and out of ditches and repair as necessary.

Ideally the horses' droppings should be removed frequently as this will help to control worm infestation. Where removal is not practical, for example on large acreages, the droppings should be harrowed regularly. This should be done during warm, dry weather (which will spread out the droppings and kill the larvae). Another aid to worm control is the grazing of cattle either with the horses or in rotation. The larvae will be destroyed in the cattle's digestive system. Cattle and sheep will also help keep paddocks tidy by eating the rougher herbage. Sheep do less damage to wet ground than cattle.

Harrowing in the spring helps to pull out dead growth and make room for new, and a field should always be harrowed before the application of fertilizer. Rolling will help to firm the soil and repair poached areas. Weed control is also best carried out in spring as soon as new shoots appear. Persistent weeds should be dug out and burnt before they seed.

Pasture needs to be rested periodically. If you have nowhere else to put your horse, divide off the paddock into two or more sections. Rest one portion, graze horses in another and, if possible, graze cattle or sheep in a third.

THE STABLED HORSE

Well-designed stabling is vitally important to the horse's health and safety, whether the horse lives in most of the time, whether he is kept on the combined system (that is part stabled, part out at grass) or whether he is stabled only occasionally.

▌ OPPOSITE **All stables should have horse-proof fastenings on the outside of the doors.**

▌ ABOVE **Roughened concrete provides a suitable surface for a busy stableyard.**

Stables

Care must be taken with the positioning and construction of stables. This applies equally to a single stable and to a large yard. Stables should be sited so that cold north and east winds cannot blow in and should be positioned on well-drained ground. When planning new stabling, various factors should be taken into consideration. These include the supply of water and electricity as well as vehicular access. It is preferable, too, to build stables near a house, in order to deter thieves.

The most popular type of stable is the loosebox, or box stall. These are usually made of wood, concrete blocks or brick and may be roofed with wood (protected by waterproof felt), tiles, slates or heavy-duty corrugated plastic. Metal should never be used for stabling because it is hot in summer and cold in winter; it is also likely to cause injuries to the horse. A loosebox must be large enough for the occupant to be able to move about, roll, lie down flat and get up again in comfort and absolute safety. A horse standing 16hh and over needs a loosebox measuring at

▌ BELOW
Good airy barn stabling provides a suitable alternative to looseboxes, especially in a hot or very cold climate. The disadvantages are the ease with which disease can spread and the fire risk.

least 12 feet x 14 feet (3.7m x 4.3m); a horse up to 16hh, 12 feet x 12 feet (3.7m x 3.7m), and a 14hh pony, 10 feet x 12 feet (3m x 3.7m). A stable of 8 feet x 8 feet (2.4m x 2.4m) is adequate for small ponies.

The roof should be sloped and fitted with effective guttering and downpipes. A high ceiling or roof is essential to prevent the horse hitting its head. If the stable has a ridge roof, the eaves should be no less than 7 feet 6 inches (2.25m) above the ground and the top of the roof should be from 12–15 feet (3.7–4.5m) high. The lowest point of a single-planed roof should be no less than 10 feet (3m) high.

Wooden kicking boards, to a height of at least 4 feet (1.2m), provide added strength and security. The stable floor should slope slightly towards the rear of the box (to aid drainage) and the surface must be hard-wearing and non-slippery. Roughened concrete is most often used. It may be covered with a special rubber material to give better purchase. Drains inside the stable are best avoided as they tend to become blocked with bedding and can also trap a horse's hoof.

For safety, the stable door must give plenty of clearance – it should be at least 4 feet (1.2m) wide and 7 feet (2.1m) high for a horse. It should be made in two halves, opening outwards, and the top half should fasten back securely for the free circulation of air and to enable the horse to see out. Only rarely is the weather so severe that it is necessary to close both halves of a stable door. The top edge of

▌ OPPOSITE TOP
A well-built block of brick stables. The overhang gives extra protection to horses and humans from extremes of weather.

▌ OPPOSITE MIDDLE
Note the protective strip on the top of the doors and the kick-over bolts at the bottom.

▌ BELOW
The inside of a barn complex. With kit and equipment conveniently to hand, this type of stabling is popular with humans though it can be a boring environment for horses.

▌ BELOW
A converted container makes a poor and potentially dangerous home for a horse. Metal is cold in winter and hot in summer and the horse could easily injure himself on the makeshift door.

SAFETY CHECKLIST

☞ Provide adequate fire extinguishers (water and foam)/fire hose/sand buckets in the stable area – your local fire prevention officer will advise on suitable precautions. Have fire extinguishers serviced regularly.

☞ Ensure that all electrical wiring is protected with suitable conduits to prevent interference by horses and rodents.

☞ Ensure that all light fittings are out of reach of the horse.

☞ Fit waterproof switches, well out of reach of the horse.

☞ Keep stable fixtures and fittings to a minimum: two rings, one to tie up the horse, one (if required) for a haynet; water bucket or automatic waterbowl; manger.

☞ Make regular checks for protruding nails, screws, splinters etc.

☞ Make regular checks of all door bolts and hinges and keep them oiled.

☞ Fit protective grilles to all windows.

☞ Keep all drains clean.

☞ Cover open drains in the stable yard area with strong grids.

the bottom door should be securely fitted with a protective strip of metal to prevent the horse chewing the wood, and the door should have a horse-proof bolt at the top and a kick-over bolt at the bottom.

The stabled horse needs a constant supply of fresh air, so good ventilation is essential. The open top door and high roof help provide this. What the horse does not need is a draughty environment. Windows, which help ventilate and light the stable, are usually positioned on the same side of the box as the door to prevent draughts. If they are to provide maximum air and light, they should not be obscured by the top door, which tends to be the case with some stabling. Windows must be fitted with protective grilles. Additional ventilation can be provided by means of ventilation cowls in the roof, or louvre boards in the eaves. Additional light may be provided by a window in the wall opposite the door. If this is also used for ventilation, it must be above the height of the horse's head to prevent cross-draughts.

Internal stabling, where lines of looseboxes are contained within a larger building (which can be an existing barn or purpose built), is popular in some countries and is particularly useful in areas which experience extremes of heat or cold. Correctly constructed, such stabling will be warm in winter and cool in summer, but care must be taken to provide good ventilation – infectious diseases are more likely to spread in this type of stabling arrangement. Doorways and centre aisles must be wide enough to enable horses to move about without banging themselves – sliding stable doors are often the best in this situation as they do not protrude into the gangways when open. The running channels must always be kept clean.

Another way of keeping horses under cover is the yard system, where a number of horses are given the run of a large barn or a partially covered area. The yard system is labour saving, since the horses can be kept on deep litter; and horses enjoy being together with the freedom to wander about. Care must be taken, however, to choose horses who get on with each other, otherwise biting and kicking will occur.

Bedding

An ample supply of bedding encourages the horse to lie down to rest, thus taking unnecessary strain off the legs and feet; it reduces the likelihood of injuries such as capped hocks when the horse does lie down; it allows the horse to roll in comfort and protects him from injury when he does so; it reduces the jarring effect on the legs and feet that may result from standing for long periods on hard flooring; it prevents the horse from slipping up; it encourages him to stale (male horses, particularly, are usually very reluctant to stale on a bare floor); it provides warmth and insulation from draughts and it helps to keep the horse and his rugs clean.

There are a number of types of suitable bedding, all of which have pros and cons. **Straw** has traditionally been the most popular – and economical – and many people still prefer it since it makes arguably the warmest, most comfortable bed and allows free drainage. It is normally easily available though it may become scarce in wet years. Wheat straw is the best for horses, being less palatable than barley or oat straw, both of which are also likely to contain awns which can get into a horse's eyes or irritate the skin.

Straw has the advantage of being much easier to dispose of than some other forms of bedding: it can be burnt (in a safe place, well away from stabling, hay stores, etc) or contractors may collect it for use as mushroom compost. The main drawback of straw is that it may be dusty or contain fungal spores, which can cause an allergic reaction in some horses, leading to respiratory problems. This in turn can affect the horse's work performance because he will not be able to take in enough oxygen. Coughing is often the first sign of problems in this respect.

It can sometimes be difficult finding a supply of small straw bales, too, particularly if you live in an area where there are few horse owners and therefore not much demand for the old type of bale. Straw is best bought in small bales because they are easier to handle. The large ones, weighing half a tonne or more, are difficult to manoeuvre and often present storage difficulties, especially for someone keeping horses on a small scale. It will take about four small bales to put down a good, thick straw bed in an average sized loosebox and upwards of half a bale a day to maintain the bed, the exact quantity depending on the amount of time that the box is occupied.

Aside from straw, **wood shavings** are probably the most popular form of

bedding nowadays. Correctly managed, they provide a clean, hygienic bed which will not be eaten by the horse. Shavings do not have spores and, provided they are dust free (having been passed through a dust extractor by the suppliers), they can be a good alternative to straw for horses with any sort of respiratory problem.

They are packed in strong plastic bags and it is therefore possible to store shavings outside, provided there has been no damage to the wrappings in transit. Shavings do have their share of disadvantages, however. They are difficult to dispose of – being slow rotting they cannot be spread on the land – and bales are fairly heavy to handle. Shavings are

also much heavier to handle when wet than straw. There is also the possibility of foreign bodies, such as sharp fragments of wood or nails, being present – though this should not be a problem with good-quality shavings. Some horses' skin may be irritated if the shavings are from wood which has been treated with chemicals and foot problems sometimes occur.

Unlike straw, which traps pockets of air, shavings pack down closely. A bed of shavings is therefore less warm than a straw bed and rather less comfortable to lie on, particularly as it is less stable than straw and more prone to exposing bare patches of floor. A shavings bed will use approximately three bales per week.

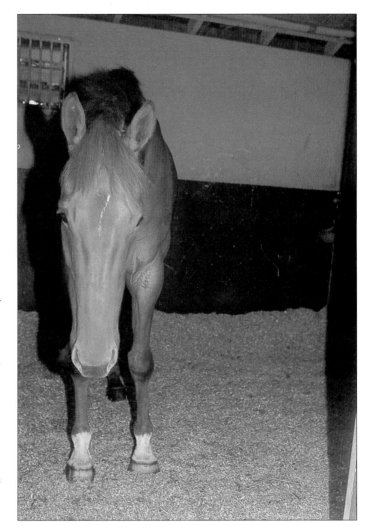

Aubiose is a fairly new and entirely natural product made from the hemp plant. It is proving particularly beneficial for horses with dust allergies and has the advantage of being exceptionally absorbent: four times more absorbent than wood shavings and twelve times more than straw. The bed is more expensive than other forms of bedding to put down initially, an average stable requiring some eight bales, but thereafter it is economical to maintain as it requires only half to one bale a week. When the bed is first laid it needs dampening with a hose or watering can to help it settle and activate its sponge-like properties.

Aubiose works by soaking up liquids in a small area at the base of the bed, in much the same way as cat litter. The top layers of the bed remain dry. It is a labour-saving form of bedding since mucking out consists simply of frequent removal of droppings and a light raking over to keep it level. It is recommended that the saturated bedding should be removed every five to ten days, depending on the horse. It is also suitable for use with the deep litter system.

Another big plus for Aubiose is the fact that it rots down to a valuable compost within five to six weeks and is therefore easy to dispose of. Its only disadvantage, apart from the initial cost, is that it is very free flowing (the particles are smaller and softer than shavings) and so it is not so easy to bank up the sides of the bed.

Shredded paper provides the most dust-free bed of all and is, as a result, often used for horses with allergies to straw or respiratory problems. It is also increasingly used for high-performance horses, such as eventers or racehorses, whose lungs need to be kept as free as possible of dust. Paper is cheaper to buy than shavings but on the other hand a deeper bed is required because it becomes saturated more quickly than either shavings or straw. On the plus side, it is light and easy to handle and

provides a really warm bed. On the minus side it is often made from printed paper and this may cause staining of the horse's coat, particularly with greys, which causes extra work for the owner or groom. It is also difficult to control a paper-bed muck heap when it is windy. Again the bed will need around three bales per week.

Peat moss may be used for bedding in areas where it is easily available . Like shavings, it is usually sold in plastic-covered bales. It, too, has its good points and its bad points. It provides a comfortable bed, is not palatable and should be reasonably easy to dispose of.

However, its main advantage over other forms of bedding is one of safety: it will not burst into flames in the event of a fire. On the other hand it is expensive, heavy to handle, needs frequent mucking out and forking over to prevent it becoming soggy and compacted and is so dark in colour that it is difficult to identify the wet areas.

Rubber matting can be used for bedding purposes but, apart from the fact that it is totally dust free when used on its own, it has more minus points than plus ones. It certainly does not look very attractive and, more important, provides

I BELOW

Rubber matting is dust free, long lasting and labour
saving but affords little comfort unless other
bedding is used on top.

I BOTTOM

Paper, being dust free and warm, is ideal for
bedding down horses with respiratory problems.
Printed paper can cause coat stains, especially on
grey horses.

little warmth or protection from
draughts. It does not absorb wet and
if it is used without a covering of other
bedding material, the droppings will be
scattered about by the horse, who will
then lie in them and, as a result, tend
always to be dirty. There is little to
prevent a horse becoming cast (the
banked-up sides of conventional beds
help in this respect). When used on its
own its chief advantage, apart from
being dust free, is its low-cost
maintenance: after the initial outlay there
is no more bedding to purchase and the
matting should last for a number of years.
Mucking out can be done by hosepipe,
and is both quick and easy.

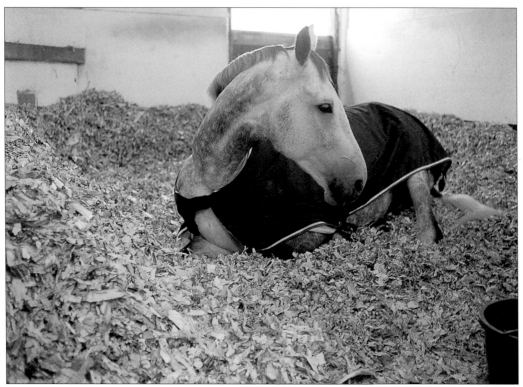

Management of Beds

Good management of beds is essential to keep the horse's environment healthy and to keep both the horse and his rugs as clean as possible. Stables can either be mucked out every day or you can adopt the deep litter or semi-deep litter system. The horse should be tied up during mucking out or, preferably, removed from the stable altogether. This protects him from any dust which may be disturbed while the bedding is being moved about and also makes the job easier.

Daily mucking out entails the removal of all droppings and soiled bedding. The best system is to take up the bed completely to allow the floor to dry while the horse is out. This is less of a chore with lightweight bedding materials such as straw and paper than with something heavier such as shavings.

You will need a wheelbarrow or a muck sheet, a fork and a strong yard broom with hard bristles. For mucking out a straw bed many people use a four-pronged fork for lifting droppings, but the same job can be accomplished with a three- or even a two-

pronged fork. Much depends upon the skill of the wielder – the fewer prongs, the lighter the fork, the less tiring the job and the faster you can work. For mucking out shavings you will need a shavings fork, which has more prongs set closer together. The advantage of using a muck sheet is that you do not normally need a shovel. Most of the soiled litter can be forked or swept on to it and any remnants can be hand lifted, provided you wear protective gloves. When a shovel is required, it should be large and lightweight.

The muck sheet or wheelbarrow is positioned across the doorway and visible droppings collected and placed on/in it. The bedding is cleared away from one corner of the box (usually the one on the same side as the door and furthest from where the horse is tied up, though if the box is large enough the other corners may be used in rotation to ensure that all corners of the floor are dried out regularly). The floor in that corner is then swept clean. The corner is used to stack all

the clean bedding – the squarer and neater the better since it will take up less room. All the droppings and wet straw are placed in the wheelbarrow or on the muck sheet and the entire floor is swept clean. Finally, a thin layer of the clean bedding is scattered across the box as standing litter. This will prevent the horse from slipping but will facilitate the drying of the floor. Assuming that the horse will stay tied up to be groomed and then exercised, the box can be left with the bed up for some time, which will help ensure that the floor – the sides as well as the centre – dries out before the bed is put down again.

An alternative, though not quite so satisfactory, method is to clear the bed completely from one wall of the box each day, thus ensuring that each bank of bedding is turned on a regular basis.

When putting down the bed again the existing bedding should be used to provide a good, deep covering to the entire floor area (right up to the door, to prevent draughts) and new bedding used to bank up the sides (with a straw bed if a

LEFT
A selection of mucking out tools: wheelbarrow, five-tined fork, shovel, shavings scoop, broom and skip. A wheelbarrow is more cumbersome to use than a muck sheet.

ABOVE
The horse should be tied up during mucking out and setting fair. (Note that, for safety, coats should be fastened while you are working with horses.)

▮ RIGHT
A muck heap sited in a three-sided bunker is easier
to manage and to keep tidy than a free-standing one.

▮ BELOW
Position the muck heap where there is good
drainage and easy access – for large vehicles as well
as wheelbarrows.

horse has a tendency to eat it, new straw
should be covered with a layer of the used
bedding which will be less palatable).
Banked sides keep out draughts, help
protect the horse from injury when he is
rolling or lying down and may help
prevent a horse becoming cast (that is
stuck with his legs in such a position that
he cannot get up again).

To keep the bed as clean as possible,
droppings should be picked up regularly
throughout the day in a container known
as a skip or skep, which may be made of
metal, plastic or rubber. At evening stables
the bed should be set fair, that is
straightened out and put tidy for the
night, care being taken to bank the sides
well and ensure that the entire floor area
is evenly covered.

To keep a horse on deep litter the

stable needs to be large (in a small one
the bed will quickly become sodden) and
well ventilated. This system saves time as it
involves the daily removal of the
droppings only, not the wet bedding
underneath. The old bed is left
undisturbed and covered with fresh
bedding each day. This type of bed needs
careful management and is better suited
to horses who are out by day as this
enables the bedding to dry out more. A
deep litter bed is warm in winter and may
stay down for as long as six months.
However, if it begins to build up too high
or to smell it must be completely removed.
The box should be thoroughly dried out
before a new bed is started. Woodwork will
tend to deteriorate more quickly with this
type of bed because of the dampness in
the lower layers.

A good compromise is the semi-deep
litter system, whereby the droppings and
the worst of the wet bedding are removed
daily and the whole box given a complete
muck out once a week or once every few
weeks. This works well with shavings beds.
With any deep-litter system, frequent
removal of droppings is essential.

Management of the muck heap is also
important. For convenience it should be
sited reasonably close to the stables, with a
dry, level approach and easy access for
large vehicles. It should be downwind of
the stables. A muck heap can be free-
standing or contained in a three-sided
bunker – breeze blocks are particularly
suitable for this purpose – which makes it
easier to keep the heap tidy. Make sure
that there is adequate drainage away from
any paths or driveways.

During mucking out the entire stable floor should
be swept clean and, if possible, allowed to dry
before the bed is put down again.

The sides of the bed should be banked well up the
stable walls to help keep out draughts and to
prevent injury when the horse lies down.

A skip is used for the periodic removal of
droppings during the day. Skips may be made of
plastic, metal or rubber.

Feeds

The horse is a herbivore, that is an eater
of plants and especially grass and herbs.
Left to live a totally natural life, the horse
will spend some twenty hours out of every
twenty-four grazing, slowly moving from
place to place in his search for satisfying
food. Horses are what are known as trickle
feeders: they have comparatively small
stomachs in relation to the size of their
large intestines and need to top up with
food at regular intervals. In the wild they
put on condition when food is plentiful
and lose it when it is not. The unnatural
conditions imposed upon horses by man –
the lack of constant access to grass and the
need to burn up energy by working –
mean that they must be fed suitable
alternatives to grass if they are to thrive.
Feeding horses is a complex subject. Like
humans, horses are individuals and vary a
good deal in the type and quantity of food
they need to maintain health and fitness.
Basically, however, the domesticated
horse's diet consists of roughage, or bulk
food, and concentrates.

ROUGHAGE

The usual way to feed roughage is in the
form of hay, which is simply dried grass.
There are two types of hay: seed hay and
meadow hay. **Seed hay** is suitable for
horses in hard work, because it is usually
more nutritious than meadow hay. It is
taken from grasses specifically sown as an
annual crop, which will include top-quality
plants such as rye grass and timothy.
Meadow hay is cut from permanent
pasture and is softer to the touch and
often greener in colour than seed hay. It
contains a greater variety of plants than
seed hay (some of which may be of
inferior quality) and is usually less
nutritious and therefore more suitable for
animals in light work.

A newer way of feeding bulk is in the
form of **haylage**, which is grass sealed in
plastic bags. It comes in different
nutritional levels and is particularly

Seed hay (left) and meadow hay (right)

Crushed oats

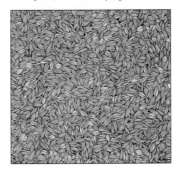

Bruised barley

Flaked maize

suitable for horses with respiratory
problems. Haylage may be mixed with
hay or replace it altogether as the horse's
bulk feed.

Chaff or **chop** is hay, either alone or
mixed with one-third proportion of oat
straw, which has been chopped into small
pieces by passing it through a chaff cutter.
It may be added to concentrates to
encourage mastication and aid digestion.

CONCENTRATES

Food such as oats and barley are known as
concentrates. These are the energy-giving
foods which, when fed in the correct
balance with the roughage, enable the
horse to perform the work required of
him without losing condition.

Oats have always been considered the
ideal cereal for feeding to horses. The
fibrous husk covering the rich seed
encourages chewing and helps prevent the
horse from eating too quickly, which can
seriously disrupt his digestive system. The
one drawback is that oats have a low
calcium-to-phosphorus ratio and the
horse's diet should therefore contain a
calcium supplement to balance the
minerals in the roughage. Oats may not be
suitable for feeding to all equine animals,
however, as they can have a heating effect,
making them difficult to control. Oats
should be lightly rolled and used within
two or three weeks thereafter, otherwise
they lose nutritional value.

Barley has a higher energy value than
oats but is lower in fibre. It may be fed
cracked, rolled, flaked (heat treated) or
micronized. It may also be fed as a mash,
which is prepared by pouring boiling
water over flaked barley and allowing it to
cool before feeding. Whole barley should
never be fed unless it has first been
cooked to soften it, otherwise it is too
indigestible. It should be covered with
boiling water and allowed to simmer for
several hours until the grain has split,
swollen and become soft.

Bran

Linseed (which must be boiled before feeding)

Soaked sugar beet

Molassed chop

Horse and pony nuts

Coarse mix

Maize is high in starch but low in protein and fibre. It is usually fed flaked or micronized. It can be very heating and should be fed only in small amounts.

Bran, a by-product of wheat, is high in fibre and often fed to horses who are off work or on a low-protein diet. It may be fed dry in small quantities, mixed with the horse's other feed, or as a mash. This is made by putting the bran, together with a handful of salt, in a bucket, pouring boiling water over it (not so much that the mash is sloppy), covering and allowing it to steam and cool.

Linseed, the seed of the flax plant, is rich in oil and often fed to improve the condition of the horse's coat. It is poisonous (it contains prussic acid) if not first boiled. The linseed is covered with cold water and

soaked overnight. The following day more water is added (about 4 pints/2 litres to 2–3oz/110g of linseed) and the mixture is brought to the boil and simmered for several hours. When the resultant jelly has cooled it may be added to a bran mash or to the horse's ordinary feed.

Sugar beet is a highly digestible source of energy and fibre. It has a good calcium-to-phosphorus ratio and may be used to correct the imbalance of those elements in cereals. Sugar beet pulp (the remains of the root vegetable after the sugar has been extracted) comes in cube form or shredded. Before feeding it is essential to soak it for at least twelve hours using at least double the amount of water to pulp. Cubes may require soaking for longer in more water. If it is not adequately soaked,

it will swell up in the horse's stomach, with potentially fatal results.

Molasses is a by-product of sugar. Dark and sticky in appearance and very palatable, it may be added in small quantities to the feed to supply energy, improve the condition of the coat and to tempt fussy feeders.

Concentrates which come in cube form or as coarse mixes are known as **compound feeds**. They are made from a variety of ingredients and are scientifically prepared to provide a balanced diet. Specially formulated compound feeds are available for foals, brood mares, competition horses, and so on. They are particularly useful for the novice horseman as a good-quality compound feed takes much of the guesswork out of feeding.

▌ LEFT
Feedstuffs should be kept in a clean feed room, in dry, rodent-proof containers. All feeds should be carefully measured.

Feeding

To work out a suitable feed ration for your horse you must take into consideration his size, his age, his type and the amount and nature of the work he is doing. Feeding is both a science and an art. Science tells us much about the principles of feeding and the nutritive value of the various feedstuffs but horses are all individuals and ultimately the proof of the pudding is in their appearance and performance. You can learn to judge the correct, healthy condition for a horse of a particular breed, age, size and build doing a particular job of work by studying similar animals to your own which are being used for similar purposes (perhaps at your riding school or in local competitions).

The ratio of bulk feed to concentrates will vary according to the nature and amount of work the horse is required to do. A horse in light work does not require a great deal of energy-giving feed (it will merely serve to make him a "hot" ride). On the other hand a horse such as a hunter or an eventer needs more energy-giving feed and less bulk. For a horse in light work (doing up to about six hours a week hacking and light schooling) and for

The following is an approximate guide to total food requirements based on height (but bear in mind that it is only approximate, since horses vary a good deal in build and a finely made animal may require less food than a heavyweight doing the same amount of work):

Height	Daily feed requirement
Under 12hh	14 – 16lb (6.3 – 7.2kg)
12 – 13hh	16 – 18lb (7.2 – 8kg)
13 – 14hh	20 – 22lb (9 – 10kg)
14 – 15hh	22 – 24lb (10 – 11kg)
15 – 16hh	24 – 26lb (11 – 12kg)
over 16hh	26 – 28lb (12 – 12.5kg)

To find a more accurate yardstick it is customary to measure feed requirements against the horse's body weight (the horse requires a total daily intake of about 2-2.5 per cent of its body weight). The best way to check his weight is to use a weighbridge. Failing that you can estimate his weight by using the following formula:

$$\frac{Girth^2 \times length\ (in\ inches)}{300} = weight\ in\ lbs$$

NB Measure the girth round the largest part of the barrel at the moment when the horse has breathed out; measure the length from the point of the shoulder to the point of the buttock.

▌ TOP LEFT
Some barn-type stabling incorporates swinging feed bowls. They are labour saving in large yards with a lot of horses to feed.

▌ ABOVE LEFT
Hook-on plastic mangers are useful for feeding horses kept at grass.

▌ LEFT
A large corner manger is a suitable way to feed the stabled horse. Mangers must be cleaned out regularly.

☛ Feed nature's way: little and often – the horse has a small stomach in relation to its size.

☛ Divide the concentrate ration (preferably mixed with chaff or other small roughage) into three or four feeds a day – never give more than 4lb (1.8kg) of concentrates in one feed.

☛ Feed at the same times each day.

☛ Wash mangers regularly with clean water.

☛ Never leave uneaten feed in the manger – if your horse regularly fails to eat up, either you are overfeeding or there is something wrong with him or the feed.

☛ Never feed directly before exercise – allow up to two hours for digestion.

☛ Never feed immediately after work – allow an hour for the horse to recover.

☛ Never make sudden changes to a horse's diet – introduce new feedstuffs gradually over a period of at least a week.

☛ Feed hay after concentrates and give the bulk of the hay at night.

☛ Never leave a horse for longer than eight hours without food.

☛ Always ensure that the horse has clean, fresh water available.

☛ Have the horse's teeth checked regularly – sharp edges must be rasped down to enable him to chew his food efficiently.

☛ Worm the horse regularly.

☛ Keep feed in clean, dry, rodent-proof bins, and hay in a waterproof feed shed, protected from damp ground.

☛ Add variety to the feed by giving succulents such as sliced apples and carrots (sliced lengthways to prevent choking), especially if the horse is a shy feeder.

most ponies the ratio should be 30 per cent concentrates to 70 per cent bulk. For a horse in medium work (doing up to ten hours work a week, including up to two hours schooling a day, some dressage, show jumping and hacking) the ratio should be 50 per cent concentrates to 50 per cent bulk. For a horse in hard work (more than ten hours a week, or including fast work such as hunting, eventing or endurance riding) the ratio should be 70 per cent concentrates to 30 per cent bulk. These are general guidelines and all horses are different, but however hard he is working the horse should never receive less than 25 per cent bulk by weight.

Horses and ponies living out at grass during the winter require the same amount of food as stabled horses in order to maintain their health and condition during bad weather. During the spring and summer (assuming that the weather is fine) good-quality grazing should provide enough nutrition for ponies and coldblooded horses doing no more than an hour or two of light work, though it is best to check their weight regularly to make sure. During the winter, grazing will do no more than provide maintenance. In severe weather it will not even do that and the horse will lose condition if he does not receive supplementary feeding.

❙ TOP LEFT
Haynets must be tied securely and high enough to prevent the horse from catching a foot in them. Feeding hay on the ground is safer and more natural.

❙ LEFT
Horses should have access to salt, to counteract any deficiency in their diet. A salt lick is a convenient way of providing it.

❙ FAR LEFT
Soaking hay in clean water for a few hours before feeding helps prevent horses inhaling mould spores.

Water

Water makes up approximately 60 per cent of an adult horse's body weight, the exact percentage depending on his age and condition. It is present in all his body fluids and is vital for the correct functioning of the blood, the digestion and the excretion process. A horse can survive for several weeks without food but only for a few days without water.

The quantity of water required by a horse on a daily basis varies according to his diet, the prevailing weather conditions, his work load and his general health. A stabled horse may drink in the region of eight gallons (37 litres) of water a day, although the amount may be as little as five gallons (20 litres) or as much as ten (40 litres). A horse at grass may drink less than a stabled horse because of the moisture content in the grazing. A horse will drink more when the weather is hot and humid or when he sweats as a result of hard work. A sick horse may be reluctant to drink.

It is vital for the stabled horse to have access to a constant supply of fresh, clean water, the only exception being before hard, fast work. Horses are extremely fussy about the water they drink and will go thirsty rather than drink dirty or tainted water.

Water for the stabled horse may be provided either in buckets or by means of an automatic water bowl. The advantage of using buckets is that you can easily check the amount of water the horse is drinking. Water buckets should be large and strong – heavy-duty rubber is the most resilient. Plastic buckets, though convenient because they are light to carry, are not the safest as they tend to split and can cause injury. Metal buckets are stronger but they, too, might cause injury to a restless horse.

Buckets should be positioned in a corner of the stable, not right by the door but not too far from it, either, so that they are easy to reach for refilling. The handle

▌ LEFT
Heavy-duty rubber water buckets are ideal for the stabled horse. They are safer and more durable than plastic.

▌ BELOW LEFT
If the horse is in the habit of knocking over his water bucket, stand it in a rubber tyre.

should be positioned away from the horse. Many horses can be trusted never to knock a bucket over, even when it is empty. Others get into the habit of playing with theirs. Some are just naturally clumsy and will knock a bucket over when moving about the box. Water buckets can be fixed

to the wall with clips or, if the stable is roomy enough, stood in a rubber tyre.

During the day water buckets should be checked and refilled regularly. Water should be replaced rather than topped up to ensure a fresh supply. At night a big horse will need two buckets so that there is no possibility of his going short. Buckets should be scrubbed out regularly with clean water.

Automatic drinking bowls, connected to the water supply and controlled by a small ballcock, are popular in large yards because they are labour saving. However, they do have several disadvantages. Compared with buckets they are quite small and may not permit a horse to enjoy a deep drink. Unless they are fitted with a plug (which should be recessed into the bottom out of the way of the horse's teeth) they are difficult to clean. Also, it is not possible to judge at a glance how much water a horse is drinking. Since water consumption, like food consumption, is an indication of the horse's state of health, this is not ideal. It is, however,

■ BELOW
An automatic drinking bowl provides an alternative to buckets. The bowl must be checked frequently to ensure that the water supply is operating correctly.

■ BELOW
The stabled horse must have constant access to clean water. A large horse will need two buckets.

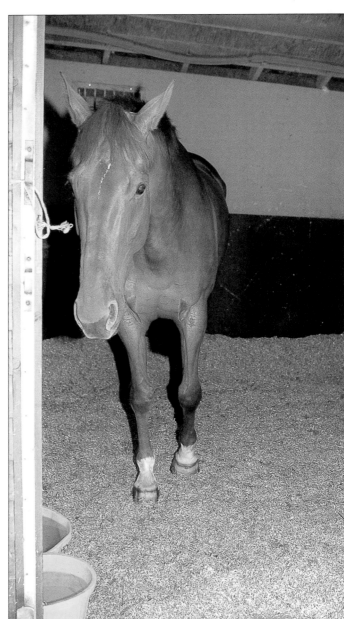

GOLDEN RULES OF WATERING

☛ Always provide the stabled horse with a constant supply of clean water.

☛ Always water before feeding.

☛ Never work a horse hard immediately after a long drink.

☛ After hard work (such as hunting or cross-country) give a horse a small quantity of water – about half a gallon (2.5 litres) every quarter of an hour until he is satisfied.

☛ When giving electrolytes (minerals to replace those lost during strenuous exercise) always offer plain water as well.

☛ Keep all water utensils clean.

☛ Check automatic water bowls every day.

possible to install drinkers fitted with a meter which overcomes this problem. All projecting fixtures in a stable are a potential source of injury to the horse and a water bowl is no exception. Conversely, there is every possibility of a bowl being damaged by the horse. Drinking bowls must be rigorously checked every day – a blocked supply will cause the horse great distress while an overflowing bowl with swamp his bedding. Precautions must be taken when fitting pipes so that they cannot freeze in winter.

Daily Care

Horses must be kept fit and healthy if they are to perform the work required of them. Keeping them that way requires daily care and attention. It is the responsibility of the owner to ensure that the horse has sufficient regular exercise of the right type and to learn how to recognize the signs of ill-health. Every horse, whether he is kept stabled or at grass, should be checked over carefully every day to ensure that he is well, sound and has no injuries or fresh lumps or bumps. Horses are creatures of habit. They thrive on a regular routine and therefore should be visited, fed, exercised and so on, at the same times each day. Some common equine ailments and minor injuries can be dealt with by the competent horseman, others will need veterinary attention. The owner must judge when to seek expert advice, bearing in mind that the sooner treatment begins, the better the chance of a cure. Regular visits from the farrier are also an essential part of horse care. There was never a truer maxim than "no foot, no horse".

Exercise

The horse needs daily exercise for the maintenance of health and, like all athletes, when he is in work he needs additional exercise to build up and maintain condition.

Where fitness of the horse is concerned exercise is always linked to feed. A horse who is kept at grass, provided the paddock is not very small, has the opportunity to

STABLE "VICES"

Being cooped up in a stable for some twenty-two hours out of every twenty-four is unnatural and boring and may lead to a horse developing bad habits, or stable "vices". These include wood chewing, box-walking (aimless walking round and round the stable), crib-biting (in which the horse takes hold of the manger or the top of the door or some other convenient object with his teeth and swallows air) or weaving (in which he stands, usually with his head over the door, and sways from side to side). Virtually all stable vices can do harm to the horse in one way or another. All can be avoided if the horse is not allowed to become bored and frustrated.

■ LEFT
The stabled horse requires regular daily exercise to keep him healthy. Hacking out helps to get him fit and enables him to relax after work.

■ OPPOSITE
For racehorses, and other horses in hard work, a carefully planned exercise programme is essential.

■ PREVIOUS PAGE OPPOSITE
Most ponies, like this Haflinger, thrive when kept at grass.

■ PREVIOUS PAGE
Despite its size, the Suffolk Punch is an economical breed to keep.

■ BELOW LEFT
In their natural state, horses and ponies such as this Exmoor mare and foal have all the exercise they need.

take all the gentle exercise he needs to stay healthy. Space and the freedom to move around at will are an intrinsic part of the horse's everyday life in the natural state so the bigger his paddock the nearer it is to his natural environment and the more contented he will be.

However, the totally grass-fed horse will not be fit to do anything other than light work in summer. By keeping the horse in a stable it is possible to monitor his food intake and gradually build up his physical fitness to enable him to carry out the work required of him. But because the stabled horse is deprived of his freedom for part, if not all, of the day a good exercise regime is essential if he is to be happy and healthy and not become unmanageable.

If possible, all stabled horses should spend part of the day turned out at grass in addition to their normal work routine. There is a danger of fit horses doing themselves harm when turned out, so it is essential to have safely fenced paddocks and to fit protective boots to guard against accidents. If for some reason it is not possible to give the stabled horse his usual exercise (for example in bad weather when it may be impossible to ride on the roads), he should be turned out for a time each day or at the very least led out and allowed to eat some grass. Another alternative to ridden exercise is to work the horse on the lunge.

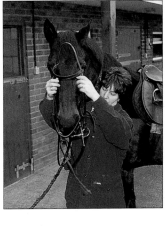

■ RIGHT
For exercise purposes
a simple snaffle bridle
and general purpose
saddle are usually
adequate.

■ BOTTOM
Horse and rider
prepared to go. If the
horse is to be ridden
on the roads, he
should be fitted with
kneeboots.

Before being exercised or worked the horse should be given a quick grooming to make him neat and tidy. Stable stains should be sponged off and all remnants of bedding removed from his mane and tail. His feet should be picked out and his shoes checked.

An all-purpose saddle is suitable for general hacking out and roadwork. A numnah will protect the saddle from grease and dirt from the horse's coat and will also be more comfortable for his back.

Keeping a bridle for everyday use will minimize the wear and tear on the bridle you use for "best", e.g. for showing or competing. The bitting and bridling arrangement will depend on the horse. Most can be hacked out safely in a snaffle with a cavesson noseband. If you do need a little more control, you may prefer to fit a Grakle or flash noseband. Whether or not you use a martingale will again depend on the horse and how difficult or otherwise he is to control.

When exercising on the roads it is advisable to fit the horse with kneeboots – fitted correctly they will not impede his action. It is all too easy for a horse to slip up on tarmac and injure his knees, yet it is surprising how few people take this simple precaution. Brushing boots are another useful means of protecting the horse's legs.

A clipped horse in winter will need an exercise sheet to keep his loins warm. This is placed under the saddle to prevent it slipping back. It should be fitted with a fillet string, which passes under the tail to prevent it blowing up in the wind.

You can exercise two horses at the same time by riding one and leading one, in which case the led horse should wear a bridle and you should lead him either by the reins or on a leather lead rein run from one bit ring, through the other and into your hand. Never lead a horse on a lunge rein which could easily become tangled, and never wind a lead rein or reins round your hand. The ridden horse must always be between the led horse and the traffic and you should always ride on the same side of the road as the direction

of the traffic. Avoid riding and leading on roads where there is anything but light traffic and never ride and lead unless the horses are traffic-proof and well behaved. For maximum control the led horse's head should be at or just behind the ridden horse's shoulder.

For more serious work – schooling, dressage, jumping and so on – the horse should wear the saddle and bridle most suited to that activity and protective boots or bandages. For jumping, fit his shoes with appropriate studs to prevent slipping.

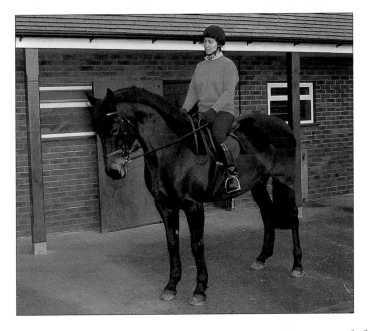

Fitness

Broadly speaking the fitness training of the horse can be divided into three distinct stages. First, there is a period of slow work designed to strengthen him up in readiness for more serious work. Second, there is the build up designed to bring him to the necessary fitness for most everyday riding activities. And third, there is the fine tuning required to bring him to a peak for physically demanding pastimes such as regular hunting, show jumping, eventing or racing.

FIRST STAGE

The period of slow work is vital and should never be rushed. The tried and tested way to make horses fit, and to prevent strains and sprains when they begin serious work, is roadwork. When the horse is first ridden after a period of rest,

▌ LEFT
Hillwork builds up muscle, particularly in the hindquarters, and improves the horse's lung and heart capacity.

▌ BOTTOM
Hacking out makes a welcome break from school work for both horse and rider.

he must have walking exercise only. Three-quarters of an hour a day is sufficient to begin with if the horse has been out at grass. Gradually, over a period of **two or three weeks** (preferably longer if the horse is ultimately going to be asked to do a lot of hard, fast work), this can be increased to an hour and a half to two hours a day.

Although this is slow work, the horse must not be allowed to slop along any old how. He should be kept going forward,

straight and in a good rhythm in order to start the process of building up muscles in the right places. The exercise route should be varied as much as possible to keep the horse alert and interested and he should have a day off each week to allow him to relax.

Trotting can begin during weeks **three to four**. To begin with the horse should walk for about thirty minutes before starting to trot. This will give his muscles time to warm up. His exercise period

▮ LEFT
By week five the horse
should be fit enough
to start a little
gymnastic jumping.

▮ BELOW LEFT
Serious schooling can
begin when the horse
has been in work for
about six weeks.

should also finish at walk, in order to cool him off. The trot should be controlled and rhythmic and in the early stages the periods of trot should be short and interspersed with longer periods of walk. As the days progress and the horse begins to feel fitter, the periods of trot can be made longer. The pace must always be controlled: trotting flat out on the roads (or any other hard surface) jars the horse's legs and can lead to injury. Uphill trotting is better than trotting on the flat because it reduces the strain placed on the front legs. At all times when trotting the rider should change the diagonal regularly and, when trotting uphill, keep the weight forward.

During **week four** some periods of schooling on the flat can be introduced. They should be no longer than about twenty minutes and cantering should be kept to a minimum. To encourage the horse to relax and to continue the building-up process, he should be taken for a hack afterwards.

Week five can see the introduction of a little hillwork, one of the finest ways of building up muscle. Hacking and flatwork should continue.

By **week six** he should be ready for a canter work-out, in which he should be allowed to stride on but without going into a wild gallop. As with trotting, uphill cantering is the most beneficial.

SECOND STAGE

Once the first stage in the fitness programme is completed the horse will be in a fit state to begin more serious work. Work on the flat, incorporating suppling exercises such as serpentines and circles, should be introduced. The schooling sessions should be kept short to begin with but may be gradually increased in length as the horse becomes more toned up. Gymnastic jumping exercises over grids and on circles and elements of circles will all help to improve his athleticism.

THIRD STAGE

The type of fitness required in a particular horse is always governed by the type of work required of him. For example a show jumper needs the muscular power to clear big fences but is never required to gallop flat out for a prolonged period. On the other hand the three-day eventer needs great stamina and endurance to be able to cope with the demands placed on him.

Getting the horse fit for sports which require speed and endurance involves longer periods of canter work. Canter work must be introduced gradually and should always be carried out on good ground to reduce the risk of injury. Short periods of canter are sufficient to begin with. Later, periods of long, steady cantering may be used to bring the horse to a high degree of fitness. Only rarely is the occasional really fast galloping necessary, as for instance with the fine tuning of a racehorse or three-day event horse. The main thing to remember is that the faster the pace the more chance there is of injury occurring.

Even when the horse reaches peak fitness for the activity required of him, he should be allowed regular periods of relaxation if he is not to become sour – hacks in the countryside or spells at liberty in the paddock. During a rest day after strenuous work the horse will appreciate being led out for a bite of grass.

■ BELOW
Mud fever usually affects the lower legs. This horse also has capped hocks and windgalls (painless fluid-filled swellings just above the fetlock joints).

■ BOTTOM LEFT
The irritation caused by sweet itch often results in the horse rubbing the mane and tail hair at the affected areas.

Common Ailments

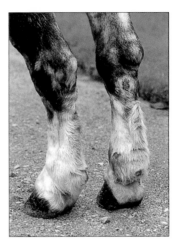

Azoturia, also known as set fast or tying-up, is a stiffening up of the large muscles of the back and hindquarters. It results from the accumulation of large amounts of lactic acid. It is not always possible to determine the reason, though too much food combined with too little exercise is a common cause. The horse begins to sweat up and has difficulty in moving forwards. The muscles feel hard to the touch and the horse will clearly be in pain. Dark, red-coloured urine may be passed. The horse should be rugged up and not moved. The veterinary surgeon should be called. He or she may prescribe drugs to relieve the pain and inflammation.

In **chronic obstructive pulmonary disease** (COPD) the airways to the horse's lungs become, as the name suggests, chronically obstructed. COPD is the result of an allergic reaction to fungal spores, for instance in the horse's hay or bedding. Symptoms include a nasal discharge followed by a cough. The horse's ability to perform hard work diminishes and in time his respiratory rate at rest increases. Treatment includes rest, fresh air, antibiotics and clean stabling with dust-free bedding and spore-free feed.

Equine influenza occurs in two main strains with numerous subtypes; a serious respiratory disease, it can prove fatal. Symptoms include a horse going off his feed, a raised temperature and general cold-type symptoms. Antibiotics may help and the horse must be rested. Horses can be vaccinated, very effectively, against many strains of flu – indeed vaccination is mandatory for most competition horses.

Grass sickness is a painful and fatal disease affecting the horse's nervous system. It is typified by loss of condition, muscle twitching, difficulty in swallowing and a green nasal discharge. In an acute case the horse may die in a few days. Others linger for weeks or months. Its cause is uncertain and it is more common in some regions than others.

Mud fever is a bacterial infection of the skin which affects the legs and/or lower body. It is most often seen on the lower legs. Raw areas develop which ooze serum and then form scabs. At the back of the pasterns and heels cracks often develop in the skin. The condition is most often seen in skin exposed to very muddy or very dry, dusty conditions. Skin with white hair is most susceptible. The best way of preventing mud fever and cracked heels is to protect the skin, when dry, with a barrier cream. Treatment involves clipping the hair from the affected area, regular washing (with antiseptic shampoo) and removal of scabs, careful drying and the use of antibiotic ointment.

COLIC

Colic is abdominal pain which may occur for a number of reasons, such as a sudden change in diet, migrating worm larvae, impaction of the intestines or, in rarer cases, a twisted gut. Signs of colic include the horse standing and looking round at, or trying to kick, its flank, sweating and/or repeated lying down and rolling.

The horse should be put in a stable on a deep bed to guard against injury if he wants to lie down and roll and the vet should be called. He or she may administer pain-relieving or relaxant drugs and/or a lubricant, depending on the type of colic. If a twisted gut is diagnosed, immediate surgery is essential to save the horse's life. Potentially life-threatening attacks of colic are accompanied by a high temperature (above 103° Fahrenheit/39°C) and raised pulse rate (above 60 per minute).

Rain scald is a skin infection caused by the same bacterium as mud fever. It occurs on the upper surfaces of the body. Like mud fever it is treated with antiseptic shampoos and the removal of the scabs which harbour the bacteria.

Ringworm is a fungal infection of the skin and hair. It occurs as small crusty, hairless patches and is infectious. An affected horse should, therefore, be isolated. Ringworm is treated with special antibiotic skin washes which should also be used on the horse's tack to kill off all traces of the infection. The stable should also be treated. Careful control is required as ringworm can affect humans, too.

Strangles is an infection of the lymph glands under the jaw caused by the bacterium *Streptococcus equi*. Affected horses have difficulty in swallowing and the glands under the jaw become swollen. The temperature may rise to as high as 106° Fahrenheit (41°C) and there is a nasal discharge. Infected horses must be kept warm and given soft food. Antibiotics

may help. The abscesses in the glands should be treated with hot fomentations – once they burst the horse's condition usually improves. The pus from burst abscesses is highly contagious and horses affected by the infection should be isolated. A policy of strict hygiene must be adopted to prevent the spread of the infection on clothing and equipment. Abscesses which burst internally are very serious since they can cause pneumonia.

Sweet itch is a skin irritation caused by hypersensitivity to the bites of midges and is therefore found chiefly during the spring and summer. It usually occurs along the mane and the base of the tail, which become inflamed and sore. The irritation is such that the horse will often rub out all the mane and tail hairs at the affected places, making the skin raw. A susceptible horse or pony will suffer from sweet itch annually and must be protected from midge bites by being stabled at dusk and dawn when the insects are most active. Benzyl benzoate is used to sooth

the sore areas and helps to repel the midges. Fly repellents will also help and mosquito netting should be fitted over open windows and doors while the horse is stabled. Special sheets that cover the entire neck and body give useful protection.

All horses should be vaccinated against **tetanus** and given a booster injection every other year. Tetanus is caused by a bacterium found in the soil and may enter the horse's system via a wound, especially a deep puncture wound. Typical symptoms are stiffness of the muscles, twitching, the horse standing in a stretched-out manner and, as the disease progresses, overreaction to sudden noises or movements. Eventually the horse is unable to stand and death occurs when the breathing muscles become affected. Some horses do recover from tetanus since the infection can be halted by the use of antibiotics and antitoxin. Early diagnosis is essential and the horse will need to rest in a quiet, dark stable.

Common Injuries

Back injuries, either to the bones or muscles of the back, are often the result of falls. Treatment involves rest and the use of anti-inflammatory drugs. Faradism (stimulation of the muscles by electricity), massage and laser therapy may also help.

A **capped elbow** – the term used for a bursal enlargement at the point of the elbow – is usually caused by the horse's shoe striking the elbow when he is lying down. The swelling is soft and is hot and painful when it first appears. A **capped hock** is a similar injury, caused by the horse striking his hock against something hard like the wall of his stable (perhaps through the use of too little bedding) or the partition in a horsebox (hock boots should be fitted to guard against this, particularly if the horse is a bad traveller). Unless the condition causes lameness or there is an infection, it will not require treatment. In the case of a capped elbow the horse should be fitted with a "sausage boot" (a protective ring) on the pastern. This protects the elbow while it is healing.

An **overreach** is an injury to the heel or the back of the tendon of the front legs caused by the horse striking itself with the toe of its own hindfoot. Overreaches should be carefully cleaned. An antibiotic dressing will help guard against infection. Overreaches can be serious – there is often extensive bruising – and are often slow to heal.

Splints are bony swellings found between the splint bones and the cannon bones. Although splints are most commonly found on the inner side of the forelegs, they can occur on either side of the leg and on the hindlegs. Splints often appear when a young horse first begins work. Conformation is a contributing factor. In many cases splints are associated

FIRST-AID KIT

The horse owner's first-aid kit
should include:

- ☛ Disinfectant – for washing wounds.

- ☛ Skin swabs – small swabs impregnated with disinfectant for cleaning wounds where there is no clean water supply.

- ☛ Wound cleansing cream or liquid.

- ☛ Wound ointment or powder.

- ☛ Wound dressings.

- ☛ Crêpe bandages.

- ☛ Adhesive bandages.

- ☛ Gamgee tissue.

- ☛ Cotton wool.

- ☛ Cold packs.

- ☛ Poultices.

- ☛ Thermometer.

- ☛ Scissors (sharp, but with rounded ends for safety).

- ☛ Fly repellent.

Swollen joints can be the result of injury, infection or a dietary problem.

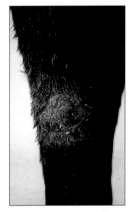

Fibrous tissue known as proud flesh may form a permanent blemish which will require surgical removal.

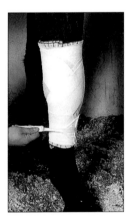

When bandaging a knee, cotton wool or Gamgee tissue should be used under the bandage.

The correct way to bandage a hock.

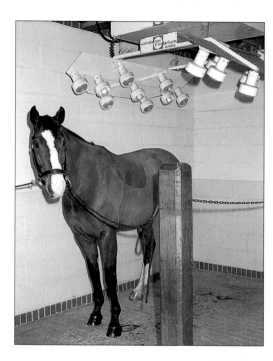

■ LEFT
Infra-red helps to relax muscles and soothe pain. This horse is enjoying a spell in a solarium.

■ BELOW LEFT AND RIGHT
Eye injuries, such as cuts and bruises, can be dangerous and require professional attention.

■ BOTTOM
Stimulation of the muscles by electricity (Faradism) is useful in the treatment of back injuries.

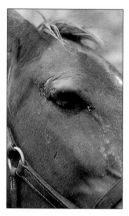

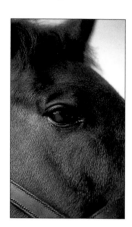

with poor foot and limb balance, in which case corrective shoeing often helps. Lameness may result, in varying degrees, while the splint is forming but often the pain associated with splints disappears in time. In the case of persistent lameness, the leg should be X-rayed to eliminate any possibility of a fracture.

Because of the strain put on the legs when galloping and jumping, **tendon injuries** are all too common in horses, particularly in the forelegs. The superficial and deep flexor tendons, which run down the back of the cannon bones, the suspensory ligament, which is immediately behind the lower part of the cannon bone, and the check ligament, situated below the knee, are all at risk. Tendon and ligament injuries are the result of sudden stress, which causes the fibres to tear. The injury causes pain, followed by heat and swelling. Cold is the most important part of the treatment: ice packs or, in an emergency, a pack of frozen peas, should be applied to the site of the injury as quickly as possible. Ice packs should be replaced frequently and the limb should be bandaged firmly, though not too tightly, for support. Laser treatment may help to reduce the swelling. The oldest – and best – treatment for all strains and

sprains is rest. A leg which has suffered a serious tendon injury is more likely to stand up to future work if the horse is given a period of twelve to eighteen months off. The veterinary surgeon can determine, by using a scanner, when a tendon injury has healed.

Horses suffer all types of **wounds** as a result of falls, accidents in the field and stable, and bites and kicks from other horses. Some, such as grazes, heal quickly provided they are kept clean and dry. Others can cause serious problems. **Puncture wounds** are often the most dangerous since bacteria may be carried deep into the wound. Although it is impossible not to notice a large, jagged laceration accompanied by a copious flow

of blood, it is easy to overlook a deep puncture wound simply because the wound to the skin is small and insignificant looking. It is important to ensure that such wounds heal from the inside out – poulticing may be necessary to draw out infection.

All wounds should be cleaned, if possible, with cold water fhough it should be remembered that continuous washing will not stop a wound from bleeding. The application of a pressure pad (such as a clean handkerchief) will help control the flow of blood while you are waiting for veterinary help. Large wounds may need stitching. If there is any doubt about the horse's vaccination status, he must be given a tetanus injection. If a wound needs covering to keep it clean, medicated gauze should be used as it will not stick to the wound. Wounds on the body, where the skin is loose, heal better than leg wounds which tend to develop proud flesh as they heal. Proud flesh is fibrous tissue, projecting beyond the level of the skin surrounding the wound and often forming a permanent blemish. The veterinary surgeon may advise using caustic preparations to arrest its development or it may need to be removed surgically.

Poulticing and Cold Treatments

The application of heat by means of a poultice helps to repair injury by stimulating the blood supply to the affected area. Heat also has a "drawing" effect, and will help to bring any pus to the surface.

Poultices may be made with kaolin, or specially impregnated padding can be bought. To make a hot kaolin poultice the tin of kaolin, with the lid loosened, is placed in a pan of boiling water for several minutes. When the kaolin is hot (no hotter than can be borne on the back of your hand) it is spread over a piece of lint, covered with gauze and applied to the injured area. To keep the heat in, polythene or aluminium foil is then wrapped over the gauze, followed by a piece of Gamgee tissue and the poultice is held in place with a bandage.

The poultice should be changed at least twice a day. All the kaolin must be removed from the wound before a new poultice is applied, otherwise the drawing effect of the new poultice will be lost. The main drawback of kaolin is that it is messy

to put on and remove. This problem can be overcome if you use ready-made poultices consisting of kaolin enclosed in a thin envelope of polythene.

Gamgee-type tissue impregnated with chemicals with drawing properties is also available. This must be activated by soaking in warm water. Like the envelope type of kaolin poultice it is easy to apply though it does leave a residue on the skin

which must be cleaned off before another poultice is applied.

Bran may be used to poultice the horse's foot in the case of problems such as a septic foot or corns. Boiling water is poured on to one or two scoops of bran to form a crumbly, not excessively wet, mixture. Test the bran for heat on the palm of the hand before applying it to the foot. The bran may be applied in a foot poultice boot, which is strapped on to the foot, or it may be placed in polythene and sacking and secured in place with a bandage. Horses sometimes try to eat bran poultices so it is advisable to add a little disinfectant to the boiling water to act as a deterrent. The poultice should be left on for twelve hours.

Tubbing is used for some foot wounds, which may require more regular applications of heat. Hand-hot water is placed in a non-metal bucket or tub and the horse's foot placed in it. Horses who are unwilling to cooperate by immersing their foot should be encouraged by having hot water gently splashed on their leg.

▌ TOP
Three types of equine boot designed to keep dressings in place on the horse's foot. Alternatively sacking, secured by a bandage, may be used.

▌ FAR LEFT
Gamgee-type tissue, impregnated with chemicals, makes an effective poultice. It is soaked in warm water before application.

▌ LEFT
Poultices should be removed at least twice a day. Any residue must be cleaned off the horse's skin before re-poulticing.

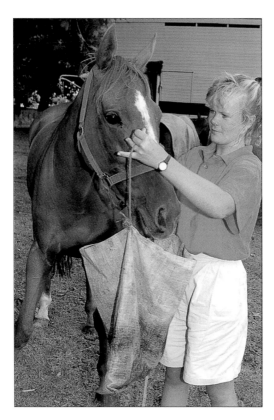

■ LEFT
Inhalants are
sometimes used when
horses have respiratory
tract problems. The
bag containing the
inhalant is fitted like a
nosebag.

■ BELOW
Hosing with cold water
helps to reduce the
swelling and heat
which accompany most
leg injuries.

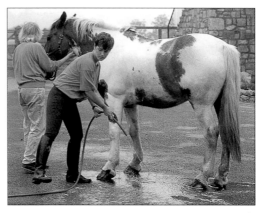

■ BELOW LEFT
Another effective
method of applying
cold treatment: a
hosepipe attached to a
"hose boot".

■ BELOW RIGHT
Hot or cold tubbing
can be carried out by
standing the horse's
foot in a bucket –
always providing he
cooperates!

Epsom salts and antiseptic may be added
to the water. Tubbing lasts for about
twenty minutes and should be carried out
at least twice a day.

Where cold treatment is required as
opposed to heat, there are various
methods. Cold water may be applied with
a hose for regular periods of about ten
minutes. The horse should be accustomed
to the feel of the water by starting at
ground level and then gradually working it
up the foot and leg. The legs should be
bandaged between hosing sessions. Where
suitable facilities are available the hose can
be bandaged to the horse's leg. He should
be given a haynet to keep him occupied.
Walking or standing a horse in a river or
in the sea is equally beneficial.

Specially designed flexible packs, which
retain their cool temperature for quite a
long time, can be obtained. They are
cooled in a freezer and bandaged into
place. Special bandages are available, too.
These are designed to absorb water and

are flexible enough to be applied even
when the water is frozen. Another way to
apply cold to a leg is to soak bandages in
cold water (care must be taken to remove
them before they start to dry out as they

might shrink). Crushed ice in a polythene
bag or, in an emergency, a packet of
frozen peas may be bandaged round a leg.
A thin layer of Gamgee should be placed
over the leg first.

Anatomy of the Foot

Lameness in horses occurs far more often in the foot than in any other part of the limbs. This is not surprising considering the amount of strain put upon the feet of domesticated horses required to pull heavy loads or carry a rider, particularly at fast speeds or over jumps.

The term foot is used to describe the hoof – the dense horny covering – and all the structures contained inside it. The external, insensitive part of the hoof comprises the wall (the outer, protective layer of the foot); the sole (a plate of hard horn just under an inch (2cm) thick; the frog (a wedge-shaped mass of soft elastic horn), and the periople (a thin layer of epidermis between the hoof wall and the skin).

The function of the sole is to give protection to the sensitive inner structures and to help support weight. The frog performs the same functions as the sole as well as providing grip and acting as a shock absorber. The periople controls evaporation from the underlying horn.

The internal part of the hoof comprises the sensitive laminae, the sensitive sole, the sensitive frog, the periopic corium and the coronary corium.

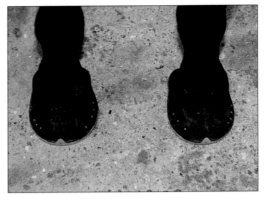

▌ LEFT
A well-matched pair of forefeet. The toe clips steady the shoes while the nails are driven in and help to ensure an accurate fit.

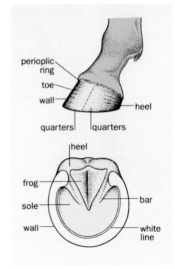

Laminae are interlocking leaf-like structures which attach the hoof to the pedal bone. Hundreds of sensitive (or primary) laminae dovetail with thousands of horny (secondary) laminae which grow outwards from the interior of the wall of the hoof.

The sensitive sole, which is attached securely to the lower surface of the pedal bone, is a thin layer of tissue which corresponds to the horny sole and supplies it with nutrition.

The sensitive frog supplies nutrition to the digital cushion on which it is moulded. This cushion is a wedge-shaped fibro-elastic pad situated in the hollow behind the heels. It has an important part to play in reducing concussion by expanding when the foot takes weight.

The periopic corium or ring situated just above the coronary corium (coronary body) supplies nutrition to the periople. The coronary corium, a thick structure situated above the sensitive laminae, lies in the coronary groove and supplies nutrition to the wall of the hoof.

On the ground surface of the sole, where the sole meets the wall, is a narrow band of soft plastic horn known as the white line. This white line is of great importance to the farrier because it indicates the position of the sensitive structures of the foot and the thickness of the wall, thus helping determine where nails can be driven into the wall to hold shoes in place without encroaching on the sensitive areas.

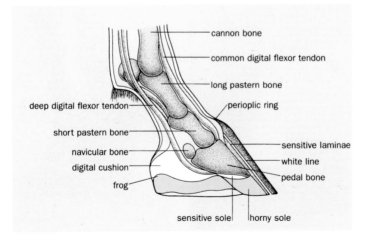

The Role of the Farrier

Horses have been shod with metal shoes for over two thousand years and although it is impossible to say for certain who first had the temerity to try nailing a shoe to the horse's hoof, it is widely assumed to have been the Celts and the Gauls.

The need to protect the feet arose when man began to use the horse as a beast of burden and for riding. The unnatural wear and tear inflicted upon the feet of the domesticated horse results in the hooves being worn down more quickly than they are renewed – this would not occur in the horse's natural state. The damage caused to the hoof is worse when travelling over hard, rough ground or in a wet environment. The latter leads to the growth of softer horn, which wears away more quickly. This explains why horses in dry, hot climates, which promote the growth of hard horn, can often do a considerable amount of work unshod without any ill effects.

The role of the farrier is of vital importance, since the horse cannot work adequately if his feet are painful. It is the farrier's job to ensure that the horse's feet are not only well and securely shod but also correctly trimmed. The horn of the hoof is constantly growing and fitting a metal shoe to the hoof prevents excess growth being worn down naturally, as is the case with the unshod horse. The average monthly growth of horn is around ¼–⅜ inch (5–9mm) and the horse needs to have his feet trimmed about every four or five weeks, depending on the rate of growth. If his old shoes are not worn, they may be refitted – these are known as "removes".

Shoes may be fitted either hot or cold. The advantage of hot shoeing is that it ensures a better fit because the shoe can be finely adjusted to fit the foot (the shoe must always be altered to fit the foot, not vice versa). The shoe is heated in the furnace and held against the prepared hoof (which is insensitive) for a short time. The imprint it leaves indicates to the farrier any necessary adjustments required. Once these have been made the shoe is plunged in cold water before being nailed on to the foot.

It is important to remember that horses who are unshod, perhaps because they are resting, still need regular attention from the farrier. Being confined in a paddock is not the same as being free to roam in search of food, and the horse's hooves will not wear down as they would in the wild.

The farrier's work is very skilful. He must be able to trim the hoof, and drive nails into the insensitive part of the hoof wall, with great precision. One slip, and the result will be a lame horse. Nor is farriery simply about the routine trimming and re-shoeing of horses. It also involves skilled remedial shoeing, which calls for a detailed knowledge of the anatomy of the horse's limbs, including the bones, the joints, the muscles, the vascular system and the nervous system. Defective action, caused by less than perfect conformation or injury, can be greatly improved by expert trimming of the foot and the fitting of specially designed shoes. In these cases, the farrier will work in conjunction with the veterinary surgeon.

At one time it was the practice for the horse to be taken to the farrier for shoeing, which meant that the farrier had all the facilities of a permanent forge on hand. Nowadays it is usually the farrier who has to travel to the horse with a mobile forge, so the onus is on the horse owner to provide him with a suitable working area.

A dry, level surface for the horse to stand on is essential, as is good lighting. In summer, when flies are a nuisance, the horse should be in a shady area, either in a building or under a tree, and it is advisable to have some fly repellent handy.

The horse's feet should be cleaned and dried beforehand and it is the owner's responsibility to ensure that the horse is as well behaved as possible. Most horses will stand quietly. But remember that feeding or moving other horses about while a horse is being shod can make him extremely restive – and the farrier's job that much more difficult.

▌ LEFT
In order to make horseshoes, the farrier must be skilled in bending, turning and shaping metal. He uses an anvil specially designed for the purpose.

The Farrier's Tools

The farrier's tools are divided into two categories: forge tools, that is those used while making shoes, and shoeing tools, that is those used while preparing the foot and nailing on the shoe.

Forge tools include the anvil, on which the metal is shaped; various hammers and tongs; the stamp, used for making nail holes in the shoes; the fullering iron, used to make a groove round the edge of the ground surface of the shoe and the pritchel, a steel punch used to finish off the nail holes and also for carrying hot shoes to the horse's foot for fitting.

Shoeing tools include hammer, pincers, trimmer and rasp. The farrier's shoeing hammer, which has a short, curved claw, is used to drive in the nails, to twist off the points of the nails and form the clenches, and to pull out nails.

When removing shoes the farrier uses a buffer (or clench cutter) to cut off the clenches or knock them up before withdrawing the nails.

Pincers are used for raising and levering off shoes and for withdrawing nails. They are also used to turn the clenches. For trimming, a hoof trimmer, cutter or parer is used. This is a tool with a pincer-like head, one side being sharp and the other flat. To remove the overgrown wall of the hoof the flat side is placed on the outside of the wall and the sharp cutting side on the inside.

When removing ragged pieces of frog or loose flakes of sole a drawing knife is used. The searcher, a similar tool but with a thinner blade, is designed for use when cutting out corns or paring away the horn round puncture wounds.

The farrier's rasp is partly coarse, partly smooth (file cut) and has serrated edges. The farrier uses the coarse side to remove excess hoof wall and for the final levelling of the bearing surface of the foot. The coarse side is also used to finish off the clenches. The file cut surface is used to finish off the shoe and to shape the clenches. Using the serrated edges the farrier removes the sharp edge of the wall (to prevent it splitting) after the shoe has been nailed on.

STUDS

Although shoes help to give the horse added grip on grass it is often essential to fit studs in the shoes as well. Studs may be permanent or of the screw-in type (in which case the shoes are provided with screw holes by the farrier). Screw-in studs

1 Having cut off or knocked up the clenches (the turned-over points of the nails), the farrier uses pincers to lever off the old shoe.

2 Excess growth of hoof is removed with a trimmer, which has one flat and one sharp side.

3 A drawing knife is used to lower the hoof wall and remove loose flakes of sole.

4 The bearing surface of the foot is levelled with a rasp before the shoe is fitted.

5 Hot shoeing ensures a better fit than cold shoeing and causes the horse no pain.

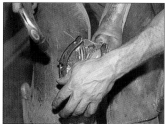

6 Nails are driven into the insensitive wall of the foot to hold the shoes in place.

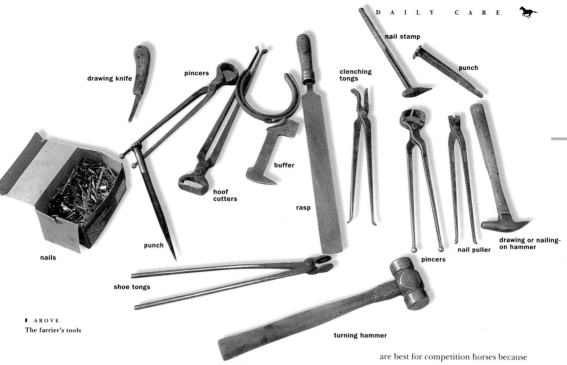

■ ABOVE
The farrier's tools

nail stamp

punch

drawing knife

pincers

clenching
tongs

buffer

hoof
cutters

rasp

nails

punch

nail puller

pincers

drawing or nailing-
on hammer

shoe tongs

turning hammer

■ RIGHT
Screw-in studs are essential for the competition
horse. After use they are removed and the holes
plugged to protect the threads. A T-tap (centre) is
used to clean out the screw holes before inserting
the studs.

are best for competition horses because
they require different types of studs
according to the work they are doing and
the state of the ground.

There is a wide range of studs available,
varying from small ones for everyday
hacking and road work (these are usually
made with a tungsten core and are very
hard wearing) to large round or square
ones suitable for use in soft going and
pointed ones which enhance the grip on
very firm ground. There are two schools of
thought about the fitting of studs: some
people fit only one stud on the outside of
each shoe. Others believe that this may
throw the foot out of balance and so fit
one on either side of the shoe.

The farrier uses the rasp to smooth the horn and
shape the clenches.

Lightweight plastic shoes are a modern
alternative to metal ones. They are attached to the
hoof with glue.

Studs are screwed into place shortly before the
horse competes. The size and shape depends on the
ground conditions.

Common Foot Problems

Corns occur most often in the front feet. A corn is a bruise of the sole in the angle between the wall of the foot and the bar (known as the "seat of corn"). Corns are caused by pressure and can be the result of a stone becoming wedged, faulty shoeing or shoes having been left on too long. The shoe should be removed and the discoloured horn pared away. The condition can be complicated by the presence of infection, in which case

poulticing will be necessary. Pressure can be relieved from the area by fitting a shoe on which the ground surface of the heel is lowered so that it does not make contact with the ground.

Laminitis (also known as "founder") is a painful condition resulting from inflammation of the laminae. The feet become hot and the horse adopts a typical leaning back stance in order to take the weight off the front of the forefeet.

Although the pathological cause is not yet completely understood, laminitis is associated with excessive concussion and the presence of inflammatory toxins which damage the blood vessels, particularly those in the feet. It is often the result of faulty diet (over-fat ponies, with overlong feet, kept on too rich pasture are the classic example) although it can also be caused by retention of the afterbirth in the broodmare.

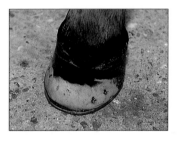

An example of the farrier's skill: this defective hoof has been artificially lengthened.

Pigeon toes (those which turn inwards) cause uneven wear on the shoes.

A sandcrack may produce lameness if the sensitive part of the foot is affected.

This leaning back stance is typical of a horse suffering from laminitis. He takes the weight on his heels to relieve the pain. Laminitis is one of the major causes of equine lameness, particularly in ponies.

Veterinary treatment is essential. If diet is the cause, the vet may advise a purgative. The horse should be stabled (standing the horse on sand is said to reduce the pain because it provides support to the feet). The vet may prescribe drugs (including pain killers) and if the horse or pony is overweight, he will advise on a suitable diet.

One of the dangers of laminitis is the possibility of pedal bone rotation. Except in the mildest cases, therefore, when the horse may be gently led out in hand, the horse must be given box rest.

Good foot care is vital. Corrective trimming will help restore the structures of the foot to their normal alignment and will limit the rotation of the pedal bone. Special shoes can also be fitted.

Navicular disease is believed to be the result of poor foot conformation and/or concussion, caused by hard work. Bony changes occur in the navicular bone, a small, shuttle-shaped bone which acts as a fulcrum for the deep flexor tendon before the tendon attaches to the under side of the pedal bone. In most cases both forefeet are affected.

A horse with navicular disease will put his foot on the ground toe-first as he attempts to avoid pressure on the affected area. In the early stages, lameness wears off during exercise but as the condition progresses the periods of lameness both increase and become more prolonged. As

pastern (high ringbone) or around the coronet (low ringbone). It is usually caused by injury. There is heat and swelling and the horse may have a shortened stride and tend to be more lame when turned sharply. Rest may help give relief in less serious cases. Where more serious injury is involved the horse may not become fully sound again, although some horses continue to work if given anti-inflammatory drugs.

of bruising of the toe area or pressure from the toe clip of a shoe. Sometimes it follows laminitis. Treatment involves cleaning out the cavity and filling it with tow. The farrier will be able to trim the foot and shoe it in such a way that further damage is avoided during movement.

A **sidebone** results when the lateral cartilages of the foot become ossified or converted into bone. The ossified

"Boxy" feet have an angle of more than 55° and are associated with upright pasterns.

Shoes with rolled toes reduce strain on the tendons and the navicular bone.

A plastic wedge raises the heel of a hoof which slopes too much.

time goes on, the horse may become prone to stumbling.

Although the condition is incurable, various treatments are employed to help relieve the pain. Corrective shoeing is used to raise the heels and reduce concussion to the navicular area. The horse may be given anticoagulants or anti-inflammatory drugs. Laser and ultrasound treatment may also be beneficial.

Pedal osteitis is inflammation of the pedal bone. It is often the result of jarring but can also develop after an attack of laminitis or following puncture injuries to the sole of the foot. It usually affects both forefeet and the horse will tend to shuffle when he moves. The demineralization of the bone is visible on X-ray. Careful shoeing can bring relief to what is usually an irreversible condition. Laser and ultrasound therapy may be beneficial.

Ringbone is an abnormal bony growth which occurs either at the centre of the

A **sandcrack** is a break in the wall of the hoof and may occur anywhere between the coronet and the ground surface of the foot. Sandcracks may be the result of injury, poor nutrition, an overdrying of the hoof (for instance in very dry weather), too much rasping during the shoeing process or neglect, for example lack of regular trimming by the farrier. Lameness may result if the crack is serious.

The farrier may be able to arrest the progress of a sandcrack by making grooves in the hoof wall to isolate the crack. Metal clips may also be used or, in the case of a deep crack, it may be necessary to fill it with a special bonding substance. Because the crack opens when weight is put on the foot as it is placed on the ground, a shoe with clips may be fitted.

Seedy toe is a condition in which the wall of the foot parts company with the sole at the white line. It may be the result

cartilages can be felt at the junction of the hair and the hoof in the area of the quarter of the foot. Sidebones are usually caused by concussion. Heavy or common-bred horses are the most susceptible. The horse may be lame while the cartilage is ossifying and sometimes lameness persists once the sidebones have developed because of pressure on the wall of the foot. The condition does not normally require treatment other than short-term rest but if lameness persists the farrier may be able to relieve the pressure with corrective shoeing and grooving of the hoof to allow expansion.

Thrush is caused by bad stable management (dirty bedding and failure to pick out the feet regularly). It is easily detected by the evil smell coming from the frog, which is moist and may have a black discharge. The affected area of the frog must be opened out to expose it to the air and treated with antiseptics.

Learning to Ride

Before Climbing Aboard

There are few more enviable sights in the world than a horse and rider enjoying a happy, trusting partnership. To be able to harness the spirit and beauty of an animal as majestic as the horse so that he is happy to work with you, and willing to do all that you ask of him, has to be one of life's greatest pleasures. A horse and rider in harmony appear to move by magic, but whilst the spectator may appreciate the words of Robert Surtees – "there is no closer secret than that between a rider and his horse" – anyone who has experienced some of the setbacks that can occur whilst trying to acquire the art of horsemanship may wonder whether these words were spoken with admiration, envy or in sheer frustration!

For some, horse riding is an occasional pastime, for others it is a lifelong passion – either way it should be a pleasure for both horse and rider. Learning to ride involves two living creatures – the rider is reliant on the horse's generosity and co-operation; the horse, in return, deserves fair and sensitive treatment from his rider.

If You Have Never
Sat on a Horse...

If you have never so much as sat on a horse or pony, there will be a great deal to take in to start with. It will help to have an overall idea in your mind of what it is you are trying to achieve.

Once you have mounted, the means of communication with the horse are through the use of the legs, seat, hands and voice. Anything that you ask the horse to do – from simply walking forwards to performing an intricate dressage movement to jumping a huge fence – is achieved by using a combination of leg, seat, hand and, sometimes, the voice. The art of riding lies in learning to feel what the horse is doing underneath you, and understanding how to influence what he does and how well he performs by mastering this subtle combination of leg, seat and hand. These means of communicating with the horse are called aids. Leg, hand and seat aids, as well as your voice, are called natural aids and they can be backed up by the artificial aids, which are the spur and whip. The spur is a short stump of blunt metal which is worn over the rider's boot just above the heel; the whip is either a short stick or a longer schooling whip.

Ultimately, riding a horse should have the same smooth feeling of power and control as driving a high-performance sports car or a speed boat. Just as a powerful car responds instantly to a light touch on the accelerator pedal, a horse should move forwards the instant he feels a light squeeze from the rider's leg. The feeling of lightness and control which power steering in a car gives you is the same feeling that a well-schooled horse should give you through the reins. Just an inclination of your hand to guide the horse in one direction or another, or a slight squeeze and hold of the rein to help gather up all his energy and power, is all that should be needed. It takes a long period of careful training for a horse to become as responsive as this, and it takes

I LEFT
When performing the half-pass you may have to do something different with each hand and leg, which is why attaining an independent seat should be the aim of all riders.

time and practice for a rider to get to the stage of being able to provide that training.

In the beginning, as a general rule of thumb, the novice rider should appreciate that it is the legs that are used first and foremost to instruct the horse to do something. The legs create the power, while the hands gently guide the horse in the right direction.

As a beginner, you will usually find yourself riding in a circle around an instructor. The hand and leg on the inside of the circle, i.e. the hand and leg nearest the instructor, are referred to as the inside hand and leg. The hand and leg on the outside of the circle are known as the outside hand and leg. If your inside hand is your left hand, i.e. you are going in an anti-clockwise direction, you are said to be riding on the left rein. If you are told to change the rein, this involves turning the

horse around and circling in the opposite direction, so that the inside hand is now your right hand, which means you are now riding on the right rein.

Your arms and hands are linked via the reins to the bit in the horse's mouth. This line of contact is all part of your communication with the horse, and to make life comfortable for him you must aim to relax your arms, so that as the horse's head and neck move you follow that movement. Ideally this is done whilst still maintaining a consistent but soft contact with the horse's mouth. The idea is not to let the reins keep going slack and then tight, but to relax your arms enough to follow what the horse's head and neck are doing whilst keeping a constant feel on the reins. The feel that you have down the reins to the horse's mouth is known as the contact, and the ultimate aim is to ride

AN INDEPENDENT SEAT

The key to all successful riding is to attain what is commonly known as "an independent seat". The means of communication with the horse are through your seat, legs, hands and voice – that is six different things and on some occasions you may have to do something different with each of them at the same time! To do this you must be able to sit securely and centrally in the saddle, whilst leaving your legs and hands free to communicate with the horse. This means being able to keep your balance without gripping with your legs, or hanging on by the reins, in all paces. Only then can your legs, seat and hands be used independently of each other to ask the horse to perform some of the more elaborate and enjoyable movements that he can offer you.

In an ideal world, any would-be horseman would first gain this independent seat by riding a horse or pony that is being lunged. To begin with you might hold on to the front of the saddle or to a neck strap to help you keep your balance, but as your body and muscles gradually become used to the movement of the horse underneath you, it becomes easier to remain relaxed and balanced. Various exercises without reins or stirrups will help to reinforce the balance and security of your

■ LEFT
Learning to ride on the lunge is one of the best ways to acquire the feel and balance that are needed to develop an independent seat. Once this is achieved, you can start to ride properly and really influence the horse.

seat until you have attained true independence of hands, seat and legs at all paces. Lungeing can be a tiring and time-consuming operation, besides which, most potential riders are in a rush to enjoy more of the thrill and excitement of horse riding. But if you really want to master the art of riding, it is time well spent, and this will be repaid when you discover how much more effective and sensitive a rider you are when you do progress to more exciting things. Remember – patience and practice are the keys to becoming a successful rider.

with a very light contact. It sometimes helps to imagine that the rein is an extension of your arm and that your hands are attached directly to the bit in the horse's mouth. As the horse's head moves your arms will have to move with him.

However ambitious or otherwise you may be, by persevering and mastering the correct techniques of horse riding, your satisfaction and enjoyment of your hobby or sport will be greatly enhanced. You may have no desire to reach the dizzy heights

of the competition world – perhaps a simple hack through the countryside is your idea of paradise – but either way, life will be more enjoyable for both you and your horse if you at least attempt to master the art of horsemanship.

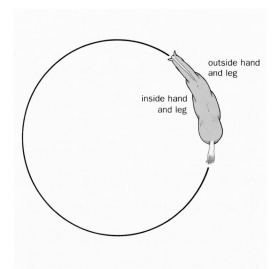

outside hand and leg

inside hand and leg

Riding on the left rein.

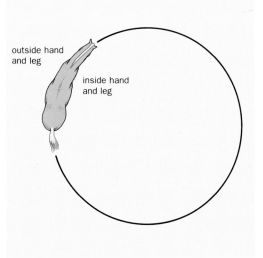

outside hand and leg

inside hand and leg

Riding on the right rein.

Understanding Horses and Ponies

The first thing that any would-be rider must appreciate is the sheer strength and bulk that a horse or pony represents. Common sense should tell even the most inexperienced person that the relationship between horse and rider cannot possibly be based on force – if it were, the horse would win every time. As a rider, you are totally dependent on the horse's co-operation, and so the partnership between horse and rider is one of mutual respect.

Much of the secret behind the successful handling of a horse or pony either from the ground or from the saddle is based on the human being in the partnership appearing both calm and confident. So before considering actually riding a horse or pony, it is well worth spending time just getting used to working with them. Most riding establishments

Spending time helping to care for and handle horses helps beginners to feel at ease with them.

Spending time grooming and preparing the horse you are going to ride is all part of building up a good partnership.

would be more than happy to accept an offer of help around the yard and this is a good opportunity to learn how to feel comfortable around horses.

A horse is happiest if he is handled confidently and positively. He is far more likely to become nervous and unsure if his handler is jittery and tentative. A horse or pony should always be handled firmly, but fairly, so that he learns what is expected of him. It is the rider's job to teach the horse

what is acceptable and what is not. The training of a horse has the same basis as the training of any other animal – when the horse does what is required he is rewarded, when he does not he is quietly reprimanded. It is vital that the handler is consistent in what he or she asks. It is not fair to drape yourself around your pony's neck, hugging and kissing him, only to turn round and wallop him when he shifts his position and accidentally steps on your toe! It is wrong to punish the horse when it was you, the handler, who put yourself in a position where you could get hurt. Although you may think it at the time, the horse would not step on you on purpose if he could avoid doing so!

Your voice is the most valuable form of communication you can have with a horse or pony. He will know from the tone of your voice whether you are pleased with him or otherwise. So it is your voice which should be used to tell the horse when he is behaving well and when he isn't. Your commands should be kept clear and

simple – if the horse does something wrong, then a stern "No" is often all it takes to let him know. A long, angry tirade will only confuse him, and wear you out. Keep it simple – "No" when he is wrong, and "Good boy" or "Good girl" when things are going well. Far too many people forget to tell the horse when they are pleased with him.

Horses, like people, have different temperaments and characters, and not every horse will get on in the same way with every person. A very sharp, nervy horse probably won't feel comfortable with an equally bolshie person – he is more likely to respond to a quieter character. An extrovert person can sometimes inspire confidence and coax a little more effort out of a horse with a more laid-back character.

NEAR SIDE, OFF SIDE

Some of the first things to learn in order to avoid confusion all round are the terms used to describe each side of the horse. If you stand facing in the same direction as the horse, his left-hand side is known as the near side, and his right-hand side is known as the off side. The horse is led from the near side; you mount and dismount from the near side. The same terms are used to describe each of the horse's limbs – if a horse is said to be lame on his off fore, this refers to the front leg on the right-hand side.

off side

near side

Where to Learn

Some children are lucky enough to be put on a pony before they can even walk – long before they are in a position to control their ponies off the leading rein, they will have developed a natural seat. This is because someone else has been in charge of the pony – all the rider has had to worry about is staying on board. It is the same principle as being lunged.

For those who haven't had that lucky start, if time and money allow, the best investment is in a course of lunge lessons at an equestrian centre with a good reputation. The advantages of this are that you will be receiving individual attention and, most importantly, you will start to acquire a deep, balanced but relaxed seat in the saddle. Lungeing will also give you the opportunity to concentrate on trying to feel how the horse is actually moving underneath you.

There is the danger of the first riding lesson being a miserable experience. Avoid any establishment where novices are put on badly schooled, bored mounts and stuck in a class with any number of other potential riders, and where inexperienced or simply incompetent instructors swagger around bawling instructions or criticism. The poor riders are expected to master

All too often a lack of communication and understanding between horse and rider leads to a lack of co-operation.

the correct riding position, keep their balance in the saddle, and manoeuvre unresponsive creatures around the arena. These new riders will either give up or become aggressive jockeys, oblivious to the reality of true horsemanship.

Lunge lessons will help the rider to develop a good seat, from which he or she will be able to communicate effectively with the horse. For any rider unable to enjoy such an opportunity, the next best thing is to opt for individual lessons, rather than group lessons. Once some of the basics have been mastered, riding in a group can be a positive and enjoyable experience, but if learning from scratch there is nothing to beat individual attention right at the beginning. This may either be at a commercial riding school or equestrian centre, or with a private individual who may give lessons using their own horses and facilities.

Always ensure that the instructor of your choice has a good reputation both for teaching ability and for being safe and responsible. In most countries there is some form of recognized teaching body and a structured system of examinations for instructors; if you have nobody to advise you, always opt for a registered and approved instructor. But if someone is highly recommended to you by more experienced riders, do not be afraid to try them even if teaching is not their profession – some people are naturally gifted teachers.

With a willing helper to lead the way, the world is yours to explore. It is a great advantage to learn to ride at such an early age. There are classes for young riders on lead reins at most local gymkhanas.

Group riding lessons are beneficial and fun once the potential rider has had a chance to master some of the basics.

Clothing and Equipment

HARD HAT

One vital item that the rider must have is a hard riding hat, also known as a crash hat or skull cap, which conforms to a recognized safety standard. Any romantic notions about feeling the wind blowing through your hair, or galloping across the prairie in your designer stetson should be dismissed – it is only fair to yourself, and to those who will have to pick up the pieces if you have an accident, that you wear the correct headgear. The design and effectiveness of riding hats has improved dramatically. A riding hat must always be worn with a safety harness to hold it in place; a traditional hard hat with an elastic chin strap is next to useless.

Hard hats come in various designs – looking like the traditional velvet hat with a built-in peak, or like a crash hat or skull cap as worn by racing jockeys and cross-country riders. The latter are more bulbous looking than the traditional type. Some of the newest styles, popularized in America, are very lightweight, vented helmets which protect the head whilst allowing the rider to stay surprisingly cool.

Whatever your standard of riding, and no matter how little or often you ride, your first priority should be to wear equipment of the highest safety standards. The highest current safety standards are the European PAS 015 and the American ASTM/SEIF 1163.

The majority of approved riding or training centres insist that their clients wear protective headgear and, similarly, whenever a rider competes he or she will generally be required to wear a proper hat. A riding hat should always be replaced once it has suffered a hard blow, either through the rider falling, or through being dropped accidentally.

RIDING BOOTS

The second most important item of clothing, from a safety point of view, is footwear. Long or short boots of some kind should be worn; it is important that they are not so wide that there is any risk of them being caught in the stirrup in the

The jockey-style crash hat or skull cap can be worn on its own, or you can fit a "silk" to it – dark blue or black for dressage and show jumping, and a colour to match your outfit for cross-country riding.

Jodhpurs are usually made of a stretchy material and are designed to be worn with short boots.

Breeches are designed to be worn with long riding boots.

The velvet riding hat is styled on the hunting cap and looks quite formal. It is particularly suitable for show-ring riding, dressage and show jumping. A stock, which is a kind of scarf or neck tie, should always be worn for cross-country riding as it does give some support to the neck in the case of a fall.

The lightweight vented helmet is fast becoming a popular choice. If it is made to the ASTM/SEIF 1163 standard, it is just as safe as any other hat made to an accepted safety standard such as the European PAS 015. In fact, the ASTM standard hats are stronger in terms of their impact resistance.

Short leather jodhpur boots can be worn with jodhpurs or with a pair of "half-chaps" to protect the rider's lower leg.

Long riding boots can be made of either rubber or leather.

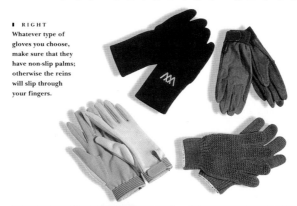

event of a fall, and they should only have a
small heel – again so that there is no risk
of the rider's foot becoming trapped.

There is a good range of casual and
affordable boots designed for leisure riding,
although they would not usually be
acceptable in the competition world. For
any form of competition riding, the
correct turnout is long boots (ideally
leather rather than rubber) or short, leather
riding boots such as jodhpur boots.

GLOVES

Most riders like to wear gloves. These
should have non-slip palms.

TROUSERS

For the sake of comfort, wear trousers
designed specifically for riding. Any
garment with a thick seam will chafe
against your skin, and anything too thin or
flimsy will simply wear through. Jodhpurs
or breeches come in a huge variety of

If spurs have to be worn they should be as short as
possible and must have a rounded or blunt end.
They should never be worn by a beginner. In fact,
they should not be worn until you have good
control of your lower leg; otherwise you will be
spurring your horse unnecessarily.

A neck strap can prove invaluable as an aid to
staying in the saddle if the horse plays up or jumps
awkwardly. Hold on to the strap with one hand to
help keep your weight deep in the saddle, making it
harder for you to be thrown off. It can also be used
as an aid to help slow the horse down.

Protective clothing is important for both horse and
rider. This rider is wearing a jockey-style crash
helmet with safety harness, a body protector and
long leather riding boots. Her horse is wearing
protective leg boots to reduce the risk of injury
through knocking into himself, or being scratched
or cut by anything whilst being ridden.

styles and colours, and can be purchased
as either competition or casual garments.

CHAPS

If short boots are to be worn, it is also
advisable to wear what are known as chaps
or half-chaps, which are shaped leggings
made from leather, suede or waterproof
material. Half-chaps are worn below the
knee and protect the lower leg. They are
usually fastened by either Velcro or a zip,
and prevent the stirrup leather rubbing
against the rider's calf. Full chaps are just
like the ones cowboys wear; they cover the
whole leg and are fastened with a belt
around the waist. As well as offering some
protection to the leg, they have the
advantage of keeping the rider warm.

BODY PROTECTOR

These are padded, vest-like garments and
are mandatory in most countries for sports
such as horse racing and the cross-country
phase of horse trials. With lightweight
breatheable materials of ever-better

quality appearing on the market each
year, they are nothing like as cumbersome
and hot as they used to be. They can be
worn either over your usual riding top,
or underneath your clothes. The ones
worn over the top tend to be the most
convenient and are available in an array of
colours and designs. In an ideal world they
would be worn whenever you rode, not just
when you intended to jump or compete.

NECK STRAP

A final, small piece of equipment that also
adds to the rider's safety is a neck strap,
which is worn by the horse. This is a
leather strap (an old stirrup leather makes
an ideal neck strap) worn loosely around
the horse's neck. It sits just above the
withers and is well positioned for you to
grab hold of if you lose your balance. Neck
straps can make the difference between
staying aboard and hitting the deck when
jumping, and have saved many a rider
from being thrown off; they also prevent a
horse from being "jabbed" in the mouth.

Sitting Comfortably

Before you even get as far as sitting on a horse there is quite
a lot of groundwork to master, such as tacking up and
mounting. Riding schools vary in their approach to tacking
up for beginners. Some have the horse ready and waiting
for his rider, others feel that tacking up is all part of the
learning process and that it will give you a few minutes of
unpressurized time in which to start to get to know your
horse. If a friend is teaching you, it is all part of the fun to
help get the horse ready.

Tacking Up

The order in which the horse is tacked up varies, but any form of boots should be put on first, once the horse's legs have been checked for signs of heat or swelling. This should have been done while the horse was being groomed, but it is good practice to double check when putting on the boots – there is no point tacking up and then finding that the horse is lame!

Whether the saddle or bridle is put on next is a matter for discussion. Some riders like to put the bridle on first, so that they have better control of the horse should he pull back and break free from his headcollar. Others like to put the saddle on first so that, having removed the horse's warm rugs, the saddle goes straight on to a warm back and the horse's muscles will remain warm underneath the saddle. On a cold day, a rug should be kept over the horse's back and quarters while he is being tacked up.

Protective boots reduce the risk of injury. Hold the boot securely in place and fasten the first strap. Then fasten the second strap firmly enough to prevent the boot slipping. Tighten the first strap if it seems looser than the second strap. These boots protect the tendon area of the legs as well as the inside of the fetlocks. Many horses are prone to knocking one leg against the inside of the opposite leg – this is called brushing – and boots prevent the horse from injuring himself as a result.

PUTTING ON THE BRIDLE

1 Whilst being tacked up or groomed, the horse is usually secured by a headcollar. Before removing the headcollar put the bridle reins over the horse's head so that you have a means of holding him.

2 Remove the headcollar by lifting the headpiece forward and then gently over the horse's ears.

3 With one hand holding the horse's nose to keep his head steady, bring the bridle up in front of his face.

4 Use your right hand to hold the bridle, lay the bit over the palm of your left hand and gently lift it up into the horse's mouth. Use your thumb to press his gum in the gap where his teeth finish which will encourage him to open his mouth.

5 Once the bit is in place, keep some tension on each side of the bridle to hold it there whilst you bring the headpiece of the bridle up and over the horse's ears. Do not allow the bit to bang against his teeth as this will make him wary next time.

6 With the headpiece in place, separate the hair of the forelock from the rest of the mane (to let the bridle sit comfortably, cut a small section out of the mane where the headpiece sits). Bring the forelock forward and lift it clear of the browband.

7 Keep your hand looped through the rein so that you have a contact with the horse, and therefore control over him, and then do up the throatlash.

8 It should not be fastened too tightly – make sure you can still get four fingers of your hand between the horse's cheek and the throatlash.

9 Fasten the noseband – in this case a drop noseband which does up below the bit rings. A cavesson noseband, used for lungeing, sits higher up the horse's nose and does up above the bit rings.

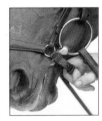

10 You should be able to place one finger between the horse's chin and the noseband.

SADDLING UP

1 Place a soft, padded numnah on the horse's back. This acts as a cushion between the horse and the saddle and can relieve pressure points and reduce the risk of rubbing. It is also a warmer layer to have against the horse's skin than the leather of the saddle.

2 Keeping the saddle well clear of the horse's back, lift it so that it is poised in the right position to be lowered on to the back. Lower the saddle into place, making sure that the saddle flap on the off side is lying flat.

3 Use your left hand to lift the numnah so that it is not pulled tight over the horse's withers. It should be tucked up to lie snugly under the pommel of the saddle, clear of the withers.

4 Most numnahs have two straps that hold them in position under the saddle. The first one is usually attached to the girth straps, so pull it over the knee roll of the saddle and put it on the strap before you do up the girth.

5 Position the strap above the buckle guard, otherwise you will not be able to pull this down into the correct position. Pull the girth strap out from the buckle guard, thread through the numnah strap, then put the strap back through the buckle guard.

6 Buckle the girth to the saddle on the off side. Return to the near side, and reach under the horse's belly to catch the girth. Thread the girth buckles through the second securing strap of the numnah and fasten them, one at a time, to each girth strap.

7 Gently tighten the girth, one buckle at a time, until you can just squeeze the flat of your hand between the horse's belly and the girth. Fasten the girth equally on each side.

8 Pull the buckle guard down so that it covers the buckles – otherwise they will gradually wear a hole through the saddle flap.

9 Smooth down under the girth so that there are no wrinkles of skin caught up which might rub. Slide your hand under the girth just clear of the saddle flap and run it down under the horse's belly, taking particular care to smooth any wrinkles in the horse's elbow area.

10 A correctly fitted jumping saddle, with the girth tightened and the stirrups run up so that they don't swing and bang against the horse's sides. A jumping saddle has forward-cut flaps and knee rolls to allow the rider to keep his or her leg on the saddle even when riding with shorter stirrups.

PUTTING ON A DRESSAGE SADDLE

1 A dressage saddle has long girth straps which do up below the saddle flap. The girth must still be tightened gradually, one buckle at a time, and the skin and hair smoothed down underneath it.

2 Dressage saddles allow your legs to hang much longer and closer to the horse's sides. This gives the best possible position for you to communicate with the horse through your legs and seat.

LEADING A TACKED-UP HORSE

I LEFT
When leading a tacked-up horse, stand on his near side and bring the reins over his head. The stirrups should be run up so that they do not swing or bang against the horse's sides. Carry the excess loop of rein and your riding stick in your left hand. Have the stick pointing backwards so that you can give the horse a tap behind the girth if he refuses to walk on. You should always wear a riding hat whenever you lead a horse.

MOUNTING FROM THE GROUND

Mounting

So now it is time to step aboard. It is essential to learn how to mount correctly from the ground but, as a general rule, it is far less stressful on the horse's back to use a mounting block or be given a leg-up. Either of these methods is also a lot safer than mounting from the ground. A great many accidents occur when riders are trying to get on their horses. If you do mount from the ground, ideally an assistant should stand on the far side of the horse and, by putting his or her hand in the stirrup iron, should use some of his or her own weight to counteract your weight swinging up from the other side. This helps to reduce the amount of twisting and pulling on the horse's spine.

1 Before attempting to get on your horse you will need to put the reins back over his head, and to let down the stirrups.

2 As you pull the stirrup irons down, keep them away from the horse's sides so that they don't knock him. When they are fully down, place them gently back against his sides.

3 Stand on the near side of the horse, facing his tail, and put both reins in your left hand. It also helps to loop a finger through the neck strap and hold on to a little piece of the mane.

4 Take the stirrup iron in your right hand and turn it to face you. The stirrup should be turned clockwise, so that once you are mounted the stirrup leather lies correctly against your leg.

5 Lift your left leg and place your foot in the stirrup iron. Put your right hand on the seat of the saddle.

6 Push with your right leg to spring off the ground and, at the same time, reach to the far side of the saddle with your right hand.

Voilà! You are now mounted on your horse. Put your right foot in the stirrup and then take up a rein in each hand.

7 Once you are high enough off the ground, you will be able to grip the far side of the saddle with your right hand and this will help you to balance. Keep bringing your right leg up until it is clear of the horse's back and hindquarters.

8 At this point start to swing your right leg over the back of the horse. Bring your right hand back to the front of the saddle and rest it on either the pommel or the horse's neck to help you support and balance your upper body.

9 As your right leg starts to come down over the off side of the horse, take your weight on your hands and arms so that you don't flop down in the saddle. Lower your seat gently into the saddle.

GETTING A LEG-UP

1 If someone is going to give you a leg-up on to your horse, you should stand on the near side facing the saddle. Take both reins and your stick in your left hand – making sure you carry the stick down over the off-side shoulder of the horse otherwise you will hit your helper in the face with it as you mount up! Rest your left hand on the horse's neck or on the pommel of the saddle, and reach up with your right hand so that it is resting near the back of the saddle.

USING A MOUNTING BLOCK

It is far less stressful for both horse and rider if you are able to get aboard by using a mounting block. The horse is led alongside the mounting block so that his near side is parallel to the block. Use the stirrup to mount in the normal way. Now that you are that much higher off the ground, there is less strain on the horse's back when you step up into the stirrup.

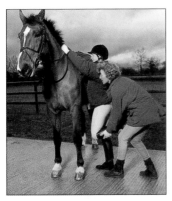

2 Bend your left leg up from the knee so that your helper can take hold of it with both hands.

3 Sink your weight down into your right leg and when your helper gives the command be ready to spring up in the air off your right leg.

4 As you spring up off your right leg, your helper will also lift your weight by lifting your left leg up. Take your weight on your hands so that you are supporting your upper body and can control the moment when you want to swing your right leg over the horse's back.

5 As you swing your right leg over the horse's back you will need to transfer your right hand from the back of the saddle to either the pommel or the top of the saddle flap on the off side. Make sure you continue to support your upper body on both your arms.

6 With your weight on your arms you can lower your seat down gently into the saddle.

Adjusting Tack

Having learned how to tack up and mount your horse, there are one or two other small adjustments you will need to make once you are on board. The first thing you must do is tighten the girth. Although this is tightened from the ground before you mount, your weight pushing the saddle down on to the horse's back will cause the girth to need retightening. Also, many horses push their stomachs out against the pressure of the girth, and only relax again once their riders are in the saddle.

It is only once you are sitting on your horse that you can feel if your stirrups are set at a comfortable length for you; they may need adjusting. When you change from riding on the flat to jumping you will also want to shorten your stirrups whilst still sitting on the horse.

1 To retighten the girth, put both reins and your stick in your right hand and bring your left leg clear of the saddle flap.

2 Reach down and lift up the saddle flap so that you have access to the girth straps.

3 Hold the saddle flap out of the way with your right hand; with your left hand, pull the buckle guard up away from the girth straps and buckles.

4 Take hold of the first girth strap and pull it up gently. Use your index finger to press the spike of the buckle through the hole.

5 Do the same to the second girth strap – make sure each is tightened by the same number of holes.

6 Pull the buckle guard back down so that it sits snugly over the girth buckles. Put the saddle flap back down and return your leg to the correct position.

HOLDING THE REINS

1 Hold the reins by allowing them to lie across the palm of your hand. The end that comes from the horse's mouth passes between your third and fourth finger.

2 It rests over the top of your first finger and is held in place by closing your thumb and fingers. You can lengthen the reins by relaxing the tension in your hand and letting them slip through your fingers.

3 This picture shows you how to hold a stick as well as your reins. When your thumb and fingers close back around the rein and stick, they are held safely in place.

ADJUSTING THE STIRRUP LEATHERS

1 Once you are in the saddle you may need to adjust your stirrup leathers in order to sit comfortably and correctly. Put the reins and stick in your right hand, and use your left hand to lift the leather flap that covers the stirrup-leather buckle.

2 Pull the free end of the stirrup leather out of its keeper if necessary, and then pull it upwards so that the buckle is released.

3 To shorten your stirrup, pull the stirrup leather upwards, as shown. To lengthen your stirrup, put your weight down into the stirrup iron and with your left hand allow the stirrup leather to slide back down through the stirrup bar.

4 When the stirrup is at the required length, push the buckle back through the appropriate hole.

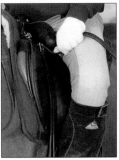

5 Make sure the stirrup-leather buckle slides back into position, hard up against the stirrup bar.

6 Push the free end of the stirrup leather back through the keeper.

7 Ensure that the leather is lying flat before repeating the procedure for the right stirrup.

POSITIONING THE STIRRUP LEATHER

Each stirrup leather should be turned outwards, rather than inwards, in order to position the stirrup iron so that your foot can go into it. This allows the stirrup leather to curve smoothly across the inside of your leg. So to put your right foot (off-side foot) in the stirrup iron, give the leather a quarter turn in a clockwise direction. For the near-side foot (left foot), turn the stirrup leather in an anti-clockwise direction.

4 You should always hold both your hands at the same height, usually just above the withers and a few inches apart. The basic rule for hand position is that there should be a straight line running from your elbow, down your arm, through the wrist and hand, down the rein to the horse's mouth. It is this rule that dictates the exact position of your hands, which will therefore alter depending on what the horse is doing with his head carriage. This hand and arm position allows you to maintain a soft, elastic but consistent contact with the horse's mouth. (See The Hands which illustrates three different but correct positions.)

Dismounting

Dismounting from the horse should also be done correctly. Do not be tempted to follow the example of countless cowboys and Indians in Wild West movies by flinging your leg over the front of the saddle. If the horse throws his head up you will, at best, be knocked off backwards or, at worst, startle the horse so that he either jumps or bolts, leading to even more painful consequences. Always remove both feet from the stirrups, lean forward and swing your right leg up and over behind the saddle. As obvious as it may sound, always check that the ground where you are about to land is safe and free of obstacles before you dismount.

GETTING OFF

1 To prepare to dismount from your horse you should take both feet out of the stirrups and put both reins, and your stick, in your left hand.

2 Rest both hands on the pommel of the saddle or on the horse's neck. Lean your upper body forward.

3 Now swing your right leg up and over the horse's back.

4 Swing your left leg back and out slightly so that it meets your right leg which has now swung over on to the near side of the horse. Use your hands on the saddle to help support your body.

5 Allow both your legs to drop to the ground together. Bend your knees as you land to absorb the impact.

6 Straighten up and you are ready to run up your stirrups, take the reins over your horse's head, and lead him back to his stable.

The Ideal Position

Once on the horse, you should try to adopt a proud and elegant posture. The ideal, classical position is like that of a person standing with their knees slightly bent, not sitting in an armchair. Your ear, shoulder, hip and heel should all be in line, with equal weight placed on each seat bone so that you are not tipped too far forward or sitting back on your buttocks. Always remember how heavy your head is in relation to the rest of your body – if you look down, or tilt your head to the side, or push it too far forward it will affect your, and therefore the horse's, balance. Your legs should hang long and loose down the horse's sides. When your foot is balanced in the stirrup, think of allowing your weight to sink down into your heel.

Although it is often frowned upon today by many who consider it unsafe, anyone who was fortunate enough to learn to ride bareback tends to adopt a correct position automatically. Often, it is the addition of the saddle and the stirrups which compromises what was otherwise a near-perfect position.

By practising the ideal position on the ground, you can start to get a good feel of what you are aiming for, before the added complication of the movement of the horse underneath you enters the equation. Similarly, while sitting on the stationary horse you can be shown how to follow the movement of his head and neck, so that you do not restrict the horse or harm him by pulling on the reins in an attempt to keep your balance.

Your foot should be balanced centrally in the stirrup, with the stirrup tread positioned under the ball of your foot and your weight lowered gently down into your heel.

If you sit a child on a pony bareback, his or her leg position will automatically be long and low as required for the classical position.

As soon as a saddle is introduced, note how the child adopts an armchair seat. The best way to acquire a natural, classical seat is to learn to ride either bareback or without stirrups.

1 You can practise the classical riding position on the ground. First stand straight, with your legs about 2 feet (0.5 m) apart, and your arms bent at the elbow as if you were holding the horse's reins.

2 Keeping your whole body straight and upright, simply bend your knees slightly – now you are in the classical dressage position. For jumping you simply bend your knees more. Your position on a horse should be as if you were standing with your knees bent, rather than as if you were sitting in a chair.

▌ LEFT
Your position in the saddle should be exactly the same as the position you have practised on the ground. See how this rider appears to be standing with her knees bent rather than sitting on the saddle. Note how there is a straight line through the rider's ear, shoulder, hip and heel. Similarly there is another straight line running from the elbow, down through the wrist and hand to the rein and eventually to the bit.

COMMON FAULTS

How not to sit! You should not allow your weight to fall on to the back of your bottom as if you were sitting on a chair. Note how, when this happens, the rider's lower leg swings forward and becomes ineffective as a result.

You should not sit with your weight pitched forward. It prevents you from sitting properly and using your legs correctly – and it is painful! Note how this position causes the lower leg to slide back.

PRACTISING A SOFT CONTACT

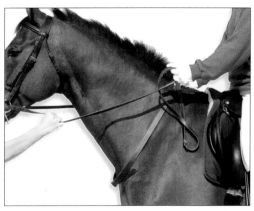

1 One of the secrets of sympathetic and effective riding is to learn how to maintain a soft but constant contact with the horse's mouth, whilst allowing him to move his head and neck freely. Take up a rein in each hand and ask a friend to hold the rein further down towards the horse's mouth.

2 Ask your friend to mimic the movement of the horse's head and neck by drawing the rein forwards and then releasing it. Concentrate on maintaining the straight line from your elbow, through your wrist and hand down the rein. Keep your elbows and wrists soft and relaxed, and allow your whole arm, from the shoulder down, to be moved by the pull on the reins.

The Hands

Never forget that your hands are attached directly via the reins to a large piece of metal in the horse's mouth. Like your own, the horse's mouth is soft and sensitive, and you must never be harsh or abusive with your hands. One of the most important ideas to grasp is that your hands belong to the horse's mouth. Although a light, consistent contact must be maintained so that you have a line of communication with the horse, that contact should be elastic. Your hands must follow the movement of the horse's head and neck. It should feel as if you are shaking hands politely with someone; there is equal pressure and movement from each party. It is not polite to clasp someone's hand roughly and shake it violently as a terrier might shake a rat! Nor is it kind to grasp the reins and swing and tug on them. An old Spanish proverb suggests that "you should ride as if with reins of silk". This can only be achieved if the whole arm stays soft and relaxed, right from the shoulder through the elbow to the hand. The elbow opens out softly to allow the hands to go forwards as the horse's head moves.

COMMON FAULTS

A common fault is to have stiff, straight arms and to turn the wrists and hands outwards. You can see from this position how harsh it all looks, and how impossible it would be to keep a sympathetic contact with the horse.

A similar error is to carry your hands so that the thumbs are pointing downwards – again this prevents you maintaining a soft, consistent contact with the horse's mouth.

The exact position of the hands, how close they are held to the withers, depends upon the horse's head carriage. There should always be a straight line from the elbow, through the wrist, down the rein to the bit; so if the horse is working with his head quite low, the hands must be carried a little lower and to either side of the withers in order to keep this straight line.

When the horse is working in a rounder outline, the hands can be carried a little higher; and when you find yourself riding a highly schooled horse who carries his head and neck higher still, your hands should be carried a few inches above the withers. The rule of thumb is to be aware of keeping the straight line from the elbow, through the rein to the horse's mouth.

You must adjust your arm position, following the horse's head and neck, so that you maintain an imaginary straight line from your elbow, through your wrist and hand, down the rein to the bit. This horse is working in a good outline in trot and you can see how the straight line is maintained.

When you encourage the horse to stretch and lower his neck, you must still keep the straight line. This rider has allowed her arms and elbows to be drawn forwards and down so that the line is maintained.

Here the horse is working with more pronounced flexion and bend through his neck. In this case you should raise your lower arms and hands slightly to maintain the line.

The Legs

The most important way that you can communicate with the horse is through the legs and seat. Your legs should hang long and relaxed around the horse's sides, with no tightness in the knee joints in particular. It is the insides of the calves which squeeze against the horse to ask him to move either forwards or across to one side or the other. If you run your hand down the inside of your leg just below the knee, you should feel the slight outward bulge of your calf muscle; it is this part of the leg which is used to communicate with the horse.

Check that your stirrup length is correct by allowing each leg to hang long and loose, and free of the stirrup. You should then only need to turn your toe up slightly to find the stirrup. This is the position that you should be aiming for,

Ask a friend to adjust the stirrup leather so that you only need to turn up your toe to find the stirrup iron. It may take some time for you to be able to ride comfortably with such a long stirrup length as your muscles will need to supple up and stretch, but this is what you are aiming for.

although at first it is likely to produce too much pull down the back of the thigh and calf muscles. Until your muscles have toned, stretched and strengthened sufficiently, it is sensible to ride with the leg in as long a position as is still comfortable. With time, and particularly as you begin to find your balance on the horse and the beginnings of an independent seat, you will gradually find it easier to ride with the leg in a longer position.

Keep your knee joint relaxed and let it fall away from the saddle slightly, which will allow the leg to hang correctly around the horse's side. Contrary to popular belief, you should not grip with the knees as doing so will effectively push your seat up and out of the saddle. Equally, if you hold your knees tightly against the saddle, you cannot squeeze the horse's sides with your legs. The knee and the toe have to be turned slightly outwards to allow the inside of the calf to press against the horse's sides; which you will need to do to apply a leg aid correctly.

A common fault is for the lower leg to be drawn back and upwards in order to press against the horse's side, but this is an

To find the correct stirrup length that will allow you to adopt the classical position for flatwork, you should sit deep in the saddle and just allow your legs to hang long and loose without putting them in the stirrups.

This is the classical position viewed from the front. You can see how the rider's legs would completely encompass the body of the horse; it is this position that allows the leg to support the horse at all times, and from which you can communicate with the horse through your leg aids.

LEFT
To apply the leg aids correctly you need to be aware of exactly what your lower leg is doing. When the horse is moving at the pace you wish him to, keep your legs gently in contact with his sides, but do not actively do anything. The lower leg and the knee joint should remain soft and relaxed.

ineffective means of communication. The lower leg must lie close to the girth; it will come into contact with the part of the horse's belly which is fractionally behind the girth. For some movements, such as turning, or when the rider wants to control the horse's hindquarters, the lower leg is used a few inches further back behind the girth. But the leg is always used in the same way – with the weight down in the heel, the knee and toe turned out slightly and with a squeeze or nudge inwards, not backwards. If you conjure up in your mind a picture of an old-fashioned, bow-legged horseman, you will have a good idea of how the rider's legs are used against the horse's sides, and why some riders end up looking bow-legged!

COMMON FAULTS

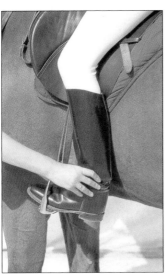

Picture one shows a bad leg position – see how the lower leg is pushed forward and away from the horse's sides. This is usually a result of the rider adopting an armchair seat in the saddle. It leads to the leg aids being incorrectly applied.

In picture two, instead of squeezing inwards this rider has drawn her lower leg back and, as a result, her weight has come out of her heel and her heel is higher than her toe. At this point it is very easy for the stirrup iron to slip off your foot. This type of leg aid is ineffective – the lower leg is simply being brushed backwards across the horse's side and is not being applied to the more sensitive area just behind the girth. A horse that is ridden like this will never be able to differentiate between an aid to move forwards and an aid to move his quarters, when the rider's lower leg is applied further back behind the girth.

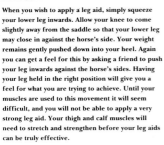

When you wish to apply a leg aid, simply squeeze your lower leg inwards. Allow your knee to come slightly away from the saddle so that your lower leg may close in against the horse's side. Your weight remains gently pushed down into your heel. Again you can get a feel for this by asking a friend to push your leg inwards against the horse's sides. Having your leg held in the right position will give you a feel for what you are trying to achieve. Until your muscles are used to this movement it will seem difficult, and you will not be able to apply a very strong leg aid. Your thigh and calf muscles will need to stretch and strengthen before your leg aids can be truly effective.

LUNGE LESSONS

Lungeing Exercises

The handler keeps a contact with the horse via the lunge line. The lunge whip can be used behind the horse's hindquarters to encourage him to move forwards, or it can be flicked towards his shoulder to keep him out on the circle. Both rider and handler should wear a riding hat; the handler should also wear gloves.

One of the best ways to encourage an independent seat is to be lunged. When the horse is lunged, the handler on the ground can control the horse's speed and direction, leaving you free to concentrate fully on your position. Lunge lessons are given at most riding establishments. It is important that the horse you ride is calm and steady on the lunge, and that the person who is lungeing you is capable and confident in what they are doing. A lungeing cavesson should be used over the horse's usual bridle. This is like a padded headcollar with a reinforced piece on the noseband which has rings attached to it. These take the lunge line. The handler should maintain a position which allows the lunge line, the lungeing whip and the horse to form a triangle.

The voice rather than the lunge whip should be used to ask the horse to move forwards. The lunge whip should only be used to back up the voice if the horse does not respond, and then should be moved quietly so that the horse does not suddenly shoot forwards. He should be allowed to settle into a steady rhythm; this

will make it easier for you to relax and find your balance. Both horse and rider should be allowed periods of rest during these exercises.

Lungeing should only ever take place on a secure surface. If you only have a field and it is hard and rutted, or deep and wet, the horse is likely to injure or strain his tendons if he is made to work on it. Lunge lessons should not last for more than 20–30 minutes, and work should be carried out in both directions. Working on a circle is tiring and stressful to the horse's limbs, and once you are tired or sore you will not be able to do anything more to improve your position. If anything, it will get worse as you tense up with effort. If you are struggling, it is much better to stop than to keep on until you reach the point of exhaustion or frustration.

RIDING WITHOUT STIRRUPS

Although work without stirrups is usually carried out on the lunge, or in an arena or *manège*, if you have the opportunity to hack out regularly, it is worth making yourself ride for a few minutes each time without stirrups. Normally, the stirrups would be crossed over in front of the saddle so that they don't bang against the horse's sides, but this is not advisable out on a hack in case you need the stirrups back in a hurry. You should only ride without stirrups on a hack at walk. At this pace they should not swing so much that they knock the horse's sides or elbows. Equally, you can quickly slip them back on if necessary. After only a few minutes of riding without stirrups, when you put your feet back in them they often feel too short – that is the time to let the stirrup leathers down a hole so that gradually you can ride at a longer length.

The triangle formed by the horse, handler, lunge line and lunge whip.

To help stretch the thigh muscles, practise this simple exercise. Bring your feet up under your bottom and hold them in position with a hand around each ankle. This has the added advantage of helping you to keep your shoulders up and straight, and it automatically puts your seat in the correct position in the saddle. When you take your stirrups back after these exercises, you may feel that you want to lengthen the stirrup leathers. This is a good sign and is the start of the path towards attaining the classical position.

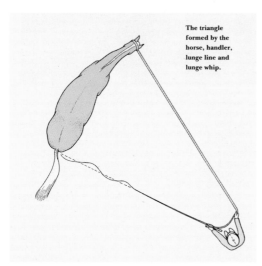

STRENGTHENING EXERCISE

1 Practise riding without stirrups and, to help build up your confidence and balance, spread your arms out to either side.

2 To help strengthen and supple your upper body, twist first round to the left...

3 ... and then back to the right.

HOLDING THE LUNGE LINE

1 It is important that whoever is going to lunge you knows how to do this safely and correctly. One of the biggest risks to the handler is getting his or her hands trapped in the lunge line should the horse panic and try to run away. The safest way to hold the lunge line is not to loop it around your hand but to do the following: lay the end of the lunge line across the palm of your hand. Do not put your hand through the loop that most lunge lines have on the end.

2 Lay the lunge line, in equal loops, backwards and forwards across the palm of your hand. Continue to loop the line across your palm until it is the desired length, i.e. you are the distance you want to be away from the horse.

3 Now you can close your hand around the loops and keep a contact with the horse as he moves. If you want to let more lunge line out so that the horse can work on a larger circle, just open your hand and allow one loop to fall away. If the horse did panic and pull away you could close your hand tight around the line and try to stop him. But if he has built up too much speed and is determined to get away, the lunge line will be pulled out of your hand, and you will be free of it. If it is looped around your hand and the horse bolts, the loops will tighten like a noose around your hand. You will either be dragged or have your fingers torn off. Either way the horse will escape if he is determined, so it is better to let him go if you have to and at least remain in one piece and in a position to retrieve him.

"ROUND THE WORLD" EXERCISE

▌ LEFT
The horse or pony you learn to ride on should be a sensible and calm one. This young rider is making the most of her pony's kind nature to have some fun, whilst also increasing her confidence on horseback. Exercises such as this one – called "Round the World" – should only ever be carried out on a quiet pony and with someone on the ground to hold the pony's head.

Mastering the Paces

Having climbed aboard, it is now time to experience some forward motion! The first thing you will suddenly be aware of is just how much the horse moves underneath you. The horse has four legs to operate and, at walk, these move one at a time. As each shoulder or hindquarter swings the appropriate leg forward, you will feel it. Each pace that the horse can offer you – walk, trot, canter and gallop – will give a different sensation of speed and motion, and you must learn to absorb it, and to remain balanced on the horse at each pace, whilst still maintaining the correct, classical position. To the outside eye, horse and rider should appear to be moving as one.

Absorbing the Movement

In an attempt to follow the movement of the horse, many riders end up trying too hard and do too much with their bodies. This, instead of creating a picture of harmony, actually looks completely unco-ordinated; the horse appears to be moving to one beat, and the rider to another. It is also uncomfortable.

The first thing to bear in mind is that your seat belongs to the saddle which, in turn, belongs to the horse's back. The saddle will mimic the movement of the horse's back and you should imagine that your seat is glued to the saddle. Sit deep in the saddle, with your weight taken equally on each seat bone. When striving for a deep, balanced seat, it sometimes helps to imagine that your legs have been cut off, about half way down the thigh; therefore it is the top half of the thighs and the seat itself which embrace the saddle. By sitting up straight and keeping the shoulders balanced above the hips, your weight sinks

down into the saddle. This allows the legs to hang long and loose around the horse's sides, with the foot supported softly by the stirrup. The arms follow the movement of the horse's head and neck, and this is achieved by keeping the elbows soft and relaxed with your shoulders remaining still. If your seat is glued to the saddle, and your shoulders, head and neck remain still, the only part of your body that is free to move is the area between your hips and your ribcage. So the hips and stomach are rocked gently forwards and back by the movement of the horse. It is by being soft and supple through the hips, the lower back and the stomach that you are able to move as one with the horse. Always remember that it is the horse that moves your body, and so your body must remain relaxed to allow it to be moved by the horse. You should not create any additional movement yourself – this is most likely to happen if your body is tense.

THE WALK

The walk is described as a four-time pace because the horse moves each leg individually; if you listen to his footfalls you hear four separate hoofbeats. In trot, the horse moves his legs in diagonal pairs, so this is known as a two-time pace.

The sequence of footfalls in walk is as follows: outside hind, outside fore, inside hind, inside fore. The horse should take strides of equal length and he should look energetic and purposeful. If you watch a horse walking you will see that his whole body is in action; the movement flows through the muscles of the hindquarters, up over the back, and through the shoulders and the neck. The horse should look supple, athletic and powerful. Although the walk is the horse's slowest pace, he does use his neck to quite a degree, which means you must be particularly aware of allowing your arms to follow the movement so that you do not restrict the horse.

MOVING WITH THE HORSE

At walk the rider allows his hips and stomach to be rocked gently forwards and back by the push of the horse's hindquarters beneath him. Notice how the rider is maintaining a straight line from the elbow, through the lower arm, and down

the rein to the bit. A light but constant contact is kept with the horse's mouth by allowing the arms to follow the natural movement of the horse's head and neck as he walks.

HALT TO WALK AND WALK TO HALT

Transitions

Changing pace on a horse, whether it be from halt to walk, or from trot to canter etc, is known as performing a transition. Like changing gear in a car, whether you are increasing or decreasing pace, it should appear smooth and effortless.

Transitions are achieved by a subtle balance of the use of the hand and leg. Use your lower leg to activate the horse's hindquarters, which is where his power comes from. You can then use your hands to guide that power in whichever direction you wish.

■ REFINING THE USE OF THE LEGS AND HANDS

To walk forwards, squeeze your legs against the horse's sides and allow your hands and arms to be drawn forwards. If the horse ignores you, give him a sharper nudge with your heels. If this is ignored, give him a tap with the schooling whip or stick behind your lower leg. If you have to

COMMON FAULTS

If the rider decides to do nothing with her legs and simply pulls on the reins in an effort to slow down you can see what happens – the horse resists the request to slow down and throws his head and neck in the air in order to fight the pull of the rider; this is described as the horse hollowing against the rider. The whole picture looks tense and uncomfortable. The rider must first ask with the legs and then only use as much hand as is absolutely necessary to achieve the desired result.

1 At halt the rider still keeps a light contact with the horse's mouth and lets the legs hang long and loose by the horse's sides. The lower leg is in contact with the horse but is not actively doing anything. Note how a straight line is maintained from the shoulder to the hip to the heel. The position would be better still if the rider kept her chin up – a common fault of many riders is the tendency to look down!

3 To prepare to return to halt, the rider squeezes her legs inwards against the horse's sides and at the same time reduces the degree to which she allows her arms to follow the movement of the horse's head and neck. On a well-schooled horse this very slight blocking of the free forward movement will be enough to halt the horse.

do this, you must be very quick to keep the soft forward movement of the hands. The horse may jump forwards if he is tapped with the whip, and he must not then be punished by being pulled in the mouth. Remember to reward the horse for obeying and going forwards. With practice, he will listen to you and a squeeze with your legs will be sufficient.

To halt the horse, squeeze with the legs but do not allow your hands to be drawn forwards so much. The horse will realize that his forward movement is being blocked and will either slow down or

2 To go forwards to walk, the rider squeezes both legs against the horse's sides and, at the same time, allows the hands and arms to go forward to follow the forward movement of the horse's head and neck. Once the horse is walking positively forwards the rider allows her legs to relax against the horse's sides. The arms and hands are drawn gently forwards and back by the movement of the horse's head and neck. This movement is led by the horse. The rider does not pull back on the reins.

4 On a less responsive horse the rider will have to continue to reduce the degree to which the hands follow the horse's head and neck to the point, where they are held still, which will completely block the forward movement. As soon as the horse halts, the rider should soften the hands as much as the horse will allow whilst still remaining at halt. Until the horse halts, the rider's legs remain actively against the horse's sides, gently pushing him up into the hands. Once he has halted, the legs relax and remain gently in contact with his sides.

shorten the steps he is taking. Continue to decrease the forward movement of the hands until, if necessary, they are returned to the normal halt position and do not move forwards at all. This complete blocking will halt the horse.

As with the leg aids, the long-term aim is to use as light and gentle an aid as possible. To begin with you may have to block completely with your hands but, with practice, the horse will become more attentive until only a slight reduction of the forward movement of the hands is enough to halt him.

Changing Direction

You cannot continue in a straight line forever, so once you are confident with forward movement you must be able to change direction.

When the legs are used together either on or fractionally behind the girth, and the hands are also moving together, the horse is kept in a straight line. To go around a corner, or to turn, the horse has to bend through his body. In order to achieve this, the hands and legs must be used individually. If one leg is allowed to slide further back behind the girth this will make the horse move his hindquarters away from the leg in question, i.e. if your right leg is used behind the girth, the horse will be encouraged to move his quarters across to the left, and vice versa. So, to make the horse turn, one leg is used in the normal place to encourage him to keep moving forwards, and the other leg is used further back behind the girth to control the hindquarters.

The horse should never be turned sharply – any turn should be thought of as part of a circle, so to turn right think about circling away to the right. Then the right hand and leg are referred to as being on the inside, while the left hand and leg are now on the outside.

TURNING RIGHT

1 Horse and rider are about to turn off a straight line and away to the right. The rider has moved the right hand a few inches away from the withers, towards the right. This is called opening the hand, and it invites the horse to turn his head and neck to the right in preparation for the turn.

2 The rider's inside (right) leg is used on the girth to keep the horse moving forwards; the outside (left) leg is used behind the girth to stop his quarters swinging too far to the left. The left hand and arm soften so that the horse keeps bending to the right. The right hand stays to the right of the withers, inviting the horse to move that way.

3 As soon as the horse has turned as far round to the right as the rider requires, the hands and legs return to their normal position.

4 To turn right, the rider's inside (right) hand is moved a little to the right of the withers – opening the hand; the inside (right) leg remains on the girth, encouraging the horse to move forwards.

5 The outside hand is softened so that the horse can bend his head and neck away to the right, whilst the outside leg is used behind the girth to control the degree to which the hindquarters move.

TURNING LEFT

1 To turn left, the rider opens the inside (left) hand a few inches to the left to invite the horse to turn his head and neck in that direction.

2 The outside (right) hand is softened forwards to allow the horse to turn away to the left, while the outside leg is used back behind the girth to control the swing of the hindquarters.

3 As soon as the horse is heading in the required direction, the rider's hands and legs return to the normal position.

4 To turn left the inside (left) hand is opened out to the left to ask the horse to turn his head and neck to the left, while the inside leg is used on the girth.

5 The outside (right) hand must be allowed to soften forwards to allow the horse to turn away to the left. The outside leg is used behind the girth in order to control the hindquarters.

▮ RIGHT
Riding forwards on
a straight line.

▮ FAR RIGHT
Bending the horse so
that he can turn right.

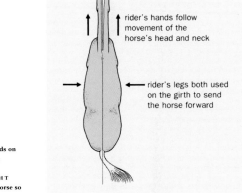

rider's hands follow movement of the horse's head and neck

rider's legs both used on the girth to send the horse forward

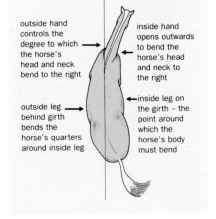

outside hand controls the degree to which the horse's head and neck bend to the right

inside hand opens outwards to bend the horse's head and neck to the right

outside leg behind girth bends the horse's quarters around inside leg

inside leg on the girth – the point around which the horse's body must bend

273

Forwards to Trot

The trot is the next pace that the horse can offer you, and many new riders find this one of the hardest to master. When the horse trots the rider feels a far more powerful force of movement from beneath than is experienced at walk. In order to feel comfortable at this pace, you must try to keep your body relaxed so that it absorbs the movement, rather than tensing up and being bounced around by the horse.

■ **THE RISING TROT**

When the horse trots you can either sit deep in the saddle the whole time – which is known as the sitting trot – or you can rise out of the saddle with each stride, in time with the beat of the trot. It is far less tiring – and more comfortable – for the new rider to learn the rising trot, than it is to master the sitting trot. Once you feel at ease at this pace, and are able to stay relaxed and balanced, then is the time to practise the sitting trot.

When the horse trots, he is springing from one diagonal pair of legs to the other. To rise to the trot, allow the spring from one pair of legs going forwards to lift your seat out of the saddle. The seat returns to the saddle as the other pair of legs springs forwards. So as the horse moves each pair of legs in a one-two, one-two, one-two beat, you are sitting and rising to the same beat: up-down, up-down, up-down.

THE TROT

The trot is a two-time pace – the horse springs from one diagonal pair of legs to the other. If you listen to his hoofbeats, you only hear two footfalls within each complete stride. The outside hind and the inside foreleg move forwards together; this is followed by a brief period of suspension, and then the inside hind and outside foreleg move forwards as a pair.

PRACTISING THE RISING TROT

1 Rising to the trot can be practised when the horse is stationary. The rider sits in the normal classical position, attempting to keep the knee-joints in particular as long and relaxed as possible. Keeping the lower legs as still as possible, the rider should think of just allowing her hips and stomach to swing forwards.

2 The seat only comes out of the saddle enough to allow the seat bones to be clear of the saddle. The hips are then allowed to return lightly to the normal sitting position. The shoulders and arms remain still – the rider should think of allowing the hips and stomach to swing forwards and up towards her elbows.

■ **RISING ON THE CORRECT DIAGONAL**

When riding in rising trot in a circle, the rider is meant to rise in time with a particular diagonal pair of the horse's legs. The easiest way to explain what this entails is for you to look down and watch the horse's outside shoulder for a few minutes once you are in trot. You should be rising out of the saddle as the outside shoulder goes forwards. As it comes back, you should sit again.

The reason for bothering to rise on the correct diagonal will become clear later when you are concerned with improving the quality of the horse's work. The horse

will find it easier to balance himself on a turn or circle if the rider is in the saddle when the inside hindleg and the outside foreleg are touching the ground. As the horse uses his legs in diagonal pairs, this is achieved by sitting as the outside shoulder comes back, and rising as it goes forwards. When you change the rein and circle in the opposite direction, it follows that you must also change the diagonal, i.e. rise as the new outside shoulder goes forwards. Changing the diagonal is achieved by sitting for an extra beat before rising again. So instead of sit-rise, sit-rise, you would sit-rise, sit-sit-rise and this will put you on the correct diagonal.

In sitting trot the rider retains the correct classical position, allowing her stomach and lower back to absorb the movement of the horse. Note the straight line through the shoulder, hip and heel, as well as the line from the elbow, down along the rein to the bit.

COMMON FAULTS

A common mistake in rising trot is actively to try to push the body up and down. This causes the shoulders and arms to bob up and down, which is disconcerting and uncomfortable for the horse as it is his mouth which suffers if there is excessive movement of the hands and arms.

Another common mistake in rising trot is for the rider's shoulders to tip forwards. This puts the rider off balance and means the hands are often rested on the horse's neck in an effort to regain balance. If the hands are resting on the neck, they cannot keep a soft but continuous contact with the horse's mouth. The shoulders must stay upright, just as they do when the rider is stationary; only the hips should move forwards. If the shoulders remain balanced and in line with the rider's heels, the rider will not be pushed off balance by the movement of the horse.

■ THE SITTING TROT

In sitting trot you should remain sitting deep in the saddle, maintaining the same classical position as when stationary and at walk. The movement of the horse is absorbed by the stomach and lower back, so that you remain deep in the saddle without being bounced up and down. As you feel the horse's legs springing forwards underneath you, try to think of allowing your ribcage to sink down towards your hips. This means that the stomach and lower back act like a concertina: as the horse springs along in trot the stomach and lower back are either contracting or expanding to absorb the movement. You must stay relaxed so that your legs can hang long and loose by the horse's sides, and your arms can still stay soft and maintain a light contact with the horse's mouth. It helps to make a conscious effort to keep breathing – you would be surprised how many riders hold their breath as soon as they concentrate too hard on something. Steady breathing helps you relax.

In sitting trot the knees should be long and loose.

Gripping with the knee makes your seat insecure.

COMMON FAULTS IN THE SITTING TROT

▌ LEFT
Back to the armchair position! How not
to sit – the lower leg has slipped forwards
and the rider is now sitting on the back of
her seat. The line from the shoulder
through the hip to the heel has been lost.

▌ LEFT
If you fall into the armchair position your
body is unable correctly to absorb the
movement of the horse. You will be
bumped up and down and, as a result, you
will find your hands and arms bobbing up
and down as well. It's uncomfortable for
both horse and rider.

FROM WALK TO TROT TO WALK

1 The horse should be walking forwards actively and attentively before the rider asks for trot. See how the rider is keeping a contact with the horse's mouth without actually pulling or restricting him. The rider's legs are in contact with the horse's sides but are not being used actively. By keeping both the legs and the hands in contact with the horse in this way, you will be keeping open your lines of communication.

2 To ask for trot, the rider squeezes both legs actively against the horse's sides and softens the hands forwards so that the horse feels free to increase the pace and go forwards into trot.

3 Once the horse is settled in trot, the rider's legs and hands return to just being in contact with the horse. The leg is there to squeeze the horse forwards should he slow down, and the hand is there to guide him.

4 To return to walk the rider sits deep in the saddle and squeezes the legs against the horse's sides. (If the rider had been in rising trot, she would return to sitting trot to achieve this.)

5 Then, instead of softening the hands forwards, she keeps the hands still so that the horse's forward movement is blocked, bringing him back to walk.

6 As soon as the horse settles in walk, the hands and legs relax sufficiently to keep just a light contact.

On into Canter

It is at canter that the new rider will first experience the true exhilaration of riding a horse. The feeling of speed and power as the horse eats up the ground with each stride gives a real buzz. But despite the increased speed, the rider generally finds this a very smooth pace.

■ CANTERING ON THE CORRECT LEG

If you watch a horse cantering in a circle, he should appear to be leading each stride with his inside foreleg. In practice, the inside foreleg is actually the last leg to be moved by the horse within each canter stride, but to the observer it does appear

▮ LEFT
In canter, the rider sits deeply in the saddle and allows the hips to be rocked forwards and back by the movement of the horse. The arms and hands must stay soft and relaxed so that they can follow the movement of the horse's head and neck. Note once more the straight line through the ear, shoulder, hip and heel, and again from the elbow, down the rein to the bit. At all paces, the correct classical position should be maintained.

THE CANTER

The canter is a three-time pace, with the legs working in the following sequence: outside hind goes forwards, then the inside hind and outside fore go forwards together, followed by the inside foreleg. There is then a period of suspension when all four feet are off the ground, before the stride pattern is repeated – outside hind, inside hind and outside fore together, then inside fore.

---

to be leading the stride. When this is the case, the horse is said to be cantering on the correct leg, or the correct lead. So when cantering on the right rein, i.e. circling to the right, the inside (right) foreleg should appear to be leading; and, when cantering on the left rein, the inside (left) foreleg appears to be leading.

To ask the horse to canter forwards on the left lead you should use the inside leg

on the girth and the outside leg behind the girth, whilst opening the left hand slightly to keep the horse bent left, and just keeping a feel on the outside rein to stop the horse simply accelerating in trot. To canter on the right lead the aids are reversed; the right leg is used on the girth, the left leg is used behind the girth, and the right hand is opened slightly to bend the horse to the right.

Cantering on the correct leg. This horse and rider are circling on the left rein and you can see how the horse's inside (left) foreleg appears to be leading.

Cantering on the wrong leg. Here you can see that, although the horse is still circling to the left, it is the outside foreleg that appears to be leading the stride.

FROM TROT TO CANTER TO TROT

1 Before asking the horse to canter, the rider must go into sitting trot and be sure that the horse is working forwards actively and attentively.

2 To ask the horse to go forwards into canter on the left rein, i.e. to canter on the left lead, the rider sits deep, presses the inside (left) leg on the girth, but asks more actively with a squeeze or a nudge of the outside leg back behind the girth. This is because it is the horse's outside hindleg that starts off the stride, so the rider activates this leg by using her own outside leg behind the girth. The inside hand is opened out slightly to the left to encourage the horse to keep a bend to the left, but the outside hand may have to keep more of a feel than usual on the outside rein to prevent the horse from simply trotting faster. In this picture the outside hind is just about to take the first step of the canter stride.

3 Once the correct canter is established, with the left leg leading, the rider just keeps her outside leg in place behind the girth to encourage the outside hind to keep initiating the canter stride. The inside leg remains on the girth, so that the horse's body is bent around the rider's inside leg as they progress around the circle.

4 The arms and hands move forwards with the movement of the horse's head and neck, and the rider sits deep in the saddle, allowing her hips to be rocked by the horse's stride.

5 In order to return to trot the rider sits deep in the saddle and closes both legs against the horse's sides.

6 The rider reduces the degree to which she allows her hands and arms to move forwards with the horse's head and neck, so that the horse's forward movement is blocked. You may have to keep a slightly stronger feel in the outside hand to help bring the horse back to trot.

7 As soon as the trot is established the rider softens her hands forwards again to follow the movement and allows her legs to hang softly by the horse's sides. She must be ready to squeeze the horse forwards again into a more active trot if he tries to slow down any more.

Influencing the Horse

There is a subtle difference between learning to ride and actually influencing the horse. The new rider will spend the early period of training simply learning how to sit correctly balanced on the horse, and mastering the basic aids which will enable horse and rider to proceed at walk, trot and canter, to halt and to circle left or right. Until you achieve this balance and the resultant independent seat, you will be little more than a passenger on the horse. Once you have acquired an independent seat, you can concern yourself with how well or otherwise your horse is performing underneath you. Riding a horse should be a pleasure for both parties – the ultimate aim is to be mounted on a co-operative horse who will respond to your lightest instruction. When this is achieved, those observing you may well marvel at that closest of secrets – the one between a rider and his horse.

Control of the Horse

Use your hands and legs to control and influence the horse's shoulders, hindquarters, head and neck. When making a turn or circling, the horse's shoulders and hindquarters are controlled by the rider's use of the legs. When combined with the hands, this can be taken further still to move the horse in a number of different ways. The rider's leg can be used behind the girth to encourage the horse to move sideways (laterally) away from the leg, or to control the swing and direction of the quarters. The use of the leg on the girth encourages the horse to bend around the leg and allows the rider to control the horse's shoulder.

MOVING TO THE LEFT

1 Whilst at halt, if the rider keeps a light feel on the outside rein (the right rein), opens out the inside rein a few inches and squeezes the horse's side with her inside leg on the girth while the outside leg remains relaxed, the horse will bend his head and neck to the left.

2 If the rider actively presses the outside (right) leg against the horse's side, but blocks the horse's forward movement by not softening her outside hand forwards, and just holds her inside leg against the horse's side behind the girth to keep the hindquarters still, the horse will step across to the left. His hindquarters remain still because the feel from the inside leg stops him stepping across with his hindlegs, but he will move his shoulders and forelegs across to the left. To straighten up again, the rider presses her left leg against the girth to push the horse's shoulders back over to the right. The left hand prevents the horse from stepping forwards, and the right hand is opened out to the right to invite the horse to step over to the right. The left leg stays back behind the girth to keep the horse's hindquarters still.

MOVING TO THE RIGHT

1 Similarly at halt, if the rider keeps a light feel on the outside (left) rein and opens the inside hand whilst pressing the inside leg against the girth, the horse will bend his head and neck to the right.

2 If the rider brings her outside (left) leg back behind the girth whilst blocking any attempt by the horse to move forwards with the outside rein, and keeps her inside (right) leg on the girth to keep the horse's shoulders stationary, then as she presses her outside leg against the horse he will swing his quarters over to the right. To straighten the horse up again the aids are then reversed – the right leg is used behind the girth to push the quarters back over to the left, whilst the right hand prevents the horse from stepping forwards. The left leg is used on the girth to make sure the shoulders remain still. Once the horse is straight again, the rider's legs and hands return to the normal position.

The Rider's Goal – To Lighten the Forehand

If you watch a horse showing off loose in a field you will see how proud and active he can look: his neck is high and arched, and he will use his hindquarters powerfully to produce round, elevated paces. As soon as a young or unschooled horse is asked to carry a rider, this picture can change dramatically: the horse's outline becomes flatter and longer, his steps lose their spring and he may lean on the bit by carrying his head and neck low, so that the rider always has a horrible, heavy feel in the hand; alternatively, he may carry his head high in an effort to evade the effect of the rider's hand on the rein and the bit. The rider has to teach the horse how to rebalance himself so that he can comfortably deal with the unbalancing effect of a rider on his back and regain his proud, elegant and light bearing.

An unbalanced horse usually takes advantage of the fact that the rider is holding the reins and will lean on the bit, so the rider is in effect helping to carry the weight of the horse. When this happens the horse is said to be on his forehand, i.e. more of the combined weight of the horse and the rider is carried on the horse's shoulders and forelegs than on the hindquarters and hindlegs. If you piled a lot of heavy weights on to the front of a car it would become heavy to handle, and similarly the horse becomes heavy in the rider's hand and is difficult to steer and control. If the weight is taken off the front of the car and loaded on to the back, suddenly the car is light and manoeuvrable in front.

The rider's aim is to encourage the horse to carry more of the weight on the hindquarters than on the forehand. In order to do this the horse has to lower his hindquarters and allow his hindlegs to step much further under his body. When he does this, his shoulders, head and neck are automatically raised and this is called lightening the forehand, or transferring the weight from the forehand to the hindquarters.

ENGAGING THE HINDQUARTERS

1 A young or unschooled horse will carry himself in a long, low outline; see how low the head and neck appear to be, and how long and flat the overall picture is as a result.

2 The rider has used her legs and seat to encourage the horse to bring his hindlegs further underneath him, and just keeps enough of a contact on the rein to prevent the horse speeding up. The effect of the rider's legs pushing the horse up into the contact maintained by the hand is that the horse starts to bend and flex his hocks more, so that they can step further underneath the body. This is called engaging the hocks or hindquarters.

3 Various schooling exercises, combined with the horse learning to become more responsive to the leg and seat aids, gradually allow the rider to encourage the horse to use his hindquarters more.

4 The horse's outline is now rounder, and the forehand has been raised slightly higher than the hindquarters so that the horse is carrying more of the weight on the hindquarters and has lightened the forehand. Asking the horse to transfer the weight in this way, from the forehand to the hindquarters, is always brought about by greater use of the rider's legs, not by pulling the horse's head and neck up and in with the reins. The rein contact should remain soft and elastic, only blocking sufficiently to prevent the horse from speeding up when the leg is applied, instead of engaging the hindquarters more as is required.

Control and Motion – Introducing Lateral Work

When first learning to ride, you are concerned primarily with being able to send the horse forwards into walk, trot, canter and gallop, and being able to halt. As your skills develop, you learn how to make the horse move sideways, either by moving his whole body or just his shoulders or hindquarters. This is known as lateral work, and is invaluable for a novice rider as it teaches him or her to feel and influence the horse's movement. For the horse, it is used as a suppling exercise and to encourage him to work more actively with his hindquarters.

Lateral movements include leg yielding, quarters-in (both described here), shoulder-in and half-pass (see Developing Lateral Work). All horses should be introduced to these exercises as part of their overall training programme. Practise them at walk and, once you have mastered control of the shoulders and hindquarters, you will realize just how manoeuvrable the horse can be.

■ **LEG YIELDING**

In this exercise the horse is asked to move forwards and sideways at the same time;

the inside hind and foreleg cross over in front of the outside hind and foreleg.

■ **QUARTERS-IN**

In this exercise the horse continues walking in a straight line but he brings his quarters in to one side. If working on a sand surface, the horse's hoofprints would leave three lines of tracks: the inside line is formed by the inside hind, the middle line is made by the inside fore and the outside hind (which follow each other), and the outside line is made by the outside fore.

■ **REIN BACK**

The rein back is when the horse is asked, quite literally, to walk backwards. It should only ever be performed in walk although, when frightened, the horse will be quite capable of running backwards at a respectable speed!

Although the rein back is not a lateral movement, it is all part of teaching horse and rider the full extent of the control and motion they can achieve.

The horse should step backwards, in a straight line, moving his legs clearly and positively in diagonal pairs – inside fore and outside hind together, followed by outside fore and inside hind together.

LEG YIELDING

■ LEFT
To leg yield across to the left, as this rider is doing, she brings her right leg behind the girth which tells the horse to move sideways; her left leg remains on the girth, encouraging the horse to keep moving forwards as well as sideways. The right hand is opened a few inches which encourages the horse to keep a slight right bend through the body; the left hand keeps enough of a feel on the rein to prevent the horse bending too far to the left and, combined with the push from the right leg behind the girth, invites the horse to step sideways. To leg yield away to the right the aids are reversed – the left leg is used behind the girth, the right leg on the girth, the right rein keeps enough contact to invite the horse to step to the right, and the left rein is opened a few inches to encourage the horse to keep a slight bend through his body.

QUARTERS-IN

RIGHT

In these pictures the horse is being asked to bring his quarters into the left whilst continuing to walk forwards in a straight line. The rider uses her outside (right) leg behind the girth to move the quarters across slightly. Her inside leg stays on the girth to encourage the horse to keep moving forwards and to prevent the shoulders moving out of line. The left hand is opened slightly which, combined with the pressure from the left leg on the girth, encourages the horse to keep a bend through his whole body. The outside hand takes up enough of a feel to keep the horse's shoulder moving forwards in a straight line.

Quarters-in to the right is achieved by reversing the aids – the left leg is used behind the girth, her right leg, now the inside leg, stays on the girth, the right hand is opened slightly and the left (outside) hand takes up enough of a feel to keep the horse's shoulders moving forwards in a straight line.

REIN BACK

1 The rein back can only be successfully performed if the horse is calm and relaxed when at the halt.

2 The rider squeezes both legs against the horse's sides, but makes sure that she blocks the horse's forward movement by not allowing her hands to move forwards. Because the legs are applied actively, the horse knows he has to move somewhere. The rein contact is telling him he cannot go forwards and so he goes backwards. Some horses, as demonstrated here, understand what is required more easily if you apply both legs behind the girth, and then lift your seat bones off the saddle. This encourages the horse to step back underneath you as required.

3 Having taken one step back with one diagonal pair of legs, the horse proceeds to step back with the remaining diagonal pair. The horse should only be asked to step backwards for a limited number of steps. As a reward, allow him to walk forwards again whilst making a fuss of him.

Acceptance of Contact

Right from the start the horse has to learn to accept, without tension or resentment, the fact that the bit in his mouth is attached, via the reins, to the rider's hands, and that there will always be a light but sympathetic contact between the two. It is vital that you achieve a balanced, independent seat so that you are not tempted to hang on to the reins in an effort to balance yourself. Your priority is to learn to follow the movement of the horse's head and neck so that you are able to keep a constant but sympathetic contact with his mouth. In the early stages of training, you should not concern yourself with how the horse is carrying his head and neck, but only with learning to feel,

BASIC PRINCIPLES

Before you can hope to achieve a lightening of the forehand, there are a number of basic principles that you and your horse must master. These form the basis of all horses' training and progression, whether or not you are dealing with a horse who has never been properly schooled, and are as follows:

■ Acceptance of the rein contact.
■ Free forward movement.
■ Maintaining a rhythm.
■ Bend and flexion through the body.
■ The use of half-halts to engage the hindquarters and rebalance the horse.
Once you have mastered these principles, you will be equipped with the means to ride your horse to the maximum of his potential.

follow and maintain the contact. Once the horse knows that the contact is constant, but kind, he will learn to accept it. Your elbows must remain soft and relaxed so that the contact can be maintained. It may be necessary to open the hands out a little wider than usual so that there is no obstruction – whatever the horse does with his head, you can follow it with your hands.

COMMON FAULTS

How often have you seen a horse slopping along like this? The rider is not keeping a contact with the horse's mouth and, although she is actively using her legs, the horse is completely ignoring the aid and continuing to plod along in a lethargic and uninterested manner.

The horse must respond the same way in all paces. Here, in trot, we can see the result of the rider failing to keep a contact with the horse's mouth, and the horse blatantly ignoring the rider's leg aids. The rider is working hard with her legs whilst the horse is being extremely lazy with his!

FOLLOWING THE HORSE'S HEAD AND NECK

1

2

■ RIGHT
In the early stages of training, the rider should not concern himself with the position of the horse's head and neck – only with learning to follow their movement so that a soft but constant contact is maintained.

Free Forward Movement

The horse also has to learn to respect the rider's legs, i.e. when you use your legs against the horse's sides, he must respond by going forwards if both legs are used together or by moving away from the leg if used as a lateral (sideways) aid. The vast majority of problems experienced both on the flat and over jumps are caused by the horse ignoring, or being slow to react to, the rider's leg aids. The horse's first reaction should always be to move forwards. Once the horse respects the leg and is willing to maintain free forward movement without you continually having to reapply the leg aids, he is said to be in front of the leg and on the aids – he is attentive and ready to react to his rider's commands instantly.

In the early stages of training, you should use your voice combined with a squeeze from both legs to ask the horse to move forwards. If the horse does not respond, use your voice again, backed up with a sharp nudge with both heels against the horse's sides. If this is still ignored, squeeze your legs against the horse, use your voice to ask him to walk on and give him a tap with the schooling whip or stick behind your leg at the same time as the leg aid is applied. You must be ready to allow forward movement with the hands, particularly if the horse jumps forward when the schooling whip is used. As soon as he moves forwards, reward him by praising him verbally. You should then relax your legs against the horse's sides. As soon as he slows down again, repeat the process. Gradually the horse will learn to respond to the first light aid.

KEEPING A SOFT CONTACT

1 Here the rider has shortened her reins sufficiently to keep a contact with the horse's mouth. She has applied the leg again and backed it up with a tap from the schooling whip. Already the picture is one of greater alertness and activity.

2 The rider maintains the contact and uses the leg once more to ask the horse to walk on a little more energetically.

3 This time the horse responds instantly; the rider's leg can relax and the horse maintains the forward movement without further nagging. Note how the horse's outline is now much rounder and shorter as he begins to lighten his forehand.

4 In trot, the rider takes up contact with the horse's mouth and backs up her leg aids with a tap from the schooling whip.

5 Immediately the horse offers much more in the way of forward impulsion. Now that he is thinking forwards, see how he lengthens his steps and voluntarily raises his head and neck into a rounder, shorter outline.

6 The rider can relax her legs and enjoy the free forward movement that the horse is offering her. But as soon as he drops back from this pace, the rider starts the process over again.

Maintaining a Rhythm

Now that the horse accepts the contact and moves forward willingly from your leg, both you and he need to learn to maintain an even rhythm in all your work. This rhythm must not be too slow or the work will lack impulsion and power; neither must it be too fast or the horse will tend to become unbalanced and will be pushed on to his forehand. Aim for a rhythm in each pace which gives you the feeling of free forward movement without feeling rushed. The ultimate aim is to use a light squeeze from the legs to ride the horse up into this rhythm; then to relax and enjoy the experience whilst the horse willingly maintains the rhythm, without continual nagging from either hand or leg.

Once the horse is responding quickly to the leg you are half way there. Some horses have naturally rhythmic paces and will automatically maintain the rhythm. Others will need a reminder from leg, voice and/or schooling whip to keep up to the rhythm, or they may need to be slowed down. Having got the horse thinking forwards, be careful not to dampen his goodwill by restricting him with the reins if he goes too fast. The use of a neck strap to slow the horse is a better method to use; it prevents the horse from learning how to lean on the bit or to fight you by shortening and tensing his neck.

By pulling on the neck strap instead of blocking with the reins, you can slow the horse down. Practise in the arena, first using the strap to bring the horse from walk to halt, and then from trot to walk etc. Once the horse understands its use, this method can be used to steady him within any pace. But remember that you must still use your legs and voice, if necessary, in the same way as you would do if you were going to use the rein contact to slow down.

USING THE NECK STRAP

1 Here the rider is introducing the neck strap by using it to bring the horse back from trot to walk. She has put the reins in one hand and holds the neck strap in the other.

2 The rider then uses her legs with a light squeeze against the horse's sides, whilst using her voice and a firm pull on the neck strap to slow the horse down. Although the rider wants to slow down, the leg is still applied because it encourages the horse to bring his hindlegs further underneath him so that he can keep his forehand light. If the leg is not used, the horse will simply shift his weight on to the forehand and will become heavy and unbalanced in the rider's hand.

3 The horse comes back quite happily to walk without the need to block with the rein. He is rewarded with a pat and praise from his rider.

4 When working in trot, if the horse has a tendency to speed up out of the desired rhythm the rider can just loop a finger through the neck strap and take a pull on it until the horse slows the rhythm down again.

5 When the horse responds, the neck strap is released and he is praised by his rider.

Bend and Flexion

■ BELOW
The horse is bringing his hocks well underneath himself, the hindquarters are lowered slightly and the poll and jaw are relaxed so that the front of the face is on the vertical.

In all the horse's work, the rider is striving to ensure that the horse's hindlegs follow in the same tracks as his front legs, i.e. his quarters are not allowed to swing out or his shoulder to fall in. This is referred to as straightness in the horse, which is a term that causes some confusion. For the horse to be straight, i.e. for his hindlegs to follow in the same tracks as his forelegs, when working on a turn or a circle he has to bend through his body; his whole body must form a slight, continual curve around the rider's inside leg. So in order to be straight the horse has to bend!

The degree of bend that the horse shows through his body is dependent on the size of circle or turn you are riding. For example, to ride a 65½ foot (20 m) circle the horse shows only a slight bend through his body, but to manoeuvre himself around a 33 foot (10 m) circle there will be a greater degree of bend.

ACHIEVING BEND

1 The rider should concentrate on making sure that the outside hand is really following the horse's movement in a soft, allowing way, whilst still maintaining a light contact. This ensures that the horse's forward momentum is not stifled by a restricting outside hand. The rider then opens the inside hand, setting it in the open position by simply tensing the muscles of the arm, not by pulling back on the rein. The inside leg is used on the girth to keep the horse pushed out on to the circle, and a firmer contact is only taken up on the outside rein if the horse falls in on the circle, i.e. allows the circle to get smaller and smaller. If he does this, the rider must keep pushing the horse out with the inside leg and draw him back out on to the original circle by using the outside rein.

2 The rider should now feel the horse bending through the body and neck; if the horse resists and does not respond by offering some bend through his body, the rider simply opens the inside rein out further and sets it there – still without pulling back on it. The inside leg is kept on, and should be backed up with a tap from the schooling whip if the horse continues to fall in on the circle rather than bend through the body.

3 As soon as the horse offers the bend, i.e. when you can see a glimpse of his inside eye and nostril, use both legs against his sides to encourage him to bring his hocks further underneath him and to flex through his topline. When you feel the horse relax his poll and jaw so that the nose is lowered and his face is on the vertical, soften the inside rein and allow it to follow the movement in the same way as the outside rein. Praise the horse verbally – this is his reward for yielding to your leg and hand. The horse is now beginning to work in self-carriage, i.e. he is carrying more weight on his hindquarters and is lightening his forehand. Note that his head and neck are higher and more arched than in picture one; this is a result of the hocks being brought further under him.

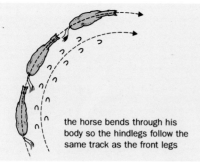

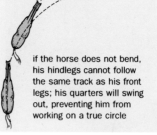

the horse bends through his body so the hindlegs follow the same track as the front legs

if the horse does not bend, his hindlegs cannot follow the same track as his front legs; his quarters will swing out, preventing him from working on a true circle

▮ LEFT
How a horse goes around a corner.

The more the horse has to bend his body the more he has to use his hocks, and the inside hindleg in particular has to step much further across and under the horse's body in order to follow in the track of the inside foreleg. Having ridden simple turns and circles, you will know that the inside leg is used on the girth with an open inside hand to encourage the horse to bend around the inside leg, whilst the outside leg is used back behind the girth to prevent the quarters swinging out. The outside hand is used to prevent the horse bending his head and neck too much to the inside. On an unschooled horse the aids have to be exaggerated

until he realizes what it is you are asking him to do. Once the horse is willing to offer you the bend through his whole body, you can ask him to flex right through his topline so that his whole outline becomes soft and round and he offers you no resistance whatsoever. The horse's topline describes the area from the top of the tail, over the hindquarters, back, withers and neck, and on up to the poll. When the horse flexes through his topline, his hindquarters are lowered as his hocks come further underneath him, he stays soft through his back, arches his neck and relaxes his poll and jaw so that the head is carried in a relaxed manner; the horse will

lower his nose so that a vertical line could be drawn down the front of his face.

The horse should be introduced to this work in trot – it is very easy to stifle his forward momentum if it is first asked for in walk. Ride forwards into trot, bearing in mind the principles of having a horse who will respond happily to your leg and settle into a rhythm without being nagged by your leg or hand.

With time and practice, you will find that the horse will become more and more responsive to the request to bend and flex. After a while, you will not need to open the inside hand in such an exaggerated fashion; simply moving the hand over

OBTAINING THE CORRECT DEGREE OF BEND

The rider should only ask for a slight bend through the horse's body and neck, so that the outside of the horse makes a continual curve around the rider's inside leg. The rider only needs to see a glimpse of the horse's inside eye and nostril to know that the bend is correct.

A common fault is for the horse to bend only through the neck from the withers, so that his body is still straight. In this position the horse can avoid having to step under himself more with his hindlegs, so his quarters will swing out as he goes around a corner. If his hocks are not underneath him, he can neither turn correctly nor flex through his topline when asked. The rider must use the outside rein to reduce the degree of bend in the neck, the outside leg to keep the hind-quarters from swinging out, and should reinforce the inside leg by tapping the horse with the schooling whip behind his or her lower leg.

Another fault is for the horse to tilt his head towards the inside. He is allowing the rider's inside hand to draw his nose to the inside but is ignoring the outside hand, so instead of bending through the neck and poll, the horse simply tilts his head to one side. More contact should be taken up with the outside rein to correct this.

BEND AND FLEXION – THE OVERALL PICTURE

1 The horse is ridden forwards into trot; the rider opens her inside hand and closes her inside leg on the girth to ask the horse to bend around her leg. The outside hand stays soft and allows the horse to move freely forwards, unless it has to be used to prevent him bending too much through the neck.

2 Here the horse has responded by curving his whole body around the rider's inside leg; see how the neck looks more relaxed and softer than in the first picture. This is because the horse is working willingly, without resistance.

3 Now that the rider has obtained the correct amount of bend, she closes both legs against the horse's sides to encourage him to be more active and step further under himself with his hindlegs. The horse is now flexing through his topline, i.e. his quarters are lowered and his back and neck are round and soft, which in turn raises and lightens his forehand.

4 The result is a picture of power with softness, and roundness with activity. See how the horse is bent around the rider's legs; he is also using his hindquarters actively which allows his forehand to be light and elevated. The increased power shows in the way the horse is stretching his front legs forwards, and matching this up behind by stepping under himself further with the hindlegs. His neck is carried higher and is more arched than in the first picture but he remains soft and light in the rider's hand. This is the start of self-carriage.

about an inch will be sufficient. Much further down the line in the horse's training, it will also only be necessary to take up a feel on the inside rein and to close the legs against the horse's sides to achieve bend and flexion.

Once the bend and flexion are established in trot, you can strive for the same result in both walk and canter. But the vital thing to remember with this training method is always to reward the horse by softening the inside hand the instant that he offers you even the tiniest degree of flexion and relaxation. To begin with it will be a case of working quite hard to ask the horse to bend and then to flex, followed by the reward of softening the inside hand as soon as he does so. He may only offer you the bend and flexion for a few strides before you have to repeat the process and ask again, but as he begins to understand what is wanted and his topline muscles up as a result of the work, he will offer it to you for longer periods.

Gradually you will be doing less asking and more rewarding; you will find yourself riding for longer with both hands soft so that the horse is working on a light contact. But you will need to be persistent and consistent in your training.

▶ RIGHT
As soon as the horse responds to the rider's aids by bending through his body and then flexing through his topline, the rider must soften the inside hand and praise the horse verbally as a reward. This is the only way that the horse can know that he has responded to the aids in the right way.

▶ RIGHT
While the inside hand is being softened, it can also be used to pat the horse's neck as further praise.

This horse has offered the rider the required degree of bend and flexion – note the arch of his neck and how his forehand appears lighter and higher than his hindquarters. You can see how he is really flexing his hock as he goes to step forwards with his hindleg and, most importantly, note how the rider has softened the inside rein so that the horse is holding this outline himself.

CORRECT USE OF THE INSIDE HAND

It is vital to ask the horse to bend his whole body around your inside leg by opening the inside hand and using the inside leg to keep the horse out on the circle. By using your hand and leg in this way, when the horse does respond he will produce a continuous bend through his body, neck and head. You may have to open your inside hand very wide, you may have to back up the inside-leg aid with a tap from the schooling whip, and your outside hand may have to take up more of a contact to stop the horse bending his neck too far to the inside, but, when the horse drops his resistance, relaxes and responds to these aids, he will be working correctly.

If the horse is slow to respond and refuses to offer the requested bend, it is very tempting to cheat! If you cross your inside hand over the horse's withers instead of opening the hand out and backing it up with the inside leg, the horse will instantly bend, but this bend will only be from the withers, it will not be right through the body. The crossing over of the rider's hand cuts off the horse's forward impulsion and cuts off the bend at the withers. So whilst you will be able to see the required glimpse of the inside eye and nostril, it will not be backed up by the correct use or position of the horse's hindquarters.

Crossing the inside hand over in this way is something that many riders, even at high levels

of competition, are tempted to do. Some do not realize that it is a false measure and are satisfied with the false bend that the horse offers them, but their future is limited and their potential will not be fully realized. The temptation to cross the hand over is simply a sign that the horse is not respecting the rider's inside leg and/or the outside hand. So instead of giving in to the temptation, use it as a reminder to yourself to use your inside leg and outside hand correctly,

even if this means not continuing with the exercise until the horse is prepared to move away from the inside leg (see Free Forward Movement). Always go back and correct the underlying fault if any training exercise is not progressing well. Never think that a short cut such as crossing the hand over or losing your temper will pay long-term dividends. Get the basics right and then you will have something permanent to build on. Be consistent, and be quick to praise your horse.

When asking the horse to bend, you must open your inside hand and use your inside leg.

If you cross your inside hand over, the horse will bend only from the wither.

Working Within Each Pace

Once both horse and rider have begun to understand the
basics of a correct and acceptable way of working in each
pace, the rider can take the horse's performance further.
Having mastered the principles of free forward
movement and obtained a degree of bend and flexion,
you can further influence the horse by seeking to
improve his paces. Plenty of horses have a pleasant
enough way of going – they are able to maintain a round
outline and a good rhythm in each pace – but this can be
nurtured to produce a horse who puts real power and
flair into his work. The use of half-halts and the introduction
of lateral work help the horse to become more balanced and
bring him nearer to working in self-carriage.

The Half-halt

The half-halt describes what happens when the rider closes his or her legs and hands momentarily against the horse. This serves to rebalance the horse in whatever pace he is working; the rider's legs push the horse's hindlegs underneath him further whilst the hand blocks any acceleration in pace which the horse might offer. The power that the legs have created is trapped by the rider's hand so that, instead of accelerating, the horse lowers his hindquarters and elevates his forehand slightly, becoming better balanced and lighter in the rider's hand. The half-halt can be used to (1) rebalance

HALF-HALT AT TROT

1 This horse is producing an active trot, and is maintaining a good outline; considering that he is only young the overall picture is soft and round. The rider is sitting quietly with the leg aid on, but only needs to maintain a light contact with the reins to the horse's mouth.

2 Now the horse is becoming unbalanced. He has probably overpowered himself with the push from his hindlegs and is poking his nose forward and starting to lean on the bit in an attempt to balance himself. The soft, round outline is disappearing.

3 To rebalance the horse, the rider uses a half-halt. She closes her legs on the horse's sides and pushes him up into her hand which, just for a second, is blocked against the horse's forward movement. In effect, the horse's body is squashed up together; his outline becomes shorter because his hindlegs are pushed further under his body so he is able to carry more weight on them, which in turn lightens and elevates his forehand.

4 The horse is rewarded by the rider relaxing the leg and softening the hand again. The softening, or giving of the rein, has been exaggerated in this picture to show that once the horse is using his hindquarters and hocks more actively he is able to carry himself and remain light in the rider's hand (self-carriage). So although the rein is completely loose, the horse is maintaining his own balance and a correct outline.

HALF-HALT AT CANTER

1 Here you can see how this horse is falling on to his forehand at canter. The impression in the picture is that the horse's weight is falling forwards and that he is leaning on the bit and, therefore, on the rider's hands for support.

2 The rider uses a half-halt to rebalance – she closes her legs against the horse's sides and blocks any forward acceleration with her hands.

3 Now the horse is balanced and light in the rider's hands. In picture one the hind-quarters appear higher than the shoulders (on the forehand). Now the shoulders are higher than the hind-quarters (the forehand is elevated and lightened).

the horse in any pace, (2) warn the horse that the rider is about to ask him to do something such as change direction and (3) build impulsion within each pace which can be stored to produce collected work, or released to produce extended work.

■ ACHIEVING THE HALF-HALT

Every horse will respond to a combination of hand and leg. You have to find out what combination is needed for your horse to obtain the desired result. Too much hand and the horse will either resist by throwing his head up, or he will simply slow down. Too much leg and the horse will try to accelerate and be pushed on to his forehand, which will unbalance him.

First, practise the half-halt at walk. At a given point, close your legs against the horse's sides and reduce the degree to which you allow your hands to follow the contact, as if you were about to halt. Just as you sense the horse is about to halt, soften

THE RIDER'S SEAT AS AN AID

The rider's body weight can be used, through the seat, to influence the horse – it can create or block the amount of impulsion that the horse is working with. If you think about using your seat as an aid too soon, there is a risk that you will simply become stiff in the body and will no longer be able to move with the horse. The use of the seat will develop naturally once you have achieved that all-important independent seat. If you think back to the use of the hands and arms, and how these stay soft and relaxed so that they follow the movement of the horse's head and neck, that is how you should think of your own body weight. Just as you can change

your hands forward again, keeping your legs on the horse's sides so that he continues in walk. Once you get the feel of how much leg and hand is needed to produce this effect of almost but not quite halting the horse, you will have achieved a half-halt. Then practise it at trot and at

the degree to which your hands follow the head and neck movement, for example when asking the horse to slow down or halt, your body weight can be used either to encourage the horse to use himself more actively, or to slow him down. Letting the seat move freely with the horse encourages active movement; reducing the degree to which the seat moves with the horse slows him down. The use of the body weight or seat should always be subtle and sympathetic. The feel for its correct use will come naturally once an independent seat has been achieved, and once you understand how and why you need to influence the horse.

canter. Each time, act as if to bring the horse back to the slower pace and, at the last second, allow him to continue in the original pace. Once you have mastered the half-halt, you can use it more subtly to forewarn the horse that he is about to be asked to do something different.

TOO MUCH HAND

If the rider makes the mistake of using too much hand and not enough leg, the horse will soon let her know by not offering the desired response. Here the rider has tried to rebalance the canter by raising and pulling back with the hands, with no back-up from the leg. The horse responds by simply falling back into trot.

Developing Lateral Work

The shoulder-in and half-pass are the most useful lateral-work exercises in terms of encouraging the horse to use his hocks more actively and effectively underneath him. The mistake that many people make is to think of them simply as requirements of a dressage test. This is not how they should be viewed – lateral work is used to improve the horse's overall way of going. These exercises teach the horse to respond to different uses of the hand and leg, to be supple through his body, and to place his hocks further underneath him in an effort to carry more of his body weight on the hindquarters rather than on the forehand.

COMMON FAULT

A common mistake is for the rider to ask for too much angle so that the horse works on four tracks instead of three, i.e. each leg is put down in a separate track. The rider has crossed her inside hand over the horse's withers so that the horse is only bending from in front of the withers, through the neck, instead of through the body and neck. The whole point of the exercise has been lost; the horse is not supple through the body, only through the neck, and the hindlegs are not being encouraged to take any extra weight at all. To correct this mistake the rider needs to take up more contact in the outside hand to reduce the bend in the neck, use the outside leg to stop the quarters swinging round any further, and the inside leg to push the shoulders back towards the track which will reduce the angle of the horse's body until he is working correctly on three tracks.

■ SHOULDER-IN

The shoulder-in is similar to quarters-in, in that the horse moves on three tracks, but here it is the shoulders that are brought in, not the quarters, as the horse continues to move forwards. The footfalls are as follows: the inside track is made by the inside foreleg, the middle track by the outside foreleg and inside hindleg together, and the outside track is made by the outside hindleg.

It is quite difficult in shoulder-in for the new rider to keep the horse moving forwards in a straight line. The horse may try to swing his quarters out one way, or may drift sideways instead of holding the position and moving forwards in a straight line. If you are working in an arena it helps to do the following: as you bring the

SHOULDER-IN

1 It is easiest to practise lateral movement in an arena so that you have a straight edge to work along; here the rider is about to ride shoulder-in in trot down the long side of the arena. She has already ridden a 33 foot (10 m) circle in trot in the corner that she is just coming from. This circle gives the rider an idea of the correct amount of bend that the horse should hold throughout the shoulder-in. To start the shoulder-in she goes to ride another 33 foot (10 m) circle, but, as soon as the horse's front legs have left the track to start the circle, she uses the outside hand to prevent him continuing on the circle, and the inside leg to keep him moving forwards along the side of the arena.

2 As the horse progresses down the long side of the arena in shoulder-in, you can clearly see how he is working on three tracks (inside fore, outside fore/inside hind, outside hind). This exercise encourages the horse to be supple as he has to maintain a bend through his body and neck; it also introduces the horse to the idea of carrying more weight on the inside hindleg. As the inside hindleg touches the ground, you can see that it is placed directly under the horse's belly and beneath the rider. So at this point the horse is carrying much of his body weight, as well as the weight of the rider, on that inside hindleg.

3 To help keep the horse moving forwards in a straight line whilst in shoulder-in, the rider should look straight ahead and think of her outside hip as pointing the way forwards.

HALF-PASS

1 To ride the half-pass, shown here in walk, the rider would turn down the long side of the arena and ask the horse to go into shoulder-in. Instead of continuing in shoulder-in, he would then use the outside leg back behind the girth to push the horse's hindquarters across until they are almost directly in line with the shoulders. The outside leg stays in place telling the horse to move sideways, whilst the inside leg also keeps him moving forwards. The outside hand controls the degree of bend through the horse's body and neck whilst the inside hand remains open, inviting the horse to step forwards and sideways.

2 In half-pass the horse must remain bent around the rider's inside leg so that he is bent in the direction in which he is moving. In this picture, the rider's outside leg can clearly be seen in use behind the girth to push the horse sideways. Half-pass can be ridden in walk, trot and canter.

3 This picture shows how, in half-pass, it is the outside hindleg which has to come across and under the horse, thereby having to take the weight of both his own body and the rider's. The exercise also encourages the horse to be supple through his body and, in particular, through his shoulders.

horse's shoulders in off the track, make sure you are looking ahead yourself and think of your outside hip as a pointer; if you imagine keeping your hip moving forwards in a straight line, the horse's outside shoulder will move forwards on the same line. The correct position for the rider in shoulder-in is for the hips to stay parallel with the horse's shoulders, but for the shoulders to be held straight as if you are riding forwards in a straight line as normal. You should look straight ahead.

■ **HALF-PASS**

In half-pass the horse moves diagonally across the arena, taking good-sized steps forwards and sideways, and keeping his body bent in the direction in which he is moving. His shoulders are allowed to be just fractionally ahead of his hindquarters as he makes this movement. His outside hind and foreleg cross over in front of his inside hind and foreleg.

COMMON FAULT

A common mistake is for the horse to try to make life easier for himself by not maintaining the correct bend. See how the horse is now bent to the outside which, in effect, means he is now simply leg yielding. The rider needs to ride the horse forwards in a straight line so that he knows straightaway that his response was not acceptable. Shoulder-in should be re-established, and the rider should use the outside leg to bring the quarters over and to keep the horse stepping sideways. As soon as the horse offers the wrong bend again, he must be ridden forwards in a straight line and the process repeated. The rider may need to tap the horse with the schooling whip just behind the inside leg to make sure he is listening to this leg and remains bent around it.

Variations Within Each Pace

The horse is capable of a number of variations of each pace, e.g. in trot or canter the horse can work in a collected, working, medium or extended pace, and he can work in collected, medium or free walk. As the horse's responsiveness to his rider increases and his training progresses, he should be able to offer all of these variations smoothly and without resistance. When asking the horse for variations within each pace, think in terms of asking for more power and impulsion rather than more speed.

MEDIUM WALK

The medium walk is the pace the horse naturally offers his rider – the sort of pace that would be produced out on a hack. The horse takes long, relaxed steps and he overtracks, which means his hind feet step further forwards than the hoofprints left by the front feet.

The medium paces require the horse to work with increased impulsion so that he takes longer, rounder steps than he would do in the working paces. He lengthens his whole frame slightly whilst still keeping a round outline.

WORKING TROT

The working trot is the pace the horse naturally offers his rider. It is an active pace with the horse maintaining a round outline whilst working in a forward-thinking rhythm. It is the sort of trot the horse would produce out hacking – relaxed but active. The same is true of the working canter.

COLLECTED TROT

In the collected paces, which can be either walk, trot or canter, the horse shortens his whole outline by lowering his hindquarters and bringing his hocks further under him, and by elevating his forehand so that his neck is raised and arched. The horse takes shorter, rounder steps, with greater elevation.

MEDIUM TROT

EXTENDED TROT

In the extended paces the horse stretches his whole frame and takes steps of maximum length with maximum impulsion. As with all the variations in pace, the horse must still remain in balance and in a rhythm. This horse could still afford to lengthen and stretch his neck a little more forwards so that the overall picture was of a longer frame.

FREE WALK

■ LEFT
The free walk is often asked for in a dressage test – the rider offers the horse a long length of rein and the horse stretches his head and neck down and takes long, relaxed steps forwards, with his hind feet overtracking his front feet. Because the horse has been taught always to expect a contact between his mouth and the rider's hand, when the rider offers him a long length of rein, he stretches his head and neck down to seek out the contact he is used to feeling. To allow the horse to stretch his head and neck fully, the rider allows her arms and hands to go forwards and down so that there is still a straight line from her elbow, through the arm, down the rein to the bit.

EXTENDED CANTER

In the extended canter the horse lengthens his whole frame and fully extends his legs to take the longest possible steps whilst still remaining in balance. The horse in these pictures needs to lengthen his neck a little more and to take his nose forwards a fraction so that he is not behind the vertical.

Achieving Collection and Extension of the Paces

Producing these variations within each pace involves bringing together the techniques and principles with which you should, by now, be familiar. Whether the horse is working in the collected, medium or extended paces, he has to maintain the same rhythm in his work. In other words, you do not slow the horse down in order to achieve collection, nor should you go faster in order to extend the horse. To achieve collection, the rider uses the half-halt so that the horse's hocks are pushed further underneath him whilst the hand prevents him from accelerating. The trapping by the rider's hand of the power produced by the use of the leg causes the horse to shorten his frame and put that power into taking shorter, higher steps. Medium or extended work is achieved by first using half-halts to collect the horse and then releasing that power and energy in varying degrees by softening the hand forwards, which enables the horse to lengthen his frame and his stride. Whether the resulting pace is medium or extended depends on the degree to which the rider softens with the hand whilst continuing to ask for more power and drive from the hindquarters. To be able to produce these variations in pace, you have to develop a feel for creating and storing energy for collected work, and for directing that energy forwards into either medium or extended work.

COLLECTING AND EXTENDING THE HORSE

1 When practising collecting and extending the horse, it is easier to work within the confines of an arena. The short side of the arena which provides two corners in close proximity to each other is a good place to ask for collection, whilst the long side, or even across the diagonal, provides room for extending the paces. This rider is using half-halts to collect the horse as he progresses through the corner of the arena and begins to turn across the diagonal. A corner is a good place to start to ask for collection, as the horse has to bring his inside hindleg further underneath him in order to negotiate the turn anyway. Note the raised, arched neck and the way the hock is being raised and flexed.

2 As the horse starts to cross the diagonal, the rider continues to collect the energy that was built up as they came through the turn. The horse's outline remains relatively high and short.

4 The outline is now lower and longer as the horse extends his limbs forwards to cover as much ground as possible with each stride.

3 Once the horse is completely straight, the rider asks the horse to extend. He continues to ask for impulsion and drive from the hindquarters by keeping his legs actively on the horse's sides, but now he releases that stored power by softening the hands forwards so that the horse can lengthen his frame and strides. Note how the horse's hindquarters are still lowered, and how the first surge of released energy has really elevated his front end as the horse begins to extend his steps.

▌ RIGHT
Teaching the horse to counter canter.

Introducing Counter Canter

Counter canter is a movement required in many dressage tests, and it demonstrates the horse's suppleness, balance and obedience. Counter canter involves the horse cantering with the left leg leading whilst being worked on the right rein, and vice versa. The horse must keep his head and neck bent over his leading foreleg, so that he is in fact bent in the opposite direction to that in which he is moving.

Counter canter is introduced by cantering on the left rein across the diagonal to the opposite track. As the horse reaches the other side and turns on to the right

COMMON FAULTS

In this picture, the horse is still cantering with the right leg leading but, instead of maintaining the bend of his head and neck to the right, he has bent to the left, i.e. he is now bent in the direction in which he is travelling. The rider must correct this by opening the right hand and closing the right leg on the girth to ask the horse to maintain the bend to the right.

Another common mistake is for the horse to bend his neck too much to the right. This causes him to lose balance and his whole body drifts back to the track instead of following the path of the 16½ foot (5 m) loop. When this happens the horse's hindlegs are not following in the same tracks as the front legs – the horse is simply falling sideways or falling out through the shoulder. If the rider now took up more contact on the outside (left) rein to straighten out the bend of the head and neck, used the left leg behind the girth to stop the quarters swinging out to the left, and opened the right hand whilst keeping the right leg on the girth to encourage the horse to bend his neck to the right, the correct counter canter would be restored.

shallow loop where horse is ridden in counter canter – still on the right leg but travelling towards the left

horse in right canter

rein, he should be asked to maintain the canter with the left leg leading for a few strides, before being brought back to trot.

Once horse and rider are comfortable with this, shallow loops can be ridden in canter down the long side of the arena; whilst the horse is on the track he is cantering as normal, whereas whilst he is negotiating the shallow loop he is in fact in counter canter, provided he maintains the original bend of his head and neck over the leading foreleg.

RIDING A 16½ FOOT (5 M) LOOP IN COUNTER CANTER

1 The horse canters around the arena on the right rein with the right leg leading as normal. Instead of continuing down the long side of the arena, the rider turns the horse off the track and rides a smooth 16½ foot (5 m) loop along the long side. As the horse negotiates the first curve of the loop he must continue to canter on the right leg.

2 With his head and neck slightly bent to the right, he starts to follow the loop around to the left. He is therefore bent away from the direction in which he is moving. The horse's body must remain straight – his hindlegs must follow in the same tracks as his forelegs, with only his head and neck showing a bend to the right.

3 As the horse follows the loop around to the left and back towards the track, he must still maintain the canter on the right lead, with his neck bent to the right.

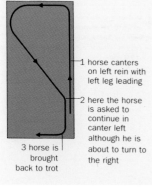

1 horse canters on left rein with left leg leading

2 here the horse is asked to continue in canter left although he is about to turn to the right

3 horse is brought back to trot

Riding a Flying Change

The flying change is when the horse changes directly from cantering with the left leg leading to cantering with the right leg leading, and vice versa. It is called for in some dressage tests and can be built upon in more advanced dressage so that the horse can literally change from one leg to the other on every stride, almost as if he were skipping! For the everyday rider, the flying change is most useful when jumping a course which requires changes of direction at canter. For example, instead of landing over a jump with the left leg leading, then having to come back to trot before picking up canter on the right lead in order to turn right to the next fence, the rider can simply land, take a few strides forwards in canter and then ask for a flying change as he turns towards the next jump.

Before the horse can be asked to perform a flying change, he must be responsive and obedient to the leg, and his canter must be balanced and able to show a degree of collection. He should willingly perform walk-to-canter transitions, be able to produce 33 foot (10 m) circles in canter, and work in counter canter before progressing to a flying change.

Some horses can tend to become excitable or nervous when they are introduced to this movement, so be sure to teach it carefully and patiently.

1 This movement is best taught by asking the horse to change from counter canter back to normal canter. This horse has been down the long side of the arena on the right rein, and has then cantered a half-circle so that he is now cantering across the diagonal with the right leg leading.

2 As the horse nears the track and the ensuing left-hand corner, the rider must indicate to the horse that he must change from right canter lead to left canter lead. The rider momentarily blocks the horse's forward momentum by closing and setting the left hand, whilst at the same time changing her leg aids from asking for right canter to asking for left canter, i.e. the rider's left leg is now applied on the girth, and the right leg used behind the girth to tell the horse to put his right hindleg down on the ground first. Remember that if the right hind starts the stride off, it is the left foreleg that appears to be leading. In this picture, you can see how the rider's left hand has blocked the horse's forward momentum so his forehand is elevated as a result.

3 In this picture, the horse is in the period of suspension that follows each canter stride, and it is only at this point that he is able to perform the flying change. So the blocking of the forward movement makes the period of suspension just a fraction longer, giving the horse time to re-arrange his legs so that he lands on the opposite lead, i.e. he changes from the right lead to the left lead. This young horse has overreacted to the rider changing the position of her leg aids (bringing her left leg back on to the girth and using her right leg behind the girth). He has flicked up his back end higher than his forehand which unbalances him. As he strengthens up and becomes more relaxed about the exercise he will make a smoother flying change.

4 As a result of the rider changing her aids from asking for canter right to asking for canter left, the horse has landed on the left lead as required and can now continue to canter around the arena on the left rein.

Riding a Dressage Test

Once you have practised everything that has been discussed in this book so far, it will be good for both you and your horse to go out and put it all to the test by riding in some dressage competitions. These can be anything from small, local affairs to affiliated competitions.

Always make the effort to learn your dressage test off by heart, but do not practise it continually on your own horse because he will learn it himself and will start to anticipate the next movement instead of waiting for your instructions. At some competitions you are allowed to have your test read out to you, but if you are having to concentrate on instructions being read out, you cannot possibly concentrate 100 per cent on getting the best out of your horse.

Your horse should be well groomed and have his mane plaited for a dressage competition. You should wear a pair of white or beige jodhpurs or breeches, long or short riding boots, a riding jacket and a shirt and tie or stock.

All dressage tests begin with the horse and rider coming down the centre line of the arena, and all but preliminary tests require the rider to halt the horse and salute the judge. This first movement is the first impression that the judge will have of you – the only thing the judge can see from that angle is how straight your horse is as he comes down the centre line. So concentrate on riding the horse forwards in a good active pace, as it is easier to ride a straight line if the horse is moving forwards with impulsion. (Think of how a bicycle wobbles if you pedal too slowly – the same happens to a horse if he lacks impulsion.) A good straight halt will earn you good marks and put the judge in a good frame of mind for the rest of your test. Be ready with both hands and legs to correct any attempt the horse may make to drift one way or the other as you squeeze him forwards from your legs into a blocking hand and into halt.

▌ RIGHT
Notice how this young rider is looking across the arena to the marker where she has to make her next move. Keeping your head up and looking ahead to where you have to go next helps improve the accuracy and timing of the different movements you have to perform.

Once the horse halts, keep a feel against his sides with your legs and down the rein with your hand. This will keep him on the aids and attentive to your next instruction. Female riders bow to the judge by putting both reins in their left hands, and bowing their heads as they drop their right hands to their sides. Male riders are usually required to remove their hats unless these are fitted with a safety harness. The reins are put in the left hand and the hat is removed with the right hand and lowered to one side as the rider bows his head. Do practise this at home, otherwise your horse is likely to shy away as you lower your hat to his side. When

Every single dressage test includes at least one – and usually two – halts and salutes. A nice straight halt and a confident, unhurried salute create a good impression, and are aspects of the test that can be practised at home.

you are ready to ride on again, concentrate first and foremost on straightness and maintaining a constant rhythm.

The various movements in a dressage test have to be carried out at the markers which are set around the arena. The correct point at which to carry out the next movement is as your shoulder is level with the marker. Always look up and think ahead to the next marker. Insist that the horse stays out on the track and uses the whole arena; do not be tempted to cut corners. If you ride the horse correctly around each corner, you will automatically be rebalancing him and asking him to use his hindlegs more actively. Remember to balance the horse during and before each new movement, with a half-halt if necessary. All tests end with another turn down the centre line and a halt and salute for the judge. No matter how well or badly the test may have gone, always perform this movement with good grace and manners. Remember that each movement in the test is marked separately, so that if you make a mistake in one movement all is not lost. If you keep your head and improve upon the mistake in the remaining movements, you will pick up marks again. Never give up – there are always more good marks to be earned. On top of all that, do make a conscious effort to smile. It will immediately fill you, and the judge, with confidence and, more importantly, it will help you to relax and to stay that way.

Preparing for Take-off

One of the best things about riding is to experience the exhilaration of riding a horse over fences. A lot of new riders are put off jumping through lack of confidence but, if you have developed any sort of feel for riding, jumping should simply be a natural and enjoyable progression.

All too often, when faced with a fence to jump, horse and rider seem to forget the basics they have been practising up until then. Balance and rhythm are abandoned as they career towards the obstacle! The secret of safe, enjoyable and successful jumping is to carry into the jumping arena the principles learnt and mastered whilst riding on the flat.

Rhythm and Balance

The two most important things for the would-be show jumper to keep in mind are rhythm and balance. If you can concentrate on keeping the horse balanced and in an even rhythm all the way to the fence, you have very little else to worry about.

You have already discovered how to encourage the horse to work in an even rhythm and to be responsive to your leg. Just because a jump appears in your path does not mean that anything changes – the horse must still be obedient enough to stay in the rhythm that you have dictated and, provided that you learn how to stay in balance with the horse throughout, clearing the fence comfortably and confidently will come naturally to both of you.

Horse and rider can practise working in a balanced rhythm by simply trotting and cantering over poles on the ground. This kind of work can be mixed in with your usual flatwork training so that the horse learns to remain calm and to apply

WORKING OVER TROT POLES

1 The horse is ridden in an active working trot through the corner and down to a line of trot poles set approximately 4 feet (1.25 m) apart, which gives the horse room to put his feet down between each pole as he takes each stride.

2 The horse must stay balanced and in the same rhythm as he approaches the line of trot poles.

3 The rider softens his hands forwards so that the horse is able to stretch his head and neck forwards as he negotiates the poles.

4 The horse should maintain exactly the same rhythm throughout the whole exercise – do not allow him to slow down at the end of the poles. Ride him through the next corner correctly, insisting he bends around your inside leg and maintains his balance and rhythm, and repeat the exercise.

WORKING THROUGH CANTER POLES

1 Exactly the same exercise should be practised in canter, except now the poles are spaced out approximately 10 feet (3 m) apart to give the horse room to canter over them.

2 The rider must keep the horse balanced and in the same rhythm through the corner and all the way up to the poles.

3 As the horse negotiates the poles, the rider simply softens the hands forwards so that the horse's head and neck are not restricted.

4 As when working over trot poles, the horse should maintain the same rhythm throughout the whole exercise.

5 As the horse completes the poles and canters on to the next corner, exactly the same rhythm and balance must be maintained throughout.

the same rules learnt on the flat to his jumping work. Far too many horses are allowed, and often encouraged, to become overexcited and go too fast when they are asked to jump. The horse should be taught to use power to clear fences, not speed.

USING POLES AND LINES OF FENCES

Trot and canter poles are often used to help introduce horse and rider to jumping. They should be spaced out in such a way that the horse can easily negotiate them, without having to stretch himself or shorten himself up. Trot poles are usually set about 4 feet (1.25 m) apart and canter poles 10 feet (3 m) apart. But if these distances do not suit your horse then, at this stage in his training, alter them to suit him. Adding lines of fences to the poles forms what is called a jumping grid. Gridwork is used to introduce the horse to the idea of jumping. Later in his training, it is used to increase his athleticism and to improve the way in which he jumps. It trains him to jump more carefully so he is less likely to injure himself or to knock fences down.

■ INSIST ON CONSISTENCY

It is only with practice and patience that you will teach the horse to carry out this exercise. Most horses thoroughly enjoy the idea of jumping but it is important to teach the horse to contain his enthusiasm so that he still remains obedient, balanced and in a rhythm.

A young horse who is being introduced to this work for the first time should have no reason to rush or get excited, provided he has been taught the basic principles throughout his flatwork training.

An older horse who already knows about jumping may get excited if he has been allowed to do so by previous riders, but practice and perseverance will teach him to keep an even rhythm.

If the horse really is inclined to rush, you should keep circling around the outside of the poles until he settles into a steady rhythm. If he still rushes as soon as he is allowed to go to the poles, simply circle him away from them again and keep repeating this exercise until he maintains the same rhythm. Alternatively, you can bring the horse back to walk and insist

that he walks over the poles until he is prepared to keep the same rhythm in both trot and canter.

The opposite problem may occur with an inexperienced or nervous horse who may want to slow down on the approach to the poles until he is confident about what they are. The first few times the horse is introduced to the exercise, he should be allowed to slow down to give him time to take everything in. After that, insist that he maintains the same rhythm. It may be worth choosing a slow rhythm in trot so that the horse does not feel he is being hassled, but do insist that the horse sticks to this rhythm throughout. Once he is confident, the pace can be picked up a little and a slightly faster rhythm maintained throughout. The horse should never be rushed through these exercises – his pace should be active and yet balanced.

In jumping it is the power of the horse that is critical, not his speed. As a rider you are trying to create and store power and energy on the way to the fence so that all that power can be used by the horse to clear the fence.

Jumping Fences

It is your job to bring the horse to the fence in a balanced rhythm, to remain in balance with him over it, and to land in balance so that you can continue to the next fence.

Most riders attempt to do far too much on the approach and over a fence, which only unbalances and distracts the horse. When jumping in canter, keep a light seat on the approach to the fence. About 22–33 yards (20–30 m) away, whilst still retaining exactly the same rhythm, lower your seat deeper into the saddle and actively close your legs against the horse's sides. Keep your shoulders slightly forwards. Having closed the legs more against the horse's sides, you may have to take a slightly stronger contact in the hand to prevent the horse accelerating. As the horse takes off over the fence, remain in the same position but close your knees and lower legs tighter against the horse's sides to help you remain still in the saddle, and stretch your hands and arms forwards to allow the horse to stretch his head and neck forwards over the fence.

BASIC TECHNIQUE

1 Here the rider is in the forward seat. Note how her seat bones are raised just off the saddle so there is less weight directly on the horse's back. This encourages the horse to remain soft through his back and to bowl along actively beneath her. The rider keeps her shoulders slightly more forward than they would be when cantering on the flat, but it is this position that allows the weight to be taken off the saddle whilst still allowing the rider to keep her balance. The lower leg is closed on the horse's sides, and the rider's weight is now taken by the stirrup iron. The horse is producing a light, active canter with his forehand nicely elevated.

2 As the rider approaches a fence, she lowers her seat into the saddle but keeps her shoulders in the forward position. The lower legs are closed more firmly against the horse's sides so that his hocks are pushed under him, but the rider's hands prevent him from accelerating. The aim is to collect the horse so that he has plenty of energy to power himself over the fence.

3 Just before the horse takes off, the rider softens her hands forwards so he can lower his head and neck to produce a supple, clean jump. The rider's seat is still deep in the saddle, her lower legs are closed against the horse's sides, her heels are pushed down and, at this point, she also allows her knees to close against the saddle to keep her body balanced as the horse jumps.

4 As the horse takes off, all the rider does is to allow her hands and arms to stretch forwards to follow the movement of the horse's head and neck. The rider remains perfectly still and balanced over the horse and, in this way, leaves the horse free to jump athletically and comfortably over the fence.

5 By adopting this technique over a fence, the rider is able to remain in balance with the horse; this means that, as they land, the two of them are still balanced and ready to face whatever comes next. If another fence were to follow immediately, they would both be in the correct position to tackle it.

6 Horse and rider look equally balanced on the approach and on landing over the fence. If horse and rider can maintain this same rhythm and balance around a whole course, they have every chance of producing a clear round, be it across country or in a show-jumping arena.

COMMON JUMPING FAULTS

GETTING IN FRONT OF THE MOVEMENT
These two pictures show one of the most common faults of which any number of riders, of all standards, are guilty. Faced with a fence, many riders seem to be overwhelmed by an irresistible desire to anticipate when the horse is going to take off and to "jump" with him! Instead of sitting quietly and maintaining their position, the rhythm and the balance, they fire their seat out of the saddle, hurl their upper body up the horse's neck and generally do about ten times more than they need to. The effect on the horse is both unbalancing and distracting. This can result in the horse hitting the fence with his front legs because the rider has loaded too much weight on to his forehand or, worse still, the horse may be tempted to put his feet back down again in front of the fence. The horse is then unable to jump at all.

You can see how easy it would be for the horse to put his front feet back down on the ground and, because the rider has come right out of the saddle and thrown all her weight forward, she would have very little chance of staying on board. In the second picture, the rider is still in a relatively weak position; her weight is balanced on her knees instead of being pushed down into the stirrups and her heels, with the result that her lower leg has slid backwards.

The rider is going to be out of balance with the horse as he lands and will not be in a very strong position to regain the balance and rhythm that they started with. If the horse stumbled as he landed, because the rider is not supporting her weight in her lower legs and heels, she would probably be thrown forwards. Again she may well fall off or at the very least she would not be able to help the horse recover as well as if she had maintained her balance.

IN TIMES OF TROUBLE!
Whilst the horse must not be allowed to rush towards his fences, it is just as important that he is not allowed to slow down to the point that he runs out of impulsion and stops. If you sense that the horse is reluctant to keep progressing forwards to a fence, you must adopt a more aggressive style of riding to encourage the horse to keep going. In this situation it is more important than ever that you keep your seat in the saddle the whole time. If you are tempted to anticipate the take-off and get in front of the movement, the reluctant jumper is presented with the ideal opportunity to stop dead!

In these pictures, the rider has pressed both legs very firmly against the horse's sides. If necessary, both heels should be used to kick the horse forwards. The seat remains deep in the saddle and the rider arches her back slightly to allow her seat as well as the legs to drive the horse forwards. The rider must not throw her hands forward at the horse as often happens – she is trying to ride the horse up into the contact so that while contact is maintained it does not actually restrict the horse's forward movement.

CHASING THE HORSE INTO THE FENCE

Another fault commonly adopted by any number of riders is to chase or rush the horse into the fence. The rider is meant to maintain the same rhythm and balance as he or she rides from fence to fence, but many people feel unable to wait for the fence. As soon as they are a few strides from it, they drive the horse forwards, immediately unbalancing the horse and pushing him on to his forehand.

This approach usually results in the horse taking off much too far away from the fence and really having to stretch to clear it. In these pictures, even the horse looks angry at this unwanted interference from his rider. If the horse is made to jump like this, he is likely to knock fences down. He is being made to use speed to clear the fences rather than power and the athleticism of his body. If he is ridden like this across country, particularly to a very upright fence, he will find it difficult to get his front legs up in the air quickly enough and risks hitting the fence; if it is a solid cross-country fence, this may well be enough to unseat his rider or, at worst, would cause the horse to fall as well.

◼ RIGHT, TOP TO BOTTOM
In the first picture the horse's canter stride is already plenty long enough, but in the second you can see that the rider has continued to drive the horse, stretching out his frame and stride even further. Compare the look of this canter to the approach made in the first pictures in this chapter. In those pictures the canter looked light and active, and the forehand was elevated. In these pictures you can see how flat and stretched out the canter is and how all the weight is falling on the forehand.

The Circle Exercise – Balance, Rhythm and Trust

Trotting poles and grids make it easier for the horse and rider to keep their rhythm and balance – the real test is whether or not they can maintain the same principles when cantering to a single fence. One of the best ways to ensure this is to practise this very simple exercise. Build a small jump somewhere that allows you room to canter in a large circle to it, say on a 33 yard (30 m) circle. Pick up a canter and just practise maintaining a good, even rhythm as you canter around the circle, bypassing the jump to begin with. When you feel settled enough to jump, make sure that you stick to the same rhythm – don't speed up or slow down just because you are thinking of jumping. As you come on to the last quarter of the circle before the jump, sit deep into the saddle, close your legs against the horse's sides and contain him in the same rhythm with your hand, and then look away from the jump. Maintain the rhythm and allow the horse to look after the jump. As you feel him take off, allow your hands and arms to go forwards to follow the contact. Have a friend standing in the middle of the circle to check you do not look at the jump.

Practise jumping at different speeds on the circle – the faster you go the further away from the fence the horse will take off, the slower you go the closer he will

FINDING THE RIGHT RHYTHM

1 On the last quarter of the circle the rider sits deep in the saddle, closes the legs and hands to collect the horse whilst still maintaining the same rhythm, and then looks away from the fence.

2 The rider continues to look away from the fence, concentrating only on keeping the same rhythm and balance. Note how the horse, left undistracted by his rider, is totally focused on the fence.

3 The horse has the fence measured up and is about to take off.

4 The rider allows his arms and hands to follow forwards whilst the horse clears the fence.

get before take-off, provided you maintain the same rhythm. This exercise will help you find the rhythm from which your horse jumps best. Once you get the idea of

trusting the horse and waiting for the fence, you can go back to looking where you are going, but return to this exercise whenever you get the urge to interfere.

LEARNING TO TRUST THE HORSE

1 Nine times out of ten, if the rider looks at the fence at this stage he or she feels obliged to interfere by either checking or chasing the horse. This simply distracts and unbalances the horse.

2 The rider is trusting her horse to do the job; note how the horse is fully concentrating on the task in hand and is about to clear the fence.

3 A horse can jump as big a fence as you wish in this way. Provided you keep the rhythm and balance, he will do the jumping.

Improving Horse and Rider's Jumping Ability

In the same way that, when learning to ride, the rider is more concerned about his or her own position and balance than about how well the horse is going, when learning to jump you must first master the art of keeping a balanced, rhythmic approach before worrying about trying to improve the horse's actual jumping ability.

Gridwork can be used to help in both instances – jumping the grids allows you to concentrate on improving your own balance and position, and can also be used to improve the horse's agility and ability over a fence.

Some horses are naturally more careful jumpers than others; some horses tend to throw long, flat jumps, whilst others may have a tendency to jump very high but with little scope to clear spreads. In either case, gridwork exercises can enhance the horse's performance.

■ GRIDWORK AND JUMPING DISTANCES

When gridwork is first introduced, the distances should be set to suit the horse. Once the horse is confident with the exercise, the distances can be altered – either lengthened or shortened – to improve the horse's technique. So with a horse who tends to throw a long, flat jump

the distance should gradually be reduced so that he has to collect himself up and use himself more athletically, while a horse who is very short striding should be encouraged to stretch out a little by using longer distances.

You may well wonder why it is necessary to alter what the horse does naturally. The reason is that, in the competition world, show jumps and cross-country fences are built to set measurements and distances. The course designer has to build fences that can be jumped safely by different sizes and types of horse, so he has to find an average distance to use and build his fences around that. For example, an average measurement used in course designing is based on the assumption that the horse will cover 4 yards (3.65 m) with every canter stride. Extra room has to be allowed for the distance away from the fence that the horse will take off, and further distance must be allowed on the other side of the fence for the horse to land. A rule of thumb is 4 yards (3.65 m) for one canter stride, plus 2 yards (1.9 m) for take-off and 2 yards (1.9 m) for landing. If the course designer wants the horse to fit in one stride between two fences, he will place the fences 8 yards (7.35 m) apart. To fit in two

strides the fences would be placed 12 yards (11 m) apart – two canter strides equal two by 4 yards (3.65 m), plus 2 yards (1.9 m) for landing over the first fence and 2 yards (1.9 m) for taking off at the second fence.

If your particular horse is to fit in the same number of strides as the course designer intended, he needs to cover the ground that the designer has based his figures on. Higher up the competition ladder, the course designer may include an extra-long or an extra-short distance, to test riders' ability to adjust the distance their horses cover. Some riders may choose to collect up their horses and fit in three strides; others may push for two.

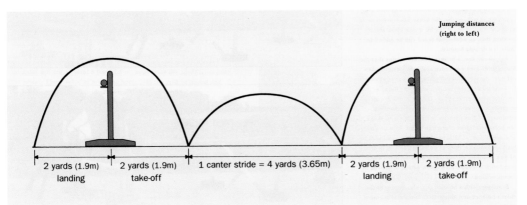

Jumping distances (right to left)

| 2 yards (1.9m) landing | 2 yards (1.9m) take-off | 1 canter stride = 4 yards (3.65m) | 2 yards (1.9m) landing | 2 yards (1.9m) take-off |

ASCENDING PARALLEL

The approach through the trot poles and the cross pole remains exactly the same. But the one-stride distance to the parallel (now ascending) has been increased. To encourage the horse to take a longer stride to help him cover the distance to the parallel, the rider simply "clicks" to the horse and closes her legs against his sides to tell him to stretch forwards. The horse responds by taking a longer stride than he did in the first grid sequence. In the last picture you can see how the horse is really using his hindquarters, and has snapped up his hindlegs to make sure he clears the back pole.

RIDER'S WEIGHT

Here the horse tackles the same grid and, from this angle, the interesting point to note is shown in the last picture. The rider has, to some degree, thrown her body weight forwards and up the horse's neck, rather than keeping her seat in the saddle. Note how she has pitched her weight to the left-hand side and look at the effect this has had on the horse's left foreleg.

Because the rider's weight is loaded over the horse's left shoulder, it is harder for the horse to bring his left foreleg up as quickly and cleanly as the right foreleg. It would therefore be very easy for the horse to knock this fence down with the trailing foreleg. To avoid this, the rider's weight must stay balanced centrally in the saddle.

DESCENDING PARALLEL

The approach to this exercise is the same as before, but the one-stride distance is shortened to less than it was in the very first grid, and the parallel is now descending. The horse has to land over the cross pole, collect and shorten his stride and then be quick and neat with his front legs to clear the front pole of the descending parallel. The previous exercise will have reminded him to be really tidy with his hindlegs, so this exercise should produce his most impressive jump. Note in the last picture how very neat and tidy this horse has been with his front legs – exactly the aim of the exercise.

■ THE DOUBLE OF PARALLELS

This exercise is aimed at helping the horse who tends to throw a high, but not necessarily very wide, jump. Two parallel fences are built one stride apart, with the distance set to suit the horse's stride, i.e. approximately 8 yards (7.35 m). The horse is cantered through this once or twice and then the distance between the two fences is shortened by simply making the two parallel fences wider – the back rail of the first fence and the front rail of the second fence are moved 1 foot (30 cm) or so towards each other. This encourages the horse to throw a wider jump than usual over the first spread; he must land and shorten himself up to fit in one stride before having to throw another scopey jump over the second spread.

INTRODUCING TWO PARALLELS

The exercise is introduced by cantering the horse to two parallels, set one stride apart at a distance to suit the horse's stride. Note how soft and sympathetic the rider's hands are – allowing the horse to use himself without restriction.

ADJUSTING TO THE JUMP

Now the spreads have been made wider so that the distance between the two fences has become shorter – the two green jump wings have been moved in towards each other. In the first picture you will see that the rider has been caught out by the huge jump that the horse has thrown – she really needed to allow her arms and hands to go forwards more so as not to restrict the horse.

Having thrown such a big jump, the horse now has to shorten and balance himself quickly in order to clear the second fence. Note the improved position of the rider's hands.

Riding Related Distances

Over a whole course of fences, two of them will often be placed on what is called a related distance. This means the designer intends the competitors to ride a set number of strides between the two. Combination fences refer to jumps which are one or two strides apart, whereas related distances refer to jumps which are anything from three to, say, six strides apart.

Gridwork exercises at home will have shown you whether or not your horse has a naturally short or long stride, and you should use this knowledge to your advantage when faced with combinations or related distances. If the horse has a naturally short stride, you will need to encourage the horse to open out his stride; you may need to ride with more pace than, say, the rider whose horse has a long, ground-covering stride. Whatever the case, when riding combinations or related distances the aim is to maintain an even stride length between the fences, not to land over the fence and then have either to check the horse or to chase him forwards towards the next element.

Watch a number of horses tackling a related distance and you will start to see how it rides best. Some riders may approach in a short, collected canter and fit in an extra stride, whilst others may let their horses jump, canter and jump out of a longer stride and fit in one stride less. If you practise the options at home you will learn which approach suits your horse, but whatever the number of strides you opt for they should be of an even length. So, to fit in the maximum number of strides, approach in a more collected canter, with a little less pace. To fit in the minimum number of strides, approach on a longer stride with more pace.

TAKING FIVE EVEN STRIDES

These two fences are set 60 feet (18.25 m) apart, and in this first exercise the rider intends to fit five strides between them. She approaches in a reasonably collected canter which encourages the horse to jump in quietly over the first fence. As she lands, the rider successfully maintains the same rhythm that she had on the approach, and this allows the horse to fit in the five even strides as required between the two fences.

TAKING FOUR EVEN STRIDES

Now the rider needs to open the horse out a little to fit in only four strides, so she approaches on a longer stride and in a stronger rhythm than previously. The horse jumps in more aggressively which helps him to make up some of the distance required. The rider again thinks about keeping the horse going forwards and up to the rhythm that she had on the approach. This allows the horse to take four strides of even length between the fences.

TOO MUCH PACE

This rider, attempting the same exercise, shows how not to do it! Her plan was to fit in five strides, but instead of coming on a quieter rhythm than normal she has ridden the horse strongly into the fence so that he throws an extravagant jump. She is now going to struggle to fit in the five strides and resorts to checking the horse back, i.e. using her hands to make the horse continually shorten his stride. In the last-but-one picture, you can see how the horse is objecting to this treatment by throwing his head up and resisting the rider's hand. The horse has kindly cleared the fence for her but could easily have knocked it down, or even refused. Once the horse throws his head up, his eye is taken off the fence and he is unable to judge what he needs to do. It also makes him tense and hollow so that he cannot be as athletic. As you can see from these pictures, instead of taking five strides of even length, this horse's strides were being gradually shortened. Having made the initial mistake of coming in with too much pace, the rider may have been wiser to allow the horse to continue in the stronger rhythm and to fit in only four strides. Practising these exercises at home will give you a feel for how to get the distance right on the day and for how best to react when things go wrong.

Cross-country
Riding

Riding across country is a true test of a horse-and-rider partnership – whether it be the genuine article when you are quite literally crossing the open countryside and jumping whatever natural hazards block your path, or the more organized version of riding a course of cross-country fences. Cross-country riding requires bravery and fitness from both horse and rider, as well as obedience and trust from the horse. Cross-country fences do not fall down, very often the horse cannot even see where he is going to land, and he cannot judge the depth of any water which he might be required to jump into. Far from being a sport for the reckless and slapdash, if the partnership is to survive it needs trust, obedience and technique.

COPING WITH AN EARLY TAKE-OFF

This rider has taken quite a risk at this widespread fence by asking her horse to take off very early. On a less scopey horse there is every chance that this sort of riding will result in a fall, as the horse may be physically unable to clear the spread of the fence and will land on it. In the first picture the rider has kept the horse balanced and in an even rhythm, but in the second picture she has suddenly opened the horse out and asked him to take off. Had she maintained the rhythm and balance all the way to the fence, the horse would have been able to fit in another stride and would have taken off a little closer to the fence. As it is, having stood the horse right off, the rider has reacted in the correct way over the fence. She has kept her body weight balanced over the middle of the horse and has slipped the reins, so that he can really stretch himself out and clear the fence.

TACKLING TWO CORNERS – 1

This horse and rider are tackling a combination of two corners set three strides apart. See how the rider lands over the first corner and, using his knowledge of his horse's stride length, he sits quietly and lets the horse take three even strides to the second corner.

TACKLING TWO CORNERS – 2

Another horse and rider tackling the same combination. Note how this rider, having landed over the first corner, knows that she has got to open her horse's stride out in order to make up the three strides to the next fence. She has sat down in the saddle and is really riding the horse forwards. Knowing her horse very well, she has even dropped the rein contact with his mouth, and thus lessened her control, to encourage him to stretch everything forwards in order to reach the fence. In this instance, it has paid off for her because she knows her horse well enough to trust him. Usually at a fence like this, which demands accuracy, you cannot afford to drop the rein contact in this way as the horse is then free to run out if he so wishes.

■ **WHEN THINGS GO WRONG**

Successful cross-country riding requires an ability to cope with the unexpected – even though you may have walked the course and know exactly how you intend riding everything, sometimes the horse has other ideas. Despite your best intentions he may jump or react differently from how you imagined. Then you need to know what to do to make the best of the situation. For example, if your horse is normally long striding you might expect him to make up the distance in a combination easily, but if there is something in that combination that makes the horse back down, such as a ditch under the jump, suddenly you may not be on the stride pattern you imagined. Experience will teach you whether it is best to shorten your horse's stride and let him fit in an extra one, or whether you are better off riding even more aggressively, forcing him to open up his stride again and to take on the fence. Some horses jump very big over ditches, or off drops, and this may alter the distance to the next fence.

Most importantly, if and when the unexpected happens, you are of most help if you can stay in balance with the horse and give him the necessary freedom of his head and neck. This all comes down to having an independent seat. If you can stay balanced without needing to hang on to the reins, and can at the same time keep thinking ahead and judging what you need to do to help the horse, you are the best asset he can have. A horse can jump out of some seemingly impossible situations, and can correct seemingly disastrous misjudgements, if his rider is not hindering him. The golden rule is to maintain rhythm and balance.

World of
the Horse

The Competition World

Competing with your horse can be as low key or as serious as you
wish to make it. Some riders make a living out of riding and
competing with horses, others simply enjoy giving the family horse
a quick wash and brush-up once a year for a local show. Whatever
you opt for within that scale, there are certain things to be aware of.
Before attempting any form of horse sport you must be sure that
your horse is fit and mature enough, both mentally and
physically, to take part. He should be sufficiently well schooled
to be obedient to your commands, and should have seen enough
in his daily hacks and general training regime not to be overawed
by the competition scene.

Most horses should be versatile enough to take part in any
number of sports at the lower levels. But if you decide to take up a
particular sport seriously, check out the requirements and skills
needed to ensure that you are both suited to that sport.

Types of Competition

■ BELOW
There are so many opportunities to compete; all abilities and tastes are catered for, from the rough and tumble of mounted games...

The wide range of horse sports that is now available means there is something to suit all types of horse and rider. From the more genteel, such as showing and dressage, to the rough and tumble of team sports such as polo and horseball, all manner of skills, both mental and physical, are tested. Some sports are judged very subjectively. Dressage and showing, for example, are reliant on the opinion of the particular judge on the day. Others are out-and-out contests of stamina and tactics, such as horse racing and endurance riding. In show jumping and cross-country-riding competitions, the skills of each horse and rider are not only pitted against their fellow competitors, but also against the questions set by the course designer. However great or small your competitive streak, there is something to suit all tastes.

■ LEFT
The main aim of competing at any level is that it should be fun. It is not so much the winning as the taking part – although everybody likes to win sometimes!

WELFARE REQUIREMENTS

■ All affiliated competitions will state the age at which horses or ponies are allowed to compete in that particular discipline. For example, event horses are not allowed to compete in one-day events until they are five years old. You will need to be aware of such restrictions before planning a competition season with your horse.

■ Competition horses must have an up-to-date vaccination certificate which proves that they have received their annual vaccination booster.

■ As a rider and competitor you have a responsibility to your horse and to other competitors to ensure that, if you suspect your horse is suffering from something contagious, he is kept isolated from other horses. Obviously if your horse is clinically ill you would not consider taking him to a competition but some diseases, such as ringworm or mild viruses, do not greatly affect the horse's general well-being. When this is the case you should not be tempted to hope for the best and still go – you must keep your horse at home, away from other horses, until he is fully recovered.

| BELOW
...to the sheer
elegance of dressage...

| RIGHT
...and the test of all-
round horsemanship,
eventing.

■ AFFILIATED AND UNAFFILIATED COMPETITIONS

Most countries have a good selection of organized horse sports, and these are usually split between what are regarded as affiliated and unaffiliated competitions. The **affiliated competitions** are generally stricter and require horse and rider to be registered as members of that particular sport's governing body.

At the top end of the scale, the International Equestrian Federation (FEI) governs all international competitions involving the sports under its jurisdiction – dressage, show jumping, carriage driving, eventing, vaulting and endurance riding.

The FEI controls their rules, and approves the programme of events at regional, championship and Olympic level.

Each country's own national federation is, in turn, answerable to the FEI. They organize competitions for all levels of experience within their own country.

Unaffiliated competitions, usually run along the same lines as the affiliated competitions, are put on by individuals who are happy about taking on the organizational responsibility. To enter these you do not need to be a registered member of any governing body, but you will need to be familiar with the affiliated

rules as these are often used. Many of the riders who compete in the affiliated competitions will take advantage of the more relaxed atmosphere at unaffiliated shows to introduce a young horse to the sport. The unaffiliated competitions also act as an introduction to the sport for novice riders.

■ RESTRICTIONS

Many sports split their competitions into classes for either different age groups of riders, or different standards or sizes of horse or pony. Pony classes are restricted either to recognized pony breeds or to any equine standing under 15hh. Showing classes are classified by size and type of horse or pony – working hunter, show hack, cob etc.

The affiliated organizations run competitions for horses of the various grades recognized by their governing body, e.g. event horses are graded from novice through to advanced, dressage horses from preliminary through to grand prix, and so on.

Local unaffiliated classes are divided up into rider age groups, size of horse or pony, or prize money or placings previously won. The novice class may be restricted to horses or ponies who have

never been placed in any competitions, the next class may be limited to horses who haven't previously won a competition. The open class, as its name suggests, is open to any grade of horse or pony and is usually the most competitive of all.

To avoid disappointment and embarrassment or, worse still, elimination, do make sure you have read the rules and regulations of any competition you intend entering and comply with them.

The happy winner of a show class salutes his appreciative audience.

Choosing a Sport

It is a good idea to find out if you enjoy and have an aptitude for a particular sport by entering unaffiliated competitions before going to the expense of registering with an affiliated body.

If, for example, you decide that dressage appeals to you, start out by competing quietly against friends and neighbours at local unaffiliated shows. Having decided that this sport really is for you, register with your national federation and start to work your way up through the grades of affiliated competition. If you have the talent, dedication and time to commit to the sport, there is nothing to stop you reaching the top. If your sights really are set on the giddy heights of world championships or the Olympics, do remember that competitors at this level not only have to qualify to take part but also have to be selected by their national federation to enter as individuals or team members.

If you are lucky enough to be able to take your sport that seriously, you should investigate the opportunities that your national federation offers. Most countries that have an affiliation to the FEI also offer training to their members, as well as competitions culminating in international championships for riders of different age groups. The sports of dressage, show

■ LEFT
When choosing a sport to take part in, it is important to consider the suitability of both your own and your horse's temperament. For some riders the excitement becomes too much – can you cope with this? Will it add to your fun or will it worry you?

■ ABOVE AND BELOW
If you wish to compete regularly then some form of transport is going to be necessary. This can be a vehicle and trailer or a horse lorry, either of which can be purchased, hired or shared. Not only will the trailer or lorry provide a safe haven for your horse in between classes, it will also tend to become the social centre of the event.

EQUIPMENT NEEDED FOR ALL EQUESTRIAN SPORTS

■ You should wear a recognized safety helmet or crash hat complete with safety harness for all horse-riding activities. If you intend riding and jumping across country, you should also wear a body protector.

■ Each sport has its own recognized and accepted style of dress. Dressage, show jumping and showing classes require the rider to be turned out in a riding jacket, jodhpurs or breeches, short or long riding boots and a hard hat. For cross-country riding, you can wear a sweat shirt or jumper instead of a riding jacket.

Polo, horseball and polocrosse require breeches and long leather boots to be worn, along with a shirt instead of a riding jacket, plus protective padding such as knee pads.

Endurance riders wear either standard jodhpurs or breeches, or more lightweight ones for hot conditions, as well as waterproofs for wet weather. They are not expected to wear riding jackets but dress according to the weather conditions.

■ Your horse or pony will need a well-fitting saddle and bridle, and it is also advisable to protect his legs against strains or knocks by using boots or bandages.

■ You will need water, buckets, sponges, sweat scrapers and towels so that the horse can be washed and dried off if he is hot and sweaty after competing.

jumping and eventing have championships specifically for pony riders, juniors and young riders. When you reach the age of twenty-one, you have to join the senior ranks.

Within the other equestrian sports there is usually a very good choice of competition designed to cover all levels of ability and ambition. In the showing world this ranges from local shows to regional competitions, right through to national championships. For some of these classes, your horse or pony may have to be registered with a breed society or showing association; these, in turn, help to govern and organize the various competitions, local and national.

Team sports such as polo, polocrosse and horseball require greater organization and facilities, as does learning the skills of vaulting. To take part usually entails joining a local club.

▮ BELOW
Whether you have a good or a bad day, you must always put your horse's or pony's needs first. Make sure he has time to relax and enjoy the experience as well.

▮ BELOW
Equestrian sports involving jumping offer variety and fun. Show jumping, for example, has classes available for anyone from leading-rein contenders, through junior classes as shown here, to international senior competitions.

TRAVELLING EQUIPMENT

Once you decide to compete regularly, unless you are very lucky in having regular competitions held within hacking distance, you will need to transport your horse in either a horse lorry or trailer. The horse must be kept safe and comfortable when travelling.
■ There should be bedding on the floor to cushion his legs and to help soak up any urine or droppings he produces.
■ He should be secured with a headcollar and rope which is tied through a piece of string attached to the fixed tie ring. This is so that, should the horse fall or struggle, he will be able to free his head and neck – otherwise he may injure himself very badly.

■ He will need a selection of rugs or blankets, chosen according to the weather conditions on the day, so that he becomes neither too hot nor too cold on the journey.
■ He should wear protective boots or bandages on his legs, a tailguard or bandage (or both) to protect his tail from rubbing, and a poll guard to protect the top of his head.
■ You should offer your horse water to drink during the journey, and a haynet, although this should be taken away at least an hour before he is due to be ridden. Take food and hay for him to eat during the day and on the journey home, and keep a check on how warm or cold he is whilst travelling.

Non-jumping
Sports

Horse sports are so varied that they are difficult to
categorize. For the purposes of this book, they are split into a
selection of non-jumping and jumping sports. To make it to
the top of any one, you need to specialize. But most riders
enjoy taking part in a number of different activities, so first
look at the different things you can try. Unless you have your
heart set on one particular sport, it is worth experimenting to
find out what really suits you and your horse. The discipline
and perfectionist nature of dressage may suit your personality,
or perhaps you would prefer the more light-hearted approach
of mounted games. Once you have outgrown those, there are
team games such as horseball, polo and polocrosse to enjoy,
or perhaps Western riding appeals to you. Whoever you are,
whatever your ability, there is bound to be something
to which you can aspire.

Mounted Games

■ BELOW
Some games rely on your pony's skills; others are down to the rider. In "Apple Bobbing" you have to retrieve an apple from a bucket of water without using your hands!

If you can envisage a cross between party games and a race on horseback, you will have some idea of what mounted games involve. Although adults do compete, it is primarily a sport for children – the energy, enthusiasm and agility that this sport requires ideally suit youngsters and their ponies. The beauty of these games is that there is one to suit every type and ability of pony and rider.

Mounted games can be organized for fun between a group of friends or as a serious form of competition, with regional, national and international championships provoking great rivalry between the various clubs and associations taking part. But at whatever level they are played, mounted games will help to develop your riding skills, your confidence in handling yourself and your pony and, most importantly, the realization that riding is fun.

■ HOW MOUNTED GAMES BEGAN

Surprisingly for a sport that is now dominated by children, mounted games were first played by adults. It was in India that the games we are familiar with today developed. They were then known as gymkhanas, which translated as gymnastic or athletic displays on horseback. The word gymkhana is still used in many countries today to describe the sport. The British Army, which was based in India in the late nineteenth century, adopted the games, although their mounts included donkeys, mules and camels. The games, such as "Kiss the Girl", "Tent Pegging" and "Grab the Hat", were a popular and light-hearted way not only of helping to keep horse and rider fit and supple, but also of fostering strong regimental loyalty.

When the soldiers returned to Britain, they introduced the games to their home country where they proved most popular with children, their small, nippy ponies being ideal mounts for the games. The Pony Club, which was formed in 1929 and quickly grew to become a world-wide organization with over 100,000 members, developed and spread the benefits of the games. Pony Club Mounted Games are now played in over twenty-five different countries at interbranch, interstate and international level.

For those who do not wish to lose out on the enjoyment of mounted games once they are over Pony Club age, there is the International Mounted Games Association. This holds an annual World Mounted Games Championship in a different host country each year, and membership of the Association goes up to the age of twenty-one.

Other opportunities to play mounted games are offered at local shows and gymkhanas, where there are classes for leading-rein competitors as well as for older children.

■ SKILLS REQUIRED

To enjoy mounted games for the fun and entertainment they offer requires no great skill on the part of horse or rider. But if you want to be the winner of many ribbons, or to make it on to a team and compete more seriously, certain skills are necessary.

Your pony will need to be fit, obedient, agile and unflappable – he will encounter

A flying start is a big advantage, whatever race you are in. Practise at home by gradually asking your pony to go straight into canter from walk, and then from halt.

asset, as is the ability to dismount at speed
without losing balance and falling over.

You must be able to control your pony
with only one hand on the reins, as the
other hand is often needed to do whatever
the game entails. If the pony can be
taught to neck rein, i.e. to respond to
pressure on the neck from the rein rather
than to a feel on the bit, controlling him
with both reins in one hand will be easy.

■ TRAINING THE MOUNTED-GAMES PONY

Obedience in the form of fast reactions is
what is required of the mounted-games
pony. He must be able to start and stop
quickly, turn tightly and, amidst all the
excitement of the race, remain stock still
while his rider carries out whatever task
the game requires.

You cannot begin to improve your
pony's responsiveness until he is working
obediently to the basic leg and hand aids.
Unless he is already at the stage where you
can quietly ask him to go forwards in walk,
trot and then canter, to halt, to turn left
or right and to move to the side, i.e. leg
yield, he is not ready to be asked to do

THE RANGE OF GAMES

Each year more and more ingenious games
are developed to test the pony's and rider's
speed, agility, co-ordination, fitness and
sense of humour!

The easiest games are designed for young
riders whose ponies are being led – musical
mats, musical chairs and musical statues.
The children are led around on their ponies
until the music stops, when they must leap
off and pounce on a chair or mat. One chair
or mat is taken away each time so that the
rider who finds him- or herself without a
chair or mat is out. In musical statues the
pony, rider and leader must remain
absolutely still when the music stops. The
first to move is out – more often than not it
is the pony who doesn't have the patience or
desire to remain still.

For those who want to test their speed
and agility there are the races. These can be
as simple as a bending race, where horse
and rider thread their way between a line of
poles, or as complex and extravagant as
such team races as the "Dragon Race".
There are even games that include the fun
of jumping. In "Chase Me Charlie", the
competitors follow each other over a jump.
If they clear it they stay in the game, if they
knock it down they are out. The jump is
raised each time until only the winner
remains. "Barrel Elimination" involves
jumping over a line of barrels. After each
round, one barrel is removed so that the
jump becomes narrower and narrower until
there is only one barrel remaining to be
jumped over. If the pony stops or runs out
to either side, he is out of the game.

all kinds of strange objects in the varied
races on offer. Most riders opt for a pony
who for most other sports would be
considered a touch too small for them,
but a smaller pony makes it easier to reach
down to deposit or retrieve objects and to
mount and dismount on the move.

As a mounted-games competitor, you
too will need to be fit and agile. Good
co-ordination and balance are called for,
as well as a good turn of speed as, in many
games, the rider may be dismounted and
leading the pony for much of the race.
Similarly, the ability to vault on to your
pony while he is cantering along is a great

▌ LEFT
It helps to be fit and supple and to have good
co-ordination. Here the rider has to retrieve a
tennis ball from the top of the cone.

NECK REINING

In countries where horses have always been used for herding livestock, such as America, Australia, New Zealand, parts of Africa and the Far East, neck reining is commonly used. This allows the rider to carry both reins in one hand. To turn the horse to the right, the rider simply brings his left hand, which is holding the reins, over to the right-hand side of the pony's neck. The reins press against the left-hand side of the pony's neck, the pony moves away from the pressure and so turns to the right. Do the opposite to turn left.

In most European countries, ponies need to be taught to respond to neck reining. If you apply the correct leg aids before you bring the rein across the pony's neck, and at the same time incline your body weight slightly in the direction you want to go, the pony will quickly get the idea of responding to neck reining.

anything beyond this. As in all things, establish the basics first and it will be easy to teach your pony any number of new skills.

THE QUICK START

To have any chance of winning you need to get a good start – your pony should be able to leap forwards from halt to full speed ahead. He will already know how to go up through the paces to canter; now he needs to speed up the process. You should first practise going forwards into trot from halt, and then try halt to canter. The correct aids should still be applied and they should be backed up by the voice, and, if necessary, a tap behind the leg with the schooling whip, rather than resorting to giving the pony a great thump with your heels. If you teach the pony to go forwards by kicking his sides with your heels, he will gradually become less responsive and will certainly be spoilt for any other activity. Treat this training in the same way as your flatwork – you are still looking for a quick response to a light aid.

THE QUICK STOP

Similarly, the pony must be able to come back rapidly from flat out to halt whenever required. This is not achieved by simply hauling hard on the reins. As in your flatwork training, ask the pony to halt by using your legs to drive him up into your hands which, on this occasion, do not soften or yield to him, so he is brought back to a halt. Using your voice to ask

him to "Whoa" will also help him to understand and respond more quickly to the request to stop. Shift your weight slightly further back in the saddle as you ask your pony to halt. This will help push his hindquarters further under him and allow him to sit down on his hocks so that, when he halts, his forehand is still light and elevated, ready for the all-important quick getaway.

In the stepping-stones race the rider has to tackle the stepping stones before vaulting on to the pony and racing for the finishing line.

pressure on the right-hand side of the
pony's neck. It is sometimes helpful to
use the reins slightly higher up the pony's
neck when you would like him to turn
particularly sharply.

GETTING USED TO THE EQUIPMENT

In a serious mounted-games competition
your pony will face any number of strange
objects. He must be prepared to go up to
whatever the target of the game is, he may
have to go under a washing-line strung
with clothes, or a post hung with
signboards – all manner of items have to
be acceptable to him. He must allow his
rider to carry flags, buckets, swords and
balloons without being worried by them.
He must be accustomed to noise and the
general hustle and bustle, including a very
noisily appreciative audience, which is all
part of a mounted-games competition.

All these strange and startling things
should be introduced to the pony at home.
As long as you give him time to realize that
none of these peculiar objects is going to

TURNING

Your pony will need to be able to turn
quickly and sharply, and this can be
practised at home by using a barrel as a
turning point. Practise first in trot, riding
up to and around the barrel, keeping your
pony as tight to the barrel as you can.
Remember that it is your outside hand
and leg that will prevent the pony from
drifting away from the barrel. Once you
have mastered a tight turn in trot using
both hands on the rein, try it in canter.
When the pony is familiar with what is
required, try it with the reins in one hand.
To turn tightly to the left around the
barrel, your right leg will be back behind
the girth to keep the pony's quarters close
to the barrel, your inside leg will be used
on the girth to make the pony bend
through his body and you will bring your
rein hand across to the left, so that there is

The "Dragon Race" is one of the most spectacular – the riders have to kill the dragon by bursting the
balloons attached to him. Then they can rescue the damsel in distress.

▌ LEFT
Mounted games are as much to do with team work
as with individual ability and success.

harm him, he will soon accept them.
There is no point using force – his trust
has to be won and this takes time and
patience. When you show your pony
something new, allow him time to make
up his own mind that it is harmless. Do
not force him to approach this strange
object too quickly. Reward and reassure
him all the time that he is prepared to
face it, even if he is still not very close to it.
Only become stronger in your riding if he
actually turns away from the object. Then
you must be positive and use your legs and
hands to turn him back. Once he is facing
it again, reward him. Let him know you
are displeased each time he tries to turn
away, and gradually he will realize that you
are determined that he will meet this new
thing. Usually curiosity takes over and he
will dare to get closer and closer. Take
things slowly – go one step at a time –
and this will ensure that your pony's
confidence and enjoyment increase.

THE CHANGEOVER

Many races require a fast changeover of
equipment – usually a baton – between
two riders. This has to be practised, firstly
to accustom the pony to the idea of
another pony and rider bearing down on
him at great speed – the last thing you
want is your pony shying away. Secondly,
both riders involved need to know how to
hand over the item without dropping it. It
should be held at arm's length so that the
receiving rider has a good view of the

target to be grabbed. The riders should be
positioned so that the receiver can grab
the baton with his or her best hand (the
right hand if he or she is right-handed)
and the first rider should not release the
grip on the baton until he or she is
positive that the second rider has taken
hold of it. It is quicker to turn around and
hand it over again than for the baton to be
dropped and the rider to have to dismount.

■ PRACTICE FOR THE RIDER

Once you are familiar with even a small
number of mounted games, you will
realize that a wide range of skills is called
for. All demand dexterity and agility, but
some demand more specialist skills. If you
are a good shot you will excel at games
such as the "Hi Lo Race", where a tennis
ball has to land in a high net, or the
"Sharpshooters' Race", where a soft ball is
thrown at a line of comic models until it
succeeds in knocking their heads off. In
the "Sack Race" you will need to be able to
race along, leading your pony, while your
feet and legs are trapped in a sack!

All these strange skills can be practised
on foot at home, with simple homemade
equipment. Practising the races on foot will
also help to promote your overall fitness
and agility, which will be all to the good
when you try them out on horseback again.

VAULTING ON AND OFF

To be a truly successful mounted-games
player you will need to master the art of

mounting and dismounting at speed. A
small pony coupled with a rider with long
legs have the advantage here, although
there is an art to vaulting on which makes
it easier than it looks. The trick is to use
the momentum created by the pony's
movement to help lift you into the saddle.
To begin with, practise mounting a
moving pony with someone leading the
pony so that he can be kept straight and at
a steady speed. You should run beside the
pony, who will be trotting or cantering,
keeping level with the pony's shoulder.
Stretch your right hand over the pony's
back and take hold of the front of the
saddle flap on the far side. Your left hand
is holding the reins and can be rested on
the pony's withers. As the pony's near-side
foreleg touches the ground, spring
upwards and swing your right leg over his
back. If your timing is good, the pony's
forward momentum will help to lift you up
into the air.

To dismount from a moving pony,
organize yourself so that you land facing
forwards and are immediately able to run
forwards so that you do not lose your
balance. If you have ever stepped off a
moving bus or carousel platform, you will
know that unless you start running as soon
as your feet touch the ground you will fall
flat on your face.

Take both feet out of the stirrups, put
your right hand on the pommel of the
saddle and your left hand on the pony's
neck. Lean forwards over the pony's neck
and swing your right leg up and over his
back. Use your hands to push your body
clear of the pony's side and to help
balance yourself as you land. Make sure
you land running.

For those competing seriously, team-
training sessions will be necessary, possibly
even with a coach; here it is possible to see
which riders and ponies are best suited to
which games, and also to discuss team
tactics – an important weapon on the
road to victory.

The Games

▮ BELOW
The "Basketball Race" is another favourite at the
Pony Club games.

As you will have gathered, any number
of mounted games can be dreamed up.
The Pony Club probably has the most
comprehensive list, which is used for their
national and international competitions. It
has a good rule book, including – to avoid
any breakdown in international relations –
an Official International Exchange Visits
rule book. Despite the fact that mounted
games are meant to be fun, they can
become very competitive, so it is always
safest to be sure everyone is agreed on
the same rules. The following is a selection
of team games. Most can be adapted to suit
team or individual competitions, but do
not feel you have to be limited to these. Let
your imagination run riot!

SACK RACE

Gallop your pony to the end of the arena
where there is an empty sack. Jump off the
pony, get inside the sack, and make your
way back to the start, hopping, shuffling
or tripping along, whilst still leading your
pony. One trick is to rest an arm across
the pony's withers as this will help support
your weight and keep you upright. The
other hand holds the sack up around you.
Jump forwards, allowing the pony to take
your weight and to carry you forwards a
little way before landing again.

An even more amusing adaptation of
this game is the "Big Sack Race". Four
team members gallop to the end of the
arena where a fifth team member is
holding a huge sack. She takes her team-
mates' ponies whilst all four of them climb
into the sack and, *en masse*, wriggle their
way back to the start.

GROOM'S RACE

This calls for an additional skill – the ability
to control two ponies at once. You have to
ride your own pony, and lead one of your
team-mates' ponies, up through a line of
bending poles. At the changeover point
your team-mate mounts her own pony, and
leads the third rider's pony back through

the line of poles. And so it goes on until all
the riders and ponies have had their turn
and are back at the start.

LAUNDRY STAKES

One pair of riders gallops to a washing-
line, carrying a basket of laundry between
them. They hang out the washing and
gallop back, handing the empty basket
to the second two members of the team.
They have to gallop to the washing-line,
remove the washing, and bring it back
safely to the start in the laundry basket.

ROPE RACE

Set off at a gallop through a line of
bending poles carrying a piece of rope
about 3 feet (1 m) long. At the end of the
arena, one of your team-mates grabs the
end of the rope and you both gallop back
through the bending poles together. At
the other end you drop your end of the
rope and a third rider picks it up; the
second and third rider hold the rope and
gallop through the bending poles, and so
on. Be careful not to allow your pony to
tread on the heels of the one in front.

■ BELOW AND OPPOSITE
The greatest opportunities to play mounted games
are provided by the Pony Club, which is an
international youth organization. These groups of
riders from many different countries are taking
part in the annual Euro Camp.

BALLOON RACE

A bunch of balloons is tied to a post.
Gallop to the post, collect a balloon,
gallop back and pass it to your
team-mate. He or she gallops with it
to the post, collects a second balloon and
hands both balloons to the third rider.
This goes on until the last team member
crosses the line with all the balloons
in his or her hand.

FISHING RACE

You are given a fishing rod, which is
actually a piece of wood with a hook on
the end. Gallop to a bin full of wooden
fish with rings in their noses, hook a fish,
gallop back to the start and hang it on a
peg. Your team-mate then sets off, catches

a fish, brings it back, and so on until all
the fish are caught.

BALL-AND-RACQUET RACE

You have to balance a tennis ball on a
tennis racquet whilst riding your pony as
fast as you can through a line of bending
poles. You then hand the racquet and ball
to your team-mate who races through the
bending poles, and so on.

STEPPING STONES

Race to a line of stepping stones – usually
a line of upturned buckets or similar –
dismount and negotiate the stepping
stones whilst leading your pony alongside.
Then remount your pony before crossing
the finishing line.

SHARPSHOOTERS' RACE

This race calls for another asset – a pony
willing to carry two riders on his back! At
the start of the race sit bareback on your
pony. When the whistle goes your team-
mate has to jump up behind you, and you
race to the far end. Your passenger jumps
off and has to throw soft balls at a row
of comic figures until their heads are
broken. Your passenger has to remount,
and you both race for the line where the
next pair of riders is ready to set off.

FIVE-FLAG RACE

Gallop with a flag in your hand to a pot
at the end of the arena. Put the flag in
the pot. On your way back, grab another
flag from a line of pots and hand it to

your team-mate. He or she gallops to the far end and puts it in the furthest pot along with the first flag. On the way back, he or she grabs another flag from the line of pots to hand to the next rider, and so on.

DRAGON RACE

This is one of the most spectacular races to watch. It requires some quite elaborate equipment in the form of the dragon, and so it usually tends to be reserved for major championships.

The centre piece is a model dragon with balloons attached to him. For added effect he is often made to puff great clouds of smoke. One team member plays the part of the damsel in distress, captured by the fearsome dragon. Her team-mates are the knights attempting to rescue her. As a gallant knight, you race to the damsel and collect a token from her, which you tie to your lance. You then attack the

---

IMPORTANT RULES

Most competitions are run under Pony Club rules. Points to note:
■ Ponies must be at least four years old, and not more than 14.2hh.
■ If you weigh more than 117 lb (53 kg) when dressed for riding, your pony must be over 12.2hh.
■ Your pony must wear a snaffle bridle and a conventional saddle; racing saddles are not allowed. Whips or spurs are not allowed; nor may you use the baton or your hand to encourage your pony to go faster.
■ Riders must wear recognized safety helmets with a proper safety harness.
■ The winner of the race is the pony who manages to get his head across the finishing line first.
■ If the race involves leading the pony, the winner is the first rider across the line provided he or she still has hold of the pony. In a race involving pairs of ponies, the placing is judged from the moment that the second pony's head crosses the line.

---

dragon by bursting a balloon. When the last knight succeeds in bursting the final balloon, the damsel is rescued and led to the finish on her pony.

BENDING RACE

In contrast to the "Dragon Race", this requires the minimum of equipment – just a line of flexible poles pushed into the ground at intervals. You have to ride your pony in and out of the poles, turn tightly at the end and either race for the finish or thread your way back through the poles. Barrels can be used instead of poles.

EGG-AND-SPOON RACE

Holding a spoon with a boiled egg resting in it, you have to race through a line of bending poles, out and back, without losing the egg.

These are just a sample of what is on offer if you take up mounted games. More important than the games themselves is the opportunity they provide to ignite a spark of interest in children, so that their enthusiasm for horses and riding, for fun or for sport, may continue long after they have outgrown the fun of mounted games.

Dressage

The simple aim of dressage is to produce a horse who can carry his rider easily, is supple, balanced, correctly muscled, active, eager and responsive to his rider's most subtle command – yet far too many people look down on dressage as an opt-out for those who are too scared to jump!

If you wish to succeed in any horse sport, you have a far greater chance of doing so if your horse is a well-schooled and responsive ride. Whatever sport or sports you decide to take part in with your horse, you should discipline yourself to practise the art of dressage, even if you never set foot or hoof in a competitive dressage arena.

Your horse cannot perform to the best of his ability, nor be a true pleasure for

you to ride, unless he has had some help and training to improve his balance and responsiveness. A horse is a far greater joy to hunt, to jump, to hack out or to compete with in any form, if he is able to balance himself so that he carries more of

his weight, and that of his rider, on his hindquarters, which in turn will lighten his forehand.

■ **THE HISTORY OF DRESSAGE**
As far back as the fourth century BC, Xenophon, a Greek, wrote a book on training the riding horse. Prior to that, most interest in training lay in driving horses for chariots, rather than in riding.

From the sixteenth century onwards, a succession of excellent European horsemen laid down the foundations of classical riding and training as we know it today. The aim of these early trainers was to improve the lightness and balance of the horse. Much of the work involved training from the ground using long reins, so that the horse learnt the movements without the hindrance of a rider. Only after that was the rider taught how not to hinder the horse!

Interest in dressage fluctuated over the following centuries. In Great Britain there was far more interest in hunting and cross-country riding which, in those days, was performed very much on a wing and a prayer. The horses jumped what they were asked to jump either because they were naturally bold or because their riders were able to use enough brute force to get what they wanted. School riding or dressage was laughed at. Typically, instead of the good influencing the bad, in this particular instance the British attitude drifted across to France after the Napoleonic Wars and

■ BELOW LEFT
Note how this rider is keeping a lovely soft contact whilst his horse remains in a nice outline and bent correctly in the direction in which they are going.

■ LEFT
This experienced and impressive combination is performing one of the more advanced dressage movements – the half-pass.

■ BELOW RIGHT
Size and layout of the dressage arenas used for lower-level tests (left) and for advanced tests.

the interest in dressage faltered there for a while. The nineteenth century saw a revival of interest in Europe. The principles laid down centuries before were refined and adapted, but the basic requirements of free forward movement, suppleness, obedience and lightness of the forehand remained and are still the aim of dressage riders today. In many other parts of the world such as America, Argentina, Africa, New Zealand and Australia, the horse was still primarily used either as a beast of burden or as a stock animal for the herding and control of large herds of livestock. But the influence of the great riding masters, particularly those of the Spanish Riding School in Vienna and the Cadre Noir in France, spread throughout the world until dressage became a truly international sport and a passion for many riders.

■ DRESSAGE AS A
COMPETITIVE SPORT
Dressage is an Olympic sport, and its governing body is the FEI. It is therefore affiliated, and there are various levels of competition for affiliated members. However, dressage is a popular and easy

sport to organize which means that many unaffiliated competitions are run by various show organizers.

Dressage tests are split into the internationally recognized FEI tests and national tests, devised by each individual country. The national tests generally start with the lowest level, preliminary or

novice, progressing through elementary to medium and advanced tests. Unaffiliated shows normally only offer classes up to elementary level, and may also make use of the simpler dressage tests taken from the sport of eventing. Most countries hold national and regional championships as well as participating in the international

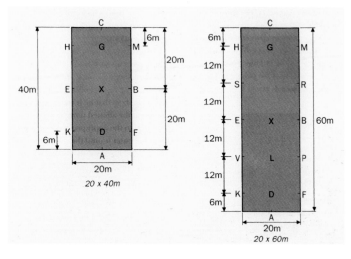

■ LEFT
As the horse progresses through the grades he is expected to show more expression in his paces. His outline should be shorter and higher, and his paces more powerful and elevated.

■ BELOW
Something to aim for – this combination won the gold medal at the 1988 Olympic Games. Nicole Uphoff on Rembrandt at Aachen.

FEI competitions. All tests are ridden in a dressage arena, which is a rectangle marked out by boards and letters. The letters signify where various movements should be carried out. The lower-level tests are performed in the minimum-sized arena of 22 x 43¾ yards (20 x 40 m), whereas more advanced tests are carried out in an international-sized arena of 22 x 65½ yards (20 x 60 m). The marker letters are always the same. At the Olympic Games and other FEI championships, the arena must have an all-weather surface of sand, but at other competitions it may be of grass, or may be indoors.

Lower-level tests are judged by just one person, who awards marks for each set

FEI TESTS

■ Prix St George
■ Intermediare 1
■ Intermediare 2
■ Grand Prix
■ Grand Prix Special
■ Free Style Test – this is the same standard as the Grand Prix but is performed to music.

movement in the test, plus an overall mark for the horse's way of going and the rider's performance. The judge stands behind the C marker, directly in line with the centre line of the arena. Higher-level competitions are judged by three or even five judges. Each judge sits to one side or the other of the centre-line judge and awards his or her own marks. These marks may well vary, as each judge will see the test ridden from a different angle. The final mark is taken as the average of all the judges' marks.

In all dressage competitions, you are given a precise time at which your test will start. You must work out how much loosening up and schooling work your horse needs so that he is well prepared for his test at the allotted time. Once you are sent over to the appropriate arena, you must not enter it until the judge signals you to start, usually with a bell or horn. You can ride around outside the arena, continuing to work on keeping your horse balanced, calm and attentive, until the judge's signal. Enter the arena at A, proceed down the centre line to X, the half-way point, halt and salute the judge. A female rider is required to put both reins

in the left hand, bow the head, and drop the right hand to the side. A male rider is expected to remove his hat and bow likewise. After this, you can proceed down the centre line and into the first movement of the appropriate test. The test always ends with another trip down the centre line to halt and salute once more. Then proceed at a free walk, giving the horse a long rein, and leave the arena at A. After that it is a case of waiting for your mark to be put up.

■ WHO CAN DO DRESSAGE?
Any rider can, and should, practise dressage, even if you choose not to compete. Once your horse is basically obedient, can maintain a rounded outline and can work in a reasonable rhythm in walk, trot and canter, he is equipped to perform the simpler dressage tests. The lower-level tests only require the horse to work in medium walk, working trot and canter, and may require some lengthening of the horse's stride. The horse must be able to produce a good halt, as all tests end with a halt and salute to the judge, and the vast majority of tests also start with one. A few of the very basic tests allow the

■ RIGHT
The aim of dressage is simply to produce a fit,
supple, obedient horse who is so responsive that his
rider appears to be doing nothing.

■ BOTTOM
16½ foot (5 m) loops.

horse to enter the arena and carry straight
on with the test. You will need to be able
to ride basic schooling movements such as
65½ or 49¼ foot (20 or 15 m) circles, and
serpentines or half-circles, but none of
these is outside the scope of a reasonably
well-schooled horse.

International tests have to be ridden
from memory, as does the dressage test in
horse trials, but lower down the scale you
are allowed to have the test read out to
you. It is well worth making the effort to
learn the test, both out of respect for the
judge who has given up a day to come and
mark you, and because to ride a really
good test you need to concentrate fully on
getting the best out of your horse, not
wondering what command is going to be
called out to you next. The movements of
the test should become second nature to
you if you are to ride your horse to the
best of your ability.

■ SKILLS REQUIRED
To be successful in any equestrian sport
you need to develop a secure independent
seat but, in dressage, it is equally important
to develop "feel". You should be able to feel
exactly what the horse is doing underneath
you. Is he straight, is he giving you the
correct bend, are his hocks really coming
underneath him, is he relaxed enough

through his neck and jaw? This feel can be
developed with experience, but some riders
are simply never able to accomplish it. Be
patient and dedicated. The correct training
of a dressage horse is a very long, careful
process – there are no short cuts.

Any horse who has been correctly
schooled is already doing dressage, and can
therefore compete, but some horses find
this discipline easier than others. A calm
temperament helps, along with a
willingness and quickness to learn. If the
horse has good conformation and naturally
good paces, he is going to find his work
easier than a horse who has an awkward
build and therefore struggles to move as
freely. The horse should be forward
thinking, and ideally he should have
naturally active hocks – some horses have
naturally "lazy" hocks and will find it harder
to use their hindquarters. Finally the ideal
dressage horse should have presence – he
should make people want to stop and watch
him. But don't be deterred if your horse
lacks some of these qualities. Careful and
consistent training can do wonders for the
most unpromising candidate – it just takes
more time and determination.

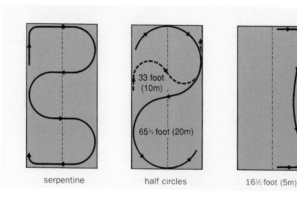

serpentine

33 foot
(10m)

65½ foot (20m)

half circles

16½ foot (5m)

The World of Showing

The showing scene probably offers a wider range of opportunities for all types and abilities than any other equestrian sport. If you are the sort of person who takes pride in appearance, manners and performance – both yours and your horse's – you will enjoy exploring the showing world.

There are no Olympics or world championships for showing, but there is ample opportunity to compete. In most countries there are regional and national championships for the different categories of show horses and ponies.

If you wish to compete at the higher-level shows, you will need to register your horse with the appropriate society. Which you register with depends on the type of horse you own and which classes you wish to compete in. It usually means registering with a breed society, a show-pony society, or a hunter or hack society or association. Small, local shows do not usually require their entrants to be registered with anyone.

■ LEFT
Mountain and moorland ponies are shown off in a more natural state than their show-pony colleagues. Their manes and tails are left full and unplaited or braided; their legs are not trimmed either. It is probably harder to produce a well-turned-out native pony than it is to produce his show-pony counterpart who may be plaited, braided, clipped and trimmed.

Different countries vary in the interest and opportunities that are afforded to showing. In terms of expense and facilities required, it is a relatively easy sport to cater for. A grass enclosure and some respected judges are all that most classes require. Generally speaking, there are classes available to suit all ages and types of horse and rider.

■ IN-HAND SHOWING

Mares and foals, yearlings, and two-, three- and four-year-old horses and ponies can all be shown "in-hand", i.e. they are led by their handlers and are judged on how smartly they are turned out, their conformation, their manners and paces, and their potential suitability for adult life. As the handler, you are expected to be

very smartly dressed yourself, and your horse should be sensible and obedient enough to stand in line with the rest of the class, and to walk and trot in-hand when he is required to do so by the judge.

Your horse should appear in the ring without a saddle, and with no boots or bandages of any sort. He can be led with either a headcollar or a bridle.

You can practise all the requirements at home, teaching your horse to halt squarely and to remain still, and to walk and trot calmly beside you when asked.

Pony and rider showing off their paces in the Working Hunter Pony class.

EQUIPMENT NEEDED

For nearly all showing classes, apart from side-saddle, you can use your normal saddle and bridle. If given the choice, a saddle which is not too forward cut is usually more appropriate. It shows off your horse's shoulders and front end rather than covering them up, and gives you more chance of impressing the judges. At higher levels of competition it may be more appropriate to wear either a top hat or a bowler hat instead of a traditional hard hat. The showing world in general strives to uphold tradition and standards, and it is worth bearing this in mind when you are buying any clothing or equipment. Keep everything clean, tidy and workmanlike and you won't go far wrong.

In many classes you have to be able to show off your horse at the gallop despite the confines of the arena. A safe, all-weather surface is provided for this show cob.

■ RIGHT
You may find yourself competing against "professional" showmen who will arrive with a whole string of horses or ponies to enter. This is Great Britain's Robert Oliver.

■ BELOW
In most showing classes all the competitors ride around together while the judge assesses them. They are then called into line, after which they may be asked to give an individual show.

■ BREED CLASSES

Some classes are restricted to particular breeds so that the entrants can be judged on their trueness to type. Each breed of horse or pony should have certain characteristics which identify him as being true to type. These characteristics are listed by the appropriate breed society. Breed classes can be judged either as in-hand or as ridden classes and, once again, turnout, manners and conformation are the key criteria.

Some breeds have very specific traits which they are judged on; for example, the Tennessee Walking Horse on his walk.

If the class is ridden, you are expected to wear jodhpurs or breeches with the appropriate short or long boots, a shirt and tie or stock, and a hunting, show or

■ ABOVE
Many of the bigger shows are held indoors, with classes going on late into the evening. Your horse will have to become accustomed to spotlights and a far more claustrophobic atmosphere than he will have experienced at an outdoor show.

■ SI...

Ridin...
used...
a lady...
comp...
with...
the n...
splen...
a co...
are h...
Addi...
hunt...
and...
com...
of as...
sado...
othe...
first...
equ...

tern...
sado...
tha...
out...
eve...
sad...
Bu...
the...
we...

suc...
giv...
he...
go...

■ LEFT
Many classes are judged in-hand, which means that the horse is led rather than ridden.

Endurance or Long-distance Riding

■ BELOW
The horse's weight is checked at the beginning and end of the ride so that the amount of condition he has lost can be judged.

There are two types of long-distance riding – endurance riding (which has FEI status) and trail riding. Trail riding does not involve racing – the idea is to complete the ride with your horse still in good condition. Trail rides vary from about 25 miles (40.25 km) to over 100 miles (160 km). Endurance riding does involve racing – it is a competition against the clock which tests the speed and stamina of the horse. It also tests the rider's horsemanship and judgement of pace, and of his or her horse's well-being. Each competition is split into a number of phases, each one being usually just under 25 miles (40 km) long. At the end of each phase the horse is checked by a veterinary surgeon for sores on his back or in his mouth, overreaches, and general well-being; his heart rate is monitored.

Competitions vary in length, but an international event which takes more than one day is usually over a minimum distance of 50–62 miles (80–100 km). A championship one-day competition usually covers nearly 100 miles (160 km)

The horse's pulse rate is monitored at intervals throughout a long-distance ride; the horse has to finish in good condition.

with a winning riding time of somewhere between ten and twelve hours.

■ DEVELOPMENT OF THE SPORT

For many centuries the horse has been used to transport man and his possessions over great distances. Most countries can boast feats of great endurance riding – there has always been someone who has wanted to go further than those before him on the back of a horse – but endurance riding as an organized competitive sport did not start in earnest until the 1950s.

Endurance riding today puts the horse's welfare first and foremost with strict veterinary checks. The organizers have the authority to eliminate any competitor whose horse shows signs of having had enough. Before this, some of the earliest long-distance races tested the horse's endurance to the limit, with equine contestants literally being ridden until they dropped. The care and attention lavished on today's endurance horses is some recompense for the suffering endured by the horses who gave their all in previous centuries.

Interest in competitive endurance riding spread most quickly in Europe and America. The first endurance rides were actually organized to demonstrate the suitability of different types of horses as cavalry mounts. It was in California in 1955 that competitive endurance riding started.

The endurance horse must learn to remain balanced, settled and in a rhythm, even on the lightest rein contact.

▌ RIGHT
All kinds of natural hazards have to be tackled.

TACTICS

To succeed as an endurance rider you will need to be happy with your own company, have a good rapport with your horse and your back-up team, and an awareness of winning tactics. Who is ahead of you, who is behind you, are you keeping up with the pace, how can you avoid overtiring your horse, how can you help him if he does tire? What is your strategy at the checkpoints and the meeting points *en route* where your horse is allowed to be refreshed? Whose horse can still put in a sprint for the finish, and how far ahead of them do you need to be to make sure you sprint over the line first?

▌ BELOW
Endurance or long-distance riding is suitable for many different types of horses.

Interest was sparked by the ride undertaken by Wendall T. Robie and a group of friends. They followed the old mining and emigrant trails over 100 miles (160 km) from Squaw Valley, through the Sierra Nevada range and on to Auburn. This trail became the world's first official

EQUIPMENT AND BACK-UP TEAM

Numnahs or gel pads are essential under saddles to reduce the risk of any rubbing or bruising, and purpose-designed endurance saddles can be purchased. Stock or Western-type saddles are popular as far as rider comfort is concerned. Many horses are ridden in hackamores (bitless bridles) to reduce the risk of sores or bruising, but these take practice and skill to use.

A good back-up team of between one and three helpers is essential during an endurance competition. They, as well as you, must be able to map read so that you all follow the same route and arrive at the same meeting points. They carry and provide everything that horse and rider may need along the way – food, water, clothing, spare tack (especially numnahs and girths as these may need changing several times during a ride), spare horseshoes, a first-aid kit, a tack-repair kit, a torch, and a grooming kit and towels.

endurance ride, and was named the Western States Trail Ride.

Today the popular sport of endurance riding, which has been approved as an international discipline since 1982, is governed by the FEI.

▌ THE ENDURANCE HORSE
The main requirements of any endurance horse are that he has strong, dense bone, strong, healthy hooves, and a willingness

and confidence to tackle whatever he is faced with because he will encounter all kinds of natural hazards on a long-distance ride. He should have a light, ground-covering action, and be balanced and sure-footed over all manner of terrain. He should be trained to settle into a steady trot or canter when required, and should accept a loose rein with minimal contact. A calm temperament means he will take less out of himself.

Western Riding

Western riding is predominant in countries where the horse is still used to work cattle, such as America, Argentina, Australia, New Zealand and parts of Africa. It also has a growing following in other countries where riders are keen to enjoy the experience of riding a light, balanced, responsive horse, along with the novelty of trying many of the Western riding skills.

■ WHAT IS WESTERN RIDING?

America is the home of Western riding, which developed directly from the needs of the early pioneers. They depended on horses for their survival – for transport, for hunting food, and later for herding and managing vast herds of cattle. They had to be able to sit comfortably, for very long hours, in the saddle. They also needed horses who were both fast and responsive and yet also calm and easy to handle. The skills that horse and rider had to learn in order to earn a living in those times form the basis of the Western-riding competitions held today.

In Western riding you adopt a longer leg position than is usual for general riding. The reins are held in one hand, leaving the other free to rope cattle, fire a gun etc, and the horse is controlled mainly by the seat and weight, rather than by hand and leg. A Western horse is not ridden in an outline. He carries himself in a relaxed, but light and balanced manner, with his rider keeping the reins virtually slack. The weight of the reins is used as an aid, rather than the contact with the horse's mouth.

Western-riding competitions test everything from how the horse feels to

■ ABOVE
In Western riding it is the seat and weight distribution of the rider that are used to control the horse, rather than the hand and leg as is usual in English riding.

■ LEFT
Western tack is designed to offer comfort, practicality and security to riders spending many hours in the saddle.

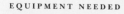

EQUIPMENT NEEDED

Many riders simply enjoy riding in the Western style – hacking or long-distance riding – without going as far as competing.

A Western or stock-type saddle adds authenticity and comfort to the proceedings but is not essential during the training of horse and rider. Similarly, a standard bridle and bit can be used, rather than the simpler Western-style bridle which may or may not be bitless. But once Western tack is used, no doubt you will want to be properly kitted out too. Cowboy boots, which have a raised, supported instep and a higher heel than a standard riding boot, along with a pair of long, leather chaps are the two essentials.

▮ RIGHT
In cattle-cutting competitions the horse has first to "cut" a selected calf out from the rest of the herd, and then to prevent the selected animal from rejoining the herd. This Quarter Horse is using his own "cattle sense" rather than his rider's instructions to keep the calf he is facing from joining the herd behind him.

ride, his ability to perform complex reining exercises and his skill at cutting out and controlling cattle, to his ability to race through a line of barrels. There are World and European Championship titles to be won, as well as numerous regional and national events to compete in.

Many Western riders get caught up in the whole Western phenomenon. As well as learning the ridden style they may also practise other "Wild West" skills, such as trick roping, whip cracking, knife and axe throwing, as well as the fast draw and gun spinning. It is amazing what sitting in a Western saddle can do to the imagination of even the most retiring rider!

■ THE WESTERN RIDING HORSE
Any horse can be converted to Western riding, but not all horses will have the temperament or inherent traits for all the Western-style competitions. The American Quarter Horse is a popular and successful choice – he has the speed, stamina, agility, intelligence and in-bred "cattle sense" to succeed. Other American types, such as the Appaloosa, the Paint horse and the Pinto, also feature strongly. But any horse with natural balance and agility, who can be taught to respond to weight and seat aids rather than being held between hand and leg as is usual in English-style riding, can be taught Western skills.

■ SKILLS REQUIRED
As a rider you must have good balance, the patience to build a rapport with your horse which allows your commands to appear invisible to the onlooker and, if you are to become involved in cattle-handling skills, the overall fitness and

In Western riding the horse is expected to be versatile and co-operative. At the Cowboy Ski Challenge in Jackson Hole, Wyoming, the horse demonstrates his ability to carry out any number of duties, from providing the power for the skiers...

365

▮ RIGHT
...to showing how
essential they were to
the survival of the
early pioneers.

▮ BELOW AND
BELOW RIGHT
The sliding halt is one
of the most dramatic
Western-riding skills.
The horse wears
special skid boots to
protect his fetlocks
and to aid the slide.

toughness which these require. For most
Western showing classes, the horse has to
be taught the jog and the lope – these are
basically a slow, smooth trot and canter.
These paces were developed for rider
comfort and to reduce wear and tear on
the horse's legs and joints. For most
equestrian disciplines, the horse is trained
to put spring and elevation into his paces,
but for Western riding the paces are
smooth and flat, with less knee and hock
action than normal. Other classes require
the horse to be taught various Western
moves – the rollback which is a fast 180°
turn, the spin or pirouette which is a 360°
turn, the side pass (lateral work), the rein

back, the sliding halt, and the flying
change.

■ SHOWING CLASSES

These are the easiest Western classes to
train for and take part in.

▌ The **Western Pleasure** class is the
simplest. The horse is judged on how
much of a pleasure he is to ride. He must
work in all paces on both reins, with the
rider keeping the reins in one hand and
a minimal contact. He is judged on how
smooth his paces and transitions are, and
on how calm and responsive he is to his
rider's commands.

▌ The **Trail** class tests the horse's ability to
cope calmly with the sort of hazards he
might encounter when riding the trail.
There are a number of tasks you and he
will have to perform in the ring, such as
opening and closing a gate, backing
through or round an obstacle, and jumping
some logs. You may have to carry an object,
and your horse may have to allow himself
to be hobbled (tied up) on his own.

▌ The **Western Riding** class imitates
some of the tasks a ranch horse might
have to carry out. The horse must
demonstrate a good walk, jog and lope,
and may have to tackle various tasks or
obstacles similar to those also found in
the trail class.

▌ The **Reining** class tests some of the most
advanced Western-riding techniques. The
horse demonstrates at speed a pattern of
various Western movements – turns,
circles, spins, flying changes, rollbacks and
sliding halts. All of these movements are
performed from the lope – the slow,
smooth canter.

■ CATTLE-HANDLING CLASSES

These require more extensive practice,
training and facilities than the Western
showing classes.

▌ In the **Cutting Horse** class, the rider
indicates to a judge which calf he is going
to separate from the herd. The calf has to
be "cut out" from the herd and driven out
into the arena. The rider must then adopt

a loose rein and leave the job of
preventing the calf from rejoining the
herd to the horse. The cutting horse
must be fast, athletic, brave and clever.
The ability to outwit and outperform the
calf is called "cow sense" and is thought
by many to be an inherited trait, rather
than an acquired skill.

▌ The **Working Cow Horse** class is judged
in two sections: first the horse performs a
reining pattern which demonstrates the
various Western movements, and then he
has to hold, manoeuvre and control a cow
within the arena, turning it several times
as well as driving it along a fence line.

▌ **Barrel Racing** is a fast, furious, grown-up
version of that most popular of mounted
games, the bending race! Horse and rider
race around a course of barrels – they are
allowed to touch the barrels but not to
knock them over.

▌ Other competitions, such as **Steer
Wrestling** and **Calf Roping**, demonstrate
and test the skills still required by the
working cow pony and rider.

Vaulting

The sport of vaulting is probably most simply described as gymnastics on horseback. Although it is now recognized as an international sport, governed by the FEI since 1982, it developed from an early teaching method which was used to accustom novice riders to the movement of the horse, and to instil a sense of balance and confidence.

Cavalry schools in particular used vaulting exercises to teach new recruits to develop their balance whilst the horse was in motion. Vaulting also served as a good fitness and strengthening exercise for riders, as well as giving them confidence when on horseback.

■ SKILLS REQUIRED

If you wish to be a vaulter you will need to have good natural balance, be naturally athletic and have an air of grace and elegance. The sport also requires confidence – it takes a brave person to carry out many of the exercises with poise.

The horse needs to be quiet-natured, strong, unflappable and able to hold a steady, rhythmic, balanced canter on the lunge throughout the exercise.

The main disadvantage of the sport is that the vaulter always requires help – someone has to be on hand to lunge the horse and, unless you are to compete only as an individual, you will need a partner or even a full team of eight to work with. Riders interested in vaulting therefore really need to join a club, although much of the actual gymnastic work can be practised on a wooden horse.

■ THE COMPETITIONS

International vaulting competitions are made up of team, individual and pair

classes. The upper age limit for team
vaulters is eighteen, but there is no upper
age limit for individuals. A team comprises
eight vaulters, one horse and one lunger,
and a reserve vaulter. Both the individual
and the team competitions include a
compulsory and a free-style test.

The horse always works on the left rein,
in canter, and must complete a circle of
no less than 42½ feet (13 m) in diameter.

There are two classes of international
competition – CVI one star, and CVI two
star. The World Championship is held
every two years, and there are also
intercontinental championships,
including classes for all-male, all-female
and mixed teams.

DISPLAY TEAMS

As well as taking part in competitions,
vaulting teams are now often called upon to
provide displays at shows and exhibitions.
Such demonstrations are certainly an
exciting, elegant and colourful way in which
to entertain a crowd of spectators.

▌ ABOVE
It takes a good athlete
to maintain the grace,
poise and balance of
a gymnast whilst on a
moving horse.

▌ LEFT
The team horse must
maintain a consistent
rhythm throughout all
the exercises.

Polo

Of all the team ball games played on horseback, polo is the most widely played and recognized. The sport of polo carries an unashamedly glamorous image. It has always been expensive to take part in, mainly because of the string of ponies that is needed if you are to be a professional player. Despite the growing number of polo clubs, and the opportunities for children to learn to play provided by the Pony Club, polo remains an expensive sport, the greatest opportunities being open to the wealthy or the very talented.

Polo is thought to have originated in Persia about two-and-a-half thousand years ago. Its popularity spread to China, Japan, Tibet and Manipur, where British soldiers learnt the game and wrote home about it. Soldiers in England started playing their own version based on the description they had been given, and British settlers took the game to Argentina. The late 1800s and early 1900s saw the foundation of many polo clubs, including London's Hurlingham which was the first in the Western world. Hurlingham's rules later became universal. Polo is now played all over the world.

■ LEFT
Polo is only too happy to flaunt its reputation for wealth and glamour. Spectators gather at the Palm Beach Polo Club.

■ THE GAME

Polo is played on a grass – or snow – pitch which is 901 feet (274 m) long by 600 feet (183 m) wide. Most of the pitch is framed with low boards to help keep the ball in play, and there is a goal at either end, 24½ feet (7.5 m) wide. Indoor polo is also growing in popularity.

There are four players in each team, each of whom has a specific role. The Number One is the front player; his job is to keep well up the pitch to take forward passes and to shoot at goal. When he is not in a position to score, he tries to keep the opposing team's back player (their Number Four) away from the goalmouth so that one of his team-mates may have a chance to score.

The Number Two is another front player; he is usually the most influential attacking player. He works closely with his Number One to keep moving the ball up the field to maximize their chances of taking a shot at goal.

The Number Three player is the link between the two forwards and the back. He is central in turning the play back from defence to attack and must be an extremely versatile player, able to defend, attack and score. He is usually the strongest and most experienced player in the team and is often the captain.

EQUIPMENT NEEDED

To play polo you must be properly dressed – breeches, long boots, helmet with optional face guard, and knee protectors. You will also need your own polo mallets.

You must have at least two ponies – there is no longer a height restriction but polo mounts are still referred to as ponies. The rules insist that ponies wear standing martingales and that they have their tails tied up so that there is no risk of them becoming caught up in anything. The polo pony needs to be brave, responsive, quick-thinking, agile, fast and tough.

■ LEFT
Practice makes perfect. Even the most complex shots can be practised without getting on a horse – at least not a real one.

■ LEFT
Polo ponies need
to be as alert and
enthusiastic as their
riders – and often
quicker thinking.

■ BELOW
A string of polo ponies is an expensive asset,
but good ponies are worth every penny to the
professional player.

■ BELOW
Polo originated in
far hotter climes than
these, but as a winter
sport continues in St
Moritz.

■ BOTTOM
Polo ponies have their
legs protected by thick
bandages during play.

The Number Four is the back player; his main task is to defend the goal but he must also be a good hitter, able to send the ball long and hard up the field to give his forwards a chance of attacking goal.

A full polo match is divided into six seven-minute periods called chukkas. One pony should only ever be used for two chukkas per game, and should never have to play two consecutive chukkas.

Each player uses a mallet (a bamboo stick with a wooden head) to drive the ball down the pitch to the opposition's goal. The opposing team is obviously doing its utmost to prevent any progress down the pitch and to turn the ball back so it can drive for a goal of its own.

All polo players are given a handicap – this varies between -2 goals and +10 goals. The handicap indicates the player's value to the team, not the actual number of goals he has or is expected to score. Teams are given overall handicaps which dictate at which level they play – high goal, medium, intermediate or low goal.

■ SKILLS REQUIRED

To succeed as a polo player you should be quick-thinking, fit, have very good co-ordination and balance, be physically and mentally tough and have good anticipation of how play is going to proceed.

There are four main playing strokes to be mastered, as well as a further eight subsidiary strokes. The four main strokes are the off-side forehander, off-side

backhander, near-side forehander and near-side backhander. These strokes can be practised on a wooden horse as well as on your pony. Would-be players spend many hours simply "stick and balling", i.e. cantering up and down a pitch, hitting a shot, chasing the ball and trying another stroke – up and down, round and round, gradually getting a better result every time.

The rules of polo are quite complex and the game itself is fast moving, with the direction of play changing all the time. As a player you need to have an intimate understanding of the rules, as well as a continual awareness of where everyone is in relation to the direction of play.

Jumping Sports

Jumping needs confidence, rhythm and balance. Once you have a fair degree of these three skills you can start to discover the world of jumping sports. Show jumping offers competitions for fun as well as for fortune seekers, and provides an excellent and safe way to practise your jumping skills and gain experience. Once you feel confident over show jumps – which fall down if you hit them – you may want to try your hand at jumping solid obstacles. Hunting and hunter trials provide you with the opportunity to do this – and when you are feeling confident enough you can progress to team chasing or eventing. For the brave and robust there is race riding – the ultimate way to jump at speed.

Hunting

There is little to beat the exhilaration of riding fast across country. You and your horse must tackle whatever is thrown in your way – balancing your horse over all kinds of terrain with the wind making your eyes stream, mud splattered in your face, encouraging him over every manner of obstacle, letting him jump out of his stride and land running, looking eagerly ahead for the next challenge.

The thrill of it usually lifts the spirits and the courage of all horsemen and women. The hedge that you sailed over effortlessly when running behind hounds may look completely unjumpable when viewed in cold blood! There is neither judge nor winner, except in the hearts and minds of those taking part. Hunting, for many, provides an opportunity to tackle much greater challenges than they might otherwise contemplate.

▌ ABOVE
Hunting etiquette requires that you and your mount are smartly and tidily turned out. Your horse's or pony's mane should be plaited (braided), your tack should be gleaming, and you should be kitted out in clean jodhpurs, boots and jacket.

▌ BELOW
The hounds are controlled by a huntsman; he is usually assisted by a whipper-in who helps to keep the hounds together as a pack.

■ DIFFERENT TYPES OF HUNTING
HUNTING QUARRY

Ever since man learnt to ride a horse he has used the horse's speed and agility to his advantage, including in his hunt for food. Today, hunting on horseback is a country sport rather than a means of survival. Hunting live quarry for sport is a controversial subject on which many people hold strong views. Some consider it has a valuable role to play in the conservation of the countryside and in the management of the wildlife it hunts; others think it is cruel and an outdated way to control wildlife. Hunt meets often attract protesters from various animal rights organizations and are often not publicized.

A wide variety of animals is hunted from horseback around the world. The most common ones are the fox and stag in

England and Ireland, the wild boar in other parts of Europe, and the coyote in North America and parts of Africa. The hunting of any of these animals relies on the co-operation and permission of the landowners whose property is crossed.

Packs of hounds are bred and trained to pick up the scent and track down the hunted animal. The hounds are controlled by a huntsman and whipper-in, who are the only people actively involved in the work of the hounds. The hunt followers, or field as they are often known, are sometimes helpful in observing the whereabouts of the hounds or the direction the hunted quarry has taken, but their main role is to help pay for the upkeep of the hunt's hounds, horses and hunting country. In return for an annual subscription and a "cap" – an additional donation to hunt funds made on the day of the hunt – the hunt follower enjoys seeing hounds at work and the thrill of the chase.

In fox hunting, after a convivial half an hour or so at the meet, the huntsman heads off with the hounds to the first cover. This is usually a piece of woodland or scrubland where a fox is likely to be found. The field follow, led by the field master whose instructions you must obey at all times – and who you should avoid overtaking! The hounds are "cast" into the cover, i.e. sent in to hunt around until they find the scent of the fox. Some days are good scenting days and the hounds can easily follow the scent; other days are not so good.

Once the hounds are on the scent of their quarry, they will follow it across all manner of country. The mounted followers keep up as best they can, the bravest and most talented jumping everything in their path, the rest finding a way around the edges of fields, through gates and along tracks. A good knowledge of the local countryside helps in the task of keeping up with the hounds. If you are crossing country that has been planted with crops, only the hounds and huntsman are allowed to take the direct line after the prey. The field have to find a way round which minimizes any damage to the crops; an intimate knowledge of your surroundings makes this easier. Etiquette demands that you follow the lead of the field master, but after a good run behind hounds the field often gets split up and strung out, and it is up to you to find the hounds again.

The hounds will either succeed in catching their prey or they will lose track

■ LEFT
Out hunting there will always be those who want
to jump obstacles and those who want to go around
them. The choice is yours, but should be based
on an appreciation of ability – yours and your
mount's – rather than on pride.

DRAG HUNTING

This involves a pack of hounds and
mounted followers but, instead of hunting
a live quarry, the hounds follow a trail that
has been laid earlier in the day by
someone dragging a bag laced with a
strong scent that the hounds have been
taught to pick up and follow.

Drag hunting gives you the chance to
ride fast across country, behind hounds.
It is safer and more predictable than
hunting live quarry because you are
following a pre-set course. The jumps will
be either safe, natural features or man-
made fences. A knowledge of the country
is not necessary as the course the hounds
take is pre-determined. Many hunts offer
days specifically for the novice or nervous,
when they will make sure the jumps
encountered are smaller than usual.

Subscriptions from the field help to pay
for the upkeep of the hounds and kennels.

BLOODHOUNDS

Hunting with bloodhounds is another
form of drag hunting. This time the
hounds are following the scent of a man

of it, or may have to be called off if the fox
crosses land that the hunt doesn't have
permission to cross. In any case the
hounds are taken to another cover to see
if they can pick up the scent of another
fox, and so it goes on.

Most hunt meets are organized for
mid-morning, and hunting continues until
late in the afternoon. At about lunchtime
"second horses" are arranged. This means
that the huntsman, whipper-in and master
will change on to fresh horses who have
been brought by lorry to a pre-arranged
point. Their first horses are taken home,
washed and dried off, rugged up, fed and
stabled. Hunt followers may also change

on to second horses if they have another
horse and have been able to organize
someone to deliver it for them.

Whilst hunting is a thrilling way of
enjoying cross-country riding, it carries a
lot of risks because there is no time to
check out what you are about to jump.
Many a horse and rider have fallen when,
having taken off over what looks like an
innocuous hedge, they see in mid-air that
there is a wire or timber fence running
alongside it on the far side. A scopey,
quick-thinking, focused horse can usually
get himself out of such a muddle, but
only with experience which can be
painful in the making.

EQUIPMENT NEEDED

Your horse should be well turned out with his mane
plaited (braided). He will need a good, strong set
of tack, as a good-quality saddle and bridle will
add to your own safety. Hunting entails long hours
in the saddle, often in bad weather conditions. The
last thing you want is for a rein or stirrup leather to
snap when you are in the middle of nowhere, riding
at a flat-out gallop and heading for a large and
solid post-and-rail fence!

Put an especially well-padded numnah under
the saddle to make it more comfortable for the
horse and to reduce the risk of him being rubbed.

Whether or not your horse wears boots to
protect his legs is a matter of personal choice.
Your horse's legs are at great risk of being knocked
or scratched out hunting, but many boots, once
they are wet and muddy and have been worn for
several hours, start to rub anyway. You will need
to decide which is the lesser of two evils.

As a rider you are expected to be smartly turned
out. You should wear traditional-coloured breeches
or jodhpurs, teamed with either long riding boots
or short jodhpur boots. You must wear either a
hacking jacket (tweed jacket) or a plain blue or
black jacket. A crash cap with blue or black velvet
silk should be worn and this should have a well-
fitting safety harness. If you wear a hacking jacket
it is correct to wear a shirt and coloured stock
(similar to a cravat or broad neck tie) held in place
with a stock pin. A plain cream or white stock
should be worn with a blue or black jacket.

Gloves should be worn and a stick carried. You
should carry in your pockets some good, thick
string, such as baling twine, and a foldaway
penknife so that you can help make repairs to any
gates or fences that get broken by the less able
jumpers in the field. A day's hunting can end up
being a very long day – find room in your pockets

for a couple of sandwiches or a bar of chocolate to
keep you going.

If you are going to hunt a lot, a hunting whip
and a pair of wire cutters are worth buying. A
hunting whip is a shaped cane with a long leather
lash on the end. The cane is useful for helping you
to open and shut gates, and the lash, if let down
so that it hangs by your horse's legs, can be used
to prevent hounds from going right underneath
your horse where they are more likely to get kicked
or trampled. A leather carrying pouch can be fitted
to your saddle in which to put a pair of wire
cutters. No matter how diligent you are, when you
are crossing unknown country it is possible to get
caught up in one of the hazards of agriculture –
wire netting or barbed wire. A pair of wire cutters is
invaluable to cut your own horse free or to help
anyone else unfortunate enough to be caught out.

■ BOTTOM
At the end of a long, hard day's hunting the field is greatly diminished. It is one of the most satisfying feelings in the world to be amongst the few left at the end of the day.

■ BELOW
Ladies traditionally only ever rode side-saddle, and the elegant picture it creates is one reason for a growing number of people returning to the habit.

who sets off some time before the hunt starts. The runner will follow a previously agreed trail, making this form of hunting as safe as drag hunting. You might find the thought of a pack of bloodhounds bearing down on a fleeing man alarming, but they will not harm him when they catch him. He will most likely be smothered in wet, warm licks by his friendly canine pursuers.

■ SKILLS REQUIRED
Hunting suits all types of horse and pony – it seems to inspire the less cautious to be even braver, but it can also cause a great deal of over-excitement. It is important to have developed a reasonably strong and secure seat and to be able to balance your horse in order to help him tackle the varied terrain and obstacles that you will encounter. Whether you are riding around a cross-country course or are genuinely crossing the country out hunting, the approach to jumping is the same: keep the horse balanced and in a rhythm. Keep in contact with the horse with your legs, seat and hands so that you can help balance him as he negotiates the unexpected.

Those brave and able enough to jump everything in their path will take the most direct line, following the lead of the field master. But there are plenty of others who will find their way around as best they can so as not to have to jump too much. Consider your own riding ability and the experience of your horse before deciding which party to join. When you do get the chance to jump, always give your horse room to see what it is you want him to do. Don't follow blindly behind the horse in front – your horse will not be able to judge the fence and, if the horse and rider in front fall or refuse, you will have a

problem. In a crowded gateway, or if there is a queue of riders waiting to jump a narrow fence, slow your horse down well beforehand, so that you don't run into the back of everyone else. Wait your turn and give your horse room to make a good, balanced approach, and the chance to see what the fence involves.

Your horse needs to be fit, as he will be required to gallop and jump, often with little chance to rest. He should be well mannered; he must accept other horses all around him. If you have even the slightest suspicion that he may panic or kick out, keep him out of the crowd. It is your responsibility to prevent your horse from hurting anyone else. A young or inexperienced horse should be introduced quietly to the hunting field. It is often a good idea to avoid the first hour of the meet when all the horses are fresh and excited, and perhaps join the hunt later in the day. Keep the horse moving and thinking forwards but do not allow him to get caught up in the crush of the field until he is used to all the sights and sounds. It is considered an unforgiveable sin to let your horse kick a hound, so be constantly aware of where the hounds are in relation to your horse. Keep his hindquarters turned away from the hounds if they approach or pass by you.

In the excitement of the chase do not overlook your horse's well-being. At all times, keep in mind how tired he might really be – horses get very caught up in the excitement of the chase and may not appear to be tired, as their excitement and adrenalin gives them additional stamina. But this should not be abused – think of how fit your horse really is, and how much galloping and jumping he has done. Do not keep him out for too long – there will always be another day. Think responsibly about what you ask him to jump. Never be tempted to jump wire – find a gate instead. Look out too for hazards such as rabbit holes and discarded farm machinery.

Hunter Trials and Team Chasing

For those who want to be judged on their cross-country-riding skills, there is the option of competing in hunter trials and team chases. In a hunter trial you may ride the course as an individual or as one of a pair. In team chasing there are four team members to motivate each other.

In hunter trials you are expected to tackle a course of cross-country fences, the height of which varies depending on the class you enter. Some competitions cater for leading-rein riders, others offer a range of classes varying from about 2 feet 6 inches to 3 feet 9 inches (0.75–1.2 m). The organizers decide upon an optimum time, which is based on horse and rider tackling the course at what is commonly described as a fair hunting pace. Within the course there is usually an additional timed section which often includes a gate that has to be opened and shut – not jumped! The winners are the horse and rider who jump clear and complete the course nearest to the optimum time – which is not revealed to the riders until after the competition. If more than one rider finishes on the optimum time, the winner is the fastest one through the timed section.

▌ ABOVE
Water is one of the most common problems encountered at a hunter trial. There is no reason why it should be feared provided it is introduced quietly and calmly. This pony looks a bit tentative and needs to gain more confidence before he is likely to tackle water with enthusiasm.

▌ BELOW LEFT
Hunter trials offer a huge variety of challenges for all ages and abilities. Even leading-rein riders can take part, provided their helpers are as agile as their ponies!

■ **SKILLS REQUIRED**

The main difference between hunting and competing in a hunter trial is that at a hunter trial you have to jump alone and in cold blood. You do not have the rush and excitement of hounds running and the rest of the field following to give you confidence. You and your horse have to be prepared to jump for the fun of it, although some classes are open to pairs in

▌ LEFT
Cross-country riding is tiring for both horse and rider, but it is always a kind and correct gesture to dismount and lead your horse or pony once you have pulled up over the finish line.

■ BELOW
This horse and rider have both taken a good soaking at the water hazard, but the joy of team chasing is that, provided the rest of the team got through, there is still a chance of winning. It just means there is a little consolation for the faller – his team will have galloped away into the distance!

■ LEFT
Competing as a pair is a good way of introducing an inexperienced or nervous horse or rider to the thrill of cross-country riding, as they can gain confidence from their partners.

Once you are up to speed it is a case of staying in that rhythm and keeping the horse balanced.

■ TEAM CHASING

Team chases are held over a variety of different-sized cross-country courses. Teams of four riders set off around the course, and progress is timed from the moment a team sets off to the moment the third rider crosses the line. So if one member of your team is left behind you are still in with a chance of winning.

The winning team is the one whose first three riders complete the course in the fastest time. Penalties are not given for falls or refusals – it is all judged on speed. For this reason the number of falls can be quite high. If the lead horse falls and the others are coming too fast and too close behind, at least one other member of the team is likely to fall also. But there is never any need to give up hope – even if one of the team stops or falls, provided the team can make up time somewhere else they still have a chance of a place. Regional and national championships are held.

which case a less confident horse can take a lead from his bolder partner. Some horses make marvellous hunters but will not jump an inch outside the hunting field. Remember to let your horse take his own line out hunting – do not just blindly follow the horse in front. If you have balanced him and helped him so that he regards hunting and cross-country jumping as fun, there is no reason why your hunter should not happily complete a hunter trial for you.

In the timed section you will have to open and shut a gate quickly without

dismounting. It should be easy if your horse has learnt to listen and respond to your hand and leg aids. You just need to be sure that your horse will rein back, and move over to the right or left when you ask him, and you can practise all these skills at home.

To win the competition you will need to have a good sense of speed and timing. If you have hunted, try to think of the speed you travel at when hounds are running, and to go at that same speed on the hunter-trial course. You will know the terrain, having already walked the course.

EQUIPMENT NEEDED

To compete in a hunter trial you need to be kitted out in your hunting attire, although most organizers allow you to wear a sweat shirt or jumper instead of a jacket. They will, however, insist that you wear a proper safety helmet and harness, as well as a body protector.

Your horse will need his usual saddle and bridle, as long as these are clean and in good condition, and his legs should be protected with either boots or bandages.

A normal riding stick or hunting whip may be carried; for hunter trials a proper hunting whip may help in opening and shutting the gate quickly in the timed section.

■ RIGHT
Team chasing involves a team of four riding fast and furiously across country. The competition is based on the time it takes for the first three team members to complete the course.

Show Jumping

The sport of show jumping involves tackling a course of artificial jumps, as opposed to natural cross-country jumps. It takes place in an arena which can be grass or have an all-weather surface, indoors or outdoors. An Olympic sport governed by the FEI, it is also a popular unaffiliated sport with any number of classes being held at local shows.

Show jumping requires accuracy and care. Almost every horse or pony can jump, but they do not all have the technique or the will to clear the fences.

Show jumping developed from the "leaping competitions" which were held at various shows in Europe and America during the late nineteenth century. There were high-jump and long-jump competitions for horse and rider but the idea of jumping a course of fences was, at the time, mainly restricted to natural cross-country fences. Jumping was first included in the Olympic Games in Paris in 1900. It incorporated the high and wide competitions plus a timed competition over a course of artificial show jumps. In 1907, the first International Horse Show was held at Olympia in London, England, and the show jumping proved to be very popular. From then on competitions were organized throughout Europe and America for major trophies such as the

▮ LEFT
Teaching your horse to go well on the flat is as important to his success as teaching him how to jump correctly; look at the beautifully round and elevated canter that this show jumper is producing – with a canter like this, jumping the fence is almost a formality.

▮ BELOW LEFT AND RIGHT
If you can invest in a few jumps of your own, or team up with some friends to share them, there is much that can be practised at home. A simple thing to practise is always looking towards the next fence. This helps you to judge your turns and your approach. Once you have taken off over a fence you should be looking towards your next target; as you ride around the course you should always be looking towards where you have to go next.

Nations Cup. This began as a military competition open to three officers of the same nationality who had to compete in uniform. Today it is open to four riders of the same nationality, male or female, military or civilian.

▮ SHOW-JUMPING COMPETITIONS

The simplest form of unaffiliated competition is the Clear-round Class. This is an excellent way of introducing an inexperienced horse and rider to the sport. Each rider pays a small fee to tackle a course of jumps. If you jump a clear round you win a rosette, but the real usefulness of the competition is that if you jump a fence badly you can turn around and jump it again. Most organizers of these classes are extremely tolerant and will even lower a fence for you if your horse continually refuses. In a proper competition you would be eliminated after three refusals.

RIGHT
RIGHT
It is important that the horse learns to jump straight, unless his rider is asking him to turn in the air. In this picture you can see that the horse is looking in the opposite direction from his rider, suggesting he has a tendency to jump crookedly. Gridwork and the use of V-poles help to teach the horse to stay straight.

The next stage is the two-round competition. Each competitor tackles the same course of fences and if you jump a clear round you go through to the jump off. This is ridden against the clock and the fastest clear round wins.

Fences in unaffiliated classes start as low as the organizer wishes. There may even be leading-rein classes with jumps only 18 inches (45 cm) high. Fences usually go up to about 3 feet 11 inches (1.2 m). Affiliated competitions start with a novice class with fences at about 3 feet 3 inches (1 m) and continue through the grades to courses with jumps which are well over 6 feet (1.8 m) high.

There are also other types of jumping classes such as "Take your own line". This involves a course of fences which each have a different value in terms of points to be won. You jump as many fences as you can in the time allowed, in any order you like, with the aim of accumulating the maximum number of points. The *Puissance* involves jumping a short course of fences; these include a wall, which is always the highest jump. The fences are gradually raised until nobody is able to clear the wall.

Derby competitions have cross-country-type obstacles in the arena, such as banks and ditches. Some shows also hold relay competitions between teams of show jumpers, or for added entertainment they may build two identical courses side by side over which competitors race. Time faults are added for knock-downs.

One of the advantages of show jumping is that jumping a course of fences does not take as much out of a horse as, say, a day's hunting or a hunter trial, so the show jumper can compete far more frequently than many other sports horses. You could compete in a couple of different classes on the same day and, provided your horse is fit enough and enjoying his work, you might compete nearly every weekend. In

EQUIPMENT NEEDED

To develop your show-jumping skills you need to have access to at least three or four sets of show-jump wings and poles. Other than that, all that is needed is a reasonably flat surface to practise on, which can be a grass paddock when ground conditions permit, or an outdoor or indoor arena with an all-weather surface. Your horse needs only his usual saddle and bridle and should wear protective boots of some sort. Most show jumpers use open-fronted boots on the front legs so that the tendon area is protected but the horse will feel the knock if he hits a pole, and short fetlock boots behind. To compete you will need to wear breeches or jodhpurs with riding boots, and a show or hacking jacket. A shirt and tie, or stock, is worn underneath the jacket.

Whilst almost any horse or pony can be persuaded to pop around a show-jumping course, once the fences get bigger you do need a horse who is athletic and balanced. There are plenty of horses who will clatter their way around a course, gaily sending poles flying without appearing to be the least bit bothered by the experience. There is a great deal you can teach a horse but, at the end of the day, he has to want to clear the top pole.

| RIGHT
Riders all develop
their own jumping
style as they gain
confidence and
experience, but one
of the things you must
always do, no matter
what your technique, is
to ensure that you give
your horse plenty of
freedom of his head
and neck. Your hands
must always move
forwards when the
horse is jumping over
the fence.

theory this offers horse and rider the chance to gain experience relatively quickly.

■ SKILLS REQUIRED

Flatwork training is as important to the show jumper as jump schooling. A balanced, rhythmic and elevated canter is essential if the horse is to jump successfully. Whatever it is you are jumping, your chances of clearing it safely are mainly reliant on how good an approach you give the horse to the fence. The horse must be able to negotiate corners and turns whilst still keeping his rhythm and balance, so he needs to be supple and responsive.

How much actual jump training you do depends on what suits your horse. Naturally careful horses are best not jumped too often – just enough to keep them in practice and their muscles toned up. A horse whose technique needs tidying up may be jumped up to three or four times a week.

Jump training rarely involves jumping huge fences. It concentrates on improving the horse's technique and ability over

smaller fences – this reduces the risk of injury or loss of confidence. Gridwork is used to make the horse more supple, and to influence his technique and the shape he makes as he goes over a fence to maximize his chance of going clear.

The distances between fences in a grid can be shortened to encourage the horse

to shorten up his stride and snap his front legs up quickly and neatly as he takes off. They can also be lengthened, which encourages the horse to stretch and to lengthen his stride and jump.

Poles can be rested on the fence or on the ground in such a way as to encourage the horse to stay straight as he jumps; many horses have a tendency to veer off to the left or right. Gridwork also gives you a chance to concentrate on tidying up your own position and to improve your balance.

The ability to lengthen or shorten your horse's stride and to react quickly when he jumps into a combination or related distance in a different way from the one that was planned, is an essential skill for the successful show jumper. Some riders have a natural eye for a stride, which means that as soon as they land over one fence they are able to gauge whether they need to alter the horse's stride length in order to meet the next fence on a good stride. Those not born with this skill can develop a good eye by practising riding different distances between fences at home, and getting a feel for the pace at which they need to approach the first

| LEFT
This little pony is
showing superb
technique – see how
tightly he has snapped
up and folded his
front legs, which gives
him every chance to
clear the fence.

Show-jumping competitions usually just involve jumping over fences. However, in Derby classes cross-country type obstacles are introduced; this is the world-famous Hickstead Derby bank.

horse and rider to progress through the grades. They can go as far as their ability, time and/or finances allow them.

For those looking for greater rewards, show jumping also offers very good opportunities. Through the FEI there is a training and team-selection programme for pony riders, juniors, young riders and seniors. There are also Pony Club and riding club competitions and championships. To be considered for team selection usually involves informing the appropriate selection committee of your interest and then entering a number of specified competitions where your performance will be noted by the selectors. If you are a likely candidate for a team place, you may be invited to attend various training courses – but remember that the ability to operate as part of a team is as important as being a good enough competitor to warrant selection.

I BELOW
In show jumping the horse has to be taught to jump *over* water, whereas in cross-country riding you are always trying to encourage your horse to jump *into* water.

fence in order to fit in the required number of strides to the next fence.

Among the most important attributes the rider needs are patience, a cool head and confidence – if you have all three of these you will no doubt succeed in whatever sport you choose!

■ OPPORTUNITIES

In all sports there are those who compete purely for their own enjoyment and entertainment, and those who compete with a view to being selected for team competitions and, who knows, maybe ultimately the Olympics. Show jumping caters extremely well for both types of competitor. For the less ambitious there are no end of unaffiliated and affiliated classes and competitions which still allow

Eventing

The sport of eventing, or horse trials as it is also known, is really a complete test of all-round horsemanship on the part of the rider, and of all-round performance on the part of the horse. Horse and rider are tested on their ability to compete in the disciplines of dressage, show jumping and cross country. The dressage test demonstrates that the horse is supple, obedient and calm; the show jumping proves his agility and carefulness over fences; the cross country proves his boldness, speed and stamina. The sport is split into one-day events and three-day events. At a one-day event the order of the phases is usually dressage, show jumping and cross country. At a three-day event the cross country, combined with some additional tests of the horse's speed and endurance, is held the day after the dressage. The show jumping is held on the final day, testing whether the horse still has the necessary energy, agility, obedience and desire to clear the show jumps following the tough test of his stamina the day before on the speed and endurance phase.

■ HOW THE SPORT DEVELOPED

Eventing was started in Europe by cavalrymen, when they were not away fighting wars! The sport was originally named "The Military". It evolved as a way of testing the skills a cavalry horse would need – the dressage represented his suitability for parade duties, the cross country reflected the need to cross any terrain to seek out, confront or escape the enemy, and the show jumping showed that after the rigours of battle the horse was still fit, willing and obedient, ready to march on to the next challenge.

The first Olympic three-day event was held in 1912. Then and for some years afterwards the sport remained the domain of the military. It spread from country to country through international military

A THREE-DAY EVENT

Day one	Dressage
Day two	Speed and endurance:
	Phase A roads and tracks
	Phase B steeplechase
	Phase C roads and tracks
	Phase D cross country
Day three	Show jumping

The sport of eventing involves three very different disciplines, all of which must be completed successfully in order to win. The dressage test comes first. Whilst this is simpler than a pure dressage test, it must be remembered that it is being ridden on a horse who has been prepared physically and mentally for the cross-country phase. He knows what is coming next, so it is harder for him to settle to the discipline of dressage.

competitions and, as events became more numerous, the interest of civilian riders was aroused. Now eventing is a popular sport in any number of countries around the world.

■ ONE-DAY AND THREE-DAY EVENTS

At a one-day event you have to complete a dressage test, a course of show jumps and a cross-country course, all on the same day. The penalties incurred in each competition, or phase, are added together, and the winner is the rider incurring the lowest number of penalties. One-day events are an end in themselves for many riders, but their true purpose is to prepare horse and rider for the more demanding three-day event.

A three-day event can actually last for four or five days, depending on the number of entrants. All the horses are stabled together at or near the event for its duration. Before the competition begins there is a veterinary inspection, where any signs of lameness, injury or illness will result in elimination before you have started. The next one or two days are taken up with everybody completing their dressage tests.

The second part of the competition – the speed and endurance section – starts on the following day. Phase A, roads and tracks, involves completing a set route within a set time. This is usually achieved comfortably at trot, although a very short-striding horse may have to canter some of the way in order to avoid time penalties. This takes you to the start of the steeple-chase, which is Phase B. All on your own

▌ OPPOSITE
In one-day events the show-jumping phase comes
after the dressage, before the cross country. At a
three-day event it is the final phase, testing the
horse's agility and obedience after the rigours and
excitement of the cross country the day before.

▌ LEFT
The cross-country
phase is the most
important, and
should be the most
influential, of the
three phases. For
most event riders it is
the favourite phase.

you have to gallop around a circuit
of steeplechase fences, again within a set
time. The finish of the steeplechase takes
you on to Phase C, another set of roads
and tracks, which is meant to serve as a
recovery period after the steeplechase. A
steady trot has to be maintained for much
of the way if you are to finish inside the
time. You then find yourself in the ten-
minute box which is a roped-off area near
the start of the cross-country course. Here
the horse is allowed to rest for ten
minutes. He is usually washed off, has his
tack re-adjusted and checked for security
and comfort, and is then walked quietly
around so that he does not stiffen up
before the cross country, which is Phase D.
In the ten-minute box, vets check the
horses over and eliminate any who are
already overly tired or are stressed.

▌ BELOW LEFT
AND RIGHT
At a three-day event,
the competitors have
to tackle two roads and
tracks phases, as well
as a steeplechase
course, before they
even set out on the
cross-country course.
There is a ten-minute
rest period between
the end of the second
roads and tracks and
the start of the cross-
country test.

After the ten-minute rest you set off on
the cross-country course, which is judged
in the same way as at a one-day event.
There are penalties for any refusals, falls
or runouts, and also for exceeding the set
time. The following day there is another
veterinary inspection where any horse who
appears to have suffered from his
exertions of the day before is withdrawn
or eliminated from the competition.

This is followed by the final phase,
the show jumping. This is usually run
in reverse order of merit, so that the
overnight leader jumps last. Any penalties
incurred for refusals, knock-downs or
exceeding the time are added to the
dressage and to the speed and endurance
penalties to give a final score. The winners
of three-day events do indeed prove
themselves and their horses to be
successful, all-round competitors.

▌ LEVELS OF COMPETITION

Eventing is governed by the FEI and there
are various levels of affiliated competition.
There are also Pony Club, Riding Club
and unaffiliated competitions although
these rarely offer classes at higher than

affiliated intermediate level. Affiliated
one-day events are graded into different
levels along such lines as novice (or below,
such as preliminary or pre-novice),
intermediate and advanced. These
classifications or grades refer to the ability
of the horse, not the rider, so in the same
novice class you may find a sixteen-year-
old riding in his or her first event
competing against the reigning Olympic
champion. For many this is all part of the
charm and attraction of the sport. It is far

more of an achievement to perform well
against such experienced riders, even if
you don't win, than it is to take first prize
in a class where you knew your rivals
weren't up to much anyway.

Affiliated three-day events are classified
as one star (novice), two star (about
intermediate level), three star
(intermediate to advanced level) and four
star (advanced and championship level).

In between the one-day events and the
three-day events are the occasional two-day

events. These are limited in number and are usually only offered at novice level, but provide a great introduction to three-day eventing for the inexperienced rider or horse. You perform your dressage and show jumping on day one, and on day two you complete a shortened speed and endurance phase. This still consists of roads and tracks, steeplechase, roads and tracks, ten-minute halt and the cross-country course, but the speeds and distances are less than for a three-day event.

Every horse has to qualify to take part in a three-day event. For each grade there are a set number of one-, two- or less rigorous three-day events which horse and rider must have completed to a set standard. You usually need to have gone clear on the cross country, or at least have

incurred only a limited number of penalties. This adds another dimension to the sport as it allows you to compete with your horse's long-term future in mind. You may well go to a one-day event and come away without a prize, but if you were able to go clear on the cross country you will have achieved a qualification towards your target of the three-day event.

■ SKILLS REQUIRED
Bearing in mind what is required for dressage, show jumping and hunter trialling will give you some idea of the myriad skills the successful event horse and rider need. But before you are put off just think of it in terms of good basic training equalling good all-round performance. If you have put some effort

into schooling your horse well on the flat, and have carried through the same principles of rhythm, balance and responsiveness into your jump training, you are well on the way to producing a capable and successful event horse. Jump training, whether over show jumps or cross-country fences, requires the same technique and skills. The only difference is the speed at which you ride across country, and the fact that the natural terrain you have to cross makes it harder to maintain your rhythm and balance than when you are jumping in an arena. An

■ ABOVE
You have to keep note of how much time you can allow yourself on the roads and tracks phases, the steeplechase and the cross-country course. Exceeding the optimum time incurs time faults. Most riders record all their times on a card which they carry on their arm, along with a stopwatch.

■ LEFT
At advanced one-day events and at three-day events the horses have to carry a minimum weight of 165 lb (75 kg). This includes the rider's clothing and the horse's saddle. If you weigh in under that, you will have to carry lead weights in a weightcloth under the saddle.

EQUIPMENT NEEDED

It is possible to compete in events with a minimal amount of tack and equipment but, because of the three disciplines involved, there is a greater chance that you will need to invest in various bits and pieces. Many horses are better ridden in different tack for each phase – a horse may perform happily in a snaffle for his dressage test but may need a double bridle or a gag for the cross country. Some horses need different tack for the show jumping as well. You should use a breastplate or girth and a safety girth with your saddle for the cross-country phase. You may also want to use different types of boots or bandages for the show-jumping and cross-country phases – show-jumping boots do not offer enough protection for cross country. If you can afford it, a dressage saddle for the dressage phase will help your seat and position enormously; some riders even opt for different show-jumping and cross-country saddles although this is a little excessive. In fact, it is now possible to buy saddles with interchangeable knee rolls which allow the same saddle to be converted from a dressage model to a jumping model.

You will need jodhpurs, breeches and boots, plus a show or hacking jacket and a recognized crash hat. You must also wear a body protector on the cross-country phase. At advanced level you are expected to perform your dressage test in a top hat and tailcoat – these are expensive when new, but can often be bought secondhand.

This horse is about to
unseat his rider,
having thrown a very
big but steep jump into
the water at
Badminton. In the
circumstances, the
rider has done well to
keep her weight back
and at the same time
has slipped the reins
to give the horse every
chance of coping with
the situation.

▮ BELOW
Blyth Tait, the 1996 Olympic gold medallist,
demonstrates how to slip the reins but still keep a
contact so that the horse has some support to help
balance him as he lands.

additional factor is the variety of fences you
will meet on a cross-country course. Once
your horse is familiar with show jumps he is
unlikely to be fazed by anything he meets
in the arena, unless you approach it badly.
But the awkward obstacles that can be built
into the natural terrain on a cross-country
course are numerous, and each time the
horse competes he may well be faced with
something he has never encountered
before. Cross-country training should
concentrate on building up confidence and
trust, and making the right decision about
the approach you should take.

Water is one hazard which seems to
cause more trouble than most. In the
horse's early training it is important that
he is never frightened in water. This
means carefully choosing any water hazard
you ask him to enter. Don't ask him to
splash through a river unless you know it
has a safe, secure bottom. If he willingly
enters water for you, and then finds
himself floundering in deep mud he is
going to be frightened and he is not going
to trust you next time you face him with
water. So do not abuse his trust and
willingness. Similarly do not allow the
overbold or exuberant horse to frighten

himself – make him approach water
quietly and calmly so that he puts in a
sensible jump which allows him to land in
a balanced and controlled manner. If your
horse is introduced to water like this, and
if you take care always to be in a good
position to support and balance him as
he lands in water, he should never have
reason to refuse to tackle a water complex.

Fitness is another necessity for both
horse and rider. As long as they are
regularly hacked out and given some
schooling and jump training, most horses
and ponies will be fit enough to
complete a novice one-day event. Once

you want to do more than this, special
attention has to be paid to the horse's
fitness and training routine. This requires
knowledge and experience of how to
achieve fitness without subjecting the
horse's vulnerable joints and limbs to
unnecessary wear and tear. You will also
need to be fit, as a tired rider is of little
help to a tired horse.

The event rider perhaps needs more
determination and persistence than other
equestrian competitors, simply because it
is a lot harder to get three things to go
well all on the same day than it is to get
one specialist discipline to come right.

▮ LEFT
Commonly known as
"hailing a cab", this
rider has thrown her
arm behind her in a
tactic which many
riders find helps them
to keep their weight
back behind the horse
when jumping down
into water.

Race Riding

Race riding, either on the flat or over fences, offers the best opportunity to experience the full power and speed that a horse can produce. The racing industry revolves around the thoroughbred horse and, to a lesser degree, the Arab horse. Point-to-pointing, the occasional unofficial horse or pony race and the growth in Arab racing all give the amateur rider the chance to experience the thrill of race riding, and the chance to race for the fun of it. Professional jockeys are either retained or employed on a freelance basis by race-horse trainers. They often work for a big training yard in order to supplement their income, exercising and schooling the race horses, as well as racing them competitively if they are offered the ride.

■ POINT-TO-POINTING

This is an amateur sport which tends to thrive wherever hunting thrives. A horse which is to go point-to-pointing has to qualify by going out hunting for a set number of days. The amateur status of the sport, and the fact that a great many who take part own just one horse which they hunt and race, all adds to its fun and social atmosphere. It is popular with spectators, even in winter when they usually end up standing around in the wet and cold, eating the traditional picnic in

■ LEFT
The ability to sit tight when the unexpected happens is a great asset. Note how this jockey has kept his upper body back and is still looking up and ahead, which is a great aid to keeping in balance when racing.

■ BELOW LEFT
Race horses have to be supreme athletes – the greatest care and attention is lavished on them to keep them in peak condition. For a change of scene, these race horses are being exercised on the beach; another day it may be over grass or all-weather gallops, or just hacking along the roads.

the car park. There are yards where the owner makes a living out of training and racing either his own or other people's point-to-pointers, and this makes some of the races very competitive.

In most point-to-points the horses jump standard brush fences which may occasionally have a ditch in front, but some courses include banks and water as well. This reflects the sport's origins when riders simply raced each other from one point, usually a church steeple, to another point somewhere in the distance. The standard of riding varies considerably; anyone who has seen the differing standards on the hunting field will know what to expect in a point-to-point race. It

is for this reason that in point-to-pointing there are more falls than in professional steeplechasing or hurdling. The point-to-point course is usually an oval-shaped track marked out over an area of grassland. The fences are well spaced out around the course and, because they make use of natural terrain, some courses are much flatter than others. Competitors quickly discover which tracks suit their particular horse best.

■ ARAB RACING

This is a well-organized sport which involves flat races between Arab horses. The racing is fast and competitive, but the sport is still small enough to allow you to

EQUIPMENT NEEDED

To ride in any of these races you will need to wear an acceptable crash hat, lightweight breeches and boots, and a jumper reflecting your racing colours. In a point-to-point you are allowed to wear hunting kit. A body protector is compulsory for some types of racing, and advisable for all types. Goggles are a handy accessory, as a faceful of mud half-way around the course does little for your ability to steer your horse home. A weightcloth will also be needed. A horse can be raced in his ordinary saddle but most jockeys opt for a lightweight racing saddle.

Despite its amateur status – which means the
greatest reward is the fun to be had rather than
the prize money to be won – the risks of point-to-
pointing are probably greater than in either
professional racing over jumps or flat racing. Falls
are frequent.

train and compete your own horse with
success. Races vary in length, which means
horses tend to specialize in either the
short, faster races, or the longer, slightly
slower ones.

■ PONY AND HORSE RACING

There are a few pony and horse races held
in most countries which give ordinary
riding horses and their jockeys a chance to
demonstrate their speed – or lack of it!
Most of these are unofficial, although a
few countries do have a national body
which registers competitors and organizes
races for them.

■ PROFESSIONAL FLAT AND JUMP RACING

The international racing scene is divided
into flat races, hurdle races, steeplechase
races and timber or cross-country races.
Flat racing is mainly to test pure speed –
many of the races are short sprints where

speed rather than stamina counts most.
Jump racing requires stamina, jumping
ability and speed.

■ SKILLS REQUIRED

To race ride you need to be fit, have good
balance and a feel for jumping at speed.
These can all be practised at home if you
intend racing just for fun. But if you want
it to be more than that, the best place to
learn is in a big racing yard, even if you
only help out there at weekends. The
more thoroughbred race horses you are
able to ride, even if only on exercise, the
better your fitness, position and balance
will become.

Flat-race jockeys are generally quite
short and also have to be lightweight.
Jump jockeys, who ride with their stirrups
a little longer, can be taller but need to
keep their weight down so that they do
not force the horse to carry more weight
than he has been allocated.

If you fancy a career with horses, a job in a good
racing yard can offer great variety, good experience
and good friends.

Dirt-track racing is common in America.

SUCCESS IS DOWN TO YOU

Competing with your horse can and should
be an enjoyable experience for both of you.
But if you take a look around you will see that
this is not always the case – unhappy horses
and riders abound at all kinds of events.
Some horses are always going to be more
talented than others; some will be more co-
operative than others. But there will also be
those who, either through lack of schooling or
understanding, or simply through bad riding,
do not fulfil their potential. Not everyone can
afford the horse or pony of their dreams.
Some think that this is exactly what they have
found, only to be disappointed when things
don't go to plan. A few horses, no matter how
well ridden, simply lack the necessary ability
or character to succeed at certain sports.

When things aren't going as well as you
would like, remember too that very few
talented riders are born – they have to be
made. Riding has to be worked at; it doesn't
just happen. You cannot be blamed for
lacking a particular skill or aptitude for a
specific sport – we are all made differently –
but you can be blamed if you don't bother to
work at your basic riding skills. So if you are
going to ride, strive to ride well. GOOD LUCK!

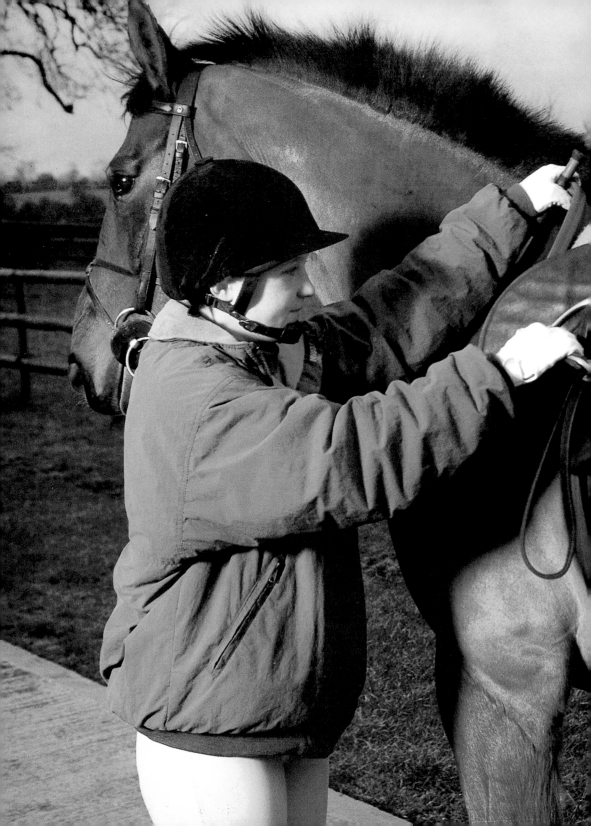

Saddlery and Equipment

The Saddle

The saddle is one of the most important pieces of equipment
for the ridden horse, and, because of the skill and craftsmanship
involved in producing a saddle, it is usually the most expensive.
The earliest type of saddle, first developed thousands of years
ago, was nothing more than a simple blanket kept in place with
breastplate and girth. The modern saddle, however, is a
sophisticated piece of equipment. It has evolved as a result of the
demands of modern equestrianism, whether it be the Western
saddle designed to withstand the rigours of cowboy life; the
dressage saddle designed to give the rider an elegant yet
effective position; or the minuscule racing saddle.
The saddle's design and fit can have a tremendous effect
on both the horse's performance and the rider's position.
An ill-fitting saddle can cause the horse considerable discomfort
and even physical damage. When choosing a new saddle,
therefore, it is always advisable to seek professional help –
a trained saddler will be able to ensure that the saddle
fits the horse correctly.

Points of the Saddle

Virtually all saddles are built upon a solid framework called a tree. This framework was traditionally made from beech wood but is now available in laminated wood, and even fibreglass and plastic. It is the shape of the tree and the placing of the metal stirrup bars riveted to the tree which determine the size and shape of the saddle. The seat of the saddle is given shape by stretching a webbing and cotton fabric over the tree. Serge or a synthetic fabric is stretched to form the seat shape and a wool or synthetic stuffing provides the padding below.

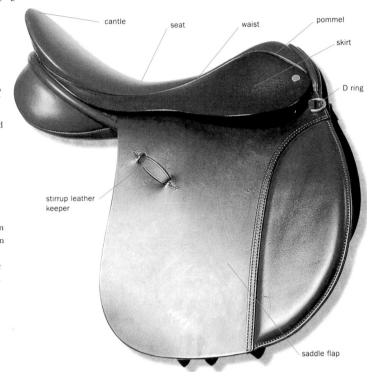

cantle seat waist pommel skirt D ring

stirrup leather keeper

saddle flap

▮ BELOW
Under the saddle flap. Most saddles have three girth straps. The first two are fixed to the web strap attached to the tree and the third is fixed independently.

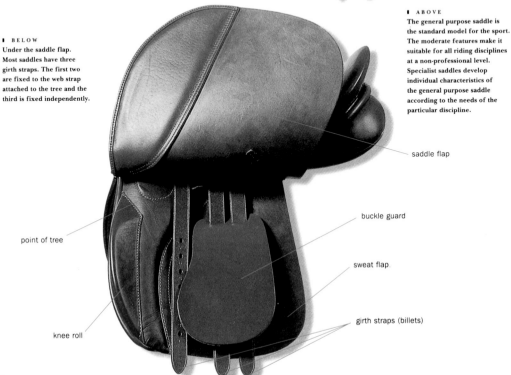

▮ ABOVE
The general purpose saddle is the standard model for the sport. The moderate features make it suitable for all riding disciplines at a non-professional level. Specialist saddles develop individual characteristics of the general purpose saddle according to the needs of the particular discipline.

saddle flap

point of tree

knee roll

buckle guard

sweat flap

girth straps (billets)

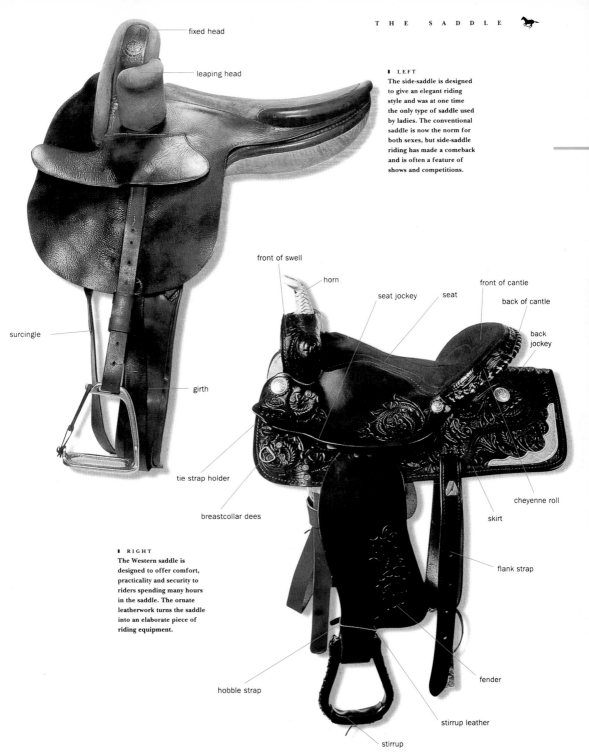

fixed head

leaping head

■ LEFT
The side-saddle is designed
to give an elegant riding
style and was at one time
the only type of saddle used
by ladies. The conventional
saddle is now the norm for
both sexes, but side-saddle
riding has made a comeback
and is often a feature of
shows and competitions.

front of swell

horn

seat jockey   seat

front of cantle

back of cantle

back
jockey

surcingle

girth

cheyenne roll

skirt

tie strap holder

breastcollar dees

flank strap

■ RIGHT
The Western saddle is
designed to offer comfort,
practicality and security to
riders spending many hours
in the saddle. The ornate
leatherwork turns the saddle
into an elaborate piece of
riding equipment.

fender

hobble strap

stirrup leather

stirrup

Riding and Competing Saddles

Saddles are available in a number of shapes and styles to suit the many equestrian disciplines at every level of competition from novice to professional.

The **leather general purpose (GP) saddle** is designed to be used across the board of riding activities. It is ideal for pleasure riding, hunting, novice cross-country and show jumping and basic dressage. A less expensive alternative to the leather saddle is the **synthetic general purpose saddle**, which is lighter in weight than the leather type, and easier to clean.

For most riders, the general purpose saddle is perfectly adequate for jumping. However, if you are riding at a competitive level and tackling larger fences, you may prefer the specialist design of the jumping saddle. The saddle flaps of the **Crosby close-contact jumping saddle** are more forward cut than those of the general purpose saddle. This enables you to keep your legs close to the saddle even when riding with a short stirrup length.

The **event saddle** is very similar in style to a general purpose saddle and can be used for all phases of horse trials, although some riders prefer to have an additional saddle for the dressage phase. Many famous riders have become involved in the design of saddles and the event saddle illustrated was developed by the international eventer, Mary King.

The **Albion Selecta** is a multi-purpose saddle which aims to combine the general purpose saddle with a dressage and a jumping saddle. It features easily removable knee pads which allow the saddle to be adapted for all riding disciplines from pleasure riding to jumping, dressage, cross-country and working hunter events.

The **polo saddle** has a relatively flat seat, extra-long sweat flaps and no knee and thigh rolls. It is designed specifically for the game of polo, during which the horse travels at speed and the rider needs to be able to move with ease to hit the ball.

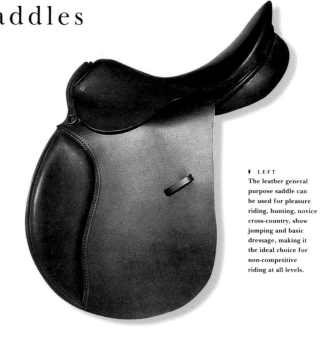

▌ LEFT
The leather general purpose saddle can be used for pleasure riding, hunting, novice cross-country, show jumping and basic dressage, making it the ideal choice for non-competitive riding at all levels.

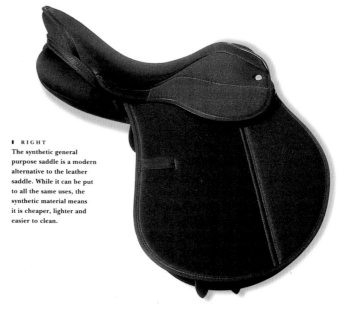

▌ RIGHT
The synthetic general purpose saddle is a modern alternative to the leather saddle. While it can be put to all the same uses, the synthetic material means it is cheaper, lighter and easier to clean.

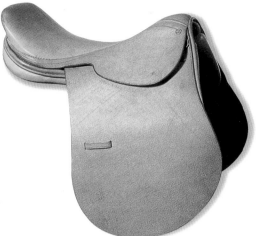

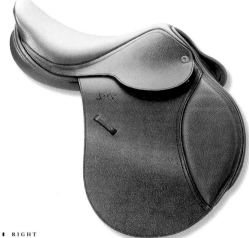

ABOVE
The polo saddle has a flat seat, extended sweat flaps and no knee or thigh rolls, all of which allow the rider freedom of movement when striking the ball.

BELOW LEFT
Event saddle. This is similar in style to the general purpose saddle and can be used for all phases of horse trials.

RIGHT
The Crosby close-contact jumping saddle. The saddle flaps are more forward cut than those of the general purpose saddle. This allows the rider to carry his legs closer to the saddle, and makes his position more secure.

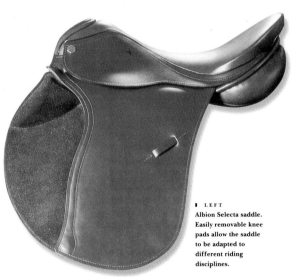

LEFT
Albion Selecta saddle. Easily removable knee pads allow the saddle to be adapted to different riding disciplines.

Showing Saddles

There are a number of saddles designed specifically to improve the horse's performance in showing competitions.

The purpose of the **showing saddle** is primarily to enhance the appearance of the show horse rather than to increase the comfort of the rider. The saddle is straight cut to show off the horse's shoulder and is simple in design, since it is the horse rather than the tack that is being judged. The showing saddle is a specialized piece of equipment and not always very comfortable; many riders prefer to use a dressage saddle for showing classes.

The **dressage saddle**, designed for riding and schooling horses on the flat rather than over jumps, has longer and straighter flaps than the general purpose saddle. This allows you to carry your legs in a longer position and closer to the horse's body. To eliminate bulk under your legs, longer girth straps (billets) are fitted and used with a short dressage girth.

The **Saddlebred saddle** is for showing American Saddlebreds and other gaited horses. It features a cut-back pommel (called a "cow-mouth") and very wide saddle flaps, which enable the rider to sit much further back in the saddle than usual.

For showing classes in which the horse is required both to jump and to be ridden on the flat, the **working hunter saddle** is ideal. The seat is deeper than the showing saddle, and padded knee rolls give a more secure seat which is helpful when jumping.

The **side-saddle,** first developed for ladies in the fourteenth century, allows the rider to carry both legs on the near (left) side of the horse, with the left foot in a stirrup and the right leg hooked over the pommel. The flat seat has a suede or doeskin cover for extra grip. Although no longer in general use, shows often feature ladies' hunter classes for side-saddle riders.

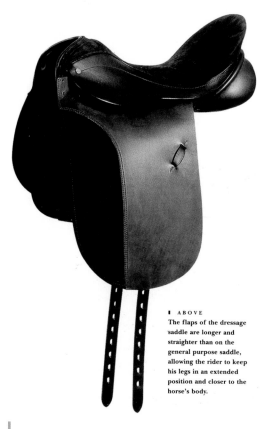

∎ ABOVE
The flaps of the dressage saddle are longer and straighter than on the general purpose saddle, allowing the rider to keep his legs in an extended position and closer to the horse's body.

∎ ABOVE
The shape of the side-saddle allows the rider to adopt a more elegant position, with both legs on the near (left) side of the horse.

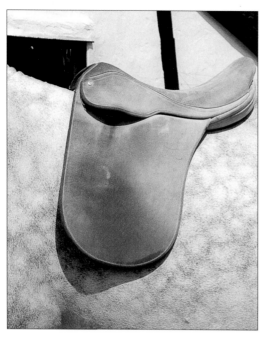

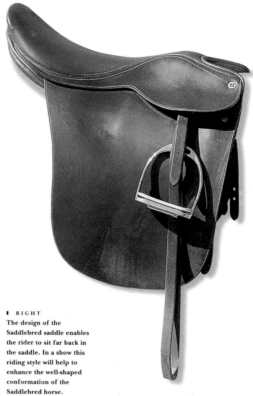

■ ABOVE
This showing saddle in
split hide, designed by
producer and rider Lynn
Rusell, is specially shaped
to suit larger show horses
such as cobs and hunters.

■ RIGHT
The working hunter saddle
is a compromise between a
showing saddle and a
jumping saddle.

■ RIGHT
The design of the
Saddlebred saddle enables
the rider to sit far back in
the saddle. In a show this
riding style will help to
enhance the well-shaped
conformation of the
Saddlebred horse.

Trail-riding and Working Saddles

Saddles which are to be ridden over long periods of time need to have an element of comfort incorporated into the design.

The **endurance saddle**, as its name suggests, is designed for long-distance rides. The seat has extra padding and the saddle panels have extra width, thereby spreading the rider's weight over a greater area and reducing the risk of localized pressure points on the horse's back. Additional D rings are fitted to the saddle so that equipment, such as lead ropes and sponges, can easily be accommodated.

The **Australian stock saddle** is a utilitarian saddle designed for the comfort of both horse and rider during the hours spent driving cattle. The weight distribution properties mean that modified versions of this saddle can also be used for endurance or trail-riding.

The **Western reining saddle** is higher in front than the standard Western saddle, preventing the rider from being thrown forward when the horse performs the characteristic sliding stop. **Western pleasure saddles** are lighter in weight than working saddles and have only one cinch attachment. Comfortable and secure, these saddles are ideal for long-distance or trail-riding.

The **parade saddle** is an ornate working saddle featuring highly intricate metal and leatherwork. These decorative saddles are specially designed for use in carnival or rodeo parades.

The **trooper** or **Cavalry saddle** is built around a steel and wood tree and is the traditional choice of the armed forces because of its strength and durability.

The **military fan saddle** is designed for working horses, such as those used by the mounted police. The saddle tree distributes the rider's weight evenly for comfort during long periods of work, often when the horse is stationary.

❚ ABOVE
The Australian stock saddle is built for comfort and durability. The rider may spend several hours driving cattle on the plains, and the even spread of his weight in the saddle will become a significant factor for both horse and rider.

❚ ABOVE
The high front of the Western reining saddle prevents the rider being thrown forward and out of the saddle when the horse performs the dramatic reining halt, which is a feature of this riding style.

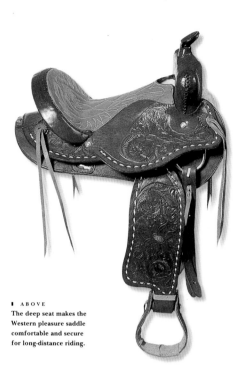

ABOVE
Endurance saddle. This is designed specifically for long-distance riding, with the comfort of both horse and rider in mind.

ABOVE
The deep seat makes the Western pleasure saddle comfortable and secure for long-distance riding.

RIGHT
The elaborate parade saddle features intricately detailed leatherwork, and makes a splendid sight at carnivals and rodeos.

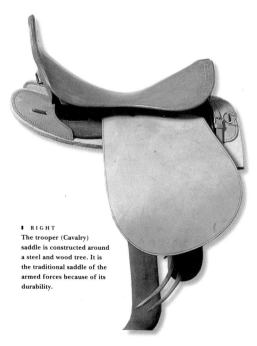

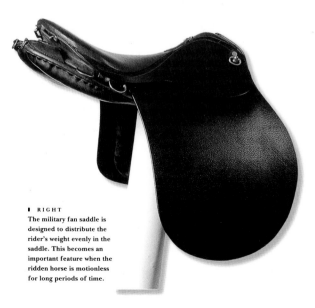

RIGHT
The trooper (Cavalry) saddle is constructed around a steel and wood tree. It is the traditional saddle of the armed forces because of its durability.

RIGHT
The military fan saddle is designed to distribute the rider's weight evenly in the saddle. This becomes an important feature when the ridden horse is motionless for long periods of time.

405

Racing Saddles

Horse racing, and flat racing in particular, requires a highly unusual riding style that makes specific demands on the saddle.

The saddle used in flat racing is crouched over rather than sat on, and for this reason it has a flat seat and is fitted with very short stirrup leathers. **Leather racing saddles** are necessarily light; they come in a variety of weights, starting from as little as 325g/11oz. Saddles for National Hunt racing (racing over jumps) are heavier and larger in size than the saddles used for flat racing. **Synthetic racing saddles** are becoming increasingly popular for dirt and all-weather track racing, where the sand used for the track's surface can cause damage to leather tack.

As the name implies, **race exercise saddles** are used when exercising racehorses rather than when actually racing them. Because the question of weight does not apply, the exercise saddle is usually heavier and larger than the racing saddle, and comes with a full or half-tree in leather or synthetic material. The full-tree saddle illustrated features "todsloan" saddle flaps, named after the American jockey James Todhunter Sloan, who pioneered the style of riding with shorter stirrup leathers.

▮ LEFT
The flat seat and short stirrup leathers are characteristic of saddles used for flat racing. The jockey rides crouched over the saddle with his head tucked well in for a more streamlined position.

▮ RIGHT
Race exercise saddles are larger and heavier than racing saddles. Exercising the horse requires a more functional saddle than the lightweight type worn for the race.

Learner Saddles

For beginners taking their first lessons in equestrianism, a specially adapted saddle can be a huge advantage, not least because of the additional safety features which these saddles incorporate.

The **pony saddle**, designed for young children and smaller ponies, has removable panels to vary the amount by which the child is "wedged in", and a hand support for extra grip. The **felt-pad saddle** also includes the safety handle feature, and this can be very helpful for nervous children. The simple design consists of a soft felt pad with a leather covering and built-in webbing girth and stirrup bars.

The **Riding for the Disabled Association (RDA) saddle** will enable physically or mentally disabled children and adults to ride in safety. The loop fitted to the front of the saddle gives the rider something to hold on to without needing to grip and pull at the reins too tightly, thereby damaging the horse's mouth.

▮ LEFT
The pony saddle makes an ideal choice for small children who are just learning to ride.

▮ LEFT
The felt-pad saddle is a beginner's saddle for children. It consists of a soft felt pad with a leather covering and built-in webbing girth and stirrup bars.

▮ RIGHT
The design of the RDA saddle enables the physically and mentally disabled to ride with safety and confidence.

407

Ceremonial Saddles

The Royal Mews at Buckingham Palace in London houses a large collection of saddles, bridles and harnesses belonging to the Royal Family. Much of the saddlery and equipment in this beautiful collection is of a unique historical interest.

Queen Elizabeth II's love of horses is well known and many of the gifts she receives are related to the subject of riding. The Portuguese ceremonial bridle was presented with a saddle to HM the Queen by the Portuguese government on a state visit to Portugal in 1957. The bridle has solid silver bit and fittings.

The Alamo saddle was presented as a gift to the Queen from the actor John Wayne, who directed and starred in the film *The Alamo*. The saddle had been used by the actor during the making of the film. The design of the saddle is highly

ornate and features tooled fenders and decorated *tapaderos* (toe covers).

Although ladies traditionally sat to the near (left) side when riding side-saddle, it was not uncommon for young ladies learning to ride to use a saddle designed for riding on the off (right) side, as demonstrated by a pair of side-saddles belonging to Princess Mary.

Queen Victoria's side-saddle was used by the monarch in the latter half of the nineteenth century. To allow for a less restrictive riding style, the design features a pommel on either side of the saddle, so that the saddle can be ridden on either the near or the off side.

A hunting saddle used by the Prince Consort, HRH Prince Albert, during the mid-nineteenth century, is elaborately detailed in gold thread and features a

holster for carrying a pair of pistols, which in those days would have been carried for the prince's personal protection.

The Kaiser's bridle, a gift from Wilhelm II of Germany, has not been used since the diamond jubilee of Queen Victoria in 1898. The lavish design features gilt trim on the bits, solid gold buckles and gold thread embellishment on the bridoon rein.

The bridle worn by Queen Elizabeth II's horse, Burmese, at the annual military ceremony, Trooping the Colour, is based on the traditional military bridle and combines a headcollar with a bridle. The detailing on the bridle is gilt and the reins are decorated with gold thread. The elaborate saddlery traditionally worn for Trooping the Colour includes gilded stirrups on the Queen's side-saddle.

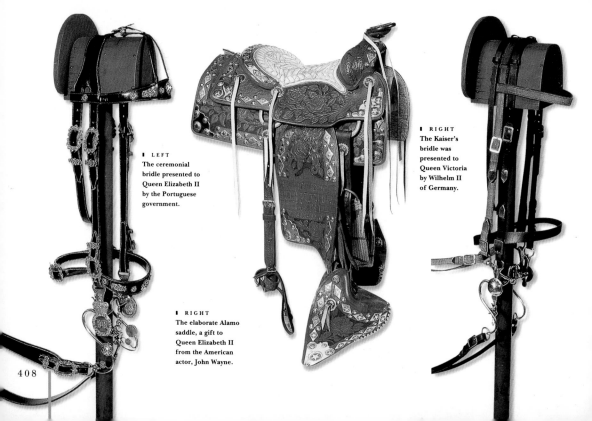

■ LEFT
The ceremonial bridle presented to Queen Elizabeth II by the Portuguese government.

■ RIGHT
The Kaiser's bridle was presented to Queen Victoria by Wilhelm II of Germany.

■ RIGHT
The elaborate Alamo saddle, a gift to Queen Elizabeth II from the American actor, John Wayne.

▌ LEFT
A highly decorative gilded stirrup from the side-saddle ridden by Queen Elizabeth II at Trooping the Colour.

▌ LEFT
A pair of side-saddles, originally belonging to Princess Mary, show how the side-saddle could be designed to let the rider sit on the off side.

▌ BELOW
The military-style bridle worn by Queen Elizabeth II's horse at Trooping the Colour.

▌ LEFT
A hunting saddle used by the Prince Consort, HRH Prince Albert, in the nineteenth century.

▌ BELOW
Queen Victoria's side-saddle, with the double pommel design, allowed the Queen to ride off either side of the saddle.

▌ BELOW
Traditional detailing on a bridle worn by Queen Elizabeth II's horse at ceremonial parades.

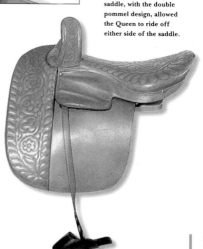

409

Girths, Cinches and Surcingles

■ ABOVE
leather Atherstone girth

■ LEFT
Atherstone girth with elastic inserts

■ ABOVE
Balding girth

GIRTHS

Girths are used to keep the saddle in place on the horse's back. They are available in leather and synthetic materials: although expensive, leather girths are very durable if well cared for, while cotton and synthetic girths are cheaper and generally less hardwearing.

The **Atherstone girth** is padded and has a contoured shape to prevent it rubbing the horse's elbow. It is an ideal choice for general or competition use. The Atherstone is also available with strong elastic inserts at one or both ends, which allows the girth to stretch as the horse expands his ribcage when galloping. Take care not to overtighten an elasticated girth as it can still cause the horse discomfort, even though it stretches.

The **Balding girth** is made of a single piece of leather split into three. It was originally developed for polo ponies: the special shape helps to minimize chafing and girth galls.

The **three-fold leather girth** has become less common since the arrival of synthetic alternatives. It comprises a single piece of leather which is folded around a piece of oiled fabric. The girth is fitted with the open side away from the horse's elbow to prevent pinching. The oiled fabric helps to keep the leather supple.

The **Humane girth** has girth tabs which slide through special loops allowing the girth to move with the horse. The **Cottage Craft girth** is an inexpensive foam-padded, cotton girth which is both comfortable for the horse and easy to wash. **Cord girths**, made from thick cotton cords, have an open design which helps to reduce sweating while the cord strands themselves help to keep the girth in place.

Neoprene girths are available for general purpose and dressage saddles. The fabric (commonly used for wet suits) does not absorb sweat and helps to reduce rubbing. **Narrow-webbing girths** are often used on show horses and ponies, as they

■ RIGHT
three-fold leather girth

■ RIGHT
Humane girth

■ RIGHT
Cottage Craft girth

■ RIGHT
neoprene girth

■ RIGHT
Wintec girth

■ RIGHT
dressage girth

■ RIGHT
Cottage Craft dressage girth

are less obtrusive than traditional girths. They consist of two narrow strips of webbing and a small section of textured rubber to prevent the girth slipping.

The **dressage girth**, also known as the **Lonsdale girth**, is shorter than a traditional girth as it is designed for use with the dressage saddle, which has longer girth tabs (billets).

The **Fitzwilliam girth**, used with a side-saddle, features an extra balance strap to prevent the saddle from slipping. The **leather stud-guard girth** is useful when competing in show-jumping events or horse trials. It is designed to prevent horses fitted with studs from injuring themselves when they snatch up their forelegs over a fence.

Racing girths are made from elastic or from webbing with elastic inserts, allowing the horse the freedom to expand his ribcage at a full gallop.

Accessories can be fitted to the girth as aids to the horse's comfort. The **fleece girth sleeve (cover)**, a soft fleece or sheepskin sleeve which slides over the girth, helps to keep the girth clean and minimize rubbing and galling. **A girth extender** is a short leather strap used to lengthen the girth. **Girth (buckle) guards** are fitted over the **girth tabs (billets)** on the saddle to prevent the girth buckles from rubbing and damaging the saddle flap. **A stud guard** is a pad of leather which is fitted to a standard girth to protect the horse when jumping, in the same way as a

■ RIGHT
narrow-webbing show girth

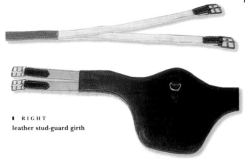

■ RIGHT
leather stud-guard girth

■ ABOVE
A racing saddle fitted with a surcingle.

■ LEFT
A surcingle fitted over the saddle for cross-country riding.

■ RIGHT
Western fleece cinch

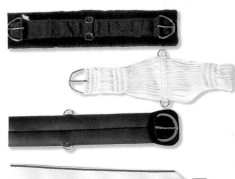

■ RIGHT
Western strand (string) cinch

■ RIGHT
neoprene cinch

■ RIGHT
all-elastic racing girth

■ RIGHT
racing girths

■ RIGHT
Fitzwilliam side saddle girth

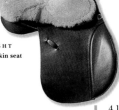

stud-guard girth. The **sheepskin seat saver** is fitted over the saddle to make it more comfortable to ride for long periods of time – ideal for endurance or trail-riding.

■ LEFT
girth extender

CINCHES AND SURCINGLES

Western saddles are held in place with cinches rather than girths. Cinches are attached to the saddle by a large buckle at each end and are available in a range of materials: **neoprene** and **padded fleece cinches** help to reduce chafing, while **strand cinches**, made from cord or woven horse hair, prevent the horse sweating.

Racing surcingles, in elastic or webbing with an elastic insert, go over the top of the saddle. They are used in addition to a racing girth to provide extra security in the event of the racing girth breaking. For the same reason, the **overgirth** or **surcingle** is fitted over the saddle for the cross-country phase of horse trials.

■ LEFT
all-elastic racing surcingle

■ LEFT
tubular racing surcingle

■ ABOVE
fleece girth sleeve (cover)

■ LEFT
leather stud guard

■ RIGHT
girth (buckle) guard

■ RIGHT
sheepskin seat saver

411

Stirrups

Stirrups, also known as irons, are available in a variety of styles but are almost always made from stainless steel, which is extremely strong. For safety, the stirrup should be wide enough to allow about 1–1.5cm/½ in on either side of the rider's foot to avoid the foot getting caught in the stirrup in the event of a fall.

The most common English stirrup is the **Prussian side open bottom**, also known as a **hunting iron**. Very useful for dressage and jumping are heavier models such as the **fillis stirrup**, which give the rider more balance. The **off-set fillis** is a popular choice for jumping. The eye of the stirrup is set to the inside, which encourages the knee and thigh to be pressed into the saddle for extra grip.

Alternatives to steel become necessary when weight is important. Contemporary choices include the **carbon-fibre stirrup** which is both light and strong, and features graphite treads for extra grip. **Polymer** and **Flexi-ride stirrups** are designed specifically for endurance and trail-riding. The rubberized material absorbs concussion, enhancing the rider's comfort when riding for long periods of time. **Cradle-bottom racing stirrups**, which are designed purely for racing, are made from lightweight aluminium.

Western stirrups consist of a wooden or Ralide frame covered in leather; a more decorative design is made from inlaid wood. For parades, a toe cover called a *tapadero* can be fitted to the stirrup. The **side-saddle stirrup** features a round eye through which the stirrup leather passes, allowing greater flexibility of movement for the rider's leg.

Rubber treads can be fitted into stirrups to provide extra grip for muddy boots or when riding in wet weather. The treads lie flat inside the stirrup, although angled or wedged treads are also available for dressage and jumping.

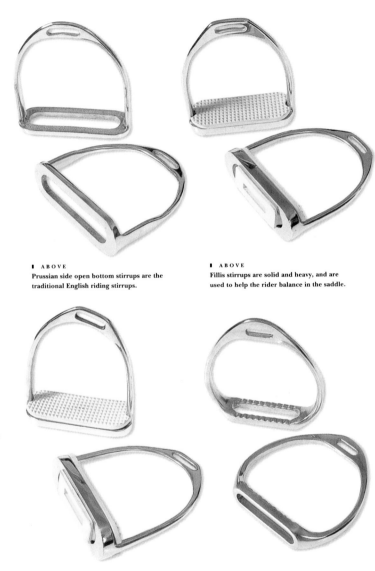

▮ ABOVE
Prussian side open bottom stirrups are the traditional English riding stirrups.

▮ ABOVE
Fillis stirrups are solid and heavy, and are used to help the rider balance in the saddle.

▮ ABOVE
The eye of the off-set fillis stirrup is set to the inside, pressing the knee towards the saddle.

▮ ABOVE
Cradle-bottom racing stirrups are made from lightweight aluminium.

Saddle

Saddle bags, pouches or p
lightweight bags which ca
the saddle, positioned be
over either side of the ho
functional accessories us
provisions needed on rid
hours or more.

The **trail pad**, a fleece
incorporated into a canv
pockets, is ideal for end
long-distance pleasure r
numnah sits comfortabl
while the canvas overlay

As its name suggests,
canteen was traditionall
the refreshments neces
fox hunting. The smart
is just the right size to l
warming liquor.

Argentinian saddle b
from wool in tradition:
used by *gauchos* to carr
for days at a time out c

■ ABOVE
leather-covered Western stirrup

■ ABOVE
inlaid wood Western stirrups

■ ABOVE
Toe covers can be fitted to ordinary
stirrups. They are commonly used in
endurance and trail-riding events and
will prevent the rider's foot sliding
through and getting stuck in the
stirrup.

■ ABOVE
Polymer and Flexi-ride stirrups are
designed to increase foot comfort
when endurance or trail-riding.

■ LEFT
Carbon-fibre
stirrups are
lightweight but
extremely strong.

■ ABOVE
The round eye of the side-saddle
stirrup allows the lower leg greater
flexibility.

■ RIGHT
Rubber treads are fitted to
stirrups to provide extra grip.

Saddle Care

A good saddle is a costly piece of equipment and it is important to look after it properly, not only because it is expensive to repair but because a damaged saddle may harm your horse's back.

incorporating thou
styrene beads. Whe
the air is pumped
the beads mould t
between the saddle

Western and po
traditionally fitted
blanket. The **Nava**
Western blanket p

HOW TO CARRY A SADDLE

> **LEFT**
> The saddle should be carried in either of the two ways shown: over the forearm with the back of the saddle nearest the elbow (*far left*), or against the side of the body with the hand holding on to the pommel (*left*).

HOW TO STORE A SADDLE

Once you have removed the saddle from the horse, it can be placed over a fence or saddle rack before being returned to the tack room. (If you leave the saddle over a stable door, the horse will most probably nudge it off.)

You can also put the saddle on the ground, pommel down and with the seat facing the wall. Place the girth between the pommel and the ground to protect the leather.

Saddles are best kept on saddle racks in a clean and dry tack room – damp conditions will damage the leather. Do not leave sweaty numnahs or girths attached to the saddle; remove and clean them before putting them away separately.

> **ABOVE**
> Aerborn Coolback
> cloth has a special
> sweat from the hors

> **ABOVE**
> The flat shock
> weight along

> **ABOVE**
> The Pro-lite
> absorb impa

HOW TO CLEAN A SADDLE

1 Place the saddle on a stand. Remove the stirrup leathers, girth and numnah. With warm water and a dampened sponge, work all over the saddle removing any mud, sweat and general dirt. Take care not to let the leather get too wet.

2 Whilst cleaning, check the saddle for wear and tear. Pay particular attention to the stitching, especially where the girth tabs (billets) are joined to the saddle.

3 Don't forget to clean the underside of the saddle as this can get sweaty even if a numnah or saddle cloth has been used.

4 Allow the leather to dry slightly before applying the saddle soap. Use a fresh sponge and work the saddle soap into the leather with a circular rubbing motion. Cover the entire surface of the saddle, including under the saddle flaps.

SADDLING UP

1 Place a numnah or saddle cloth on the horse's back, making sure it is positioned sufficiently high up the horse's withers.

2 Lift the saddle over the horse's back and carefully lower it into position on top of the numnah or saddle cloth. Ensure both saddle flaps are lying flat against the horse's sides.

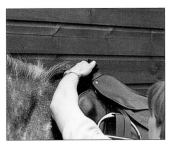

3 Pull the numnah or saddle cloth up into the gullet of the saddle so that it is clear of the horse's withers.

4 Numnahs usually have straps to anchor them to the saddle and stop them from slipping. Attach the top straps to the saddle's girth tabs (billets) through which the girth is fitted above the girth guard before doing up the girth.

5 Buckle the girth to the off side (right) of the saddle first and pass it through the bottom strap on the numnah. Move back to the near side (left) of the horse, reach underneath him and take hold of the girth.

6 Pass the girth through the retaining strap on the numnah before buckling to the saddle girth tabs on the near side.

5 Remove dirt and grease from the stirrup leathers with a sponge. Apply the saddle soap and check the stitching for wear. Check that the leathers have not stretched: because we mount from the near side, one leather will become longer than the other if they are not switched regularly.

7 Tighten up the girth gradually (it should be equal on both sides) until there is just room to fit the flat of your hand between the girth and the horse's side. Picking up the horse's feet, one at a time, and pulling them forward will also help you to judge if the girth is comfortable for the horse.

8 Once the girth has been tightened, slide the buckle guard down over the girth buckles to prevent them from rubbing against and damaging the saddle flaps. Slide your hand round the horse's belly under the girth to ensure that there are no wrinkles in the horse's skin.

Bridles and Bits

Along with the saddle, the bridle and bit are the most important pieces of equipment for the ridden horse. Combined with the rider's legs, voice and body position, the bridle and bit provide that important line of communication which allows you to control the horse.

Bridles are traditionally made of leather. However, synthetic bridles, which come in a choice of vivid colours, are becoming much more popular, especially in the sports of flat racing and endurance riding.

The variety of bits available can be bewildering, and choosing the right bit for a horse is almost a science in itself. To simplify matters, bits are divided into five groups which are categorized by their action, based on the area of the horse's head to which pressure is applied. The five groups are: snaffles, doubles, pelhams, gag snaffles and bitless bridles. It is important to make an accurate judgment over your choice of bit: a bit that is too weak will result in the rider having no control over the horse, while one that is too severe will encourage the horse to fight against it.

Western Bridle

The traditional Western bridle is fastened with narrow leather thongs, which enabled the cowboy to carry out running repairs on any items of broken tack himself when he was miles from the nearest saddler. Western bridles are referred to as either "one-ear" or "split-ear". The headpiece (crownpiece) of a split-ear bridle is made from a single piece of leather which has slits cut into it to fit over each ear. This is to prevent the bridle from being pulled off accidentally. The one-ear bridle incorporates a definite loop which fits over one of the horse's ear. The reins of the Western bridle are not joined at the end. This is to avoid the risk of the horse getting a foot caught in the reins if they trail on the ground.

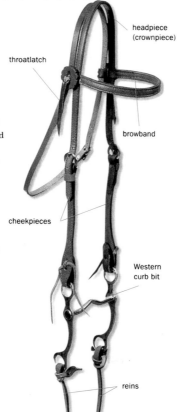

headpiece (crownpiece)

throatlatch

browband

cheekpieces

Western curb bit

reins

Endurance 2-in-1 Bridle

The endurance bridle is a combination of a headcollar (crownpiece) and a standard bridle. The cheekpieces and reins can be quickly unclipped to leave just the headcollar in place. The headcollar can also be ridden as a Scawbrig, a type of bitless bridle, by attaching the reins to the noseband. The endurance bridle (also known as the combination bridle) has proved popular with endurance riders because of its practical design: the bit can be removed quickly to give the horse a drink during competition, while the reins very usefully double as a lead rope.

THE MAIN POINTS OF CONTROL

Bits, bitless bridles and certain types of nosebands will all act on specific parts of the horse's head.

The poll – the headpiece (crownpiece) of the bridle applies pressure here when a gag or curb bit is used.

The nose – bitless bridles and specific types of nosebands affect the nose.

The mouthcorners – snaffle bits bring pressure on the corners of the horse's mouth and lips.

Side of the face – bits with full cheeks, D rings or large racing rings affect this area.

Curb groove – the curb chain fitted with a pelham or Weymouth bit affects the curb groove.

Roof of the mouth – bits with ported mouthpieces affect this area.

Tongue – all bits apply pressure to the tongue.

Bars – all bits affect the bars, a sensitive part of the horse's mouth between the incisors and premolar teeth.

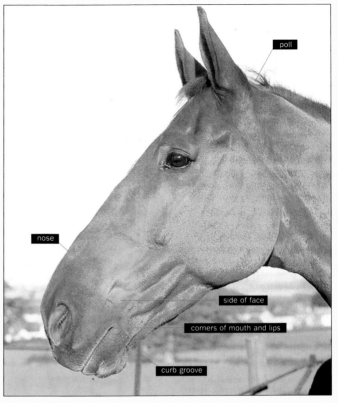

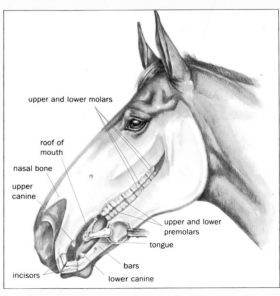

Training Aids and Gadgets

There is a saying that gadgets and training aids are fine in the hands of experts but that experts have no need for them. This may apply in an ideal world but every horseman or woman, however expert, will encounter problems when schooling and training horses and may occasionally need additional help in the form of an aid or a gadget.

A training aid is a piece of equipment used to develop a well-schooled, obedient horse to improve his performance, while a gadget is a piece of equipment which prevents or restrains an aspect of the horse's behaviour which makes him dangerous or difficult to ride.

A degree of skill is required when using training aids or gadgets. The equipment must be fitted correctly, and you must be aware of its strength and severity. Only use it when it is specifically required, never as a matter of course. Training aids and gadgets in the wrong hands can damage the horse physically and psychologically.

Martingales

Martingales are designed to assist the bridle in controlling the horse. They prevent the horse from raising his head beyond the point at which the rider can control him.

The **running martingale** consists of a neck strap and a second strap which is attached to the girth and passes between the horse's front legs before dividing into two pieces. At the end of each of these straps is a small metal ring through which the reins pass. **Rein stops** should be fitted to the reins, below the bit, to prevent the martingale rings from getting caught on the bit. When the horse carries his head in the correct position no pressure is felt. However, when he raises his head above a certain point, the martingale restricts the movement of the reins which in turn causes the bit to bear down on the bars of the horse's mouth. The running martingale should be fitted so that the rings are in line with the withers to prevent it putting any pressure on the

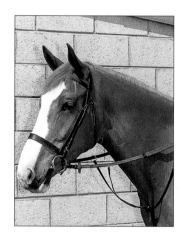

▌ **ABOVE**
running martingale

▌ **BELOW LEFT**
combined breastplate and martingale

▌ **BELOW RIGHT**
bib martingale

reins when the horse's head is held in the correct position. It should not be used in conjunction with a curb bit.

The **bib martingale** is a variation on the running martingale. The two straps of the martingale are joined by a triangle of leather. This is to prevent an excitable horse from getting caught up in the straps; the design is often used on racehorses.

The **combined breastplate and martingale** is a traditional heavyweight hunting-style breastplate used to stop the saddle from slipping back. The breastplate has a central ring to which a running martingale attachment is fixed.

The **standing martingale** has a single strap which is attached to the girth, passes between the horse's front legs and is fixed to the back of the noseband (a cavesson or the cavesson part of a flash noseband). Like the running martingale, it has a neck strap. When correctly fitted it should be possible to push the martingale strap up into the horse's gullet.

❚ LEFT AND
BELOW
The Irish
martingale is
used to prevent
the reins being
thrown over the
horse's head in
the event of
a fall. It is
often used on
racehorses, as
shown here on
Desert Orchid.

A **rubber martingale stop** should always be fitted to running and standing martingales to stop the martingale from slipping through the neck strap, which could result in the horse getting a foot caught in the straps.

The **Market Harborough** consists of a leather strap attached to the girth, which passes between the horse's front legs before dividing into two straps with a clip at each end. These straps pass through the bit rings and are clipped on to one of a series of rings on the side of the reins. Like the running martingale, the Market Harborough will only put pressure on the bit (and as a consequence on the bars of the horse's mouth) if the horse brings his head up beyond a certain point. The Market Harborough should only be used with an ordinary snaffle.

The **Irish martingale**, unlike other martingales, has no direct action on the horse's head carriage. It consists of a short piece of leather with a ring at either end

through which the reins pass. The Irish martingale is used to prevent the reins from being pulled over the horse's head in the event of a fall. It can also be used for horses who have a habit of suddenly tossing their heads in the air – "star gazers" – resulting in the reins being thrown over their heads.

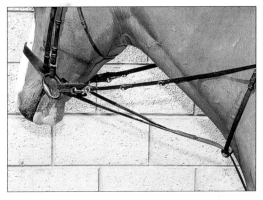

❚ LEFT
Market Harborough
martingale

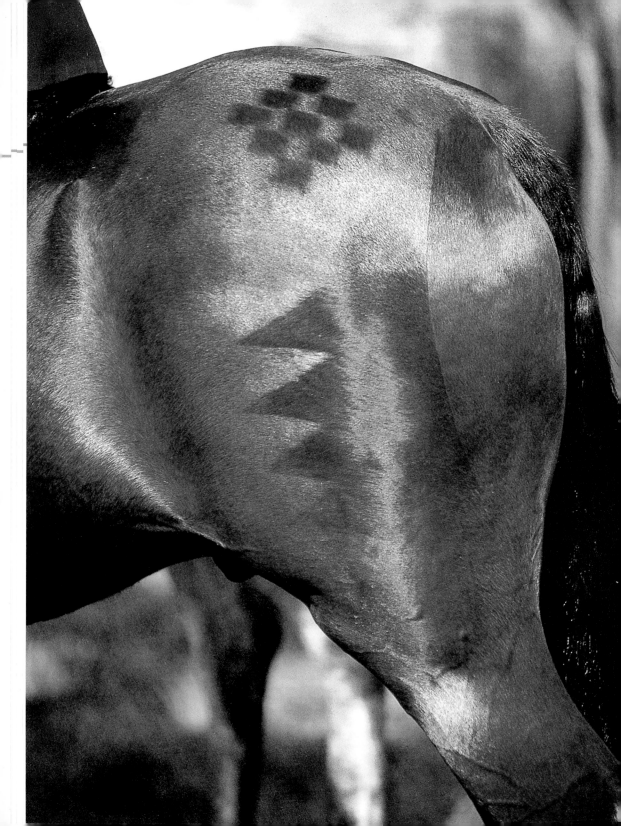

Grooming Equipment

Regular grooming is an essential part of good horse management. It is not simply a question of making the horse look smart. Far more important is the fact that thorough brushing helps keep the horse healthy by removing accumulated dust, dead skin and hair, and helping to keep the pores open and clean. During hard work the horse's skin excretes waste matter in the form of sweat. It is important that the skin and coat are kept clean to enable this system to work efficiently. A good, strenuous grooming also serves as a massage, improving the horse's muscle tone. In addition, grooming helps to keep the horse's tack and rugs clean, which in turn prevents sores. While the stabled horse needs daily grooming both before and after exercise, the grass-kept horse requires far less attention. Although the areas under the saddle and bridle must always be cleaned before tacking up, only the worst of the mud or grease should be removed elsewhere for appearances' sake. Horses and ponies who live out need the natural grease and dirt in their coats to help keep them warm and dry, especially in winter.

Grooming Technique

The stabled horse needs a thorough grooming every day. This is best carried out after exercise when the horse is warm. The pores of the skin will be open and grease and dirt will be easier to remove. The horse should be tied up during grooming.

Each **foot** should be picked up and carefully cleaned out with the hoof pick. The pick should be used from the horse's heel towards the toe to avoid damaging the frog. Dirt from the feet should be placed in a skip, not in the horse's bed.

The body brush is used to clean the horse's entire **body,** starting with the neck and working down to the shoulders and the front legs, along the body, over the hindquarters and down the hindlegs. Use the brush – in the left hand for the nearside, in the right hand for the offside

– with brisk, firm strokes and after every few strokes clean the bristles on the metal curry comb, which is held in the other hand. Periodically the dirt should be tapped from the curry comb. This should be done in the doorway or just outside the stable, not into the bedding. Care should be taken when grooming not to bang the horse's bony projections, for example those of the hips and legs, and the brush should not be used with too much pressure over the loins. Having completed

one side, move round to the other side of the horse and repeat the process.

The body brush is also used to clean the **head,** which should be done very gently. The horse should not be tied up for this, in case he pulls back. The headcollar should be fastened round his neck, leaving his nose free.

Brush out the **mane** and **tail** with the body brush, taking care not to break the hairs. The tail should be held away from the horse's body with your free hand and

■ LEFT
A very sweaty or dirty horse may be washed down provided he can be dried quickly to prevent chilling. Excess water is removed with a sweat scraper.

1 The body brush is used to give the entire body a thorough grooming. It should be used in the direction of the lie of the coat.

2 The curry comb is held in the spare hand and used for cleaning the body brush – never use it on the horse.

3 The hoof wall should be kept clean – a stiff brush may be used to remove mud and other forms of dirt.

1 Grooming begins with picking out the feet. The hoof pick shold always be used from the heel towards the toe.

2 Remnants of dirt may be removed from the area round the frog with a brush.

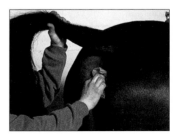

3 The dock should be sponged each time the horse is groomed. Use a different sponge from the one used for the eyes and nose.

1 Tail bandages are made of elasticated cotton and are about 3 inches (8cm) wide and 10 feet (3m) long.

2 The bandage is started high up, as near as possible to the top of the dock.

3 A loose flap is left at the top and then turned down and bandaged over. This helps prevent slipping.

4 The bandage is applied down the length of the dock and up again. It should not be fitted too tightly

5 The bandage is secured with tapes and the dock should be eased into its natural shape.

brushed out a lock at a time. Any tangles should be teased out with the fingers. A very muddy tail will need washing. To finish off the mane and tail, dip the bristles of the water brush in clean water (not the horse's drinking water) and go lightly over the mane to "lay" it down smoothly. Do the same to the top hairs of the tail. A pulled tail should be bandaged for an hour or so afterwards to keep it tidy.

Use a damp sponge to clean the horse's **eyes** and **nostrils** and another for the **dock.** In the case of geldings the **sheath** will need sponging out once every couple of weeks or so to remove the greasy discharge which accumulates and can cause the horse discomfort. Special solutions can be obtained for this purpose or you can use a mild soap and warm water. Use the same sponge that is used for cleaning his dock. The easiest time to give him a thorough clean in this area is when he is staling. Do it carefully and gently – and beware of being kicked should the horse object. If you are unable to catch the moment when the horse is staling, clean out the sheath by gently inserting the sponge inside it and cleaning all round. Rinse the whole area several times and dry off with a towel.

The finishing touch to the whole grooming process is applied by running a damp stable rubber or other cloth over the entire coat to add a final polish. Wisping with a hay wisp or pad, when done, takes place after regular grooming since its purpose is not to clean but to **massage.** The pad or wisp is applied in

GROOMING TIPS

☛ Never try to groom a sweaty horse – walk him about until he is dry.

☛ Never try to brush off wet mud – either hose it off or let it dry first.

☛ To dry off a wet horse in the stable cover him with a sheet or rug made of "breathable" material or put a layer of straw along his back and quarters with a rug over the top (this is known as "thatching").

☛ To remove dried mud use a dandy brush or rubber curry comb but not too roughly – it may be necessary to remove mud from sensitive areas of skin, such as inside the hindlegs, with your hand.

☛ In cold weather keep a clipped horse warm during grooming by turning his rugs back and forward (as when quartering) rather than removing them altogether.

☛ Give all rugs and blankets a thorough shaking every week – it is pointless to put dusty rugs back on to a clean horse.

☛ Never stand directly behind a horse.

☛ Never sit or kneel on the floor to reach the lower parts – always squat or bend so that you can move quickly if he does.

☛ Keep a watchful eye open for any skin injuries or tell-tail lumps or bumps, particularly on the legs, which could warn of impending soundness problems.

☛ With the grass-kept horse clean the area under the saddle and brush off the worst of the mud for appearances' sake but do not attempt regular, thorough grooming.

much the same way as a brush, but with a firmer thump (though not too hard). It is used on the large muscular areas of the horse (the neck, shoulders and quarters). It is said to improve the circulation and muscle tone. It should never be used on the more tender areas, such as the loins, nor on the bony areas, such as the legs.

A thorough grooming will take from half to three-quarters of an hour, depending on the initial cleanliness of the horse's skin and coat – and the strength and endurance of the groom! Grooming is most effective if you stand a little away from the horse in order to put your weight behind the brush.

A less comprehensive type of grooming called **quartering** is used to prepare the horse in the morning for exercise. Its purpose is to remove any surface dirt accumulated during the night and to make the horse generally presentable. Quartering involves unfastening his rugs, turning them back over his loins and giving his front half a quick brush over, then turning his rugs forward and doing the same to his hind end. Any stains and bedding marks should be removed, if necessary by using a damp sponge or water brush. The damp areas should be dried off with a stable rubber or a towel. The mane and tail should be brushed through and all traces of bedding removed. The feet should be picked clean and the eyes, nostrils and dock sponged. Quartering takes between ten and twenty minutes, depending on the horse's size and how dirty he is.

Clipping and Trimming

Clipping horses is hard work and can be dangerous. It should never be carried out alone. The beginner should learn the techniques by watching an expert at work. If in doubt, find someone else to clip your horse, at least to begin with so that you can find out how he behaves.

Having decided on the type of clip, all lines (for example the leg lines and saddle patch) should be marked on the horse's coat with chalk or a damp piece of saddle soap. To mark the saddle patch put the horse's usual saddle on his back, without its fittings, make sure it is in the position where it lies when he is being ridden, and draw round it. It is better to make the saddle patch a little larger than it will finally need to be to make allowance for any mistakes when clipping the edges. A badly positioned saddle patch will spoil the look of the horse.

Start clipping at the front of the horse, on the neck or shoulder, and work your way backwards section by section. The clippers should be used against the lie of the coat (broadly speaking from the back of the horse towards the front) with long, sweeping strokes. Each stroke should be parallel to the one above or below it and should slightly overlap the previous one.

Take care when clipping the top line of the neck not to cut into the mane. Clip a short bridle path out of the mane just

▐ RIGHT
Essential clipping and trimming equipment: electric clippers, electric and battery driven trimmers, spare clipper blades, oil, small brush (for cleaning clogged blades) and screwdriver (for changing fuses if necessary).

behind the ears where the headpiece of the bridle lies. This does not need to be very long: 2 inches (5cm) is adequate.

After the neck and shoulders clip the body and finally the hindquarters. Be particularly careful when clipping awkward places such as the delicate skin below the stifle and the folds between the front legs. The stifle skin should be held with your spare hand to straighten out the folds. An assistant should hold each foreleg up and forward in turn to stretch the folds of skin. Holding up a foreleg will also help prevent a horse from fidgeting or kicking. When clipping between the hindlegs be particularly watchful in case the horse does try to kick out. Keeping hold of his tail will help to prevent this.

The most difficult part of the horse to clip well is the head. If a horse is really frightened of having the clippers near his

head it is far better to leave it unclipped. If the horse's head is to be clipped, first remove the headcollar. If he will not stand still without some form of restraint a halter is easier to work round with the clippers than a headcollar. Where you start will depend very much on the horse but the cheeks are probably the best place. Rest the clippers, switched off, against the cheekbone for a few moments until the horse becomes used to their presence. Then if he does not object switch on and work carefully over both cheeks, underneath from the chin to the throat, up over the front of the head and over the forehead. Because the head is so bony the clippers should be used as lightly as possible to reduce vibration. Be particularly careful when working near the eye.

Some people clip off the horse's whiskers round his muzzle but since these

The mane is shortened and thinned by means of pulling, using a mane comb. Remove only a few hairs at a time to prevent soreness and damp the mane down afterwards.

To neaten an untidy tail, pull hair from the sides and centre of the dock, preferably when the horse is warm and the pores are open.

A mane comb and sharp, round-ended scissors are used to trim excess hair from the pasterns and fetlocks of unclipped legs. Take care not to leave "steps" of hair.

▌ RIGHT
Holding up a foreleg
smooths out skin
creases and also stops
the horse fidgeting.

▌ MIDDLE RIGHT
Proceed carefully and
gently when clipping
the head.

▌ BOTTOM RIGHT
Holding the tail helps
prevent a horse from
kicking. The tail is
bandaged to keep it
clear of the clipper
blades.

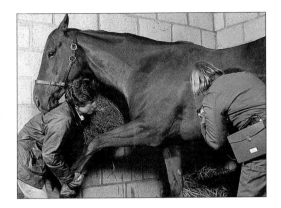

CLIPPING AND TRIMMING TIPS

☞ During clipping feel the underside of the blades every few minutes – if they are becoming hot, switch off and allow them to cool down before continuing.

☞ During clipping clean and oil the blades every ten to fifteen minutes.

☞ During clipping keep the horse warm by throwing a rug over the clipped areas – a cold horse will fidget more than a warm one.

☞ Always clip in good light conditions – start in the morning.

☞ Never try to clip a sweaty or dirty horse.

☞ For the best results do not clip until the horse's winter coat has "set" (i.e. is fully grown) – usually mid-autumn.

☞ To gauge the correct position and angle of leg lines measure one hand's width from where the foreleg joins the chest (for the V) and two hands' widths below the elbow; measure four hands' widths below the top of the stifle on the hindleg and two hands' widths above the point of the hock.

☞ Accustom a nervous horse to the feel of clippers by running hand clippers (i.e. non-motorized ones) over him.

☞ Have clippers serviced, and the blades reground, regularly.

☞ Ask your veterinary surgeon to administer a sedative to a horse who is really dangerous to clip.

☞ Pull manes and tails when the horse is warm, either on a hot day or after exercise – the hair will come out more easily while the pores are open, which is easier for you and more comfortable for the horse.

☞ Pull hair, whenever possible, from the underside of the mane – this will encourage it to lie flat.

are used as sensors it is preferable, and kinder, to leave them alone.

To trim the ears, hold each one in turn and run the clippers along the outside edge only. Never try to clip the hair from inside the ear as the horse needs this as protection from insects and dirt. Never clip the eyelashes. Be careful when clipping the top of the head not to cut into the forelock.

If the horse's legs are left unclipped it will probably be necessary to trim his fetlocks and pasterns to make him look tidy. Use a mane comb and scissors (with rounded ends for safety) to remove excess feather, taking care not to create "steps" of hair but to leave a smooth line. Trim any thick hair from around the coronet.

If the horse's head is left unclipped, long hairs around the jaw may also be removed with scissors and comb. Scissors may be used to trim the long hairs from the edge of the ears.

Manes are kept neat by means of pulling, which involves plucking out strands of hair until the mane is the desired length and thickness. If the horse finds this too uncomfortable, it is possible to tidy up the mane with a thinning comb but never be tempted to use scissors which will give a very unsatisfactory result. Pulling can usually be achieved if you take your time and do only a small section of the mane at a time, spreading the whole job over a number of days.

An untidy tail can also be improved by pulling out some of the hairs from the top of the dock. Hair should be removed from the sides and, to a lesser extent, from the

centre. As with the mane, it is best to remove a few hairs each day to prevent soreness. After pulling, the tail should be dampened with a water brush and bandaged to make the hair lie flat (do not leave the bandage on overnight). A pulled

tail will need regular pulling if it is to keep its neat shape. A horse who lives out during the winter should not have his tail pulled – the hair at the top of the dock is there to protect him from rain and snow. To trim the bottom of the tail, raise the horse's dock to the position where he carries it when he is on the move. With your other hand hold the hair at the bottom of the tail and then cut off the hair to the required length. The end of the tail should be parallel to the ground when the horse is moving.

Horse Clothing and Equipment

The ridden horse needs a variety of clothing and equipment to keep him warm, clean and dry, and to protect him from injury. Rugs are a necessity for clipped horses and for fine-skinned, hot-blooded types such as Thoroughbreds. Modern rugs are lighter in weight than their predecessors, making them more comfortable for horses to wear and easier to clean. They are also more effective at keeping the horse warm, dry, cool or clean.

There is always a risk that a horse may be injured during exercise or when he is competing or travelling to and from shows. To minimize the risk there is a range of equipment and clothing available to protect him literally from head to tail.

Sheets and Coolers

BELOW
A linen summer (stable) sheet can be used to keep
the stabled horse clean during warmer weather.

SHEETS

Sheets are made from lighter materials
than turnout or stable rugs. A sheet can
be used either in the summer months
when the temperatures are higher, or
immediately before or after exercise.

Summer (stable) sheets, made from
linen or cotton, are lightweight rugs used
to help keep the stabled horse clean.

Paddock sheets are shaped rugs in
cotton or wool, so-called because they are
used to keep racehorses warm while being
paraded in the paddock before the race.
The paddock rug is held in place with a
surcingle and breastgirth. It can double as
an exercise sheet, also called a half-sheet
or quarter-sheet, to keep the racehorse's
hindquarters warm during early morning
exercise on the gallops.

Many exercise sheets are designed to
keep the horse warm and dry while active,
and are particularly useful for clipped
horses. The synthetic polypropylene fabric
used for the **wicking exercise sheet** will
only allow moisture to pass through if
the horse begins to sweat. This type of
exercise sheet is worn under the saddle.

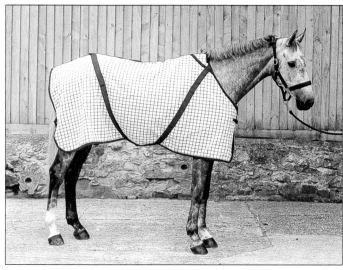

BELOW
paddock sheet

COOLERS

Coolers are multi-purpose rugs, often
incorporating the latest developments in
fabric technology. They allow the horse
to dry off quickly after exercise or bathing
without the risk of catching a chill because
of a wicking effect which allows moisture
to pass from the horse's body through the
fabric. Cooler rugs are ideal for those
horses with a tendency to sweat profusely
when travelling.

The non-absorbent breathable fabric
of the **Coolmasta rug** makes it suitable
for use as an anti-sweat rug, a travelling
rug or a stable rug. The polypropylene
fabric of the **Universal wicking rug** allows
dampness from the horse's body to pass
through the rug to prevent chills, as does
the **fleece rug**. The **Combi sweat (anti-
sweat) rug and fly sheet (scrim)** is a fine-
mesh rug. The knit of the cotton fabric
creates air pockets which help the horse
to dry off quickly. These rugs can be used
on a stabled horse under a lightweight
summer sheet to speed up the drying
process after exercise.

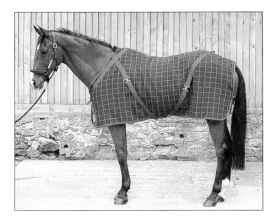

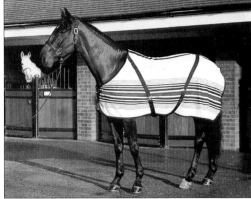

▌ ABOVE LEFT
Universal wicking rug. A multi-purpose rug which
lets body moisture through the fabric to prevent
the horse catching a chill.

▌ ABOVE RIGHT
Coolmasta synthetic rug. A cooler which is versatile
enough to be used as summer (stable) sheet,
anti-sweat rug, travel or day rug.

▌ RIGHT
Fleece rug. While moisture evaporates away
through the rug, the fleece fabric ensures that
the horse's body temperature does not drop.

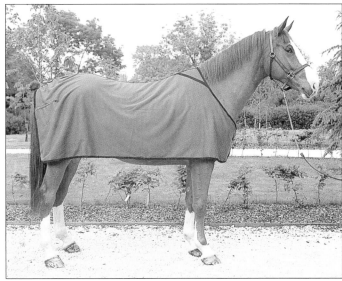

▌ BELOW
Combi sweat (anti-sweat) rug and fly sheet (scrim).
A fine mesh rug which can be used under a summer
sheet to speed up drying.

▌ BELOW RIGHT
Rain sheet. This waterproof rug (cover) will keep
the horse dry at shows and competitions.

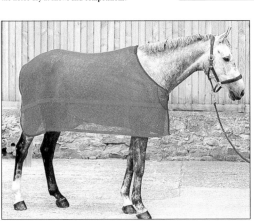

Specialist Sheets and Rugs

▮ BELOW
Continental waterproof exercise sheet

Besides the basic types of rug, an increasing number of rug products are available for more specific needs.

Exercise sheets will keep thin-skinned horses warm and dry during exercise sessions. The **continental waterproof exercise sheet** has a lightweight outer shell with a twill lining and can be fitted over the saddle in wet weather. The **fluorescent exercise sheet** ensures that both horse and rider are easily seen by other road users, and is especially useful for anyone who has to ride on roads at times of poor visibility.

The **rain sheet** is a lightweight synthetic sheet which covers the horse from ears to tail. The sheet will keep the horse dry at competitions and shows but should not be used on horses turned out in the field.

New-born foals do not normally require rugs. However, the **quilted foal rug** can be very useful in helping to keep a sickly foal warm in the stable.

The **rug bib (blanket bib)** is fitted under the rug to prevent it from rubbing the horse's shoulders, leading to sores and bare patches in his coat.

Hoods can be fitted to rugs to provide extra warmth and to help keep the horse clean. The **outdoor hood**, made from a synthetic material, can be fitted to a turnout rug. The **lycra hood** is used in the stable to keep the horse clean.

Chest extenders are panels of fabric with straps which can be buckled on to the horse's existing rug to provide a better fit.

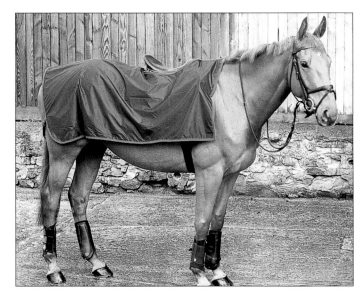

▮ BELOW
Continental waterproof exercise sheet

▮ BELOW LEFT
fluorescent exercise sheet

▮ BELOW RIGHT
wicking exercise sheet

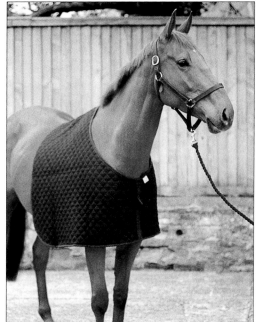

▌ ABOVE
A rug bib is fitted
under the rug to
prevent the rug
from rubbing.

▌ ABOVE
golden stripe horse blanket

▌ BELOW
lycra hood

▌ BELOW
under rug

Fitting a Rug

Whatever type of rug you use, it is important that it is fitted correctly. Rugs are often left on for long periods of time and an ill-fitting rug can cause rubbing and discomfort. Rugs are sized according to their length, with the measurement based on the length of the horse taken from the centre of the chest to the tail.

HOW TO PUT ON A RUG

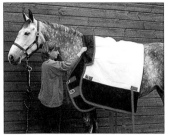

1 Stand on the near (left) side of the horse. Fold the blanket in half widthways and place it over the horse's neck. Fold the rug back over the horse's hindquarters.

2 Fasten the cross surcingles, but not too tightly: there should be room for the width of a hand between the horse's belly and the straps. These straps should be fastened first so that there is no risk of the rug ending up hanging around the horse's neck, or worse still, his legs.

HOW TO REMOVE A RUG

To remove the rug, undo the leg straps first, then the chest straps and finally the cross surcingles. Fold the front of the rug over the horse's hindquarters and slide off carefully.

3 Next fasten the chest straps: there should be room for a hand's width at the chest.

4 Finally, fasten the leg straps. Fitted correctly, the straps should hang clear of the horse's legs so that they do not rub, but should not be loose enough for the horse to get his leg caught.

■ RIGHT
Modern turnout rugs allow horses to spend time out in their field whatever the weather. It is important to remember that turned out horses should have their rugs checked at least once a day, as the rug can slip and become uncomfortable for the horse.

Rug Rollers and Surcingles

Most modern stable rugs have surcingles already fitted but separate rollers and surcingles can be used to keep in place those rugs which do not incorporate their own. A separate roller or surcingle is also necessary when more than one rug at a time is worn, to keep them both in place.

Rollers and surcingles should be fitted snugly enough to secure the rug, but they should not be so tight as to be uncomfortable for the horse after long periods of time. Correctly tightened, there should be just enough room to allow four fingers between the roller or surcingle and the rug.

Surcingles used to secure rugs differ significantly from surcingles used to secure saddles, since the needs of the turned out horse and the ridden horse are not the same. The **rug surcingle** is designed for comfort. It is wrapped in protective padding and replaces the buckles and clasps of the saddle surcingle with thick rounded straps, to allow the horse the freedom to sit or roll.

The **elasticated surcingle** fits around the horse's girth. If you are using one of these, it is a good idea to fit a pad over the withers to prevent pressure sores. The **elasticated roller** has padding built in to the area in contact with the withers, as does the **jute surcingle**, which fastens with strong leather straps.

The **anti-cast roller**, made from webbing and leather, has a large metal hoop on the top which prevents the horse from getting cast or wedged when rolling in his stable (stall).

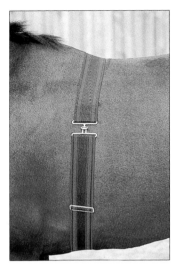

Elasticated surcingle. This type should be used with a pad over the withers to prevent pressure sores.

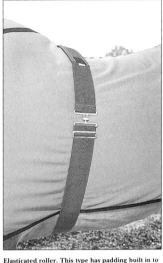

Elasticated roller. This type has padding built in to protect the withers.

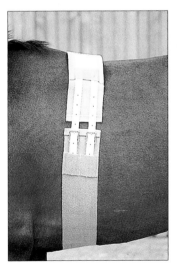

Jute surcingle. This type has built-in padding and fastens with strong leather straps.

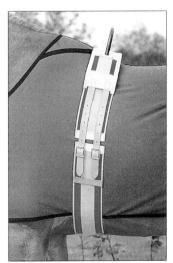

Webbing anti-cast roller. The large metal hoop on the top prevents the horse from getting cast.

Boots

Boots are designed to protect the horse's legs when travelling, turned out or being ridden, and a wide choice is available. Many equestrian activities place extreme demands on the horse's legs and protection is needed to prevent injury. Some horses are also predisposed conformationally to striking themselves accidentally while being exercised.

Brushing boots, also referred to as **splint boots**, have a reinforced pad along the inside of the boot to prevent injuries caused when one leg knocks against the other. The boot should start just below the knee and finish just below the fetlock (or ankle) joint. **Hind brushing boots** are longer than **fore brushing boots** to protect the hind cannon bone. **Leather brushing boots** have buckle and strap fastenings. They are tougher than synthetic boots but must be looked after to maintain their condition. **Synthetic brushing boots** are held in place with Velcro straps. They are lightweight and easily washed.

Leather brushing boots. These are used to prevent injuries inflicted as the horse is being brushed.

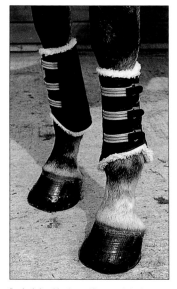

Synthetic brushing boots. These particular boots are fleece lined to prevent rubbing.

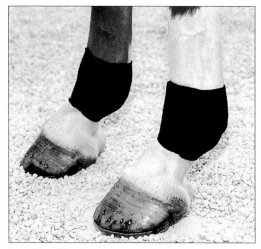

Sesamoid boots. These boots protect the base of the horse's fetlock.

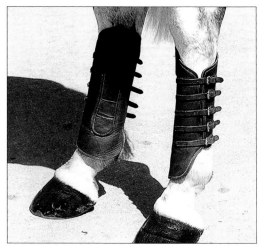

Speedicut boots. These are fitted to the hind legs to prevent injuries if the horse were to accidentally kick himself while galloping.

Speedicut boots are fitted to the hind legs and are designed to protect against injuries that occur when one leg strikes another during fast work. When the horse is travelling at high speed, the vulnerable area is the upper part of the leg, hence the boot's extra length.

Tendon boots are designed to protect the tendons which run down the back of the horse's lower foreleg, so are normally open-fronted. The boots should start high enough to protect the tendon and extend low enough to protect the fetlock joint. Leather tendon boots have buckle and strap fastenings and may be lined with sheepskin to prevent rubbing. Synthetic tendon boots usually have strap and clip fastenings.

Open-fronted boots are popular with show jumpers because they protect the vulnerable part of the horse's leg while still allowing him to feel the poles of the jump.

Sesamoid boots protect the base of the fetlock joint and are often used on

■ BELOW
Leather tendon boots protect the tendons which run down the back of the horse's leg.

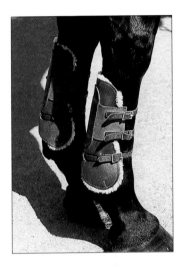

■ BELOW
Synthetic tendon boots are cheaper and easier to clean than the leather boots.

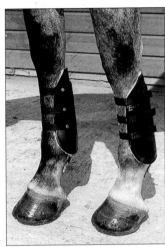

racehorses that are trained or run on all-weather or dirt tracks. The base of the fetlock would be damaged if unprotected as it touches the ground as the result of the forces exerted when galloping.

Fetlock boots are shortened versions of brushing boots, fitted to the hindlegs. Skid boots are used for Western riding, and are fitted to prevent fetlock injuries which can occur when the horse makes sliding halts.

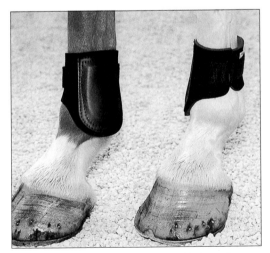

Fetlock boots. These are a shortened version of the brushing boot, and are normally fitted to the hindlegs only.

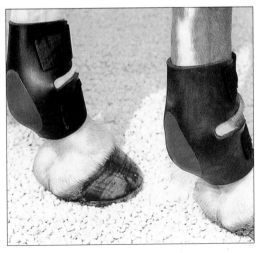

Skid boots. These are fitted to prevent injuries to the fetlock when the horse comes to a sliding halt.

Free knee boots prevent damage to the horse's knees when jumping. Because of their design – they can flip up – they are not suitable for road work or travelling. Skeleton knee boots have a lower strap fitted which prevents the pad from flipping up in the event of the horse falling. They are not suitable for jumping as there is a risk that the horse could get a hoof caught in the back strap.

The coronet ring, also called an anti-brushing ring, is fitted to one of a pair of legs to prevent brushing injuries. A sausage boot, also referred to as a shoe-boil boot, is used on stabled horses to prevent injury to the elbow when the horse lies down.

Overreach boots, or bell boots, prevent overreach injuries. An overreach is caused by the toe of the hind foot striking into the heel or coronet of the front foot. Pull-on rubber overreach boots can be difficult to get on but, once on, stay in place well. A disadvantage of this type of overreach boot is that they can flip up, in which case they will not protect the heel and coronet. Velcro-fastened rubber overreach boots are easier to put on and take off. Petal boots are less likely to flip up because of their segmented design. They are made up of a series of tough plastic segments or petals which are attached to a strap fitted around the coronet.

Covering boots are felt shoes which fit over the mare's hind feet. They are used on mares being covered, to avoid risking injury to the stallion should the mare try to kick him.

I LEFT
Free knee boots. Because of their design, these boots are not suitable for roadwork or travelling.

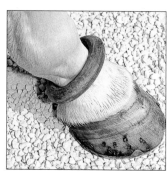

I ABOVE
Coronet ring. This is fitted to one leg to prevent brushing injuries.

I ABOVE
Skeleton knee boots. These have a lower strap fitted which prevents the pad flipping up.

I RIGHT
Sausage boot. These are used on stabled horses to prevent injuries to the elbow.

■ LEFT
Protection is necessary to guard against the hazards
encountered during the cross-country phase of a
one-day event. Because the horse is jumping fixed
objects, it is vital that his legs are protected with
boots or bandages.

■ ABOVE
Mare's covering boots. These felt shoes are fitted
over the mare's hind feet to protect the stallion
should she lash out at him.

■ ABOVE
Velcro-fastened rubber overreach boots. This type
is easier to put on and take off than the pull-on
variety of overreach boot.

■ RIGHT
Pull-on rubber
overreach boots.
These moulded boots
will sit securely on the
hoof, but they do flip
up easily and can offer
no protection when
this happens.

■ LEFT
Petal boots are made
up of a series of tough
plastic segments which
are attached to a strap.

EXERCISE BOOTS

Exercise boots, such as brushing boots, are much more convenient to use than exercise bandages (polo wraps) as they are quicker and easier to put on.

▮ BELOW
Skid boots are worn by reining horses to protect the base of the fetlock joint from injury as he comes to a sliding halt.

FITTING BRUSHING BOOTS

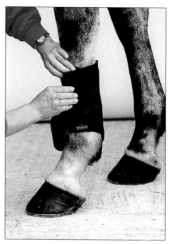

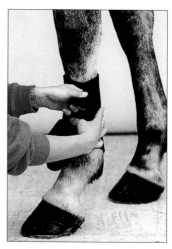

1 Never kneel down when putting on or taking off boots – always crouch so that you can get out of the way quickly should the horse suddenly move. When fitting boots with two straps, fasten the top strap first.

2 On most boots, straps fasten from the front to the back. For boots with more than two straps, fasten the middle strap first, then the top strap and finally the bottom strap or straps.

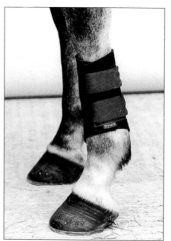

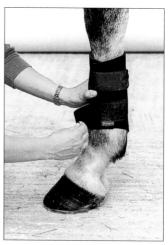

3 Be careful not to over-tighten boots as this is uncomfortable for the horse and can damage the tendons in his lower legs.

4 When removing boots, undo the bottom strap before unfastening the top one.

THERAPY BOOTS

These boots are designed to keep in place poultices, which are used to draw out dirt from a wound, and otherwise to assist in the treatment of injuries.

Rubber over-shoes fit over the horse's foot. One of these can be used to cover a foot bandage or poultice, or to protect the unshod hoof during ridden work. The **Tenderfoot sox** is used to hold a foot poultice in place.

A **tendon-hosing boot** fitted to the horse's lower leg allows cold water to be trickled down the leg to help reduce swelling caused by stresses, strains or injuries. If something more than a trickle is needed **aqua boots**, covering the entire lower leg and foot, are attached to a compressor which forces water to move around inside, massaging the lower leg.

Magnetic therapy boots are available in various designs. They incorporate thin, flexible magnetic pads which, when placed over the injured area, are said to assist in the repair of muscle, tendon or bone damage.

❚ LEFT
rubber over-shoe

❚ LEFT
magnetic therapy
boots

❚ BELOW LEFT
tendon-hosing boot

❚ BELOW RIGHT
aqua boots.

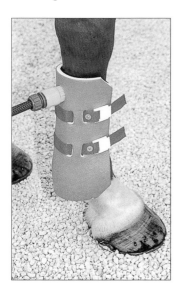

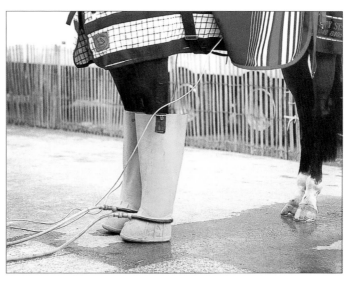

Bandages and Pads

BANDAGES

Like boots, bandages can be used to protect the horse's legs during exercise or travelling as well as for first-aid purposes.

Travelling or **stable bandages** are non-stretch bandages usually made of wool or acrylic and used for warmth and protection. To prevent pressure sores developing on the leg, they should always be used with padding underneath.

Exercise or **tail bandages** are lighter in weight than stable bandages. They are usually slightly elasticated and are held in place with ties. When used to protect the leg during competitions, in particular horse trials, they can be stitched in place. They will help to smooth the tail hair down as well as protecting the tail while the horse is travelling to the competition.

Polo wraps are made from strong, shock-absorbent felt. Unlike traditional bandages, polo wraps do not require padding underneath.

A **cohesive bandage** is a stretchy bandage which sticks to itself. It can be used as an alternative to an exercise bandage or for holding dressings and poultices in place.

PADS

Bandages should never be applied directly to the leg (except for polo bandages) but should be used with bandage pads to help reduce the risk of pressure sores developing on the legs.

Felt pads are hardwearing and shock absorbent, but they do not mould easily to the shape of the horse's leg. **Cotton quilted pads** are easily washable and hardwearing but, like felt, do not mould easily to the horse's leg. **Porter boots** are hard-shelled leg protectors which mould to the shape of the horse's leg and are held in place with an exercise bandage. They are used instead of pads to protect the leg from injury during competitions.

❚ LEFT
travelling or stable bandages

❚ BELOW LEFT
exercise or tail bandage

❚ BELOW RIGHT
polo wraps

❚ ABOVE LEFT
stable bandages

❚ ABOVE RIGHT
Porter protector

❚ LEFT
cohesive bandage

PUTTING ON AN EXERCISE BANDAGE

EXERCISE BANDAGES

Exercise bandages and polo wraps are used to protect the horse's legs during exercise or work. A great deal of skill is required to apply bandages which are neither too tight (which can lead to damaged tendons), nor too loose (when they can unravel and cause the horse to fall). Exercise bandages must always be applied over some sort of padding, such as a Gamgee, Fybagee or Porter boot.

1 Place the padding around the leg, making sure that the edge of the pad lies between the tendons, on the outside of the leg. The padding should start just below the knee or hock and finish just below the fetlock joint. Wrap the pad around the leg firmly, from front to back, making sure that there are no lumps or wrinkles.

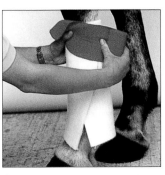

2 Bandage in the same direction as the padding and start just below the padding at the top.

3 Do one complete turn with the bandage around the top of the padding before working down the leg. Exercise bandages are elasticated so be careful not to pull the bandage in too tightly.

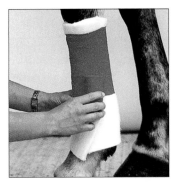

4 Make sure that the bandage stays smooth and that the tension is even.

5 At the bottom of the leg the bandage should follow the same angle as the fetlock joint so that it forms a V at the front of the leg. This will ensure that the movement of the fetlock is not restricted.

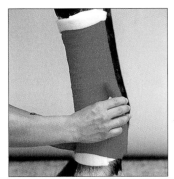

6 Continue to wrap the bandage around the leg, working back up to the top of the padding.

7 Secure the bandage by fastening the ties with a simple knot. The knot should be flat and sit on the outside of the leg. For competitions, stitch the bandage to ensure that it stays in place. Cover the stitched end with insulating tape.

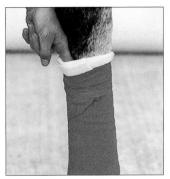

8 The bandage should be firm enough not to slide down but not so tight that it could damage the tendons. You should just be able to slide your finger inside the bandage.

Travelling Equipment

Special clothing can be used to protect the horse from injuries incurred during transportation in a horse truck or trailer.

A **tail guard** prevents the horse from rubbing his tail when travelling. Linen and cotton tail guards are secured with strips tied to the surcingle. The padded tail guard is fitted with Velcro fastenings.

Shaped travel boots can be used instead of travelling bandages to protect the front and hindlegs, from the coronet up to the knee and hock. **Travel boots** are simple square wraps which give protection to the lower leg.

Hock boots, made from leather and felt, are fitted over the top of travel bandages to protect the hock from injury, in the same way that **knee pads** are used to protect the knees. **Felt travel pads** under travel bandages will do the same job.

A **poll guard**, made from leather with a felt lining, provides protection for the sensitive poll area of the horse's head. It is attached to the headcollar or halter.

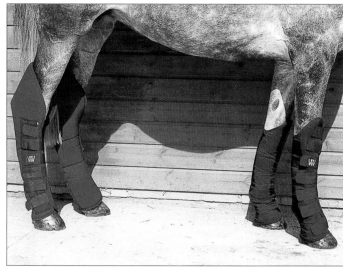

Shaped travel boots. These are designed for front or hindlegs to protect them from the coronet right up to the knee or hock.

Travel boots. These simple square padded wraps are effective in protecting the lower leg.

Hock boots. These are fitted to protect the hock joint from injury during transit.

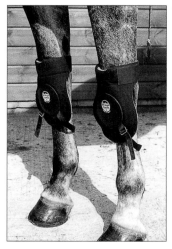

Knee pads. These can be used with travel bandages to protect the knees from damage.

HORSE DRESSED FOR TRAVELLING

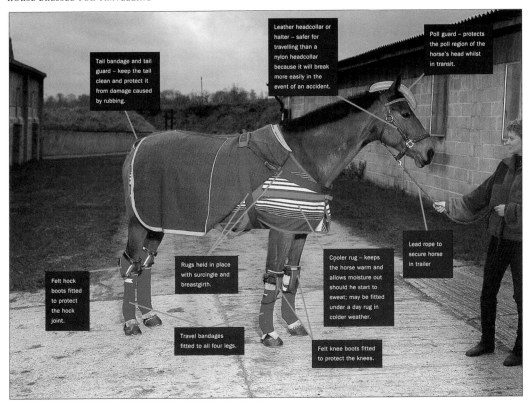

Tail bandage and tail guard – keep the tail clean and protect it from damage caused by rubbing.

Leather headcollar or halter – safer for travelling than a nylon headcollar because it will break more easily in the event of an accident.

Poll guard – protects the poll region of the horse's head whilst in transit.

Lead rope to secure horse in trailer

Felt hock boots fitted to protect the hock joint.

Rugs held in place with surcingle and breastgirth.

Cooler rug – keeps the horse warm and allows moisture out should he start to sweat; may be fitted under a day rug in colder weather.

Travel bandages fitted to all four legs.

Felt knee boots fitted to protect the knees.

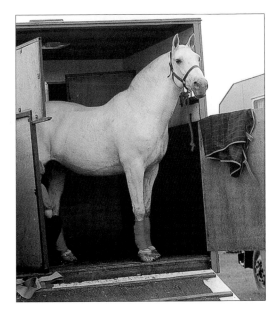

■ LEFT
Horses are very vulnerable to minor injuries when travelling on the roads. While a complete set of travelling equipment is not always necessary, your horse should be fitted with leg protection and a rug. Regular safety checks should also be made on the trailer itself.

Shaped travel pads can be used in conjunction with travel bandages to protect specific parts of the legs when the horse is in transit.

Corrective Equipment

The following pieces of equipment may be used on the horse to discourage or prevent bad habits when he is stabled or turned out to grass.

A **plastic muzzle** may be used on a horse who is on a strict diet but needs to be turned out. The muzzle prevents him from eating large amounts of food, while the holes in the design allow him to breathe and drink. Plastic muzzles are also useful for horses who bite, chew their rugs or eat their bedding. The design of the **leather muzzle**, made of thick strips, allows the horse to breathe and drink but, like the plastic muzzle, it prevents him from nibbling his rug and biting.

A **bib** is attached to the headcollar and sits below the horse's chin. Like the muzzle, it is fitted to prevent the horse from chewing his rugs or bandages. A much more restrictive item is the **neck cradle**, which should be used only as a last resort to stop a horse from chewing.

A **cribbing collar** is a strong leather strap which is fitted tightly around the horse's throat to prevent him from crib biting and wind-sucking. The collar will not cure the condition, but will stop him doing it while it is fitted.

The design of the leather muzzle allows the horse to breathe and drink but will not allow him to bite and chew.

A plastic muzzle may be used on a horse on a diet who nonetheless needs to be turned out.

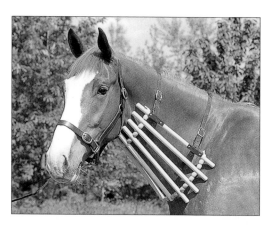

▌ LEFT
The neck cradle offers a last ditch attempt to stop a horse chewing rugs or bandages.

Cribbing collar. This is fitted around the horse's throat to prevent crib biting and wind-sucking.

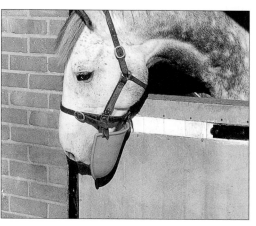

▌ LEFT
The plastic bib is a mildly restrictive piece of equipment which will help to dissuade the horse from chewing his clothing.

490

What are Vices?

There are a number of pieces of equipment used on horses to prevent or discourage vices (as described on the opposite page) but what are vices and what causes a horse to exhibit them? A vice is chronic, habitual behaviour displayed by the horse, for example box walking, weaving (when the horse rocks from side to side swaying its head), windsucking (the horse sucks in air and swallows it) or crib biting (similar to windsucking except that the horse will also take hold of an object with his teeth).

Most vices are displayed by stabled horses (although not exclusively) and are thought to be a result of boredom or nervousness on the part of the horse. It is also possible that vices are copied by one horse from another.

Before resorting to equipment to stop a vice, it is always worth investigating the possible causes. For example, if a horse is bored being kept in his stable for long periods, try turning him out for part of the day, or increasing the amount of hay in his diet to keep him occupied.

If a horse persistently chews his rugs or bandages it is possible that they may be irritating him in some way. His bandages may have been applied too tightly or his rug may be irritating his skin. In any case it is always worth trying to eliminate the possible causes of a vice before trying to treat the symptoms.

▮ LEFT
It is always better to prevent vices rather than deal with them once the bad habits have formed. Horses can easily get bored if they are kept in a stable all day, and this can lead to chronic stress-induced behaviour. Make sure your horse is turned out as much as possible, to give him exercise and to add variety to his routine.

▮ BELOW
Check your horse and his rugs. If they are chewed, it may be a sign that the horse is uncomfortable or that his skin is irritated. It may help to remove the rug for a time, loosen it, or try a different material.

▮ ABOVE
If your horse is stabled for long periods, make sure he has fresh supplies of hay. This is not only good for his diet, but will also keep him occupied.

The Rider's Clothes

Like the horse, the rider requires specialist clothing for his
or her safety and comfort. There is a wide variety of riding
clothing available, with new designs and developments always
coming on to the market. However, there are a few basic items
which are essential for anyone who rides. A protective riding
hat should always be worn when riding, lungeing or long
reining horses, to reduce the risk of injury to the head. The
wearing of a body protector is also a sensible precaution when
jumping or riding horses which you know to be
unpredictable. Riding boots (short or long) should be worn,
because they are designed to prevent the rider's foot getting
caught in the stirrup in the event of a fall. Many riders choose
to wear gloves: those which have non-slip palms are better as
they prevent the reins from slipping through the hands.
Gloves, however, should always be worn when lungeing, long
reining or leading horses by hand, to prevent injury to the
hands should the horse suddenly pull away. Jodhpurs or
breeches are a sensible choice for riding as their design
prevents rubbing caused by the saddle or stirrup leathers.

Clothes

When working with horses, whether you are on the ground or riding, safety is the keynote. Horses are big, strong animals and there is always an element of danger, however calm and placid they might normally be. Therefore care should be taken even when choosing clothes for mundane, everyday chores such as mucking out.

Neat clothing which is well fitting without being too tight is the easiest to move around in. A long-sleeved shirt with a sweatshirt or sweater, depending on the weather, and a pair of comfortable trousers, jeans or jodhpurs are ideal for stable work. Avoid overtight trousers as they make bending down difficult. Dark colours will stay looking smart longer. Long sleeves are preferable to short ones since they give some protection from nips from equine teeth. Sleeveless suntops and vests should definitely be avoided.

Footwear is of great importance since a misplaced hoof can do a great deal of damage to a human foot. "Trainers" give little protection, nor do most rubber boots, though sturdy Wellingtons are as good as anything for mucking out, particularly if you wear thick walking-boot socks inside. At other times a pair of leather jodhpur boots will probably afford the best protection and will certainly enable you to move more quickly than when wearing Wellingtons. Some boots are now fitted with protective toecaps.

Coats and body warmers, when worn, should be kept fastened – a flapping coat can frighten a nervous horse and there is also the danger that it might become caught up on some "foreign body". Some horses are nervous of noisy waterproof fabrics, so avoid wearing them around the stables.

Long hair should be tied up, again to avoid the possibility of scaring a horse or becoming caught up. This is particularly important in windy weather. Avoid wearing jewellery: rings, earrings,

noserings and the like can all cause nasty injuries if they become caught up.

Most well-trained horses are safe to lead about, in and out of their stables, down to the paddock, etc. But if you have any doubts whatsoever about a horse's good behaviour (when handling a young horse, for example) take precautions: wear a hard hat, correctly fastened, in case he rears up and strikes out, boots to protect your feet and a pair of gloves.

▌ ABOVE
A sweatshirt, breeches, boots and a hard hat make a suitable outfit for everyday exercise.

▌ LEFT
Neat, workmanlike clothes enable you to carry out daily chores in comfort and safety.

Safety Gear

Riding has always been and always will be a risk sport. But modern safety equipment is constantly improving and everyone who rides should ensure that they wear the best available protective gear, which includes hat, body protector and boots.

The most vulnerable part of the rider is the head and it is irresponsible to get on to a horse, or to lunge or long rein or otherwise handle an unpredictable young

LEFT
Fluorescent clothing is a wise safety precaution when riding on the roads. The message on the tabard helps to alert drivers.

SAFETY CHECKLIST

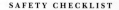

- Wear a correctly fitting hard hat with the chin strap fastened at all times when mounted.

- Replace a hat that has been subjected to impact in a fall – it may not give sufficient protection next time.

- Always ride in your own hat – a borrowed hat is unlikely to fit you correctly.

- Wear safe footwear at all times when mounted.

- Always use the correct stirrup iron size – about 1 inch (2.5cm) wider than your boot – to prevent your foot becoming stuck.

- Wear fluorescent garments – hat cover, tabard/body warmer etc – fitted with retro-reflective strips when riding on the roads and fit your horse with similar high visibility leg bands.

- Avoid riding on the roads in poor visibility and after dark.

- Never ride in jewellery.

- Always fasten tiepins horizontally or at an angle, never vertically.

- Always ride with your coat fastened.

- Never take off a coat or sweater while mounted – while you are taking your arms out of the sleeves you will have no control over the horse should he make an unexpected move.

- If you have less than perfect eyesight, wear soft contact lenses if possible. If not, seek your optician's advice on the safest type of spectacles.

horse, without wearing a **hard hat** securely fastened with a **chin strap**. Your country's national federation (for example in Britain the British Horse Society, in the United States the American Horse Shows Association) will advise on the most up-to-date safety standards. The **jockey skull**, or **crash hat**, is generally considered to give maximum protection and is therefore recommended (and obligatory under the rules of most sports) for all riding which involves fast work or jumping. The **chin harness** must be correctly adjusted and fastened at all times. It may be worn on the point of the chin, with a chin cup, or under the chin, whichever is most comfortable. The alternative is the traditional **hunting cap** which must have a soft peak (a hard peak can cause facial, head or neck injuries in a fall). All riding

hats should be correctly fitted (many retailers are trained in hat fitting).

Body protectors are designed to protect the torso and the shoulders in the event of a fall. They should fit well, feel comfortable and not restrict the rider's movement.

Riding boots and **jodhpur boots** are designed to prevent the foot from sliding right through the stirrup iron or otherwise becoming caught up in the iron in the event of a fall – a potentially fatal situation. They have smooth soles and a clearly defined heel. Leather boots afford the best protection from knocks, for example when riding across country, but rubber ones fashioned in the same style are suitable for everyday riding. Wellington boots, trainers and other boots or shoes with ridged soles and little or no heel should never be worn for riding.

LEFT
A jockey skull or "crash hat", with a correctly adjusted chin harness, gives the head maximum protection. It is fitted with a silk cover.

LEFT
A body protector should be worn when jumping fixed fences and by people needing special protection (for example, an older person with more brittle bones).

Riding Clothes

By and large all riding clothes are designed for comfort and protection. Only with the odd item of equipment (such as the top hat for dressage) is clothing dictated by fashion.

Most riding clothes are based on hunting attire, which evolved over a long period and led to the design of an entire outfit which would give protection from wet, cold and the many knocks experienced when travelling at speed across country. Long leather boots keep the feet and lower legs dry and give maximum protection from painful encounters with gateposts or other fixed objects. Breeches keep the upper legs warm and dry and protect the insides of the knees from chafing against the saddle. A well-fitting jacket made of a good stout tweed or twill gives warmth and a certain amount of waterproofing while at the same time affording complete freedom of movement – essential for all riding, but particularly for jumping and riding at speed. Gloves keep the hands warm and dry and give a secure grip on the reins. A hunting tie or stock helps protect the neck in the event of a fall. A hard hat, correctly secured with a chin harness, protects the most vulnerable part of all, the head.

For everyday riding there is a wealth of suitable clothing to choose from which is both cheaper than more formal attire and suited to frequent immersion in the washing machine. **Jodhpurs**, which extend down the leg to the ankle, and are usually worn with short, elastic-sided leather jodhpur boots, are cooler in summer than breeches and long boots. They come in a range of materials, from lightweight cotton suitable for hot climates to thermal material for wear in extremes of cold. Instead of jodhpur boots, jodhpurs may be worn with **half-chaps**, which cover the leg from below the knee to the foot, or with full **chaps**, which extend up to the thigh.

Close-fitting **riding trousers** are also suitable for everyday wear. Like jodhpurs,

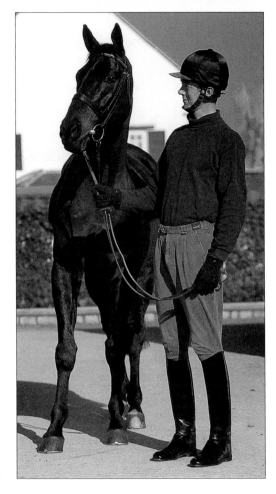

▍ LEFT
Everyday riding clothes should be neat and safe. Dark colours are more practical than the light shades worn with traditional hunting dress.

▍ BELOW LEFT
Chaps are a good alternative to boots. This rider is prepared for roadwork – note the fluorescent tabard and the horse's protective boots.

they come with "strappings" – reinforcements at the knee and thigh. Some garments are also fitted with an inset seat panel made in an extra-grip material.

Rubber **riding boots** are a cheaper alternative to leather ones, though they can be cold in winter, when an inner sole

or an extra pair of socks may be required.

Casual **riding coats** such as waxed or quilted jackets, blousons and body warmers are fine for everyday riding and may be worn with a shirt and/or sweatshirt or sweater. Modern waterproof materials are light and comfortable to wear and the more expensive ones have the advantage of being "breathable". Waterproofs come in a range of lengths and may have added features such as storm collar and cuffs, fleecy lining and pommel flap. Noisy waterproof materials should be avoided as horses tend to be frightened of them, particularly on a windy day.

There are **gloves** for every occasion, specially designed for the rider. Special features include reinforced rein fingers, pimple palm grips and lycra inserts for extra flexibility.

Clothes for Competition

For most forms of competitive riding it is usual to wear a riding coat with breeches and boots, a shirt with a collar and tie or collarless shirt with a hunting tie or stock. The rules of some sports also stipulate the wearing of spurs. A hat is obligatory and although the bowler hat (derby) is still seen in show classes and the top hat in dressage, the trend is more and more to the safer type of hunting cap and, even more so, the jockey skull. The latter is usually worn with a dark-coloured silk cover.

For cross-country riding the jacket is replaced by a sweater or shirt, according to the weather, which may be in the rider's own colours, as may the hat silk.

Endurance riding is one area where tradition holds less sway, partly because the sport is of fairly recent origin (at least in an organized competitive way) and also because at the higher echelons riders are not only in the saddle for very long periods but also spend some of the time on their feet, running alongside their horses to give them a breather. Breeches and boots would be too hot and uncomfortable so this is the one sport where runningshoes are permitted. However, as a safety precaution, riders are required to use enclosed-type stirrup irons to prevent their feet slipping right through.

LEFT
Correct dress for top-level dressage includes a top hat, tail coat and waistcoat.

BELOW
Most riding gear, for women as well as men, is based on clothes developed for the hunting field.

BOTTOM LEFT
The clothes worn for endurance riding are less formal than in other competitive sports.

Whips and Spurs

Whips and spurs (referred to as artificial aids) can be used by the rider to reinforce the leg aids.

The rider uses a whip just behind his or her leg if the horse does not respond to a command from the leg. Whips should only be used in these circumstances and not as an alternative to the leg, or as a punishment.

Shorter, thicker whips are used for show jumping and cross country. Longer, finer whips are ideal for schooling horses on the flat, because they can be used to give a gentle flick without the rider having to take his or her hands off the reins.

Hunting whips are not used on the horse, but are traditionally carried out hunting. They usually have a bent top which is very useful for pulling gates shut,

LEFT
This cross-country rider is carrying a short, thick whip, only to be used if the horse does not respond to a command from the leg.

and a plaited leather thong and cord lash which is carried looped round. For showing horses, a simple malacca or leather-covered cane is often carried.

Spurs can be worn to emphasize the rider's leg aids. The most common type of spur used for English riding is called a Prince of Wales spur. It has a short blunt-ended neck which, when fitted, points downward. The spur fits snugly around the back of the rider's boot and is held in place with a strap. Spurs are also available with rowels (small metal discs fitted to the tip of the spurs) which give them a much sharper action. Spurs should only be used by experienced riders who have an independent seat and can maintain control when the spur is applied to the horse.

LEFT
A dressage whip is longer and allows the rider to use the whip without letting go of the reins.

▮ LEFT
The hunting whip is
not used on the horse,
but is carried as a
hunting tradition, and
is sometimes used for
pulling gates shut. It is
much longer than the
show-jumping or cross-
country whip.

▮ ABOVE
Spurs, like whips, can be used to emphasize the
rider's leg aids. They should only be used by
experienced riders.

▮ RIGHT
A show-jumping whip, used for encouraging the
horse to move forward if he doesn't respond to the
rider's leg aids.

499

Suppliers and Acknowledgements

The authors would like to thank the many individuals and breed societies who kindly provided information for use in the breeds section of this book, particularly:

The American Morgan Horse Association, Inc; The American Paint Horse Association; The American Saddlebred Horse Association, Inc; The British Spotted Pony Society; Vivienne Burdon; The Cleveland Bay Horse Society; The Clydesdale Horse Society of Great Britain and Ireland; The Exmoor Pony Society; The Hackney Horse Society; The Haflinger Society of Great Britain; The Highland Pony Society; The Irish Draught Horse Society (GB); Sylvia Loch (author of *The Royal Horse of Europe*, J.A. Allen, 1986); The Lusitano Breed Society of Great Britain; The Palomino Horse Association of America, Inc; The Pinto Horse Association of America, Inc; Valerie Russell; The Suffolk Horse Society; The Walkaloosa Horse Association; The Walking Horse Owners' Association of America, Inc; The Welsh Pony and Cob Society.

We are grateful to the following for allowing their horses, ponies and stables to be photographed:

HORSES: EUROPE
Arab – Sariah Arabians, Dorking, Surrey
Barb – Haras Regional de Marrakech, Morocco
Thoroughbred – Mrs M Blackburn, c/o Catherston Stud, Whitchurch, Hampshire
Anglo-Arab – Woodlander Stud, Raglan, Gwent
Danish Warmblood – Catherston Stud, Whitchurch, Hampshire
Ariègeois – Bob Langrish, photographer
Norman Cob – Haras National Le Lion d'Angers, Loire, France

Camargue – Laurent Serre, Camargue, France
Selle Français – Haras National Le Lion d'Angers, Loire, France
French Trotter – Haras National Le Lion d'Angers, Loire, France
Percheron – Haras National Le Lion d'Angers, Loire, France
Breton – Haras National Le Lion d'Angers, Loire, France
Hanoverian – Mrs S Bray, Nuneaton, Warwickshire
Holstein – Mr Luetzow, Wokingham, Berkshire
Oldenburg – I Brendel, Trenthide, Dorset
Westphalian – Marlow Building Co Ltd, Marlow, Buckinghamshire
Hackney – Georgina Turner, Ipswich, Suffolk
Shire – Lingwood Shire, Brentwood, Essex
Suffolk – Randy Hiscock, Shaftesbury, Dorset
Shagya Arab – Sonia Lindsay, Okehampton, Devon
Icelandic – Edda Hestar, Salisbury, Wiltshire
Friesian – Harrods, London
Gelderland – Mr Luetzow, Wokingham, Berkshire
Dutch Warmblood – Mrs C Hughes, Doncaster

Don – Russian Horse Society, Epsom, Surrey (standing) Mrs June Connolly, Droitwich, West Midlands (action)
Budenny – Mrs Marcus, Beoley, Redditch, Hereford & Worcester (action)
Kabardin – Mrs June Connolly, Droitwich, West Midlands
Orlov – George Bowman Jnr, Penrith, Cumbria
Vladimir – Russian Horse Society, Epsom, Surrey
North Swedish – Jan Gyllensten, photographer, Sweden
Akhal-Teke – Viscountess Bury, Plumpton, Sussex
Knabstrup – Mrs Ann Peruzzi-Smith, Diss, Norfolk

HORSES: UNITED STATES
Morgan – Betty Gray, Orange Lake, Florida
Quarter Horse – Quiet Oaks Farm, Ocala, Florida & Derby Daze Farm, Ocala, Florida
Saddlebred – Boca Raton Equestrian Center, Del Ray Beach
Standardbred – David McDuffee & Tom Walsh Jnr, South Florida Trotting Center
Missouri Fox Trotter – Sandy Hart, Winter Haven, Florida

Tennessee Walking Horse – Mrs Carol Worsham, Dunnellon, Florida
Mustang – Cindy Bowman, Dunnellon, Florida
Peruvian Paso – Annette Ward, Alachua, Florida
Pony of the Americas – Cynthia Bunnell, Eustis, Florida
American Shetland – Caroline Proctor, Ocala, Florida
Palomino – Holmes Quarter Horses, Brandon, Florida
Appaloosa – Classic Acres Farm, Ocala, Florida
Paint – Brooke Hamlin, Ocala, Florida

PONIES
Haflinger – Millslade Farm Stud, Bridgwater, Somerset
Exmoor – Mrs J Freeman, Wareside, Hertfordshire
New Forest – Shirley Young, Salisbury, Wiltshire
Shetland – Mr & Mrs E House, Bincombe Shetlands, Bridgwater, Somerset
Dales – Mrs B Powell, Farnham, Surrey
Connemara & Welsh Cob – Miss S Clark, Dorking, Surrey
Fjord – Mrs Murray, Ottery St Mary, Devon
Caspian – Henden Caspian Stud, Chippenham, Wiltshire

STABLE MANAGEMENT
Catherston Stud, Whitchurch, Hampshire
Stretcholt Farm Stud, Bridgwater, Somerset.

We would also like to thank the following for facilities and equipment, and for riding for photographs:

FACILITIES AND EQUIPMENT
Philip Wellon for the use of land at Vine Farm; Aubiose UK Ltd for the outdoor arena; HAC TAC Ltd for supplying close-contact breeches.

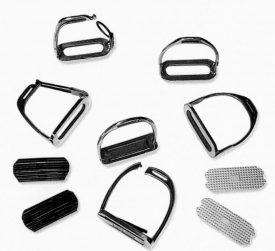

RIDERS
Amanda Colbourne, Thomas
Cooper, Janine Cornish,
Charles Daniel, Kate Eckley,
Janice Peglar, Sarah Rees-Elford,
and Jeremy Russell.

The following companies supplied
the tack and equipment featured
in this book:

UNITED KINGDOM
Aerborn Equestrian Ltd
Pegasus House
198 Sneiton Dale
Nottingham NG2 4HJ

Albion Saddlemakers Co Ltd
Albion House
55 Caldmore Road
Walsall
West Midlands WS1 3NA

Clyst Equestrian Ltd
Teko House
Furnham Road
Chard
Somerset TA20 1AX

Keenthorne Saddlery
Nether Stowey
Bridgwater
Somerset

Miller Crosby Ltd
30 Birchbrook Industrial Estate
Shenstone
Nr Lichfield
Staffordshire WS14 0DT

Proteq™ Worldwide Ltd
Graingers
West Ashling
Chichester
West Sussex PO18 8DN

The Royal Mews
Buckingham Palace
London SW1W

Shires Equestrian Products
15 Southern Avenue
Leominster
Herefordshire HR6 0QF

Stylo Matchmakers
International Ltd
Holybrook Mill
Harrogate Road
Greengates
Bradford
West Yorkshire BD10 0QW

Wychanger Barton Saddlery
The Haywain
Burlescombe
Nr Tiverton
Devon EX16 7JY

UNITED STATES
Whitman Saddle Manufacturing
5272 West Michigan
Kalamazoo
MI 49006

Libertyville Saddle Shop Inc.
P.O. Box M
Libertyville
IL 60048-4913

Fennell's Horse Supplies
Red Mile Road
Lexington
KY 40504

Drury's Saddlery and Supplies
1638 Danville Road
Harrodsburg
KY 40330

We are also grateful to the
following for allowing their
equipment, horses and stables
to be photographed:

Betty Howett
Bossington Stables
Bossington
Nr Minehead
Somerset

Mrs Mary King
School House
Salcombe Regis
Devon EX10 0JQ

Bob Mayhew
Dumpford Manor Farm
Trotton
Hampshire GU31 5JR

Lynn Russell
Durfold Farm
Plaistow Road
Surrey EV8 4PQ

Sarah Rowe
4 Cleal Cottages
Broadway
Ilminster
Somerset TA19 9RD

Margaret Swords
White Horse Lodge
Over Stowey
Bridgwater
Somerset

Hannah Washer
Fulbrook Cottage
Fiddington
Nr Bridgwater
Somerset

Megan Williams
The Moat House
Longdon
Nr Tewkesbury
Gloucestershire

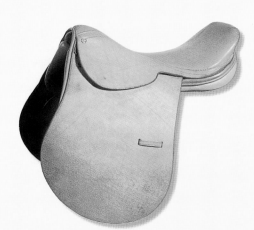

Index

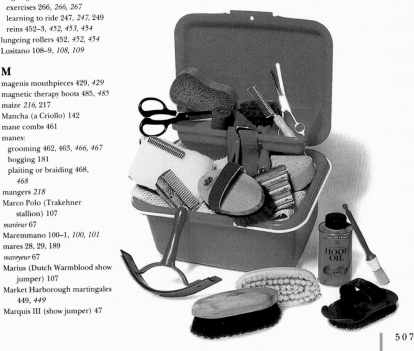